O Tempora! O Mores!

Oklahoma Series in Classical Culture

Series Editor

Ward W. Briggs, Jr., *University of South Carolina*

Advisory Board

O Tempora! O Mores!

Cicero's *Catilinarian Orations*

A Student Edition with Historical Essays

Susan O. Shapiro

University of Oklahoma Press : Norman

Library of Congress Cataloging-in-Publication Data

Cicero, Marcus Tullius.
  [In Catilinam]
  O tempora! O mores! : Cicero's Catilinarian orations : a student edition with historical
essays / [edited] by Susan O. Shapiro.
      p. cm. — (Oklahoma series in classical culture ; v. 30)
  Includes bibliographical references.
  Text in Latin; commentary in English.
  ISBN 978-0-8061-3662-2 (paper)
  1. Latin language—Readers. 2. Speeches, addresses, etc., Latin. 3. Speeches, addresses,
etc., Latin—History and criticism. 4. Rome—History—Conspiracy of Catiline, 65–62 B.C.—
Sources. I. Shapiro, Susan O. (Susan Olfson), 1951– II. Title. III. Series.
  PA6279.C2 2005
  478.6'421—dc22

                                                                    2004058833

*O Tempora! O Mores! Cicero's "Catilinarian Orations": A Student Edition with Historical
Essays* is Volume 30 in the Oklahoma Series in Classical Culture.

The paper in this book meets the guidelines for permanence and durability of the Committee on
Production Guidelines for Book Longevity of the Council on Library Resources, Inc. ∞

For my Latin students
Cum docemus, discimus.

Maps

1. The Roman Forum and Surrounding Area
   in the Late Republic   205
2. Rome   206
3. Italy   207
4. The Roman World in the Time of Cicero   208

Preface

In 63 B.C. Lucius Sergius Catilina, a Roman nobleman, formed a conspiracy with several other members of the upper classes to overthrow the Roman Republic. They gathered an army of some 10,000 men in northern Italy, attempted to form an alliance with Rome's enemies in Gaul, and planned to burn the city and murder key officials while their army attacked from the north. Cicero, who was consul that year, exposed their plot before they could put it into effect and documented his defeat of the conspiracy in four *Orations against Catiline*, which he later published. The *First Catilinarian Oration* is well known and deservedly famous; but, while the other three speeches are familiar to scholars, most students do not even know they exist. This is a pity, because the *Third Oration* is a fast-paced, cloak-and-dagger drama, while the *Second* and *Fourth Orations* provide a fascinating look at a critical event in Roman Republican history. This textbook aims to make all of Cicero's *Catilinarian Orations* available to the intermediate Latin student, along with the necessary interpretive tools to make the speeches accessible and enjoyable.

The purpose of the book is twofold. First, the text and grammatical commentary will make a significant addition to the number of Latin texts available to intermediate students. Second, the historical essays and appendices will bring a new dimension to college-level Latin study that has previously been lacking. Most intermediate Latin textbooks are reprints of earlier editions, written in the late nineteenth and early twentieth centuries and aimed primarily at junior high or high school students, who are generally not interested in detailed historical analysis. Today's intermediate Latin students are likely to be juniors or seniors in college, and they are eager to learn about the history and politics behind the texts they are translating. Although these students are capable of understanding complex political and social issues, most intermediate Latin textbooks provide only a cursory background to the text. College-level Latin students demand a more in-depth approach, and I hope they will find the historical essays both valuable and stimulating.

This text is designed to be flexible and to fit into a variety of pedagogical approaches. Professors can assign any one of the *Catilinarian Orations* independently, or they may wish to assign excerpts from all four speeches. The historical essays also do not need to be read in their entirety. Each essay is divided into nine short sections; individual sections can be assigned for class discussion at different times. The first essay, which gives historical background to the late Republic, may not need to be read by the entire class; it may simply be used as a resource for those students who need it. The vocabulary, maps, bibliography, and three appendices also add to the book's flexibility and completeness.

Why would a patrician, a member of Rome's exclusive inner circle, want to overthrow his own government, a government controlled by men very much like himself? How could he attract scores of upper-class Romans and thousands of ordinary citizens to participate in his ill-advised scheme? How was Cicero able to disarm such an entrenched conspiracy without any fighting inside the city, especially at a time when political violence was rapidly increasing? This book aims to ask these questions competently and to provide students with the tools that they need to figure out some possible answers.

Acknowledgments

Although I have consulted several commentaries on Cicero's *Catilinarians*, I am particularly indebted to Karl Frerichs' thorough treatment of Cicero's *First Catilinarian Oration* and Charles E. Bennett's masterful commentary on all four *Catilinarians* in his *Selections from Cicero*. I am truly grateful for the insights into Ciceronian grammar that these and other commentators have given me. The text is from A. C. Clark's *Oxford Classical Text* (1907), and I would like to thank Oxford University Press for permission to use it here. I have made a few minor changes in punctuation and spelling, to make the Latin more accessible to intermediate readers.

I would like to thank Xavier University, which provided support for the start of this project in the form of a Junior Faculty Research Fellowship in the summer of 2001, and Utah State University, which provided a Women and Gender Research Institute Grant in the summer of 2002 and a Dean's Research Opportunity Grant to help with the preparation of the maps.

The encouragement of friends and colleagues has been most helpful in preparing this commentary. Rob Ulery used an early version with his Latin class at Wake Forest University and provided several corrections and suggestions, as did John Gruber-Miller, who tested a later version at Cornell College. Darryl Phillips read both historical essays, which have been considerably improved by his thoughtful suggestions. Judith de Luce provided encouragement for the project at several stages of its development, and I very much appreciate her support.

I am greatly indebted to John Drayton, director of the University of Oklahoma Press, for the enthusiasm with which he received the project and for his assistance throughout the editing process. Jennifer Cunningham and Marian Stewart, editors at the Press, provided excellent advice on matters both large and small, and Kathy Lewis, the copyeditor, gave the manuscript scrupulous attention. The maps were very ably prepared by Bill Nelson. I would especially like to thank the two anonymous readers for the Press for their keen interest in this project, as well as their judicious criticism. The responsibility for all errors and omissions of course remains my own.

I am extremely grateful for the support of my colleagues in the History Department at Utah State University, particularly Mark Damen and Fran Titchener in the Classics Program, Norm Jones, chair of the Department, and Dan McInerney, who kept pushing me to ask the "so what?" question. The advice and support of my husband, Philip Parisi, has helped me immeasurably in this, as in everything I do.

Finally, I would like to dedicate this commentary to my Latin students at Xavier and Utah State University, whose questions inspired me to write it and whose energy helped me carry it through to completion. I would like to express my special appreciation to Rebecca Muich, my research assistant at Xavier University. Becky's high level of commitment to this project and her maturity beyond her years (not to mention her unerring skill at turning my chicken-scratchings into beautifully typed notes) allowed me to quickly transform the germ of an idea into a workable classroom text. I would also like to give a special thanks to my boisterous and engaging Latin 3100 class at Utah State in the fall semester of 2003, whose enthusiasm for spotting typographical errors was almost as great as their passion for reading Cicero!

Cicero's *Catilinarian Orations* and Commentary

theatricality

Text of Cicero's *Catilinarian Orations*

IN L. CATILINAM ORATIO PRIMA
HABITA IN SENATV

[1]   Quo usque tandem abutere, Catilina, patientia nostra? Quam
diu etiam furor iste tuus nos eludet? quem ad finem sese effrenata
iactabit audacia? Nihilne te nocturnum praesidium Palati, nihil
urbis vigiliae, nihil timor populi, nihil concursus bonorum omnium,
nihil hic munitissimus habendi senatus locus, nihil horum ora   5
voltusque moverunt? Patere tua consilia non sentis, constrictam iam
horum omnium scientia teneri coniurationem tuam non vides? Quid
proxima, quid superiore nocte egeris, ubi fueris, quos convocaveris,
quid consili ceperis, quem nostrum ignorare arbitraris?

[2]   O tempora, O mores! Senatus haec intellegit, consul videt; hic   10
tamen vivit. Vivit? immo vero etiam in senatum venit, fit publici
consili particeps, notat et designat oculis ad caedem unum quemque
nostrum. Nos autem, fortes viri, satis facere rei publicae videmur, si
istius furorem ac tela vitamus. Ad mortem te, Catilina, duci iussu
consulis iam pridem oportebat, in te conferri pestem quam tu in nos   15
omnis iam diu machinaris.

[3]   An vero vir amplissimus, P. Scipio, pontifex maximus, Ti.
Gracchum mediocriter labefactantem statum rei publicae privatus
interfecit: Catilinam orbem terrae caede atque incendiis vastare
cupientem nos consules perferemus? Nam illa nimis antiqua   20
praetereo, quod C. Servilius Ahala Sp. Maelium novis rebus
studentem manu sua occidit. Fuit, fuit ista quondam in hac re
publica virtus ut viri fortes acrioribus suppliciis civem perniciosum
quam acerbissimum hostem coercerent. Habemus senatus
consultum in te, Catilina, vehemens et grave. Non deest rei publicae   25

consilium neque auctoritas huius ordinis: nos, nos, dico aperte, consules desumus.

[4] Decrevit quondam senatus uti L. Opimius consul videret ne quid res publica detrimenti caperet: nox nulla intercessit; interfectus est propter quasdam seditionum suspiciones C. 30 Gracchus, clarissimo patre, avo, maioribus; occisus est cum liberis M. Fulvius consularis. Simili senatus consulto C. Mario et L. Valerio consulibus est permissa res publica: num unum diem postea L. Saturninum tribunum plebis et C. Servilium praetorem mors ac rei publicae poena remorata est? At vero nos vicesimum iam diem 35 patimur hebescere aciem horum auctoritatis. Habemus enim eius modi senatus consultum, verum inclusum in tabulis, tamquam in vagina reconditum, quo ex senatus consulto confestim te interfectum esse, Catilina, convenit. Vivis, et vivis non ad deponendam, sed ad confirmandam audaciam. 40

Cupio, patres conscripti, me esse clementem, cupio in tantis rei publicae periculis non dissolutum videri, sed iam me ipse inertiae nequitiaeque condemno.

[5] Castra sunt in Italia contra populum Romanum in Etruriae faucibus conlocata, crescit in dies singulos hostium numerus; eorum 45 autem castrorum imperatorem ducemque hostium intra moenia atque adeo in senatu videtis intestinam aliquam cotidie perniciem rei publicae molientem. Si te iam, Catilina, comprehendi, si interfici iussero, credo, erit verendum mihi ne non hoc potius omnes boni serius a me quam quisquam crudelius factum esse dicat. Verum ego 50 hoc quod iam pridem factum esse oportuit certa de causa nondum adducor ut faciam. Tum denique interficiere, cum iam nemo tam improbus, tam perditus, tam tui similis inveniri poterit qui id non iure factum esse fateatur.

[6] Quam diu quisquam erit qui te defendere audeat, vives, et 55 vives ita ut nunc vivis, multis meis et firmis praesidiis obsessus, ne commovere te contra rem publicam possis. Multorum te etiam oculi et aures non sentientem, sicut adhuc fecerunt, speculabuntur atque custodient.

Etenim quid est, Catilina, quod iam amplius exspectes, si   60
neque nox tenebris obscurare coetus nefarios nec privata domus
parietibus continere voces coniurationis tuae potest, si inlustrantur,
si erumpunt omnia? Muta iam istam mentem, mihi crede,
obliviscere caedis atque incendiorum. Teneris undique; luce sunt
clariora nobis tua consilia omnia, quae iam mecum licet   65
recognoscas.

[7] Meministine me ante diem XII Kalendas Novembris dicere in
senatu fore in armis certo die, qui dies futurus esset ante diem VI
Kal. Novembris, C. Manlium, audaciae satellitem atque administrum
tuae? Num me fefellit, Catilina, non modo res tanta, tam atrox   70
tamque incredibilis, verum (id quod multo magis est admirandum),
dies? Dixi ego idem in senatu caedem te optimatium contulisse in
ante diem V Kalendas Novembris, tum cum multi principes civitatis
Roma non tam sui conservandi quam tuorum consiliorum
reprimendorum causa profugerunt. Num infitiari potes te illo ipso   75
die meis praesidiis, mea diligentia circumclusum, commovere te
contra rem publicam non potuisse, cum tu discessu ceterorum
nostra tamen qui remansissemus caede contentum te esse dicebas?

[8] Quid? cum te Praeneste Kalendis ipsis Novembribus
occupaturum nocturno impetu esse confideres, sensistin illam   80
coloniam meo iussu meis praesidiis, custodiis, vigiliis esse munitam?
Nihil agis, nihil moliris, nihil cogitas quod non ego non modo
audiam sed etiam videam planeque sentiam.

Recognosce mecum tandem noctem illam superiorem; iam
intelleges multo me vigilare acrius ad salutem quam te ad perniciem   85
rei publicae. Dico te priore nocte venisse inter falcarios—non agam
obscure—in M. Laecae domum; convenisse eodem compluris
eiusdem amentiae scelerisque socios. Num negare audes? quid
taces? Convincam, si negas. Video enim esse hic in senatu quosdam
qui tecum una fuerunt.   90

[9] O di immortales! Ubinam gentium sumus? quam rem
publicam habemus? in qua urbe vivimus? Hic, hic sunt in nostro
numero, patres conscripti, in hoc orbis terrae sanctissimo

gravissimoque consilio, qui de nostro omnium interitu, qui de huius
urbis atque adeo de orbis terrarum exitio cogitent. Hos ego video   95
consul et de re publica sententiam rogo, et quos ferro trucidari
oportebat, eos nondum voce volnero! Fuisti igitur apud Laecam illa
nocte, Catilina, distribuisti partis Italiae, statuisti quo quemque
proficisci placeret, delegisti quos Romae relinqueres, quos tecum
educeres, discripsisti urbis partis ad incendia, confirmasti te ipsum   100
iam esse exiturum, dixisti paulum tibi esse etiam nunc morae, quod
ego viverem. Reperti sunt duo equites Romani qui te ista cura
liberarent et se illa ipsa nocte paulo ante lucem me in meo lecto
interfecturos esse pollicerentur.

[10]   Haec ego omnia vixdum etiam coetu vestro dimisso comperi;   105
domum meam maioribus praesidiis munivi atque firmavi, exclusi
eos quos tu ad me salutatum mane miseras, cum illi ipsi venissent
quos ego iam multis ac summis viris ad me id temporis venturos
esse praedixeram.

Quae cum ita sint, Catilina, perge quo coepisti: egredere   110
aliquando ex urbe; patent portae; proficiscere. Nimium diu te
imperatorem tua illa Manliana castra desiderant. Educ tecum etiam
omnis tuos, si minus, quam plurimos; purga urbem. Magno me
metu liberaveris, modo inter me atque te murus intersit. Nobiscum
versari iam diutius non potes; non feram, non patiar, non sinam.   115

[11]   Magna dis immortalibus habenda est atque huic ipsi Iovi
Statori, antiquissimo custodi huius urbis, gratia, quod hanc tam
taetram, tam horribilem tamque infestam rei publicae pestem
totiens iam effugimus. Non est saepius in uno homine summa salus
periclitanda rei publicae. Quam diu mihi consuli designato,   120
Catilina, insidiatus es, non publico me praesidio, sed privata
diligentia defendi. Cum proximis comitiis consularibus me
consulem in campo et competitores tuos interficere voluisti,
compressi conatus tuos nefarios amicorum praesidio et copiis nullo
tumultu publice concitato; denique, quotienscumque me petisti, per   125
me tibi obstiti, quamquam videbam perniciem meam cum magna
calamitate rei publicae esse coniunctam.

[12]   Nunc iam aperte rem publicam universam petis, templa
deorum immortalium, tecta urbis, vitam omnium civium, Italiam

totam ad exitium et vastitatem vocas. Qua re, quoniam id quod est   130
primum, et quod huius imperi disciplinaeque maiorum proprium
est, facere nondum audeo, faciam id quod est ad severitatem lenius,
ad communem salutem utilius. Nam si te interfici iussero, residebit
in re publica reliqua coniuratorum manus; sin tu, quod te iam
dudum hortor, exieris, exhaurietur ex urbe tuorum comitum magna   135
et perniciosa sentina rei publicae.

[13]   Quid est, Catilina? num dubitas id me imperante facere quod
iam tua sponte faciebas? Exire ex urbe iubet consul hostem.
Interrogas me, num in exsilium? Non iubeo, sed, si me consulis,
suadeo. Quid est enim, Catilina, quod te iam in hac urbe delectare   140
possit? in qua nemo est extra istam coniurationem perditorum
hominum qui te non metuat, nemo qui non oderit. Quae nota
domesticae turpitudinis non inusta vitae tuae est? Quod privatarum
rerum dedecus non haeret in fama? Quae libido ab oculis, quod
facinus a manibus umquam tuis, quod flagitium a toto corpore   145
afuit? Cui tu adulescentulo quem corruptelarum inlecebris
inretisses non aut ad audaciam ferrum aut ad libidinem facem
praetulisti?

[14]   Quid vero? nuper cum morte superioris uxoris novis nuptiis
locum vacuefecisses, nonne etiam alio incredibili scelere hoc scelus   150
cumulavisti? Quod ego praetermitto et facile patior sileri, ne in hac
civitate tanti facinoris immanitas aut exstitisse aut non vindicata
esse videatur. Praetermitto ruinas fortunarum tuarum quas omnis
proximis Idibus tibi impendere senties: ad illa venio quae non ad
privatam ignominiam vitiorum tuorum, non ad domesticam tuam   155
difficultatem ac turpitudinem, sed ad summam rem publicam atque
ad omnium nostrum vitam salutemque pertinent.

[15]   Potestne tibi haec lux, Catilina, aut huius caeli spiritus esse
iucundus, cum scias esse horum neminem qui nesciat te pridie
Kalendas Ianuarias Lepido et Tullo consulibus stetisse in comitio   160
cum telo, manum consulum et principum civitatis interficiendorum
causa paravisse, sceleri ac furori tuo non mentem aliquam aut
timorem tuum sed fortunam populi Romani obstitisse? Ac iam illa
omitto—neque enim sunt aut obscura aut non multa commissa

postea—quotiens tu me designatum, quotiens vero consulem   165
interficere conatus es! quot ego tuas petitiones ita coniectas ut
vitari posse non viderentur parva quadam declinatione et, ut aiunt,
corpore effugi! Nihil agis, nihil adsequeris, neque tamen conari ac
velle desistis.

[16]   Quotiens iam tibi extorta est ista sica de manibus, quotiens   170
excidit casu aliquo et elapsa est! Quae quidem quibus abs te initiata
sacris ac devota sit nescio, quod eam necesse putas esse in consulis
corpore defigere.

Nunc vero quae tua est ista vita? Sic enim iam tecum loquar,
non ut odio permotus esse videar, quo debeo, sed ut misericordia,   175
quae tibi nulla debetur. Venisti paulo ante in senatum. Quis te ex
hac tanta frequentia, tot ex tuis amicis ac necessariis salutavit? Si
hoc post hominum memoriam contigit nemini, vocis exspectas
contumeliam, cum sis gravissimo iudicio taciturnitatis oppressus?
Quid? quod adventu tuo ista subsellia vacuefacta sunt, quod omnes   180
consulares qui tibi persaepe ad caedem constituti fuerunt, simul
atque adsedisti, partem istam subselliorum nudam atque inanem
reliquerunt, quo tandem animo tibi ferendum putas?

[17]   Servi mehercule mei si me isto pacto metuerent ut te metuunt
omnes cives tui, domum meam relinquendam putarem: tu tibi   185
urbem non arbitraris? Et si me meis civibus iniuria suspectum tam
graviter atque offensum viderem, carere me aspectu civium quam
infestis omnium oculis conspici mallem: tu, cum conscientia
scelerum tuorum agnoscas odium omnium iustum et iam diu tibi
debitum, dubitas quorum mentis sensusque volneras, eorum   190
aspectum praesentiamque vitare? Si te parentes timerent atque
odissent tui neque eos ratione ulla placare posses, ut opinor, ab
eorum oculis aliquo concederes. Nunc te patria, quae communis est
parens omnium nostrum, odit ac metuit et iam diu nihil te iudicat
nisi de parricidio suo cogitare: huius tu neque auctoritatem   195
verebere nec iudicium sequere nec vim pertimesces?

[18]   Quae tecum, Catilina, sic agit et quodam modo tacita loquitur:
"Nullum iam aliquot annis facinus exstitit nisi per te, nullum
flagitium sine te; tibi uni multorum civium neces, tibi vexatio

direptioque sociorum impunita fuit ac libera; tu non solum ad   200
neglegendas leges et quaestiones verum etiam ad evertendas
perfringendasque valuisti. Superiora illa, quamquam ferenda non
fuerunt, tamen ut potui tuli; nunc vero me totam esse in metu
propter unum te, quicquid increpuerit, Catilinam timeri, nullum
videri contra me consilium iniri posse quod a tuo scelere abhorreat,   205
non est ferendum. Quam ob rem discede atque hunc mihi timorem
eripe; si est verus, ne opprimar, sin falsus, ut tandem aliquando
timere desinam."

[19]   Haec si tecum, ut dixi, patria loquatur, nonne impetrare
debeat, etiam si vim adhibere non possit? Quid, quod tu te in   210
custodiam dedisti, quod vitandae suspicionis causa ad M'. Lepidum
te habitare velle dixisti? A quo non receptus etiam ad me venire
ausus es, atque ut domi meae te adservarem rogasti. Cum a me
quoque id responsum tulisses, me nullo modo posse isdem
parietibus tuto esse tecum, quia magno in periculo essem quod   215
isdem moenibus contineremur, ad Q. Metellum praetorem venisti. A
quo repudiatus ad sodalem tuum, virum optimum, M. Metellum
demigrasti, quem tu videlicet et ad custodiendum te diligentissimum
et ad suspicandum sagacissimum et ad vindicandum fortissimum
fore putasti. Sed quam longe videtur a carcere atque a vinculis   220
abesse debere qui se ipse iam dignum custodia iudicarit?

[20]   Quae cum ita sint, Catilina, dubitas, si emori aequo animo non
potes, abire in aliquas terras et vitam istam multis suppliciis iustis
debitisque ereptam fugae solitudinique mandare? "Refer" inquis
"ad senatum"; id enim postulas et, si hic ordo placere sibi decreverit   225
te ire in exsilium, obtemperaturum te esse dicis. Non referam, id
quod abhorret a meis moribus, et tamen faciam ut intellegas quid hi
de te sentiant. Egredere ex urbe, Catilina, libera rem publicam
metu, in exsilium, si hanc vocem exspectas, proficiscere. Quid est?
ecquid attendis, ecquid animadvertis horum silentium? Patiuntur,   230
tacent. Quid exspectas auctoritatem loquentium, quorum
voluntatem tacitorum perspicis?

[21]   At si hoc idem huic adulescenti optimo P. Sestio, si fortissimo
viro M. Marcello dixissem, iam mihi consuli hoc ipso in templo

senatus iure optimo vim et manus intulisset. De te autem, Catilina,   235
cum quiescunt, probant; cum patiuntur, decernunt; cum tacent,
clamant. Neque hi solum (quorum tibi auctoritas est videlicet cara,
vita vilissima), sed etiam illi equites Romani, honestissimi atque
optimi viri, ceterique fortissimi cives qui circumstant senatum,
quorum tu et frequentiam videre et studia perspicere et voces paulo   240
ante exaudire potuisti. Quorum ego vix abs te iam diu manus ac tela
contineo, eosdem facile adducam ut te haec quae vastare iam
pridem studes relinquentem usque ad portas prosequantur.

[22]   Quamquam quid loquor? te ut ulla res frangat, tu ut umquam
te corrigas, tu ut ullam fugam meditere, tu ut ullum exsilium   245
cogites? Utinam tibi istam mentem di immortales duint! Tametsi
video, si mea voce perterritus, ire in exsilium animum induxeris,
quanta tempestas invidiae nobis, si minus in praesens tempus
recenti memoria scelerum tuorum, at in posteritatem impendeat.
Sed est tanti, dum modo tua ista sit privata calamitas, et a rei   250
publicae periculis seiungatur. Sed tu ut vitiis tuis commoveare, ut
legum poenas pertimescas, ut temporibus rei publicae cedas non est
postulandum. Neque enim is es, Catilina, ut te aut pudor a
turpitudine aut metus a periculo aut ratio a furore revocarit.

[23]   Quam ob rem, ut saepe iam dixi, proficiscere ac, si mihi inimico,   255
ut praedicas, tuo conflare vis invidiam, recta perge in exsilium. Vix
feram sermones hominum, si id feceris; vix molem istius invidiae, si
in exsilium iussu consulis iveris, sustinebo. Sin autem servire meae
laudi et gloriae mavis, egredere cum importuna sceleratorum manu,
confer te ad Manlium, concita perditos cives, secerne te a bonis,   260
infer patriae bellum, exsulta impio latrocinio, ut a me non eiectus ad
alienos, sed invitatus ad tuos isse videaris.

[24]   Quamquam quid ego te invitem, a quo iam sciam esse
praemissos qui tibi ad Forum Aurelium praestolarentur armati, cui
sciam pactam et constitutam cum Manlio diem, a quo etiam aquilam   265
illam argenteam quam tibi ac tuis omnibus confido perniciosam ac
funestam futuram, cui domi tuae sacrarium sceleratum constitutum
fuit, sciam esse praemissam? Tu ut illa carere diutius possis, quam

venerari ad caedem proficiscens solebas, a cuius altaribus saepe
istam impiam dexteram ad necem civium transtulisti?   270

[25]   Ibis tandem aliquando quo te iam pridem tua ista cupiditas
effrenata ac furiosa rapiebat; neque enim tibi haec res adfert
dolorem, sed quandam incredibilem voluptatem. Ad hanc te
amentiam natura peperit, voluntas exercuit, fortuna servavit.
Numquam tu non modo otium sed ne bellum quidem nisi nefarium   275
concupisti. Nactus es ex perditis atque ab omni non modo fortuna
verum etiam spe derelictis conflatam improborum manum.

[26]   Hic tu qua laetitia perfruere, quibus gaudiis exsultabis, quanta
in voluptate bacchabere, cum in tanto numero tuorum neque audies
virum bonum quemquam neque videbis! Ad huius vitae studium   280
meditati illi sunt (qui feruntur) labores tui; iacere humi non solum
ad obsidendum stuprum verum etiam ad facinus obeundum,
vigilare non solum insidiantem somno maritorum verum etiam
bonis otiosorum. Habes ubi ostentes tuam illam praeclaram
patientiam famis, frigoris, inopiae rerum omnium quibus te brevi   285
tempore confectum esse senties.

[27]   Tantum profeci, cum te a consulatu reppuli, ut exsul potius
temptare quam consul vexare rem publicam posses, atque ut id
quod esset a te scelerate susceptum latrocinium potius quam bellum
nominaretur.   290
    Nunc, ut a me, patres conscripti, quandam prope iustam
patriae querimoniam detester ac deprecer, percipite, quaeso,
diligenter quae dicam, et ea penitus animis vestris mentibusque
mandate. Etenim si mecum patria, quae mihi vita mea multo est
carior, si cuncta Italia, si omnis res publica loquatur: "M. Tulli, quid   295
agis? Tune eum quem esse hostem comperisti, quem ducem belli
futurum vides, quem exspectari imperatorem in castris hostium
sentis, auctorem sceleris, principem coniurationis, evocatorem
servorum et civium perditorum, exire patiere, ut abs te non emissus
ex urbe, sed immissus in urbem esse videatur? Nonne hunc in   300
vincla duci, non ad mortem rapi, non summo supplicio mactari
imperabis? Quid tandem te impedit? mosne maiorum?

[28]   "At persaepe etiam privati in hac re publica perniciosos civis morte multarunt. An leges quae de civium Romanorum supplicio rogatae sunt? At numquam in hac urbe qui a re publica defecerunt   305
civium iura tenuerunt. An invidiam posteritatis times? Praeclaram vero populo Romano refers gratiam qui te, hominem per te cognitum, nulla commendatione maiorum tam mature ad summum imperium per omnis honorum gradus extulit, si propter invidiam aut alicuius periculi metum salutem civium tuorum neglegis.   310

[29]   "Sed si quis est invidiae metus, non est vehementius severitatis ac fortitudinis invidia quam inertiae ac nequitiae pertimescenda. An, cum bello vastabitur Italia, vexabuntur urbes, tecta ardebunt, tum te non existimas invidiae incendio conflagraturum?"
His ego sanctissimis rei publicae vocibus et eorum hominum   315
qui hoc idem sentiunt mentibus pauca respondebo: Ego, si hoc optimum factu iudicarem, patres conscripti, Catilinam morte multari, unius usuram horae gladiatori isti ad vivendum non dedissem. Etenim si summi viri et clarissimi cives Saturnini et Gracchorum et Flacci et superiorum complurium sanguine non   320
modo se non contaminarunt sed etiam honestarunt, certe verendum mihi non erat ne quid hoc parricida civium interfecto invidiae mihi in posteritatem redundaret. Quod si ea mihi maxime impenderet, tamen hoc animo fui semper ut invidiam virtute partam gloriam, non invidiam putarem.   325

[30]   Quamquam non nulli sunt in hoc ordine qui aut ea quae imminent non videant aut ea quae vident dissimulent; qui spem Catilinae mollibus sententiis aluerunt coniurationemque nascentem non credendo conroboraverunt; quorum auctoritate multi non solum improbi verum etiam imperiti, si in hunc animadvertissem,   330
crudeliter et regie factum esse dicerent. Nunc intellego, si iste, quo intendit, in Manliana castra pervenerit, neminem tam stultum fore qui non videat coniurationem esse factam, neminem tam improbum qui non fateatur. Hoc autem uno interfecto intellego hanc rei publicae pestem paulisper reprimi, non in perpetuum comprimi   335
posse. Quod si sese eiecerit secumque suos eduxerit et eodem ceteros undique conlectos naufragos adgregarit, exstinguetur atque

delebitur non modo haec tam adulta rei publicae pestis verum etiam stirps ac semen malorum omnium.

[31] Etenim iam diu, patres conscripti, in his periculis coniurationis insidiisque versamur, sed nescio quo pacto omnium scelerum ac veteris furoris et audaciae maturitas in nostri consulatus tempus erupit. Nunc si (ex tanto latrocinio) iste unus tolletur, videbimur fortasse ad breve quoddam tempus cura et metu esse relevati, periculum autem residebit et erit inclusum penitus in venis atque in visceribus rei publicae. Ut saepe homines aegri morbo gravi, cum aestu febrique iactantur, si aquam gelidam biberunt, primo relevari videntur, deinde multo gravius vehementiusque adflictantur, sic hic morbus qui est in re publica, relevatus istius poena, vehementius reliquis vivis ingravescet.

[32] Qua re secedant improbi, secernant se a bonis, unum in locum congregentur, muro denique, quod saepe iam dixi, secernantur (a nobis;) desinant insidiari domi suae consuli, circumstare tribunal praetoris urbani, obsidere cum gladiis curiam, malleolos et faces ad inflammandam urbem comparare; sit denique inscriptum in fronte unius cuiusque quid de re publica sentiat. Polliceor hoc vobis, patres conscripti, tantam in nobis consulibus fore diligentiam, tantam in vobis auctoritatem, tantam in equitibus Romanis virtutem, tantam in omnibus bonis consensionem ut Catilinae profectione omnia patefacta, inlustrata, oppressa, vindicata esse videatis.

[33] Hisce ominibus, Catilina, cum summa rei publicae salute, cum tua peste ac pernicie cumque eorum exitio qui se tecum omni scelere parricidioque iunxerunt, proficiscere ad impium bellum ac nefarium. Tu, Iuppiter, qui isdem quibus haec urbs auspiciis a Romulo es constitutus, quem Statorem huius urbis atque imperi vere nominamus, hunc et huius socios a tuis ceterisque templis, a tectis urbis ac moenibus, a vita fortunisque civium omnium arcebis et homines bonorum inimicos, hostis patriae, latrones Italiae scelerum foedere inter se ac nefaria societate coniunctos aeternis suppliciis vivos mortuosque mactabis.

340

345

350

355

360

365

370

IN L. CATILINAM ORATIO SECVNDA
HABITA AD POPVLVM

[1] Tandem aliquando, Quirites, L. Catilinam, furentem audacia, scelus anhelantem, pestem patriae nefarie molientem, vobis atque huic urbi ferro flammaque minitantem ex urbe vel eiecimus vel emisimus vel ipsum egredientem verbis prosecuti sumus. Abiit, excessit, evasit, erupit. Nulla iam pernicies a monstro illo atque   5
prodigio moenibus ipsis intra moenia comparabitur. Atque hunc quidem unum huius belli domestici ducem sine controversia vicimus. Non enim iam inter latera nostra sica illa versabitur, non in campo, non in foro, non in curia, non denique intra domesticos parietes pertimescemus. Loco ille motus est, cum est ex urbe   10
depulsus. Palam iam cum hoste nullo impediente bellum iustum geremus. Sine dubio perdidimus hominem magnificeque vicimus, cum illum ex occultis insidiis in apertum latrocinium coniecimus.

[2] Quod vero non cruentum mucronem, ut voluit, extulit, quod vivis nobis egressus est, quod ei ferrum e manibus extorsimus, quod   15
incolumis civis, quod stantem urbem reliquit, quanto tandem illum maerore esse adflictum et profligatum putatis? Iacet ille nunc prostratus, Quirites, et se perculsum atque abiectum esse sentit et retorquet oculos profecto saepe ad hanc urbem quam e suis faucibus ereptam esse luget: quae quidem mihi laetari videtur, quod   20
tantam pestem evomuerit forasque proiecerit.

[3] Ac si quis est talis qualis esse omnis oportebat, qui in hoc ipso in quo exsultat et triumphat oratio mea me vehementer accuset, quod tam capitalem hostem non comprehenderim potius quam emiserim, non est ista mea culpa, Quirites, sed temporum.   25
Interfectum esse L. Catilinam et gravissimo supplicio adfectum iam pridem oportebat, idque a me et mos maiorum et huius imperi severitas et res publica postulabat. Sed quam multos fuisse putatis, qui quae ego deferrem non crederent, quam multos qui propter stultitiam non putarent, quam multos qui etiam defenderent, quam   30
multos qui propter improbitatem faverent? Ac si illo sublato depelli a vobis omne periculum iudicarem, iam pridem ego L. Catilinam (non modo invidiae meae verum etiam vitae periculo) sustulissem.

[4]   Sed cum viderem, ne vobis quidem omnibus etiam tum re
probata, si illum (ut erat meritus), morte multassem, fore ut eius   35
socios invidia oppressus persequi non possem, rem huc deduxi ut
tum palam pugnare possetis cum hostem aperte videretis. Quem
quidem ego hostem, Quirites, quam vehementer foris esse timendum
putem, licet hinc intellegatis, quod etiam illud moleste fero quod ex
urbe parum comitatus exierit. Utinam ille omnis secum suas copias   40
eduxisset! Tongilium mihi eduxit quem amare in praetexta
coeperat, Publicium et Minucium quorum aes alienum, contractum
in popina, nullum rei publicae motum adferre poterat: reliquit quos
viros, quanto aere alieno, quam valentis, quam nobilis!

[5]   Itaque ego illum exercitum prae Gallicanis legionibus et hoc   45
dilectu quem in agro Piceno et Gallico Q. Metellus habuit, et his
copiis quae a nobis cotidie comparantur, magno opere contemno,
conlectum ex senibus desperatis, ex agresti luxuria, ex rusticis
decoctoribus, ex eis qui vadimonia deserere quam illum exercitum
maluerunt; quibus ego non modo si aciem exercitus nostri, verum   50
etiam si edictum praetoris ostendero, concident. Hos quos video
volitare in foro, quos stare ad curiam, quos etiam in senatum venire,
qui nitent unguentis, qui fulgent purpura, mallem secum suos
milites eduxisset: qui si hic permanent, mementote non tam
exercitum illum esse nobis quam hos qui exercitum deseruerunt   55
pertimescendos. Atque hoc etiam sunt timendi magis quod quid
cogitent me scire sentiunt neque tamen permoventur.

[6]   Video cui sit Apulia attributa, quis habeat Etruriam, quis
agrum Picenum, quis Gallicum, quis sibi has urbanas insidias caedis
atque incendiorum depoposcerit. Omnia superioris noctis consilia   60
ad me perlata esse sentiunt; patefeci in senatu hesterno die; Catilina
ipse pertimuit, profugit: hi quid exspectant? Ne illi vehementer
errant, si illam meam pristinam lenitatem perpetuam sperant
futuram.
        Quod exspectavi, iam sum adsecutus ut vos omnes factam esse   65
aperte coniurationem contra rem publicam videretis; nisi vero si
quis est qui Catilinae similis cum Catilina sentire non putet. Non est
iam lenitati locus; severitatem res ipsa flagitat. Unum etiam nunc
concedam: exeant, proficiscantur, ne patiantur desiderio sui

Catilinam miserum tabescere. Demonstrabo iter: Aurelia via   70
profectus est; si accelerare volent, ad vesperam consequentur.

[7] O fortunatam rem publicam, si quidem hanc sentinam urbis
eiecerit! Uno me hercule Catilina exhausto, levata mihi et recreata
res publica videtur. Quid enim mali aut sceleris fingi aut cogitari
potest quod non ille conceperit? Quis tota Italia veneficus, quis   75
gladiator, quis latro, quis sicarius, quis parricida, quis
testamentorum subiector, quis circumscriptor, quis ganeo, quis
nepos, quis adulter, quae mulier infamis, quis corruptor iuventutis,
quis corruptus, quis perditus inveniri potest qui se cum Catilina non
familiarissime vixisse fateatur? Quae caedes per hosce annos sine   80
illo facta est, quod nefarium stuprum non per illum?

[8] Iam vero quae tanta umquam in ullo iuventutis inlecebra fuit
quanta in illo? Qui alios ipse amabat turpissime, aliorum amori
flagitiosissime serviebat, aliis fructum libidinum, aliis mortem
parentum non modo impellendo verum etiam adiuvando   85
pollicebatur. Nunc vero quam subito non solum ex urbe verum
etiam ex agris ingentem numerum perditorum hominum conlegerat!
Nemo, non modo Romae sed ne ullo quidem in angulo totius Italiae,
oppressus aere alieno fuit quem non ad hoc incredibile sceleris
foedus asciverit.   90

[9] Atque ut eius diversa studia in dissimili ratione perspicere
possitis, nemo est in ludo gladiatorio paulo ad facinus audacior qui
se non intimum Catilinae esse fateatur, nemo in scaena levior et
nequior qui se non eiusdem prope sodalem fuisse commemoret.
Atque idem tamen stuprorum et scelerum exercitatione, adsuefactus   95
frigore et fame et siti et vigiliis perferendis, fortis ab istis
praedicabatur, cum industriae subsidia atque instrumenta virtutis in
libidine audaciaque consumeret.

[10] Hunc vero si secuti erunt sui comites, si ex urbe exierint
desperatorum hominum flagitiosi greges, o nos beatos, o rem   100
publicam fortunatam, o praeclaram laudem consulatus mei! Non
enim iam sunt mediocres hominum libidines, non humanae et
tolerandae audaciae; nihil cogitant nisi caedem, nisi incendia, nisi

rapinas. Patrimonia sua profuderunt, fortunas suas obligaverunt; res eos iam pridem, fides nuper deficere coepit: eadem tamen illa, 105 quae erat in abundantia, libido permanet. Quod si in vino et alea comissationes solum et scorta quaererent, essent illi quidem desperandi, sed tamen essent ferendi: hoc vero quis ferre possit, inertis homines fortissimis viris insidiari, stultissimos prudentissimis, ebrios sobriis, dormientis vigilantibus? Qui mihi 110 accubantes in conviviis, complexi mulieres impudicas, vino languidi, conferti cibo, sertis redimiti, unguentis obliti, debilitati stupris eructant sermonibus suis caedem bonorum atque urbis incendia.

[11]   Quibus ego confido impendere fatum aliquod et poenam iam diu improbitati, nequitiae, sceleri, libidini debitam aut instare iam 115 plane aut certe appropinquare. Quos si meus consulatus, quoniam sanare non potest, sustulerit, non breve nescio quod tempus sed multa saecula propagarit rei publicae. Nulla enim est natio quam pertimescamus, nullus rex qui bellum populo Romano facere possit. Omnia sunt externa unius virtute terra marique pacata: domesticum 120 bellum manet, intus insidiae sunt, intus inclusum periculum est, intus est hostis. Cum luxuria nobis, cum amentia, cum scelere certandum est. Huic ego me bello ducem profiteor, Quirites; suscipio inimicitias hominum perditorum; quae sanari poterunt quacumque ratione sanabo, quae resecanda erunt non patiar ad 125 perniciem civitatis manere. Proinde aut exeant aut quiescant aut, si et in urbe et in eadem mente permanent, ea quae merentur exspectent.

[12]   At etiam sunt qui dicant, Quirites, a me eiectum esse Catilinam. Quod ego si verbo adsequi possem, istos ipsos eicerem 130 qui haec loquuntur. Homo enim videlicet timidus aut etiam permodestus vocem consulis ferre non potuit; simul atque ire in exsilium iussus est, paruit. Quin hesterno die, cum domi meae paene interfectus essem, senatum in aedem Iovis Statoris convocavi, rem omnem ad patres conscriptos detuli. Quo cum Catilina venisset, 135 quis eum senator appellavit, quis salutavit, quis denique ita aspexit ut perditum civem ac non potius ut importunissimum hostem? Quin etiam principes eius ordinis partem illam subselliorum ad quam ille accesserat nudam atque inanem reliquerunt.

[13]   Hic ego, vehemens ille consul qui verbo civis in exsilium eicio,   140
quaesivi a Catilina in nocturno conventu ad M. Laecam fuisset
necne. Cum ille homo audacissimus conscientia convictus, primo
reticuisset, patefeci cetera: quid ea nocte egisset, ubi fuisset, quid in
proximam constituisset, quem ad modum esset ei ratio totius belli
descripta edocui. Cum haesitaret, cum teneretur, quaesivi quid   145
dubitaret proficisci eo quo iam pridem pararet, cum arma, cum
securis, cum fascis, cum tubas, cum signa militaria, cum aquilam
illam argenteam cui ille etiam sacrarium domi suae fecerat scirem
esse praemissam.

[14]   In exsilium eiciebam quem iam ingressum esse in bellum   150
videram? Etenim, credo, Manlius iste centurio qui in agro Faesulano
castra posuit, bellum populo Romano suo nomine indixit, et illa
castra nunc non Catilinam ducem exspectant, et ille eiectus in
exsilium, se Massiliam, ut aiunt, non in haec castra confert.

O condicionem miseram non modo administrandae verum   155
etiam conservandae rei publicae! Nunc si L. Catilina consiliis,
laboribus, periculis meis circumclusus ac debilitatus subito
pertimuerit, sententiam mutaverit, deseruerit suos, consilium belli
faciendi abiecerit, et ex hoc cursu sceleris ac belli iter ad fugam
atque in exsilium converterit, non ille a me spoliatus armis audaciae,   160
non obstupefactus ac perterritus mea diligentia, non de spe
conatuque depulsus, sed indemnatus innocens in exsilium eiectus a
consule vi et minis esse dicetur: et erunt qui illum, si hoc fecerit,
non improbum sed miserum, me non diligentissimum consulem sed
crudelissimum tyrannum existimari velint!   165

[15]   Est mihi tanti, Quirites, huius invidiae falsae atque iniquae
tempestatem subire, dum modo a vobis huius horribilis belli ac
nefarii periculum depellatur. Dicatur sane eiectus esse a me, dum
modo eat in exsilium. Sed mihi credite, non est iturus. Numquam
ego ab dis immortalibus optabo, Quirites, invidiae meae relevandae   170
causa ut L. Catilinam ducere exercitum hostium atque in armis
volitare audiatis, sed triduo tamen audietis; multoque magis illud
timeo ne mihi sit invidiosum aliquando, quod illum emiserim potius
quam quod eiecerim. Sed cum sint homines qui illum, cum
profectus sit, eiectum esse dicant, idem, si interfectus esset, quid   175
dicerent?

[16]   Quamquam isti qui Catilinam Massiliam ire dictitant non tam
hoc queruntur quam verentur. Nemo est istorum tam misericors
qui illum non ad Manlium quam ad Massiliensis ire malit. Ille
autem, si me hercule hoc quod agit numquam antea cogitasset,   180
tamen latrocinantem se interfici mallet quam exsulem vivere. Nunc
vero, cum ei nihil adhuc praeter ipsius voluntatem cogitationemque
acciderit (nisi quod vivis nobis Roma profectus est), optemus potius
ut eat in exsilium quam queramur.

[17]   Sed cur tam diu de uno hoste loquimur et de eo hoste qui iam   185
fatetur se esse hostem, et quem, quia (quod semper volui), murus
interest, non timeo: de his qui dissimulant, qui Romae remanent, qui
nobiscum sunt nihil dicimus? Quos quidem ego, si ullo modo fieri
possit, non tam ulcisci studeo quam sanare sibi ipsos, placare rei
publicae. Neque id qua re fieri non possit, si iam me audire volent,   190
intellego. Exponam enim vobis, Quirites, ex quibus generibus
hominum istae copiae comparentur; deinde singulis medicinam
consili atque orationis meae, si quam potero, adferam.

[18]   Unum genus est eorum qui, magno in aere alieno, maiores
etiam possessiones habent; quarum amore adducti, dissolvi nullo   195
modo possunt. Horum hominum species est honestissima—sunt
enim locupletes—voluntas vero et causa impudentissima. Tu agris,
tu aedificiis, tu argento, tu familia, tu rebus omnibus ornatus et
copiosus sis, et dubites de possessione detrahere, adquirere ad
fidem? Quid enim exspectas? Bellum? Quid ergo? In vastatione   200
omnium tuas possessiones sacrosanctas futuras putes? An tabulas
novas? Errant qui istas a Catilina exspectant: meo beneficio tabulae
novae proferuntur, verum auctionariae; neque enim isti qui
possessiones habent alia ratione ulla salvi esse possunt. Quod si
maturius facere voluissent neque (id quod stultissimum est), certare   205
cum usuris fructibus praediorum, et locupletioribus his et
melioribus civibus uteremur. Sed hosce homines minime puto
pertimescendos, quod aut deduci de sententia possunt aut, si
permanebunt, magis mihi videntur vota facturi contra rem publicam
quam arma laturi.   210

[19]   Alterum genus est eorum qui, quamquam premuntur aere
alieno, dominationem tamen exspectant, rerum potiri volunt,

honores quos quieta re publica desperant perturbata se consequi
posse arbitrantur. Quibus hoc praecipiendum videtur, unum scilicet
et idem quod reliquis omnibus, ut desperent id quod conantur se   215
consequi posse: primum omnium me ipsum vigilare, adesse,
providere rei publicae; deinde magnos animos esse in bonis viris,
magnam concordiam <ordinum>, maximam multitudinem, magnas
praeterea militum copias; deos denique immortalis huic invicto
populo, clarissimo imperio, pulcherrimae urbi contra tantam vim   220
sceleris praesentis auxilium esse laturos. Quod si iam sint id quod
summo furore cupiunt adepti, num illi in cinere urbis et in sanguine
civium, quae mente conscelerata ac nefaria concupiverunt, consules
se aut dictatores aut etiam reges sperant futuros? Non vident id se
cupere quod, si adepti sint, fugitivo alicui aut gladiatori concedi sit   225
necesse?

[20] Tertium genus est aetate iam adfectum, sed tamen
exercitatione robustum; quo ex genere iste est Manlius cui nunc
Catilina succedit. Hi sunt homines ex eis coloniis quas Sulla
constituit; quas ego universas civium esse optimorum et   230
fortissimorum virorum sentio, sed tamen ei sunt coloni qui se
insperatis ac repentinis pecuniis sumptuosius insolentiusque
iactarunt. Hi dum aedificant tamquam beati, dum praediis lectis,
familiis magnis, conviviis apparatis delectantur, in tantum aes
alienum inciderunt ut, si salvi esse velint, Sulla sit eis ab inferis   235
excitandus: qui etiam non nullos agrestis homines tenuis atque
egentis in eandem illam spem rapinarum veterum impulerunt. Quos
ego utrosque in eodem genere praedatorum direptorumque pono,
sed eos hoc moneo, desinant furere ac proscriptiones et dictaturas
cogitare. Tantus enim illorum temporum dolor inustus est civitati   240
ut iam ista non modo homines sed ne pecudes quidem mihi
passurae esse videantur.

[21]   Quartum genus est sane varium et mixtum et turbulentum; qui
iam pridem premuntur, qui numquam emergunt, qui partim inertia,
partim male gerendo negotio, partim etiam sumptibus, in vetere   245
aere alieno vacillant; qui vadimoniis, iudiciis, proscriptione
bonorum defetigati permulti et ex urbe et ex agris se in illa castra
conferre dicuntur. Hosce ego non tam milites acris quam

infitiatores lentos esse arbitror. Qui homines quam primum, si stare
non possunt, conruant, sed ita ut non modo civitas sed ne vicini   250
quidem proximi sentiant. Nam illud non intellego, quam ob rem, si
vivere honeste non possunt, perire turpiter velint, aut cur minore
dolore perituros se cum multis quam si soli pereant arbitrentur.

[22]   Quintum genus est parricidarum, sicariorum, denique omnium
facinerosorum. Quos ego a Catilina non revoco; nam neque ab eo   255
divelli possunt et pereant sane in latrocinio, quoniam sunt ita multi
ut eos carcer capere non possit. Postremum autem genus est non
solum numero verum etiam genere ipso atque vita quod proprium
Catilinae est, de eius dilectu, immo vero de complexu eius ac sinu;
quos pexo capillo, nitidos, aut imberbis aut bene barbatos videtis,   260
manicatis et talaribus tunicis, velis amictos, non togis; quorum
omnis industria vitae et vigilandi labor in antelucanis cenis
expromitur.

[23]   In his gregibus omnes aleatores, omnes adulteri, omnes impuri
impudicique versantur. Hi pueri tam lepidi ac delicati non solum   265
amare et amari neque saltare et cantare sed etiam sicas vibrare et
spargere venena didicerunt. Qui nisi exeunt, nisi pereunt, etiam si
Catilina perierit, scitote hoc in re publica seminarium Catilinarum
futurum. Verum tamen quid sibi isti miseri volunt? num suas secum
mulierculas sunt in castra ducturi? Quem ad modum autem   270
illis carere poterunt, his praesertim iam noctibus? Quo autem pacto
illi Appenninum atque illas pruinas ac nivis perferent? Nisi idcirco
se facilius hiemem toleraturos putant, quod nudi in conviviis saltare
didicerunt.

[24]   O bellum magno opere pertimescendum, cum hanc sit   275
habiturus Catilina scortorum cohortem praetoriam! Instruite nunc,
Quirites, contra has tam praeclaras Catilinae copias, vestra praesidia
vestrosque exercitus. Et primum gladiatori illi confecto et saucio
consules imperatoresque vestros opponite; deinde contra illam
naufragorum eiectam ac debilitatam manum, florem totius Italiae ac   280
robur educite. Iam vero urbes coloniarum ac municipiorum
respondebunt Catilinae tumulis silvestribus. Neque ego ceteras
copias, ornamenta, praesidia vestra cum illius latronis inopia atque
egestate conferre debeo.

[25]   Sed si, omissis his rebus quibus nos suppeditamur, eget ille,   285
senatu, equitibus Romanis, urbe, aerario, vectigalibus, cuncta Italia,
provinciis omnibus, exteris nationibus; si his rebus omissis causas
ipsas quae inter se confligunt contendere velimus, ex eo ipso quam
valde illi iaceant intellegere possumus. Ex hac enim parte pudor
pugnat, illinc petulantia; hinc pudicitia, illinc stuprum; hinc fides,   290
illinc fraudatio; hinc pietas, illinc scelus; hinc constantia, illinc
furor; hinc honestas, illinc turpitudo; hinc continentia, illinc libido;
hinc denique aequitas, temperantia, fortitudo, prudentia, virtutes
omnes certant cum iniquitate, luxuria, ignavia, temeritate, cum vitiis
omnibus; postremo copia cum egestate, bona ratio cum perdita,   295
mens sana cum amentia, bona denique spes cum omnium rerum
desperatione confligit. In eius modi certamine ac proelio nonne, si
hominum studia deficiant, di ipsi immortales cogant ab his
praeclarissimis virtutibus tot et tanta vitia superari?

[26]   Quae cum ita sint, Quirites, vos, quem ad modum iam antea   300
dixi, vestra tecta vigiliis custodiisque defendite; mihi ut urbi sine
vestro metu ac sine ullo tumultu satis esset praesidi consultum
atque provisum est. Coloni omnes municipesque vestri certiores a
me facti de hac nocturna excursione Catilinae, facile urbis suas
finisque defendent; gladiatores, quam sibi ille manum certissimam   305
fore putavit, quamquam animo meliore sunt quam pars patriciorum,
potestate tamen nostra continebuntur. Q. Metellus quem ego (hoc
prospiciens) in agrum Gallicum Picenumque praemisi, aut opprimet
hominem aut eius omnis motus conatusque prohibebit. Reliquis
autem de rebus constituendis, maturandis, agendis iam ad senatum   310
referemus, quem vocari videtis.

[27]   Nunc illos qui in urbe remanserunt atque adeo qui contra
urbis salutem omniumque vestrum in urbe a Catilina relicti sunt,
quamquam sunt hostes, tamen, quia nati sunt cives, monitos etiam
atque etiam volo. Mea lenitas adhuc si cui solutior visa est, hoc   315
exspectavit ut id quod latebat erumperet. Quod reliquum est, iam
non possum oblivisci meam hanc esse patriam, me horum esse
consulem, mihi aut cum his vivendum aut pro his esse moriendum.
Nullus est portis custos, nullus insidiator viae: si qui exire volunt,
conivere possum; qui vero se in urbe commoverit, cuius ego non   320

modo factum sed vel inceptum ullum conatumve contra patriam
deprehendero; sentiet in hac urbe esse consules vigilantis, esse
egregios magistratus, esse fortem senatum, esse arma, esse carcerem
quem vindicem nefariorum ac manifestorum scelerum maiores
nostri esse voluerunt.   325

[28]   Atque haec omnia sic agentur ut maximae res minimo motu,
pericula summa nullo tumultu, bellum intestinum ac domesticum
post hominum memoriam crudelissimum et maximum me uno
togato duce et imperatore sedetur. Quod ego sic administrabo,
Quirites, ut (si ullo modo fieri poterit), ne improbus quidem   330
quisquam in hac urbe poenam sui sceleris sufferat. Sed si vis
manifestae audaciae, si impendens patriae periculum me necessario
de hac animi lenitate deduxerit, illud profecto perficiam quod in
tanto et tam insidioso bello vix optandum videtur, ut neque bonus
quisquam intereat paucorumque poena vos omnes salvi esse   335
possitis.

[29]   Quae quidem ego neque mea prudentia neque humanis
consiliis fretus polliceor vobis, Quirites, sed multis et non dubiis
deorum immortalium significationibus, quibus ego ducibus in hanc
spem sententiamque sum ingressus; qui iam non procul (ut   340
quondam solebant), ab externo hoste atque longinquo, sed hic
praesentes, suo numine atque auxilio sua templa atque urbis tecta
defendunt. Quos vos, Quirites, precari, venerari, implorare debetis
ut, quam urbem pulcherrimam florentissimam potentissimamque
esse voluerunt, hanc omnibus hostium copiis terra marique   345
superatis a perditissimorum civium nefario scelere defendant.

IN L. CATILINAM ORATIO TERTIA
HABITA AD POPVLVM

[1] Rem publicam, Quirites, vitamque omnium vestrum, bona,
fortunas, coniuges liberosque vestros atque hoc domicilium
clarissimi imperi, fortunatissimam pulcherrimamque urbem,
hodierno die deorum immortalium summo erga vos amore,
laboribus, consiliis, periculis meis e flamma atque ferro ac paene ex   5
faucibus fati ereptam et vobis conservatam ac restitutam videtis.

[2] Et si non minus nobis iucundi atque inlustres sunt ei dies
quibus conservamur, quam illi quibus nascimur, quod salutis certa
laetitia est, nascendi incerta condicio et quod sine sensu nascimur,
cum voluptate servamur, profecto, quoniam illum qui hanc urbem   10
condidit ad deos immortalis benevolentia famaque sustulimus, esse
apud vos posterosque vestros in honore debebit is qui eandem hanc
urbem conditam amplificatamque servavit. Nam toti urbi, templis,
delubris, tectis ac moenibus subiectos prope iam ignis
circumdatosque restinximus, idemque gladios in rem publicam   15
destrictos rettudimus mucronesque eorum a iugulis vestris
deiecimus.

[3] Quae quoniam in senatu inlustrata, patefacta, comperta sunt
per me, vobis iam exponam breviter ut et quanta et quam manifesta
et qua ratione investigata et comprehensa sint vos qui et ignoratis et   20
exspectatis scire possitis.
    Principio, ut Catilina paucis ante diebus erupit ex urbe, cum
sceleris sui socios, huiusce nefarii belli acerrimos duces Romae
reliquisset, semper vigilavi et providi, Quirites, quem ad modum in
tantis et tam absconditis insidiis salvi esse possemus. Nam tum cum   25
ex urbe Catilinam eiciebam—non enim iam vereor huius verbi
invidiam, cum illa magis sit timenda, quod vivus exierit—sed tum
cum illum exterminari volebam, aut reliquam coniuratorum manum
simul exituram aut eos qui restitissent infirmos sine illo ac debilis
fore putabam.   30

[4] Atque ego, ut vidi, quos maximo furore et scelere esse
inflammatos sciebam, eos nobiscum esse et Romae remansisse, in eo

omnis dies noctesque consumpsi ut quid agerent, quid molirent
sentirem ac viderem, ut (quoniam auribus vestris propter
incredibilem magnitudinem sceleris minorem fidem faceret oratio
mea), rem ita comprehenderem ut tum demum animis saluti vestrae
provideretis cum oculis maleficium ipsum videretis. Itaque ut
comperi legatos Allobrogum, belli Transalpini et tumultus Gallici
excitandi causa, a P. Lentulo esse sollicitatos, eosque in Galliam ad   40
suos civis eodemque itinere cum litteris mandatisque ad Catilinam
esse missos, comitemque eis adiunctum esse T. Volturcium, atque
huic esse ad Catilinam datas litteras, facultatem mihi oblatam putavi
ut (quod erat difficillimum quodque ego semper optabam ab dis
immortalibus) tota res non solum a me sed etiam a senatu et a vobis
manifesto deprenderetur.   45

[5]   Itaque hesterno die L. Flaccum et C. Pomptinum praetores,
fortissimos atque amantissimos rei publicae viros, ad me vocavi, rem
exposui, quid fieri placeret ostendi. Illi autem, qui omnia de re
publica praeclara atque egregia sentirent, sine recusatione ac sine
ulla mora negotium susceperunt et, cum advesperasceret, occulte ad   50
pontem Mulvium pervenerunt atque ibi in proximis villis ita
bipertito fuerunt ut Tiberis inter eos et pons interesset. Eodem
autem et ipsi sine cuiusquam suspicione multos fortis viros
eduxerant, et ego ex praefectura Reatina compluris delectos
adulescentis quorum opera utor adsidue in rei publicae praesidio   55
cum gladiis miseram.

[6]   Interim tertia fere vigilia exacta, cum iam pontem Mulvium
magno comitatu legati Allobroges ingredi inciperent unaque
Volturcius, fit in eos impetus; ducuntur et ab illis gladii et a nostris.
Res praetoribus erat nota solis, ignorabatur a ceteris. Tum   60
interventu Pomptini atque Flacci pugna quae erat commissa sedatur.
Litterae quaecumque erant in eo comitatu integris signis praetoribus
traduntur; ipsi comprehensi ad me, cum iam dilucesceret,
deducuntur. Atque horum omnium scelerum improbissimum
machinatorem, Cimbrum Gabinium, statim ad me nihil dum   65
suspicantem vocavi; deinde item arcessitus est L. Statilius et post
eum Cethegus; tardissime autem Lentulus venit, credo quod in
litteris dandis praeter consuetudinem proxima nocte vigilarat.

[7] Cum summis et clarissimis huius civitatis viris (qui audita re frequentes ad me mane convenerant) litteras a me prius aperiri 70 quam ad senatum deferri placeret, ne, si nihil esset inventum, temere a me tantus tumultus iniectus civitati videretur, negavi me esse facturum ut de periculo publico non ad consilium publicum rem integram deferrem. Etenim, Quirites, si ea quae erant ad me delata, reperta non essent, tamen ego non arbitrabar in tantis rei 75 publicae periculis esse mihi nimiam diligentiam pertimescendam. Senatum frequentem celeriter, ut vidistis, coegi.

[8] Atque interea statim admonitu Allobrogum, C. Sulpicium praetorem, fortem virum, misi qui ex aedibus Cethegi si quid telorum esset efferret; ex quibus ille maximum sicarum numerum et 80 gladiorum extulit.

Introduxi Volturcium sine Gallis; fidem publicam iussu senatus dedi; hortatus sum ut ea quae sciret sine timore indicaret. Tum ille dixit (cum vix se ex magno timore recreasset) a P. Lentulo se habere ad Catilinam mandata et litteras ut servorum praesidio uteretur, ut 85 ad urbem quam primum cum exercitu accederet; id autem eo consilio ut (cum urbem ex omnibus partibus quem ad modum descriptum distributumque erat incendissent caedemque infinitam civium fecissent) praesto esset ille qui et fugientis exciperet et se cum his urbanis ducibus coniungeret. 90

[9] Introducti autem Galli ius iurandum sibi et litteras a P. Lentulo, Cethego, Statilio ad suam gentem datas esse dixerunt, atque ita sibi ab his et a L. Cassio esse praescriptum ut equitatum in Italiam quam primum mitterent; pedestris sibi copias non defuturas. Lentulum autem sibi confirmasse ex fatis Sibyllinis haruspicumque 95 responsis se esse tertium illum Cornelium ad quem regnum huius urbis atque imperium pervenire esset necesse: Cinnam ante se et Sullam fuisse. Eundemque dixisse fatalem hunc annum esse ad interitum huius urbis atque imperi qui esset annus decimus post virginum absolutionem, post Capitoli autem incensionem vicesimum. 100

[10] Hanc autem Cethego cum ceteris controversiam fuisse dixerunt quod Lentulo et aliis Saturnalibus caedem fieri atque

urbem incendi placeret, Cethego nimium id longum videretur. Ac
ne longum sit, Quirites, tabellas proferri iussimus quae a quoque
dicebantur datae. Primo ostendimus Cethego: signum cognovit. Nos   105
linum incidimus; legimus. Erat scriptum ipsius manu Allobrogum
senatui et populo sese quae eorum legatis confirmasset facturum
esse; orare ut item illi facerent quae sibi eorum legati recepissent.
Tum Cethegus, qui paulo ante aliquid tamen de gladiis ac sicis quae
apud ipsum erant deprehensa respondisset dixissetque se semper   110
bonorum ferramentorum studiosum fuisse, recitatis litteris
debilitatus atque abiectus conscientia, repente conticuit.
Introductus Statilius cognovit et signum et manum suam. Recitatae
sunt tabellae in eandem fere sententiam; confessus est. Tum ostendi
tabellas Lentulo et quaesivi cognosceretne signum. Adnuit. "Est   115
vero" inquam "notum quidem signum, imago avi tui, clarissimi viri,
qui amavit unice patriam et civis suos; quae quidem te a tanto
scelere (etiam muta) revocare debuit."

[11]   Leguntur eadem ratione ad senatum Allobrogum populumque
litterae. Si quid de his rebus dicere vellet, feci potestatem. Atque   120
ille primo quidem negavit; post autem aliquanto, toto iam indicio
exposito atque edito, surrexit, quaesivit a Gallis quid sibi esset cum
eis, quam ob rem domum suam venissent, itemque a Volturcio. Qui
cum illi breviter constanterque respondissent per quem ad eum
quotiensque venissent, quaesissentque ab eo nihilne secum esset de   125
fatis Sibyllinis locutus, tum ille subito scelere demens, quanta
conscientiae vis esset ostendit. Nam, cum id posset infitiari, repente
praeter opinionem omnium, confessus est. Ita eum non modo
ingenium illud et dicendi exercitatio (qua semper valuit) sed etiam
(propter vim sceleris manifesti atque deprehensi) impudentia qua   130
superabat omnis improbitasque defecit.

[12]   Volturcius vero subito litteras proferri atque aperiri iubet quas
sibi a Lentulo ad Catilinam datas esse dicebat. Atque ibi
vehementissime perturbatus Lentulus tamen et signum et manum
suam cognovit. Erant autem sine nomine, sed ita: "Quis sim scies ex   135
eo quem ad te misi. Cura ut vir sis et cogita quem in locum sis
progressus. Vide ecquid tibi iam sit necesse et cura ut omnium tibi

auxilia adiungas, etiam infimorum." Gabinius deinde introductus, cum primo impudenter respondere coepisset, ad extremum nihil ex eis quae Galli insimulabant negavit.   140

[13] Ac mihi quidem, Quirites, cum illa certissima visa sunt argumenta atque indicia sceleris, tabellae, signa, manus, denique unius cuiusque confessio, tum multo certiora illa, color, oculi, voltus, taciturnitas. Sic enim obstupuerant, sic terram intuebantur, sic furtim non numquam inter sese aspiciebant ut non iam ab aliis   145 indicari sed indicare se ipsi viderentur.

   Indiciis expositis atque editis, Quirites, senatum consului de summa re publica quid fieri placeret. Dictae sunt a principibus acerrimae ac fortissimae sententiae, quas senatus sine ulla varietate est secutus. Et quoniam nondum est perscriptum senatus   150 consultum, ex memoria vobis, Quirites, quid senatus censuerit exponam.

[14] Primum mihi gratiae verbis amplissimis aguntur, quod virtute, consilio, providentia mea res publica maximis periculis sit liberata. Deinde L. Flaccus et C. Pomptinus praetores, quod eorum opera forti   155 fidelique usus essem, merito ac iure laudantur. Atque etiam viro forti, conlegae meo, laus impertitur, quod eos, qui huius coniurationis participes fuissent, a suis et a rei publicae consiliis removisset. Atque ita censuerunt ut P. Lentulus, cum se praetura abdicasset, in custodiam traderetur; itemque uti C. Cethegus, L.   160 Statilius, P. Gabinius qui omnes praesentes erant in custodiam traderentur; atque idem hoc decretum est in L. Cassium qui sibi procurationem incendendae urbis depoposcerat, in M. Ceparium cui ad sollicitandos pastores Apuliam attributam esse erat indicatum, in P. Furium qui est ex eis colonis quos Faesulas L. Sulla deduxit, in Q.   165 Annium Chilonem qui una cum hoc Furio semper erat in hac Allobrogum sollicitatione versatus, in P. Umbrenum, libertinum hominem, a quo primum Gallos ad Gabinium perductos esse constabat. Atque ea lenitate senatus est usus, Quirites, ut ex tanta coniuratione tantaque hac multitudine domesticorum hostium   170 novem hominum perditissimorum poena re publica conservata reliquorum mentis sanari posse arbitraretur.

[15]   Atque etiam supplicatio dis immortalibus pro singulari eorum merito meo nomine decreta est, quod mihi primum post hanc urbem conditam togato contigit, et his decreta verbis est: "quod   175
urbem incendiis, caede civis, Italiam bello liberassem." Quae supplicatio si cum ceteris supplicationibus conferatur, hoc interest, quod ceterae bene gesta, haec una conservata re publica constituta est. Atque illud quod faciendum primum fuit, factum atque transactum est. Nam P. Lentulus, quamquam patefactis indiciis,   180
confessionibus suis, iudicio senatus, non modo praetoris ius verum etiam civis amiserat, tamen magistratu se abdicavit, ut quae religio C. Mario, clarissimo viro, non fuerat quo minus C. Glauciam de quo nihil nominatim erat decretum praetorem occideret, ea nos religione in privato P. Lentulo puniendo liberaremur.   185

[16]   Nunc quoniam, Quirites, consceleratissimi periculosissimique belli nefarios duces captos iam et comprehensos tenetis, existimare debetis omnis Catilinae copias, omnis spes atque opes his depulsis urbis periculis concidisse. Quem quidem ego cum ex urbe pellebam, hoc providebam animo, Quirites, remoto Catilina non mihi esse P.   190
Lentuli somnum nec L. Cassi adipes nec C. Cethegi furiosam temeritatem pertimescendam. Ille erat unus timendus ex istis omnibus, sed tam diu dum urbis moenibus continebatur. Omnia norat, omnium aditus tenebat; appellare, temptare, sollicitare poterat, audebat. Erat ei consilium ad facinus aptum, consilio   195
autem neque lingua neque manus deerat. Iam ad certas res conficiendas certos homines delectos ac descriptos habebat. Neque vero, cum aliquid mandarat, confectum putabat: nihil erat quod non ipse obiret, occurreret, vigilaret, laboraret; frigus, sitim, famem ferre poterat.   200

[17]   Hunc ego hominem tam acrem, tam audacem, tam paratum, tam callidum, tam in scelere vigilantem, tam in perditis rebus diligentem, nisi ex domesticis insidiis in castrense latrocinium compulissem—dicam id quod sentio, Quirites—non facile hanc tantam molem mali a cervicibus vestris depulissem. Non ille nobis   205
Saturnalia constituisset, neque tanto ante exiti ac fati diem rei publicae denuntiavisset neque commisisset ut signum, ut litterae

suae, testes manifesti sceleris deprehenderentur. Quae nunc illo
absente sic gesta sunt ut nullum in privata domo furtum umquam
sit tam palam inventum quam haec in tota re publica coniuratio   210
manifesto comprehensa est. Quod si Catilina in urbe ad hanc diem
remansisset, quamquam, quoad fuit, omnibus eius consiliis occurri
atque obstiti, tamen, ut levissime dicam, dimicandum nobis cum illo
fuisset, neque nos umquam, cum ille in urbe hostis esset, tantis
periculis rem publicam tanta pace, tanto otio, tanto silentio   215
liberassemus.

[18]   Quamquam haec omnia, Quirites, ita sunt a me administrata ut
deorum immortalium nutu atque consilio et gesta et provisa esse
videantur. Idque cum coniectura consequi possumus (quod vix
videtur humani consili tantarum rerum gubernatio esse potuisse),   220
tum vero ita praesentes his temporibus, opem et auxilium nobis
tulerunt ut eos paene oculis videre possimus. Nam ut illa omittam,
visas nocturno tempore ab occidente faces ardoremque caeli, ut
fulminum iactus, ut terrae motus relinquam, ut omittam cetera quae
tam multa nobis consulibus facta sunt ut haec quae nunc fiunt   225
canere di immortales viderentur, hoc certe, Quirites, quod sum
dicturus neque praetermittendum neque relinquendum est.

[19]   Nam profecto memoria tenetis, Cotta et Torquato consulibus,
compluris in Capitolio res de caelo esse percussas, cum et simulacra
deorum depulsa sunt et statuae veterum hominum deiectae et   230
legum aera liquefacta et tactus etiam ille qui hanc urbem condidit
Romulus, quem inauratum in Capitolio, parvum atque lactantem,
uberibus lupinis inhiantem fuisse meministis. Quo quidem tempore
cum haruspices ex tota Etruria convenissent, caedis atque incendia
et legum interitum et bellum civile ac domesticum et totius urbis   235
atque imperi occasum appropinquare dixerunt, nisi di immortales
omni ratione placati, suo numine prope fata ipsa flexissent.

[20]   Itaque illorum responsis tum et ludi per decem dies facti sunt
neque res ulla quae ad placandos deos pertineret praetermissa est.
Idemque iusserunt simulacrum Iovis facere maius et in excelso   240
conlocare et contra atque antea fuerat ad orientem convertere; ac se
sperare dixerunt, si illud signum quod videtis solis ortum et forum

curiamque conspiceret, fore ut ea consilia quae clam essent inita
contra salutem urbis atque imperi inlustrarentur ut a senatu
populoque Romano perspici possent. Atque illud signum   245
conlocandum consules illi locaverunt; sed tanta fuit operis tarditas
ut neque superioribus consulibus neque nobis ante hodiernum diem
conlocaretur.

[21]   Hic quis potest esse tam aversus a vero, tam praeceps, tam
mente captus qui neget haec omnia quae videmus praecipueque   250
hanc urbem deorum immortalium nutu ac potestate administrari?
Etenim cum esset ita responsum, caedis, incendia, interitum rei
publicae comparari, et ea per civis (quae tum propter
magnitudinem scelerum non nullis incredibilia videbantur), ea non
modo cogitata a nefariis civibus verum etiam suscepta esse sensistis. 255
Illud vero nonne ita praesens est ut nutu Iovis Optimi Maximi
factum esse videatur, ut, cum hodierno die mane per forum meo
iussu et coniurati et eorum indices in aedem Concordiae ducerentur,
eo ipso tempore signum statueretur? Quo conlocato atque ad vos
senatumque converso, omnia et senatus et vos quae erant contra   260
salutem omnium cogitata inlustrata et patefacta vidistis.

[22]   Quo etiam maiore sunt isti odio supplicioque digni qui non
solum vestris domiciliis atque tectis sed etiam deorum templis atque
delubris sunt funestos ac nefarios ignis inferre conati. Quibus ego si
me restitisse dicam, nimium mihi sumam et non sim ferendus: ille,   265
ille Iuppiter restitit; ille Capitolium, ille haec templa, ille cunctam
urbem, ille vos omnis salvos esse voluit. Dis ego immortalibus
ducibus hanc mentem voluntatemque suscepi atque ad haec tanta
indicia perveni. Iam vero illa Allobrogum sollicitatio, iam ab
Lentulo ceterisque domesticis hostibus, tam dementer tantae res   270
creditae et ignotis et barbaris commissaeque litterae numquam
essent profecto, nisi ab dis immortalibus huic tantae audaciae
consilium esset ereptum. Quid vero? ut homines Galli ex civitate
male pacata, quae gens una restat quae bellum populo Romano
facere posse et non nolle videatur, spem imperi ac rerum   275
maximarum ultro sibi a patriciis hominibus oblatam neglegerent
vestramque salutem suis opibus anteponerent, id non divinitus esse
factum putatis, praesertim qui nos non pugnando sed tacendo
superare potuerint?

[23] Quam ob rem, Quirites, quoniam ad omnia pulvinaria   280
supplicatio decreta est, celebratote illos dies cum coniugibus ac
liberis vestris. Nam multi saepe honores dis immortalibus iusti
habiti sunt ac debiti, sed profecto iustiores numquam. Erepti enim
estis ex crudelissimo ac miserrimo interitu, erepti sine caede, sine
sanguine, sine exercitu, sine dimicatione; togati me uno togato duce   285
et imperatore vicistis.

[24]   Etenim recordamini, Quirites, omnis civilis dissensiones, non
solum eas quas audistis sed eas quas vosmet ipsi meministis atque
vidistis. L. Sulla P. Sulpicium oppressit: C. Marium, custodem huius
urbis, multosque fortis viros partim eiecit ex civitate, partim   290
interemit. Cn. Octavius consul armis expulit ex urbe conlegam:
omnis hic locus acervis corporum et civium sanguine redundavit.
Superavit postea Cinna cum Mario: tum vero clarissimis viris
interfectis lumina civitatis exstincta sunt. Ultus est huius victoriae
crudelitatem postea Sulla: ne dici quidem opus est quanta   295
deminutione civium et quanta calamitate rei publicae. Dissensit M.
Lepidus a clarissimo et fortissimo viro Q. Catulo: attulit non tam
ipsius interitus rei publicae luctum quam ceterorum.

[25]   Atque illae tamen omnes dissensiones erant eius modi quae
non ad delendam sed ad commutandam rem publicam pertinerent.   300
Non illi nullam esse rem publicam sed in ea quae esset se esse
principes, neque hanc urbem conflagrare sed se in hac urbe florere
voluerunt. Atque illae tamen omnes dissensiones, quarum nulla
exitium rei publicae quaesivit, eius modi fuerunt ut non
reconciliatione concordiae sed internicione civium diiudicatae sint.   305
In hoc autem uno post hominum memoriam maximo
crudelissimoque bello, quale bellum nulla umquam barbaria cum
sua gente gessit, quo in bello lex haec fuit a Lentulo, Catilina,
Cethego, Cassio constituta ut omnes qui salva urbe salvi esse possent
in hostium numero ducerentur, ita me gessi, Quirites, ut salvi omnes   310
conservaremini, et, cum hostes vestri tantum civium superfuturum
putassent quantum infinitae caedi restitisset, tantum autem urbis
quantum flamma obire non potuisset, et urbem et civis integros
incolumisque servavi.

[26]   Quibus pro tantis rebus, Quirites, nullum ego a vobis   315
praemium virtutis, nullum insigne honoris, nullum monumentum
laudis postulabo praeterquam huius diei memoriam sempiternam.
In animis ego vestris omnis triumphos meos, omnia ornamenta
honoris, monumenta gloriae, laudis insignia condi et conlocari volo.
Nihil me mutum potest delectare, nihil tacitum, nihil denique eius   320
modi quod etiam minus digni adsequi possint. Memoria vestra,
Quirites, nostrae res alentur, sermonibus crescent, litterarum
monumentis inveterascent et conroborabuntur; eandemque diem
intellego, quam spero aeternam fore, propagatam esse et ad salutem
urbis et ad memoriam consulatus mei, unoque tempore in hac re   325
publica duos civis exstitisse quorum alter finis vestri imperi non
terrae sed caeli regionibus terminaret, alter huius imperi
domicilium sedisque servaret.

[27]   Sed quoniam earum rerum quas ego gessi non eadem est
fortuna atque condicio quae illorum qui externa bella gesserunt   330
(quod mihi cum eis vivendum est quos vici ac subegi, illi hostis aut
interfectos aut oppressos reliquerunt), vestrum est, Quirites, si
ceteris facta sua recte prosunt, mihi mea ne quando obsint
providere. Mentes enim hominum audacissimorum sceleratae ac
nefariae ne vobis nocere possent ego providi, ne mihi noceant   335
vestrum est providere. Quamquam, Quirites, mihi quidem ipsi nihil
ab istis iam noceri potest. Magnum enim est in bonis praesidium
quod mihi in perpetuum comparatum est, magna in re publica
dignitas quae me semper tacita defendet, magna vis conscientiae
quam qui neglegunt, cum me violare volent, se indicabunt.   340

[28]   Est enim nobis is animus, Quirites, ut non modo nullius
audaciae cedamus sed etiam omnis improbos ultro semper
lacessamus. Quod si omnis impetus domesticorum hostium
depulsus a vobis se in me unum converterit, vobis erit videndum,
Quirites, qua condicione posthac eos esse velitis qui se pro salute   345
vestra obtulerint invidiae periculisque omnibus: mihi quidem ipsi
quid est quod iam ad vitae fructum possit adquiri, cum praesertim
neque in honore vestro neque in gloria virtutis quicquam videam
altius quo mihi libeat ascendere?

[29]   Illud perficiam profecto, Quirites, ut ea quae gessi in consulatu   350
privatus tuear atque ornem, ut, si qua est invidia in conservanda re
publica suscepta, laedat invidos, mihi valeat ad gloriam. Denique
ita me in re publica tractabo ut meminerim semper quae gesserim,
curemque ut ea virtute non casu gesta esse videantur. Vos, Quirites,
quoniam iam est nox, venerati Iovem, illum custodem huius urbis ac   355
vestrum, in vestra tecta discedite et ea (quamquam iam est
periculum depulsum) tamen aeque ac priore nocte custodiis
vigiliisque defendite. Id ne vobis diutius faciendum sit atque ut in
perpetua pace esse possitis providebo, Quirites.

IN L. CATILINAM ORATIO QVARTA
HABITA IN SENATV

[1]   Video, patres conscripti, in me omnium vestrum ora atque oculos esse conversos, video vos non solum de vestro ac rei publicae verum etiam, si id depulsum sit, de meo periculo esse sollicitos. Est mihi iucunda in malis et grata in dolore vestra erga me voluntas, sed eam per deos immortalis deponite atque obliti salutis meae de vobis   5 ac de vestris liberis cogitate. Mihi si haec condicio consulatus data est ut omnis acerbitates, omnis dolores cruciatusque perferrem, feram non solum fortiter verum etiam libenter, dum modo meis laboribus vobis populoque Romano dignitas salusque pariatur.

[2]   Ego sum ille consul, patres conscripti, cui non forum (in quo   10 omnis aequitas continetur), non campus (consularibus auspiciis consecratus), non curia (summum auxilium omnium gentium), non domus (commune perfugium), non lectus (ad quietem datus), non denique haec sedes honoris umquam vacua mortis periculo atque insidiis fuit. Ego multa tacui, multa pertuli, multa concessi, multa   15 meo quodam dolore in vestro timore sanavi. Nunc si hunc exitum consulatus mei di immortales esse voluerunt ut vos populumque Romanum ex caede miserrima, coniuges liberosque vestros virginesque Vestalis ex acerbissima vexatione, templa atque delubra, hanc pulcherrimam patriam omnium nostrum ex foedissima   20 flamma, totam Italiam ex bello et vastitate eriperem, quaecumque mihi uni proponetur fortuna subeatur. Etenim si P. Lentulus suum nomen inductus a vatibus fatale ad perniciem rei publicae fore putavit, cur ego non laeter meum consulatum ad salutem populi Romani prope fatalem exstitisse?   25

[3]   Qua re, patres conscripti, consulite vobis, prospicite patriae, conservate vos, coniuges, liberos fortunasque vestras, populi Romani nomen salutemque defendite; mihi parcere ac de me cogitare desinite. Nam primum debeo sperare omnis deos qui huic urbi praesident pro eo mihi ac mereor relaturos esse gratiam;   30 deinde, si quid obtigerit, aequo animo paratoque moriar. Nam neque turpis mors forti viro potest accidere neque immatura consulari nec misera sapienti. Nec tamen ego sum ille ferreus qui

fratris carissimi atque amantissimi praesentis maerore non movear
horumque omnium lacrimis a quibus me circumsessum videtis.   35
Neque meam mentem non domum saepe revocat exanimata uxor et
abiecta metu filia et parvolus filius, quem mihi videtur amplecti res
publica tamquam obsidem consulatus mei, neque ille qui exspectans
huius exitum diei stat in conspectu meo gener. Moveor his rebus
omnibus, sed in eam partem uti salvi sint vobiscum omnes, etiam si   40
me vis aliqua oppresserit, potius quam et illi et nos una rei publicae
peste pereamus.

[4]   Qua re, patres conscripti, incumbite ad salutem rei publicae,
circumspicite omnis procellas quae impendent nisi providetis. Non
Ti. Gracchus quod iterum tribunus plebis fieri voluit, non C.   45
Gracchus quod agrarios concitare conatus est, non L. Saturninus
quod C. Memmium occidit, in discrimen aliquod atque in vestrae
severitatis iudicium adducitur: tenentur ei qui ad urbis incendium,
ad vestram omnium caedem, ad Catilinam accipiendum Romae
restiterunt. Tenentur litterae, signa, manus, denique unius cuiusque   50
confessio: sollicitantur Allobroges, servitia excitantur, Catilina
arcessitur, id est initum consilium ut interfectis omnibus nemo ne
ad deplorandum quidem populi Romani nomen atque ad
lamentandam tanti imperi calamitatem relinquatur.

[5]   Haec omnia indices detulerunt, rei confessi sunt, vos multis   55
iam iudiciis iudicavistis, primum quod mihi gratias egistis
singularibus verbis et mea virtute atque diligentia perditorum
hominum coniurationem patefactam esse decrevistis, deinde quod P.
Lentulum se abdicare praetura coegistis; tum quod eum et ceteros
(de quibus iudicastis) in custodiam dandos censuistis, maximeque   60
quod meo nomine supplicationem decrevistis, qui honos togato
habitus ante me est nemini; postremo hesterno die praemia legatis
Allobrogum Titoque Volturcio dedistis amplissima. Quae sunt
omnia eius modi ut ei qui in custodiam nominatim dati sunt sine
ulla dubitatione a vobis damnati esse videantur.   65

[6]   Sed ego institui referre ad vos, patres conscripti, tamquam
integrum, et de facto quid iudicetis et de poena quid censeatis. Illa
praedicam quae sunt consulis. Ego magnum in re publica versari

[11]   Quam ob rem, sive hoc statueritis, dederitis mihi comitem ad   140
contionem populo carum atque iucundum, sive Silani sententiam
sequi malueritis, facile me atque vos crudelitatis vituperatione
populus Romanus liberabit, atque obtinebo eam multo leniorem
fuisse. Quamquam, patres conscripti, quae potest esse in tanti
sceleris immanitate punienda crudelitas? Ego enim de meo sensu   145
iudico. Nam ita mihi salva re publica vobiscum perfrui liceat ut ego,
quod in hac causa vehementior sum, non atrocitate animi moveor—
quis enim est me mitior?—sed singulari quadam humanitate et
misericordia. Videor enim mihi videre hanc urbem, lucem orbis
terrarum atque arcem omnium gentium, subito uno incendio   150
concidentem. Cerno animo sepulta in patria miseros atque
insepultos acervos civium, versatur mihi ante oculos aspectus
Cethegi et furor in vestra caede bacchantis.

[12]   Cum vero mihi proposui regnantem Lentulum, sicut ipse se ex
fatis sperasse confessus est, purpuratum esse huic Gabinium, cum   155
exercitu venisse Catilinam, tum lamentationem matrum familias,
tum fugam virginum atque puerorum ac vexationem virginum
Vestalium perhorresco, et, quia mihi vehementer haec videntur
misera atque miseranda, idcirco in eos qui ea perficere voluerunt
me severum vehementemque praebebo. Etenim quaero, si quis   160
pater familias, liberis suis a servo interfectis, uxore occisa, incensa
domo, supplicium de servis non quam acerbissimum sumpserit,
utrum is clemens ac misericors an inhumanissimus et crudelissimus
esse videatur? Mihi vero importunus ac ferreus qui non dolore et
cruciatu nocentis suum dolorem cruciatumque lenierit. Sic nos in   165
his hominibus (qui nos, qui coniuges, qui liberos nostros trucidare
voluerunt, qui singulas unius cuiusque nostrum domos et hoc
universum rei publicae domicilium delere conati sunt, qui id
egerunt ut gentem Allobrogum in vestigiis huius urbis atque in
cinere deflagrati imperi conlocarent), si vehementissimi fuerimus,   170
misericordes habebimur; sin remissiores esse voluerimus, summae
nobis crudelitatis in patriae civiumque pernicie fama subeunda est.

[13]   Nisi vero cuipiam L. Caesar, vir fortissimus et amantissimus rei
publicae, crudelior nudius tertius visus est, cum sororis suae,

feminae lectissimae, virum praesentem et audientem vita   175
privandum esse dixit, cum avum suum iussu consulis interfectum
filiumque eius impuberem legatum a patre missum in carcere
necatum esse dixit. Quorum quod simile factum, quod initum
delendae rei publicae consilium? Largitionis voluntas tum in re
publica versata est et partium quaedam contentio. Atque illo   180
tempore huius avus Lentuli, vir clarissimus, armatus Gracchum est
persecutus. Ille etiam grave tum volnus accepit, ne quid de summa
rei publicae minueretur; hic ad evertenda fundamenta rei publicae
Gallos arcessit, servitia concitat, Catilinam vocat, attribuit nos
trucidandos Cethego et ceteros civis interficiendos Gabinio, urbem   185
inflammandam Cassio, totam Italiam vastandam diripiendamque
Catilinae. Vereamini minus, censeo, ne in hoc scelere tam immani
ac nefando aliquid severius statuisse videamini: multo magis est
verendum ne remissione poenae crudeles in patriam quam ne
severitate animadversionis nimis vehementes in acerbissimos hostis   190
fuisse videamur.

[14]   Sed ea quae exaudio, patres conscripti, dissimulare non
possum. Iaciuntur enim voces quae perveniunt ad auris meas
eorum qui vereri videntur ut habeam satis praesidi ad ea quae vos
statueritis hodierno die transigenda. Omnia et provisa et parata et   195
constituta sunt, patres conscripti, cum mea summa cura atque
diligentia tum multo etiam maiore populi Romani ad summum
imperium retinendum et ad communis fortunas conservandas
voluntate. Omnes adsunt omnium ordinum homines, omnium
generum, omnium denique aetatum; plenum est forum, plena   200
templa circum forum, pleni omnes aditus huius templi ac loci.
Causa est enim post urbem conditam haec inventa sola in qua
omnes sentirent unum atque idem praeter eos qui, cum sibi viderent
esse pereundum, cum omnibus potius quam soli perire voluerunt.

[15]   Hosce ego homines excipio et secerno libenter, neque in   205
improborum civium sed in acerbissimorum hostium numero
habendos puto. Ceteri vero, di immortales! qua frequentia, quo
studio, qua virtute ad communem salutem dignitatemque
consentiunt! Quid ego hic equites Romanos commemorem? qui
vobis ita summam ordinis consilique concedunt ut vobiscum de   210

amore rei publicae certent; quos ex multorum annorum dissensione huius ordinis ad societatem concordiamque revocatos hodiernus dies vobiscum atque haec causa coniungit. Quam si coniunctionem in consulatu confirmatam meo, perpetuam in re publica tenuerimus, confirmo vobis nullum posthac malum civile ac domesticum ad 215 ullam rei publicae partem esse venturum. Pari studio defendendae rei publicae convenisse video tribunos aerarios, fortissimos viros; scribas item universos quos, cum casu hic dies ad aerarium frequentasset, video ab exspectatione sortis ad salutem communem esse conversos. 220

[16] Omnis ingenuorum adest multitudo, etiam tenuissimorum. Quis est enim cui non haec templa, aspectus urbis, possessio libertatis, lux denique haec ipsa et commune patriae solum, cum sit carum tum vero dulce atque iucundum?

Operae pretium est, patres conscripti, libertinorum hominum 225 studia cognoscere qui, sua virtute fortunam huius civitatis consecuti, vere hanc suam patriam esse iudicant quam quidam hic nati, et summo nati loco, non patriam suam sed urbem hostium esse iudicaverunt. Sed quid ego hosce ordines atque homines commemoro quos privatae fortunae, quos communis res publica, 230 quos denique libertas ea quae dulcissima est ad salutem patriae defendendam excitavit? Servus est nemo, qui modo tolerabili condicione sit servitutis, qui non audaciam civium perhorrescat, qui non haec stare cupiat, qui non, quantum audet et quantum potest, conferat ad salutem voluntatis. 235

[17] Qua re si quem vestrum forte commovet hoc quod auditum est, lenonem quendam Lentuli concursare circum tabernas, pretio sperare sollicitari posse animos egentium atque imperitorum, est id quidem coeptum atque temptatum, sed nulli sunt inventi tam aut fortuna miseri aut voluntate perditi qui non illum ipsum sellae 240 atque operis et quaestus cotidiani locum, qui non cubile ac lectulum suum, qui denique non cursum hunc otiosum vitae suae salvum esse velint. Multo vero maxima pars eorum qui in tabernis sunt, immo vero—id enim potius est dicendum—genus hoc universum amantissimum est oti. Etenim omne instrumentum, omnis opera 245 atque quaestus frequentia civium sustentatur, alitur otio; quorum si

quaestus occlusis tabernis minui solet, quid tandem incensis futurum fuit?

[18]   Quae cum ita sint, patres conscripti, vobis populi Romani praesidia non desunt: vos ne populo Romano deesse videamini   250
providete. Habetis consulem ex plurimis periculis et insidiis atque ex media morte non ad vitam suam sed ad salutem vestram reservatum. Omnes ordines ad conservandam rem publicam mente, voluntate, voce consentiunt. Obsessa facibus et telis impiae coniurationis vobis supplex manus tendit patria communis, vobis se,   255
vobis vitam omnium civium, vobis arcem et Capitolium, vobis aras Penatium, vobis illum ignem Vestae sempiternum, vobis omnium deorum templa atque delubra, vobis muros atque urbis tecta commendat. Praeterea de vestra vita, de coniugum vestrarum atque liberorum anima, de fortunis omnium, de sedibus, de focis vestris   260
hodierno die vobis iudicandum est.

[19]   Habetis ducem memorem vestri, oblitum sui, quae non semper facultas datur; habetis omnis ordines, omnis homines, universum populum Romanum, id quod in civili causa hodierno die primum videmus, unum atque idem sentientem. Cogitate quantis laboribus   265
fundatum imperium, quanta virtute stabilitam libertatem, quanta deorum benignitate auctas exaggeratasque fortunas una nox paene delerit. Id ne umquam posthac non modo non confici sed ne cogitari quidem possit a civibus hodierno die providendum est. Atque haec, non ut vos qui mihi studio paene praecurritis excitarem,   270
locutus sum, sed ut mea vox, quae debet esse in re publica princeps, officio functa consulari videretur.

[20]   Nunc ante quam ad sententiam redeo, de me pauca dicam. Ego, quanta manus est coniuratorum, quam videtis esse permagnam, tantam me inimicorum multitudinem suscepisse video; sed eam   275
turpem iudico et infirmam et abiectam. Quod si aliquando alicuius furore et scelere concitata manus ista plus valuerit quam vestra ac rei publicae dignitas, me tamen meorum factorum atque consiliorum numquam, patres conscripti, paenitebit. Etenim mors, quam illi fortasse minitantur, omnibus est parata: vitae tantam   280
laudem (quanta vos me vestris decretis honestastis) nemo est

adsecutus; ceteris enim semper bene gesta, mihi uni conservata re
publica gratulationem decrevistis.

[21]   Sit Scipio clarus ille cuius consilio atque virtute Hannibal in
Africam redire atque Italia decedere coactus est, ornetur alter   285
eximia laude Africanus qui duas urbis huic imperio infestissimas
Karthaginem Numantiamque delevit, habeatur vir egregius Paulus
ille cuius currum rex potentissimus quondam et nobilissimus Perses
honestavit, sit aeterna gloria Marius qui bis Italiam obsidione et
metu servitutis liberavit, anteponatur omnibus Pompeius cuius res   290
gestae atque virtutes isdem quibus solis cursus regionibus ac
terminis continentur: erit profecto inter horum laudes aliquid loci
nostrae gloriae, nisi forte maius est patefacere nobis provincias quo
exire possimus, quam curare ut etiam illi qui absunt habeant quo
victores revertantur.   295

[22]   Quamquam est uno loco condicio melior externae victoriae
quam domesticae, quod hostes alienigenae aut oppressi serviunt aut
recepti beneficio se obligatos putant, qui autem ex numero civium,
dementia aliqua depravati, hostes patriae semel esse coeperunt, eos,
cum a pernicie rei publicae reppuleris, nec vi coercere nec beneficio   300
placare possis. Qua re mihi cum perditis civibus aeternum bellum
susceptum esse video. Id ego vestro bonorumque omnium auxilio
memoriaque tantorum periculorum, quae non modo in hoc populo
qui servatus est sed in omnium gentium sermonibus ac mentibus
semper haerebit, a me atque a meis facile propulsari posse confido.   305
Neque ulla profecto tanta vis reperietur quae coniunctionem
vestram equitumque Romanorum et tantam conspirationem
bonorum omnium confringere et labefactare possit.

[23]   Quae cum ita sint, pro imperio, pro exercitu, pro provincia
quam neglexi, pro triumpho ceterisque laudis insignibus quae sunt a   310
me propter urbis vestraeque salutis custodiam repudiata, pro
clientelis hospitiisque provincialibus quae tamen urbanis opibus
non minore labore tueor quam comparo, pro his igitur omnibus
rebus, pro meis in vos singularibus studiis proque hac quam
perspicitis ad conservandam rem publicam diligentia, nihil a vobis   315
nisi huius temporis totiusque mei consulatus memoriam postulo:

quae dum erit in vestris fixa mentibus, tutissimo me muro saeptum esse arbitrabor. Quod si meam spem vis improborum fefellerit atque superaverit, commendo vobis parvum meum filium, cui profecto satis erit praesidi non solum ad salutem verum etiam ad   320 dignitatem, si eius qui haec omnia suo solius periculo conservarit illum filium esse memineritis.

[24]   Quapropter de summa salute vestra populique Romani, de vestris coniugibus ac liberis, de aris ac focis, de fanis atque templis, de totius urbis tectis ac sedibus, de imperio ac libertate, de salute   325 Italiae, de universa re publica decernite diligenter, ut instituistis, ac fortiter. Habetis eum consulem qui et parere vestris decretis non dubitet et ea quae statueritis, quoad vivet, defendere et per se ipsum praestare possit.

Notes to the Commentary

The relevant sections of Bennett's *New Latin Grammar* (B) and Gildersleeve and Lodge's *Latin Grammar* (G) are noted in the grammatical commentaries, but students can easily locate the corresponding sections in any standard Latin grammar.

The Latin text is printed in **boldface** type. Suggested English translations are in *italics*. Key rhetorical terms are printed in BOLDFACE AND SMALL CAPS; students will find these terms defined in Appendix C.

Latin words that are not in Cicero's text but are understood (and are required to complete the meaning) are added in square brackets: [ ]. Brackets are also used in the suggested translations to indicate words that are understood (and are important for the meaning) but are not present in the text.

Abbreviations

B   Bennett (1908).
BC   Sallust, *Bellum Catilinae*.
BJ   Sallust, *Bellum Jugurthinum*.
CAH 9[1] *The Cambridge Ancient History*. Vol. 9. Ed. B. S. Cook, F. E. Adcock, and M. P. Charlesworth. Cambridge: Cambridge University Press, 1932.
CAH 9[2] *The Cambridge Ancient History*. 2nd ed. Vol. 9. Ed. J. A. Cook, A. Lintott, and E. Rawson. Cambridge: Cambridge University Press, 1994.
Cat.   Cicero, *The Catilinarian Orations*.
G   Gildersleeve and Lodge (1895).
OCD[3]   *The Oxford Classical Dictionary*. 3rd ed. Ed. S. Hornblower and A. Spawforth. Oxford: Oxford University Press, 1996.
RE   *Paulys Realencyclopädie der classischen Altertumswissenschaft*. Rev. ed. Ed. Wilhelm Kroll and Kurt Witte et al. Stuttgart: Verlag J. B. Metzler, 1994.
SCU   **senatus consultum ultimum.**

Commentary

Cicero's *First Catilinarian Oration*
Delivered November 8, 63 B.C., before the
Senate in the Temple of Jupiter Stator

Chapter 1

1 **Quo usque:** *How long?* (literally, *all the way to where?*). **tandem:** here **tandem** serves to emphasize the urgency of the question; translate: *I ask you.* **abutere:** alternative form for **abuteris** (second person singular future indicative of deponent **abutor**). The alternative second person singular passive ending for **-ris** is **-re**; it is most frequently used with the future indicative, as here. **patientia nostra:** ablative with **abutere** (B218, G407).

2 **quem ad finem:** *to what end? how long?*

3 **Nihilne:** *In no way? Not at all?* This **nihil** and the others in lines 3–5 are used adverbially (B176.3a, G442n2).

3–6 **praesidium, vigiliae, timor, concursus, locus, ora voltusque:** these nouns, along with their modifiers, are all subjects of the verb **moverunt**; **te** is the direct object for each subject; **nihil** is repeated in each phrase. Translate: *Does the night guard on the Palatine move you not at all? Do the night watches of the city move you not at all?* (etc.). Note Cicero's use of ANAPHORA here to emphasize that Catiline *should* be moved by these extraordinary defensive measures.

3 **nocturnum praesidium Palati:** *the night guard of the Palatine [Hill].* This was an unusual measure designed to safeguard the Palatine Hill, where many of the leading senators had their homes, in the wake of rumors that Catiline was planning a massacre of Rome's most prominent citizens (see Historical Essay II.5).

4 **concursus bonorum omnium:** *the coming together of all good men* (i.e., for the defense of the government). Many supporters had probably gathered outside the Temple of Jupiter Stator, where the Senate was meeting.

5 **hic munitissimus . . . locus:** This was the Temple of Jupiter Stator (see Map 2). Cicero chose to convene the Senate here because it could easily be fortified; the Senate's usual meeting place was the Curia, or Senate House, situated on the northern edge of the Comitium (see Map 1). **habendi senatus:** genitive with **locus**; **habendi** is a gerundive modifying **senatus** (B339, G427). **horum:** *of these men* (i.e., the senators).

6 **Patere:** infinitive in indirect statement, dependent on **sentis**.

6–7 **constrictam . . . vides:** order for translation, **non vides tuam coniurationem [esse] constrictam [et] teneri scientia horum omnium? constrictam [esse]** and **teneri** are infinitives in indirect statement following **vides; scientia** is ablative of means.

7–9 **Quid, quid, ubi, quos, quid:** each of these interrogatives introduces an indirect question, following the direct question, **quem nostrum ignorare arbitraris** (B300, G467). You can translate the sentence with the direct question first, or you can translate it as written, with the indirect questions first. The entire first paragraph of this speech is composed of RHETORICAL QUESTIONS.

8 proxima: i.e., **proxima [nocte]**, November 7; ablative of time when (B230, G393). **superiore nocte:** *on the night before last*, November 6. **egeris, fueris, convocaveris:** subjunctives in indirect question (B300, G467).

9 quid consili: *what plan*; literally; *what of plan*; **consili** is partitive genitive (genitive of the whole) (B201.1, G369). On the night of November 6 Catiline and some of his chief conspirators met at the house of M. Porcius Laeca and planned to massacre leading citizens and set fires throughout the city in coordination with an attack on Rome by Manlius' troops at Faesulae (see Historical Essay II.5).

Chapter 2

10 O tempora, O mores!: accusative of exclamation (B183, G343). In this exclamation, which has since become famous, Cicero laments the sorry state of the Republic, in which a citizen could plot against the state and not be punished for it. **haec:** neuter plural (i.e., the evidence of Catiline's conspiracy).

11 immo vero: *in fact*; **immo vero** is used to correct or strengthen a previous statement.

12 unum quemque: *each and every one.*

13 nostrum: partitive genitive (genitive of the whole) (B201.1, G368). **fortes viri:** an example of IRONY. **videmur:** *video* in the passive voice often means *to seem*.

14–5 te ... duci ... oportebat: *you ought to have been led* or (more literally) *it was fitting that you be led*. **Oportet** is an impersonal verb meaning *it is fitting*; it takes the accusative of person and an infinitive. Latin frequently uses a past tense of **oportet** with a present infinitive to indicate that something should (already) have happened.

15 iam pridem: *now for a long time*. **in te conferri pestem:** order for translation, **[iam pridem] pestem [oportebat] conferri in te. quam:** the relative pronoun; **pestem** is the antecedent.

16 omnis: masculine accusative plural, agreeing with **nos**; **-is** is an alternative accusative plural ending for third declension adjectives and third declension i-stem nouns (see B37, B68–70, G56, G57.5, G78n2, G83n1).

Chapter 3

17 An: *Or is it the case that?* **An** usually introduces the second member of a double question (*either . . . or*), but sometimes it introduces a single question and can have the force of **-ne, nonne,** or **num** (B162.4a, G457.1). Here it has the force of **nonne**, expecting a yes answer. **pontifex maximus:** the chief priest at Rome and the leader of the college (group) of sixteen **pontifices**. The **pontifices** controlled the religious calendar and established the holy days and intercalary months; they were also responsible for recording the most important events of each year.

17–19 P. Scipio . . . Ti. Gracchum . . . interfecit: in 133 B.C. Scipio Nasica, leading a crowd of senators and their supporters, killed Tiberius Gracchus and many of his followers. For more on this watershed event, see Historical Essay, I.2.

17 P. = Publius; Ti. = Tiberius. For a complete list of Roman names and their abbreviations, see B373, G p. 493.

18 privatus: Publius Scipio Nasica (consul in 138 B.C.), was only a private citizen (i.e., he was not a public official) when he led the senatorial mob that attacked Tiberius Gracchus and his followers. Cicero is contrasting the present situation, in which he holds the office of consul and presumably has a greater right to take action against Catiline. **mediocriter labefactantem statum:** Tiberius Gracchus caused only moderate harm to the Republic in comparison to Catiline, and yet Tiberius was killed.

19 Catilinam: note the ASYNDETON between these two clauses.

19–20 Catilinam ... perferemus: order for translation, **nos consules perferemus Catilinam cupientem vastare orbem terrae caede atque incendiis. Cupientem** (present active participle, masculine accusative singular) agrees with **Catilinam**; **vastare** is a complementary infinitive with **cupientem**; **orbem** is the direct object of **vastare**; **perferemus** is future indicative. This is a **RHETORICAL QUESTION**, following **An** at the beginning of the sentence.

21 **praetereo**: *I pass over*. Cicero claims to pass over the following incident because it is too ancient, but by mentioning it anyway he actually emphasizes it, an example of **PRAETERITIO**. **quod**: *the fact that* (B299.1a, G525.2). **novis rebus**: res novae meant political change or revolution; the dative is dependent on **studentem** (a present active participle agreeing with **Spurium Maelium**).

21–22 **C. Servilius Ahala Sp. Maelium . . . occidit**: this is an incident from the early period of the Republic. During a period of famine in 439 B.C., Spurius Maelius, a wealthy plebeian, was said to have furnished grain to the poor at his own expense. Because of this he was suspected of aiming at a tyranny (**regnum**) and was killed by Gaius Servilius Ahala, who was supposedly the cavalry commander (**magister equitum**) under the dictator Cincinnatus but who may have actually been a private citizen; see Lintott (1970).

22 **Fuit, fuit**: note Cicero's use of **ITERATIO**.

22–23 **ista . . . virtus**: *such virtue*. Here **ista** is not pejorative (negative) but simply describes the kind of virtue that Cicero claims once existed in the Republic.

23–24 **ut . . . coercerent**: a result clause.

24 **quam**: *than*; take with the comparative **acrioribus**. Cicero harkens back to the (mainly mythical) "good old days," when Roman citizens were held to a higher standard of behavior than noncitizens; thus citizens who attacked the Republic would be punished more harshly than a foreign enemy.

24–25 **senatus consultum**: *a decree of the Senate*. Cicero is referring to the decree that was later known as the **senatus consultum ultimum** (SCU), giving the consuls the right

to declare martial law and order the summary execution of citizens. The legality of the SCU was an issue (see Historical Essays I.4 and II.3).

26 **nos, nos**: note the **ITERATIO**. Cicero had gotten the SCU against Catiline on October 21, but he had not yet acted upon it. There were several reasons for Cicero's delay. First, Cicero did not yet have direct evidence tying Catiline to the conspiracy (he explains how he later acquired this evidence in the *Third Catilinarian Oration*). Second, as becomes clear later in this speech (e.g., *Cat.* 1.30), several senators seem to have been supporting Catiline, and Cicero was unwilling to act without the Senate's full backing.

Chapter 4

28 **Decrevit quondam senatus**: this was in 121 B.C., the first use of the so-called **senatus consultum ultimum** (SCU). For a full discussion of this incident, see Historical Essay I.4.

28–29 **uti . . . videret, ne . . . caperet**: indirect commands (B295, G546). **consul videret ne quid res publica detrimenti caperet**: order for translation, **consul videret ne res publica caperet [ali]quid detrimenti**. This became the standard formula for the SCU (see Historical Essay I.4).

29 **[ali]quid . . . detrimenti**: *something of harm* (i.e., *some harm*); **detrimenti** is partitive genitive (B201, G369). **nox nulla intercessit**: *not a single night intervened* (i.e., between the passing of the SCU and the consul's action).

30–31 **interfectus est . . . C. Gracchus**: in 121 B.C., (see Historical Essay I.4).

30 **propter quasdam seditionum suspiciones**: Gaius Gracchus was killed merely on suspicion of treasonous actions, as opposed to the clear evidence of Catiline's intentions. In fact, Cicero did not yet have clear evidence of Catiline's intentions.

31 **clarissimo patre, avo, maioribus**: ablatives of description (or quality) with Gaius Gracchus (B224, G400).

31–32 occisus est cum liberis M. Fulvius consularis: Marcus Fulvius Flaccus had been consul in 125 B.C.; **consularis** is the regular term for someone who had previously been a consul. Fulvius was one of Gracchus' strongest supporters. The fact that Opimius killed both of Flaccus' sons (the youngest one had simply served as his father's messenger) stands as a testament to his cruelty (see Historical Essay I.4).

32 Simili senatus consulto: simili consulto is ablative of means. The Senate passed the SCU for the second time against L. Saturninus and C. Servilius Glaucia (usually known as Glaucia) in 100 B.C. when C. Marius and L. Valerius were consuls (see Historical Essay I.5).

32–33 C. Mario . . . consulibus: datives with **est permissa** (*was entrusted to*).

33 num: *surely not?* (introduces a direct question expecting a negative answer). **unum diem:** *for a single day*; accusative of duration of time (B181, G336).

34–35 mors ac rei publicae poena remorata est: *death and the penalty of the Republic was delayed for* + accusative person. **rei publicae poena:** *the penalty of the Republic*; **rei publicae** is subjective genitive (B199, G363.1). In this case, the penalty was death.

35 vicesimum iam diem: accusative of duration of time (B181, G336). The Senate had passed the SCU on October 21, which was actually only eighteen days earlier.

36 aciem horum auctoritatis: *the edge of the authority of these men* (the senators). Cicero compares the SCU to a sword whose edge is becoming dull (an example of **METAPHOR**).

37 inclusum in tabulis: the SCU is locked up in the Senate's records (i.e., it is not yet put into use).

37–38 tamquam in vagina reconditum: *as though hidden in a scabbard.* Cicero continues to compare the SCU to a sword.

38 quo ex senatus consulto: order for translation, **ex quo consulto senatus**: *in accordance with this decree of the Senate.* Latin often uses

a relative pronoun (**quo**) where English prefers a demonstrative pronoun (**eo**).

38–39 te interfectum esse . . . convenit: *it is fitting for you to have been put to death* (i.e., *you ought to have been put to death*). **convenit** is an impersonal verb that takes accusative person and infinitive; the use of a perfect rather than a present infinitive is unusual (B270.2a, G280.2).

39–40 non ad deponendam [audaciam] sed ad confirmandam audaciam: *not for laying aside your boldness, but for strengthening it.* The gerundive in the accusative with **ad** can be used to express purpose (B338.3 and B339.2, G432).

41 patres conscripti: *senators*; this was the regular way of addressing the senators. The original expression was probably **patres et conscripti**: *fathers and enrolled*; it may go back to the early Republic, at a time when new senators were chosen. The older senators were called **patres,** while the newer ones were probably called **conscripti** (*enrolled*). But **patres et conscripti** eventually became shortened to **patres conscripti,** and the origin of the phrase was forgotten.

42–43 me ipse . . . condemno: *I myself condemn myself;* **ipse** is nominative and is used for emphasis.

43 inertiae nequitiaeque: verbs of accusing, convicting, and acquitting take the genitive of the charge (B208, G378).

Chapter 5

44–45 Castra sunt . . . conlocata: this was Manlius' camp at Faesulae in Etruria, the modern Fiesole, near Florence (see Map 3).

45 in dies singulos: *day by day.*

45–46 eorum . . . castrorum imperatorem ducemque: this was Catiline, who was directing the movements of Manlius' men from Rome.

47 intestinam aliquam . . . perniciem: the direct object of **molientem** (line 48).

48 molientem: present active participle, agreeing with **imperatorem ducemque** (line 46).

48–49 Si te iam . . . iussero: iussero is future perfect indicative of **iubeo** and goes with both if-clauses. Order for translation: **Si iam [iussero] te, Catilina, comprehendi, si iussero [te] interfici**.

49 erit verendum mihi: *it will have to be feared by me* (i.e., *I will have to fear*); an impersonal periphrastic construction in the future tense.

49–50 ne non . . . dicat: a negative clause of fearing after **erit verendum mihi**, with **ne non** (*that not*) instead of **ut** (see B296.2a, G500.2). Order for translation, **ne non omnes boni [dicant] hoc factum esse serius a me potius quam quisquam dicat [hoc factum esse] crudelius.** Translation: *(I suppose I shall have to fear), not that all good men may say this was done too late by me, rather than that anyone may say this was done too cruelly.* Cicero hesitates to kill Catiline because of two different and opposing fears. On the one hand, he fears that all good men may say he waited too long to kill him; on the other hand, some of Catiline's powerful supporters may say that he killed Catiline too cruelly (i.e., without a proper trial). In this sentence Cicero compares the two fears and explains that he is <u>more afraid</u> of the second fear (that someone may complain he killed Catiline too cruelly) than the first (that good men may say he waited to long to kill him). Cicero's fears were borne out five years later, in 58 B.C., when he was banished for putting five of the conspirators to death without a trial (see Historical Essay II.8).

50–52 Verum ego ⌢ faciam: order for translation, **Verum egó cérta ⌒de causā nondum adducor ut faciam hoc quod iam pridem oportuit factum esse‖ nondum adducor ut faciam:** *I am not yet induced to do;* literally, *I am not yet induced that I should do*; indirect command (B295, G546). **iam pridem factum esse oportuit:** *long ago should have been done*; see the note on **oportebat**, lines 14–15 above. **certa de causa:** the reason is Cicero's fear (mentioned above and reiterated below) that, if he kills Catiline, one of

Catiline's supporters may say that he acted too cruelly.

52 Tum . . . cum: *At that time . . . when*; correlatives. **interficiere = interficieris,** future passive indicative; see note on **abutere,** line 1 above.

52–53 tam . . . tam . . . tam: an example of ANAPHORA.

53–54 qui . . . non . . . fateatur: *who does not admit*; relative clause of characteristic showing result (B284.2a, G631.1). Cicero will refrain from killing Catiline until there is no one left who would not admit that he was killed justly.

Chapter 6

55 Quam diu: *As long as.* **qui . . . audeat:** relative clause of characteristic (B283.2, G631.2).

56–57 ne . . . possis: negative purpose clause (B282, G545.3).

57 commovere te: *set yourself in motion* (i.e., *take action*).

58 sentientem: present active participle, agreeing with **te**; literally *you, not being aware* (i.e., *although you are not aware of it*).

60 quid est . . . quod iam amplius exspectes: order for translation, **quid amplius est [id] quod iam exspectes:** *what more is it that you now are waiting for?* **quod . . . exspectes** is a relative clause of characteristic.

61 neque nox . . . nec privata domus: both nouns are subjects of **potest** (line 62).

63 omnia: subject of both **inlustrantur** (line 62) and **erumpunt. Muta:** imperative of **muto, mutare.**

64 obliviscere: imperative of **obliviscor.** Remember that deponents have imperatives that look like active infinitives. **Obliviscor** takes a genitive object, as do most verbs of remembering and forgetting (B206, G376). **luce:** ablative of comparison with **clariora** (line 65).

65–66 quae . . . recognoscas: order for translation, **quae iam licet [ut] recognoscas**

cum me. Licet (*it is permitted that*) takes ut
+ subjunctive, but sometimes the ut is omitted
(see B295.6 and 295.8).

Chapter 7

67 Meministine: *Do you remember?* Memini
has only perfect forms, so the perfect tense is
translated as present. This verb introduces
indirect discourse. ante diem XII Kalendas
Novembris: *on October 21.* On the Roman
calendar, see B371–72, G, p. 491. Novembris
is not the genitive of a noun, but an adjective
agreeing with Kalendas.

67–68 in senatu: at this Senate meeting on
October 21, the Senate passed the SCU
against Catiline and Manlius (see Historical
Essay II.5).

68–70 fore in armis . . . administrum tuae:
this is also in indirect discourse. Order for
translation, C. Manlium, satellitem atque
administrum tuae audaciae, [futurum
esse] in armis certo die, qui dies futurus
esset ante diem VI Kalendas Novembris.

68 fore = futurum esse.

68–69 ante diem VI Kalendas Novembris:
October 27.

70 Num me fefellit, Catilina: *Nor did . . .
deceive me, did it, Catiline?* Where English
would say "I was not mistaken about . . . "
Latin says "[nominative subject] did not
deceive me." The subject of fefellit is the rest
of the sentence.

70–72 Num me fefellit . . . dies?: it is probably best to translate this sentence in the following order: Non modo res tanta, tam atrox,
tamque incredibilis [non] me fefellit, verum
(id quod multo magis est admirandum) dies
[non me fefellit]. non modo . . . verum: *not
only . . . but even.*

72 Dixi ego idem: *I also said*; Literally, *The
same I said.* This adverbial use of idem is
quite common. contulisse: perfect active
infinitive of confero. Confero in + a date: *to
assign to* (a date), *to determine for* (a date).

73 ante diem V Kalendas Novembris:
October 28. tum cum: *at a time when.*

74 Roma: ablative of separation with
profugerunt (line 75).

74–75 non tam . . . causa: causa in the ablative takes a preceding genitive and means *for
the sake of.* This clause explains why the
leading citizens left Rome on October 28,
and should be translated in the following
order: non tam sui conservandi causa
quam tuorum consiliorum reprimendorum causa. non tam . . . quam: *not so much
. . . as much as.*

76 meis praesidiis, mea diligentia: ablative
of means with circumclusum.

77 discessu ceterorum: ablative of time
when.

78 nostra . . . qui remansissemus caede:
with the slaughter of us who had remained.
Literally, *with our slaughter, [we] who had
remained.* The antecedent of qui is implied
by nostra, which is here substituting for
nostri (*of us*).

Chapter 8

79 Quid?: Quid here functions as a transi-
tional particle, calling attention to the question that follows. Translate: *What about the
fact that . . . ?* Praeneste: accusative direct
object of occupaturum . . . esse (line 80).
Praeneste (modern Palestrina) was an ancient
Etruscan town about 20 miles southeast of
Rome. Its hilltop site and strong fortifications
gave it strategic importance. In the 80s B.C.
Praeneste supported Marius and was sacked
by Sulla in 82, after which it became a
Roman colony (colonia). Kalendis ipsis
Novembribus: *November 1.*

80 occupaturum . . . esse: future active
participle in indirect discourse after confideres (*you were confident that*). sensistin =
sensistine.

81 meis praesidiis, custodiis, vigiliis: the
omission of connective words (ASYNDETON)
produces a forceful, rapid-fire effect.

82 Nihil . . . nihil . . . nihil: ANAPHORA,
TRICOLON, and CLIMAX.

82–83 non . . . non modo . . . sed etiam: the

first **non** negates each of the following three verbs. The second **non** is part of the correlative construction, **non modo . . . sed etiam:** *You do nothing, you plan nothing, you think nothing that I do not not only hear [about], but also see and plainly know.* Or more smoothly: *I not only hear [about] but also see and plainly know everything you do, everything you attempt, everything you think.*

84 **noctem illam superiorem**: *that night before last* (i.e., November 6).

85 **quam**: *than*, after the comparative **acrius**. **ad salutem** (i.e., **ad salutem rei publicae**) ad + accusative can show purpose. Translate: *for the safety of the Republic.*

86 **priore = superiore**. **inter falcarios**: *into the scythe-makers' quarter*, a district in Rome. **agam = loquar**.

87 **M. Laecae**: Marcus Laeca was a senator and one of the chief conspirators. **eodem** (adv.): *to the same place*. **compluris**: accusative plural, agreeing with **socios** (line 88).

88 **quid:** *why?*

90 **tecum una**: *together with you.* Cicero is aware that a number of the senators were tacitly supporting Catiline.

Chapter 9

91 **Ubinam gentium**: *Where in the world?* Literally, *Where of peoples?* For this use of the partitive genitive, see B201.3, G372n3.

93–94 **hoc . . . consilio**: i.e., the Senate.

94 **qui**: *[those] who*; the antecedent of **qui** is understood from the omitted plural subject of **sunt** (line 92). **nostro omnium interitu = interitu omnium nostrum**.

95 **cogitent:** subjunctive in a relative clause of characteristic.

96 **sententiam rogo**: it was customary for the consul or other presiding magistrate to call on individual senators and ask their opinion on the topic at hand; see Appendix A.

96–97 **quos ferro trucidari oportebat:** *those who deserved to be killed by the sword*;

those who should have been killed by the sword. For the use of **oportebat,** see the note on lines 14–15 above. The antecedent of **quos** is **eos** in line 97.

98 **partis:** accusative plural. **quo:** *to where, whither*; interrogative adverb introducing an indirect question. **quemque:** *each one* (i.e., each of the chief conspirators).

99 **quos Romae relinqueres:** relative clause of characteristic (B283, G631) or purpose (B282.2, G630). **Romae:** locative case (B21.1c and B232; G23n and G411).

100 **confirmasti = confirmavisti**.

101 **paulum . . . morae:** *a small amount of delay*; **paulum** is a neuter noun here; **morae** is partitive genitive (B201, G369). **quod:** *the fact that* (B299, G525).

102 **duo equites Romani:** we learn from Sallust (*BC* 28) that their names were C. Cornelius and L. Vargunteius (see Historical Essay II.5).

102–104 **qui . . . liberarent et . . . pollicerentur:** relative clause of characteristic (B283) or purpose (B282.2).

103 **in meo lecto:** *on my couch*. The conspirators planned to kill Cicero under the pretext of making a formal morning call or **salutatio** (see Historical Essay II.5).

Chapter 10

105 **vixdum etiam coetu vestro dimisso:** ablative absolute, *with your meeting scarcely having been dismissed.*

107 **ad me salutatum:** *to greet me*; a supine in the accusative showing purpose. The supine is a fourth declension neuter noun formed from the fourth principal part of a verb; it has only two forms, accusative and ablative singular. For usage, see B340, G434–36.

108 **multis ac summis viris:** *to many and eminent men*; dative of indirect object with **praedixeram** (line 109). **id temporis = eo tempore**.

108–109 **venturos esse:** *would come;* future active infinitive of **venio**, agreeing with

quos; infinitive in indirect discourse after **praedixeram**.

110 Quae cum ita sint: *Since these things are so.* Literally, *Since which things are so.* Latin frequently uses a relative pronoun at the beginning of a sentence (e.g., *which things*) where English prefers a demonstrative pronoun (*these things*). **perge:** imperative of **pergo. quo** (adv.): *to where, whither.* **egredere:** imperative of **egredior**; deponents have imperatives that look like active infinitives.

111 aliquando (adv.): *finally, at last.*

111–12 diu . . . desiderant: *has long been desiring*; the present tense is sometimes used to describe an action that began in the past and continues in the present (see B259.4, G230).

112 tua illa Manliana castra: *that Manlian camp of yours*; subject of **desiderant**. Manlius' camp was in Faesulae, in Etruria (see Map 3). **Educ:** imperative; for the form, see B116.3, G130.5a.

113 omnis: accusative plural; **-is** is an alternative ending for **-es** in the accusative plural of i-stem third declension nouns. **si minus:** *if less than all.* **quam plurimos:** *as many as possible*; **quam** + superlative: as _____ as possible.

113–14 Magno . . . metu: ablative of separation with **liberaveris**.

114 modo: *provided only that*; a clause of proviso (B310.II, G573). **murus:** *the wall of a city, city wall.*

115 iam diutius: *any longer.* **non feram, non patiar, non sinam: TRICOLON, ASYNDETON,** and **ANAPHORA**.

Chapter 11

116 dis: dative plural of **deus**.

116–17 Magna . . . gratia: *great thanks.* Cicero provides emphasis by separating the adjective from the noun it modifies, a figure called **HYPERBATON. Magna . . . habenda est . . . gratia:** *Great thanks must be given +* dative person. **ipsi Iovi Statori:** Cicero had

called this Senate meeting in the Temple of Jupiter Stator. Romulus was said to have promised a temple to Jupiter Stator (the Stayer) if he would halt the Sabines' advance on Rome after the rape of the Sabine women. Jupiter duly halted the battle, but the temple was not built until sometime after 294 B.C.

117 quod: *because.*

119–20 Non est saepius . . . rei publicae: order for translation, **summa salus rei publicae non periclitanda est saepius in uno homine**.

119 saepius: *very often.* **in uno homine:** *in one man* (i.e., because of one man). Cicero is referring to Catiline.

120 Quam diu: *As long as.* **consuli designato:** *consul elect.* Consular elections regularly took place in July, but the new consuls did not take office until the following January 1. Between the time they were elected and the time they took office, the new consuls were known as **consules designati**.

122 proximis comitiis consularibus: *at the most recent consular elections.* These were probably held in July of 63 B.C. Cicero had postponed them because of a threatening speech that Catiline had made, but they were probably postponed for only a few days, (see Historical Essay II.4).

122–23 me consulem . . . et competitores tuos interficere voluisti: Cicero attended this election surrounded by a private bodyguard, with his breastplate conspicuously peeking out from under his toga. Cicero may well have exaggerated the threat of violence from Catiline in order to influence the voting. In any case, Catiline lost his second and final consular election (see Historical Essay II.4).

123 in campo: the consular elections were held in the Campus Martius, a large grassy plain north of the Capitoline Hill (see Map 2).

124 amicorum praesidio et copiis: as noted above, Cicero appeared at the elections with a bodyguard composed of his friends and supporters. **compressi conatus tuos nefarios: conatus** is accusative plural. There is no evidence (beyond Cicero's own assertion) that

Catiline had planned any violent attacks at these elections.

124–25 nullo tumultu publice concitato: *with no public disturbance having been incited*; **publice** is an adverb.

125 petisti: a shortened (syncopated) form of **petivisti** (G131).

125–26 per me: *through my own efforts.*

Chapter 12

130 Qua re: *Wherefore, For which reason*; literally, *because of which thing.*

130–31 id quod est primum: *that which is first* (i.e., that which should be done first: the execution of Catiline).

131–32 et quod huius imperi disciplinaeque maiorum proprium est: *and [that] which is appropriate to this [= my] authority and to the teaching of the ancestors.* Cicero is apparently referring to the SCU that the Senate has voted against Catiline.

132 facere nondum audeo: the direct object of **facere** is **id quod est primum** (lines 130–31). Cicero does not yet dare to kill Catiline, partly for the reason that he states in the next sentence, but also because he does not have irrefutable proof that Catiline is linked with the conspiracy. **ad severitatem:** *as regards strictness.*

133 iussero: future perfect indicative of **iubeo** in a future more vivid condition (G595); it is best translated into English as a present.

134 sin: *but if* (si + ne).

134–35 sin tu . . . exieris: order for translation, **sin tu exieris, [id] quod hortor te iam dudum**; **exieris** is a shortened (syncopated) form of **exiveris**, the future perfect indicative of **exeo**. **quod te iam dudum hortor:** *[a thing] which I have been urging you to do for a long time now.* Temporal expressions such as **iam** and **iam dudum** are frequently used with the present tense to describe an event that began in the past and continues into the present (B259.4).

135–36 exhaurietur . . . sentina: in this METAPHOR Catiline and his followers are compared to bilge-water, the filthy water that collects and stagnates in the bottom of a ship. If Catiline leaves Rome and takes his followers with him, the dregs will be drained from Rome as bilge-water is drained from a ship.

Chapter 13

137 num: *surely not?* **dubitas:** dubito + infinitive, *to hesitate to do something.*

137–38 id . . . quod iam . . . faciebas: *that which you were already beginning to do.* **Faciebas** is an inceptive imperfect (B260.3). Catiline was already planning to leave the city when Cicero ordered him to do so.

138 tua sponte: *of your own accord.*

141–42 possit, metuat, oderit: subjunctives in relative clauses of characteristic.

142–43 nota . . . non inusta . . . est: this METAPHOR may be drawn from the practice of branding the foreheads of runaway slaves and criminals (after they had been recaptured) with the letter "F" for **fugitivus**.

144–46 libido, facinus, flagitium: these three nouns are all subjects of **afuit; afuit** is singular because it agrees with its closest subject.

146–48 Cui tu adulescentulo . . . praetulisti: order for translation, **Cui adulescentulo quem inretisses inlecebris corruptelarum non praetulisti ferrum ad audaciam aut [praetulisti] facem ad libidinem?** *To what youth whom you had ensnared with the enticements of corruption did you not offer a sword for [his] boldness or [carry] a torch for [his] pleasure?* **Cui adulescentulo** is dative with the compound verb **praetulisti; quem . . . inretisses** is a relative clause of characteristic. Cicero is accusing Catiline of corrupting young men with the attractions of illicit pleasures and then encouraging them to further exploits of violence and lust. The expression "to carry a torch for" meaning "to provide the opportunity for" came from the practice of slaves who carried a torch for their masters when they traveled at night.

Chapter 14

149 **morte:** ablative of means.

149–50 **cum morte superioris uxoris novis nuptiis locum vacuefecisses:** *when you had cleared a place for a new marriage by the death of your former wife.* Both here and elsewhere (e.g., *In toga candida* 91–92C), Cicero accuses Catiline of several acts of domestic murder, incest, and adultery. Such accusations were common in political invective, however, and there is no corroborating evidence to support these charges (see Historical Essay II.1).

150 **nonne etiam:** *didn't you also . . . ?* **Nonne** expects an affirmative answer.

151 **Quod ego praetermitto:** *Which [crime] I disregard.* By stating that he will not mention Catiline's other domestic crimes, Cicero actually directs our attention to them; an example of **PRAETERITIO.**

151–53 **ne . . . videatur:** a negative purpose clause, explaining why Cicero will not give details about Catiline's other alleged domestic crimes. A more likely reason is that Cicero does not have the evidence to support the charges. Translate: *in order that the enormity of so great a crime may not seem to have existed in this so great a state, or [if it did exist], in order that it may not seem to have gone unpunished.*

152 **tanti facinoris immanitas:** *the enormity of so great a crime* (i.e., a crime of such enormity).

153 **ruinas fortunarum tuarum:** Catiline had run for the consulship of 62 B.C. promising **novae tabulae** (*new account books*; i.e., the cancellation of debt). High levels of debt were a problem at all levels of Roman society at that time (see Historical Essay II.4). The question of Catiline's own financial situation is not clear, however. In a letter that he left with a friend after leaving town on the night of November 8 (following this speech), Catiline claims that he could easily pay his own debts. But in a campaign speech to supporters, just before the election, Catiline had said that "the only trustworthy defender of

the wretched is one who is wretched himself" (see Historical Essay II.4). **ruinas fortunarum tuarum quas omnis:** literally, *the ruins of your fortunes, all of which*; grammatically **omnis** modifies **quas**, but logically it goes with **ruinas** (i.e., *the total ruin of your fortunes, which*).

154 **proximis Idibus:** debts and interest on loans were often due on the Kalends and the Ides. Cicero implies that Catiline will not be able to pay his debts and so will soon become bankrupt.

154–55 **non ad privatam ignominiam** (i.e., **non [pertinent] ad privatam ignominiam**): **pertinent** (line 157) also goes with **ad domesticam tuam difficultatem** (lines 155–56) and with **ad summam rem publicam** (line 156), as well as with **ad omnium nostrum vitam salutemque** (line 157).

156 **summam rem publicam:** *the highest welfare of the state.*

Chapter 15

158 **huius caeli spiritus:** *the breath of this air* (i.e., life).

159 **cum scias:** *since you know.* **horum:** i.e., the senators.

159–63 **nesciat . . . obstitisse:** **nesciat** governs the following three infinitives (**stetisse, paravisse, obstitisse**) in indirect discourse. Cicero is here alluding to the so-called First Catilinarian Conspiracy, a supposed plot to kill the consuls and leaders of the state on January 1, 65 B.C. The alleged plot was never carried out. There is some disagreement among scholars as to whether such a conspiracy actually existed, but most scholars now agree that, if it did exist, Catiline was not a part of it (see Historical Essay II.1).

159–60 **pridie Kalendas Ianuarias:** *the day before the Kalends of January,* December 29. Before Julius Caesar reformed the calendar in 46 B.C., March, May, July, and October had thirty-one days, February had twenty-eight, and the rest of the months had twenty-nine (see G, pp. 491–92).

160 **Lepido et Tullo consulibus:** *when Lepidus and Tullus were consuls*; i.e. in the year 66 B.C. **in comitio:** *in the comitium.* The **Comitium** was an open space where public meetings were held; it was located in the Forum between the **Curia Hostilia** (Senate house) and the **Rostra** (speaker's platform) (see Map 1).

161 **cum telo:** it was against the law to carry a weapon inside the city walls.

162 **sceleri ac furori:** datives with **obstitisse** (line 163). **mentem aliquam:** *a change of mind, a change of plans.*

163–66 **illa omitto . . . conatus es:** an example of **PRAETERITIO**.

164 **neque enim sunt aut obscura:** *for they are not hidden* (i.e., everyone knows about them). **neque enim sunt aut . . . aut:** *for they are not . . . and*; **aut . . . aut** usually mean *either . . . or*, but occasionally they are used to join two clauses (translated *and*), as here. **non multa:** *a few.* Cicero is using **LITOTES** here, implying that there were numerous occasions on which Catiline tried to kill him.

164–65 **aut non multa commissa postea:** *and [quite] a few [crimes were] committed [by you] afterward.*

165 **quotiens:** *how many times!* Note the break in grammatical construction (**ANACOLUTHON**). **me designatum . . . consulem:** *[when] I [was] consul elect . . . [when I was] consul.*

166 **quot . . . tuas petitiones:** *how many of your attempts*; this phrase is the direct object of **effugi** (line 168).

166–67 **ita coniectas ut . . . viderentur:** *aimed in such a way that they seemed*; result clause.

166–68 **petitiones, declinatione, corpore:** these are technical terms connected with the gladiator's art. Cicero is pointing out that he has sidestepped or avoided Catiline's attacks without the use of force.

167–68 **parva quadam declinatione et . . . corpore:** *by a certain small sideways movement and body* (i.e., *by a certain small side-*

ways movement of the body). The use of two words to express one idea (**declinatione et . . . corpore**) is called **HENDIADYS**.

Chapter 16

171 **Quae:** refers to **ista sica** in line 170.

171–72 **Quae quidem . . . nescio:** order for translation, **quidem nescio quibus sacris ista sica initiata ac devota sit abs te:** *indeed I know not by what sacred rites that dagger has been consecrated and dedicated by you.* (The words **ista sica** have been substituted for **quae** here.)

172 **quod:** *that.*

172–73 **quod . . . defigere:** *that you think it necessary to plant it in the body of a consul.* Cicero ironically suggests that Catiline, in accordance with ancient custom, had vowed to dedicate his dagger to some god after he had plunged it into a consul's body.

175 **non ut . . . videar . . . sed ut . . . :** probably purpose clauses; for the use of **non ut**, see B282.1c. **quo:** i.e., **odio**.

175–76 **non ut odio . . . debetur:** order for translation, **non ut videar permotus esse odio, quo debeo [permotus esse], sed ut [videar permotus esse] misericordia, quae non debetur tibi.** (**Non** has been substituted for **nulla**.)

176 **nulla = non.**

178 **hoc:** i.e., a senator not being greeted by any of his colleagues. **post** (prep. + acc.): here **post** means *within*.

178–79 **vocis . . . contumeliam:** *a reprimand of the voice* (i.e., a spoken reprimand).

180 **Quid? quod:** *What about the fact that?* (see B299, G525).

181 **constituti fuerunt = constituti sunt:** *have been selected.* **tibi:** *by you*; dative of agent with a passive verb (B189.2, G354). **ad caedem:** *for slaughter.*

181–82 **simul atque:** *as soon as.*

183 **quo tandem animo tibi [hoc esse] ferendum putas?:** *with what disposition, finally, do you think you ought to bear [this]?*

The **hoc** (understood) refers to the first half of the sentence, the fact that all the senators moved away from Catiline as soon as he sat down.

Chapter 17

184–85 si . . . metuerent . . . putarem: imperfect subjunctives in a present contrary-to-fact condition (B304, G597).

184 isto pacto . . . ut: *in that way as.*

185 omnes cives tui: *all your citizens* (i.e., all your fellow citizens). **relinquendam = relinquendam esse.**

185–86 tu tibi urbem non arbitraris?: order for translation, **tu non arbitraris urbem [relinquendam esse] tibi?**

185 tibi: dative of agent (B189, G354).

186–88 Et si . . . viderem, . . . mallem: another present contrary-to-fact condition.

186 iniuria (ablative singular as adverb): *unjustly.* **meis civibus:** either dative of reference (*suspect to my fellow citizens*) or dative of agent (*suspected by my fellow citizens*).

187 quam: *rather than,* following the implied comparative in **mallem** (line 188).

187–88 carere me aspectu . . . mallem: order for translation, **mallem me carere aspectu civium quam [me] conspici infestis oculis omnium.**

188 conscientia: ablative of means.

188–89 cum . . . agnoscas: *since you recognize that.*

189 iustum = iustum esse.

190 debitum = debitum esse.

190–91 dubitas . . . vitare?: order for translation, **dubitas vitare aspectum praesentiamque eorum, quorum mentis sensusque volneras?**

190 dubitas: dubito + infinitive = *to hesitate.* **mentis:** accusative plural; **-is** is an alternative accusative plural ending for **-es** in third declension i-stem nouns. **volneras = vulneras.**

191–93 Si te parentes timerent atque odissent . . . neque . . . posses . . . concederes: another present contrary-to-fact condition.

Timerent, odissent, and **posses** all govern the protasis (if-clause); **concederes** governs the apodosis (then-clause). **Odissent** is in the pluperfect (rather than the imperfect) subjunctive, because **odi** is a defective verb that has only perfect forms.

192 neque . . . posses: *and you could not.* **ratione ulla:** *in any way.*

193 aliquo (adv.): *to someplace.* **Nunc:** *But as it is.* After a contrary-to-fact condition, **nunc** is always logical, never temporal.

193–95 Nunc te patria . . . cogitare: order for translation, **Nunc [tua] patria . . . odit ac metuit [te] et iudicat te iam diu cogitare nihil nisi de parricidio suo.**

194 iam diu: *for a long time now.*

195 de parricidio suo: *about its own parricide* (i.e., about its own destruction). The fatherland is personified as an actual parent here; Cicero continues the PERSONIFICATION in chapter 18, by making the fatherland speak to Catiline directly.

195–96 neque . . . nec . . . nec: an example of TRICOLON.

196 verebere = vereberis; second person singular future indicative of **vereor. sequere = sequeris;** second person singular future indicative of **sequor.**

Chapter 18

197 Quae: *Who,* referring to the fatherland; PERSONIFICATION. **agit:** *pleads.* **quodam modo:** *in a certain way.* **tacita:** *silent, although silent.* The fatherland pleads with Catiline (in a sense), even though it is silent; an example of OXYMORON (paradox).

198 aliquot annis: *for several years;* ablative of time within which (B231, G393). **Nullum . . . facinus exstitit nisi per te:** this entire sentence is an example of HYBERBOLE (exaggeration).

199 tibi uni: *for you alone, in your case alone.*

199–200 tibi uni . . . libera: order for translation, **tibi uni neces multorum civium [fuit impunita ac libera]; tibi [uni]**

vexatio direptioque sociorum fuit impunita ac libera.

199 **multorum civium neces:** in the previous year (64 B.C.) Catiline had been tried on charges of having committed murders during Sulla's proscriptions, but he was acquitted (see Historical Essay II.1).

199–200 **vexatio direptioque sociorum:** in 65 B.C. Catiline was tried and acquitted on charges of having extorted large amounts of money from Africa when he was governor of that province, (see Historical Essay II.1).

200–202 **tu . . . ad evertendas perfringendasque valuisti:** *you are strong not only for neglecting the laws and courts, but also for overturning and violating them* (i.e., *you are able not only to overturn and neglect,* etc.); **HYPERBOLE.**

201 **quaestiones:** the **quaestiones perpetuae** were standing jury courts, each having jurisdiction over a particular type of crime; see Appendix A.

202–203 **quamquam ferenda non fuerunt:** *although they should not have been tolerated;* passive periphrastic in the perfect tense.

203 **ut potui:** *as best I could* (the fatherland is speaking).

203–205 **esse, timeri, videri:** these infinitives are all subjects of **non est ferendum** (line 206). Translate: *It should not be tolerated that I am completely in fear on account of you alone, it should not be tolerated that whatever makes a sound,* etc.

204 **quicquid increpuerit, Catilinam timeri:** *whatever makes a sound, Catiline is feared.* Cicero implies that whenever there is the least disturbance, people immediately suspect Catiline; **HYPERBOLE.**

205 **quod . . . abhorreat:** *that is apart;* relative clause of characteristic.

206 **Quam ob rem:** *For this reason, Wherefore.* **mihi:** dative of separation (B188.2d, G347.5).

207 **verus . . . falsus:** both refer to **timorem** (line 206).

207–208 **ne opprimar . . . ut . . . desinam:** two purpose clauses, dependent upon the main verb, **eripe.**

Chapter 19

209–10 **si . . . loquatur, nonne . . . debeat, etiam si . . . non possit?:** a future-less-vivid condition, with an additional protasis (if-clause) tacked on at the end; or the second protasis could be seen as a potential subjunctive (B303 and B280.2, G596 and G257.2).

209 **nonne:** *would not?* (expects an affirmative answer).

210 **Quid, quod:** *What about the fact that?*

210–11 **tu te in custodiam dedisti:** Catiline had recently been charged with public violence and had offered to place himself in the custody of various senators who would then be responsible for bringing him to court. This practice was called **custodia libera.** As it turned out, Catiline left Rome after Cicero made this speech, so he was never brought to trial (see Historical Essay II.5).

211 **quod:** *what about the fact that?* **vitandae suspicionis causa:** **causa** in the ablative takes a preceding genitive and means *for the sake of.* **ad M'. Lepidum:** *at the house of Manius Lepidus.*

213 **ut . . . adservarem:** indirect command after **rogasti** (B295, G553). **rogasti = rogavisti** (syncopation) (B116.1).

214 **id responsum:** explained by what follows. **nullo modo:** *in no way.*

214–15 **isdem parietibus:** *within the same house walls.*

215 **tuto:** the adverb.

215–16 **quia . . . essem quod . . . contineremur:** dependent clauses in indirect discourse have their verbs in the subjunctive (B314, G650). Note the contrast between **parietibus** (*house walls*) and **moenibus** (*city walls*).

216 **ad Q. Metellum:** *to the house of Quintus Metellus;* he was praetor at that time (63 B.C.) and consul three years later.

217 **ad sodalem tuum:** *to [the house of] your pal.* **virum optimum:** an example of

IRONY; Marcus Metellus seems not to have been very highly regarded.

218 demigrasti = demigravisti (syncopation) (B116.1).

218–20 quem tu . . . putasti: order for translation, **quem tu videlicet putasti fore diligentissimum ad custodiendum te, et [tu putasti fore] sagacissimum ad suspicandum [te], et [tu putasti fore] fortissimum ad vindicandum [te]**; an example of TRICOLON as well as IRONY.

218–19 ad custodiendum te . . . ad suspicandum [te] . . . ad vindicandum [te]: ad + accusative of the gerund (or gerundive) shows purpose. Translate: *for guarding you,* etc.

220 putasti = putavisti (syncopation). **fore = futurum esse**.

220–21 Sed quam longe . . . iudicarit?: order for translation, **Sed quam longe videtur [aliquis] debere abesse a carcere atque a vinculis, qui ipse iam iudicarit se dignum custodia?** For nominative forms with **videtur**, see G528R2.

220 quam longe: *how far.*

221 iudicarit = iudicaverit (syncopation); perfect subjunctive in a relative clause of characteristic. **dignum custodia: dignum +** ablative: *worthy of.*

Chapter 20

222 Quae cum ita sint: *Since things are this way.*

222–24 dubitas . . . abire . . . et . . . mandare: dubito + infinitive: to *hesitate.*

222 aequo animo: *with a calm spirit, calmly.* Cicero seems to imply that Catiline will be found guilty (and perhaps condemned to death) if he stays in Rome. Most likely Cicero is bluffing here; Catiline still had powerful supporters in the city.

223–24 vitam istam . . . mandare: order for translation, **[dubitas] mandare istam vitam (ereptam multis iustis debitisque suppliciis) fugae solitudinique?**

224–25 "Refer" . . . "ad senatum": *Bring the matter before the Senate.* **Refero** is the regular term for bringing a matter before the Senate for consideration.

225 si hic ordo placere sibi decreverit: *if this order* (i.e., the Senate) *will have decreed that it is pleasing to itself.*

226 obtemperaturum te esse dicis: *you say that you will obey.*

226–27 id quod abhorret a meis moribus: *a thing which is inconsistent with my custom.* The Senate had no legal power to send a citizen into exile, so Cicero may mean that it is inconsistent with his custom to introduce improper measures before the Senate. But it is also true that Catiline would be under no legal obligation to obey such a decree, and Cicero may simply have wanted to avoid such a situation.

228–29 Egredere, libera, proficiscere: imperatives.

229 hanc vocem: *this voice, this spoken request* (i.e., to go into exile).

230 ecquid attendis, ecquid animadvertis horum silentium?: *do you notice anything? do you observe any silence of these men at all?* Cicero uses **ecquid** first as an interrogative pronoun and then as an interrogative adjective.

231 Quid: *Why?*

231–32 Quid . . . perspicis: *Why do you wait for the decision of those speaking, whose will, although silent, you perceive?* Literally, *whose will, silent . . .*

Chapter 21

233–55 At si . . . si . . . dixissem, . . . intulisset: pluperfect subjunctives in a past contrary-to-fact condition; **dixissem** should be taken with both si-clauses.

233 hoc idem: *this same thing* (i.e., **in exsilium proficiscere** in line 229). **P. Sestio:** Publius Sestius was a quaestor at this time. In 56 B.C. Sestius was prosecuted for **ambitus** (electoral bribery) and **vis** (public violence) and was successfully defended by Cicero, among others (see *Pro Sestio*). **fortissimo:** *most honorable.*

234 **M. Marcello:** Marcus Marcellus later became consul in the crucial year of 51 B.C. and openly opposed Caesar. He sided with Pompey in the civil war that followed, but was eventually pardoned by Caesar at a Senate meeting in 46 B.C., after which Cicero gave a speech of gratitude (*Pro Marcello*). **hoc ipso in templo:** *in this very temple.* The Senate would not hesitate to use violence to defend these honorable men, even in a sacred place such as this one; the Senate was then meeting in the Temple of Jupiter Stator.

235 **iure optimo:** *with complete justice.* **vim et manus:** *violent hands;* **HENDIADYS.**

236–37 **cum quiescunt, probant; cum patiuntur, decernunt; cum tacent, clamant:** note the **TRICOLON** and **OXYMORON.** Cicero apparently has only lukewarm support from the Senate, but he is making the most of the fact that none of the senators is willing to speak out openly in Catiline's favor (see Historical Essay II.5).

237 **Neque hi solum:** *Not only these men* (i.e., the senators). Cicero means that not only the senators but other Romans also want Catiline to leave the city. **quorum tibi auctoritas est videlicet cara:** Cicero is probably referring to Catiline's offer to abide by a possible Senate vote to exile him (lines 224–26).

238 **vita vilissima:** nominative. **equites Romani:** the equestrian order ranked second only to the senatorial in status. Many equestrians, unlike senators (who were the landowning political elite), were closely and directly engaged in business (see Historical Essay I.3).

239 **ceterique fortissimi cives:** Cicero later formed the ideal of a **concordia ordinum** (a union of right-thinking men from all classes who would come together and save the Republic), based on the support he received from all classes of citizens against Catiline; see the *Fourth Catilinarian Oration*, especially chapters 14–16, and Historical Essay II.8. **qui circumstant senatum:** the doors to Senate meetings were left open so that ordinary citizens could hear the debates.

240–41 **voces paulo ante exaudire potuisti:** apparently the crowd outside the Senate meeting had voiced support for something that Cicero had said a little earlier.

242–43 **eosdem facile adducam ut te . . . usque ad portas prosequantur:** *I will easily persuade these same men to escort you all the way to the city gates.* The ut-clause is an indirect command (B295, G546). **te . . . relinquentem:** order for translation, **te relinquentem haec quae iam pridem studes vastare;** **haec** refers to the buildings and homes in the city that Catiline had planned to burn and destroy.

243 **studes:** the present tense is frequently used with **iam pridem** and similar expressions to denote an action that began in the past and continues in the present (B259.4).

Chapter 22

244 **Quamquam:** *And yet.* **quid:** *why?*

244–46 **te ut ulla res frangat, tu ut umquam te corrigas, tu ut ullum fugam mediteris, tu ut ullum exsilium cogites?:** *As if anything would break you! As if you would ever correct yourself!* (etc.). These are exclamatory questions, a type of **RHETORICAL QUESTION;** their format is **ut** + the subjunctive. As can be seen from this example, exclamatory questions deny that the stated result could ever occur (see G558). These exclamatory questions also exemplify both **ANAPHORA** and **ASYNDETON.**

245 **mediteris = mediteris;** second person singular present subjunctive

246 **Utinam . . . di immortales duint!:** *Would that the immortal gods might give . . .!* **Duint** is an archaic form of the present subjunctive of **do, dare** (equivalent to **dent**), probably used to increase the solemnity of Cicero's invocation. **Utinam** + present subjunctive (*would that*) is the regular way to express a possible wish (B279.1, G261). **mentem:** *intention, plan.* **Tametsi:** *Nevertheless.*

247–49 **video, si mea voce . . . impendeat:** order for translation, **si [tu], perterritus mea** voce, induxeris animum ire in exsilium, video quanta tempestas invidiae impendeat nobis, si minus in praesens tempus recenti memoria scelerum tuorum, at in posteritatem. In a future-less-vivid condition, the perfect subjunctive (**induxeris**) can be translated as present (B303, G596).

247 si . . . animum induxeris: *if you should persuade yourself, if you should decide.*

247–49 video . . . quanta tempestas invidiae nobis . . . impendeat: *I see how great a storm of hatred hangs over us*; indirect question. Both here and elsewhere in the *Catilinarian Orations* (e.g., *Cat.* 2.15, lines 166–69) Cicero acknowledges that banishing or harming Catiline would be an unpopular act.

249 recenti memoria: *on account of the fresh memory*, ablative of cause (B219, G408).

250 est tanti: *it is of so great a value* (i.e., it is worth the risk of unpopularity); genitive of indefinite price or value (B203.3, G380R). dum modo: *provided only that*; a clause of proviso (**dum** or **dum modo** + subjunctive) (B310.II, G573).

251–53 Sed tu ut . . . non est postulandum: translate **non est postulandum** as an impersonal passive periphrastic (*it is not to be demanded that*) and translate the three **ut**-clauses as indirect commands, dependent on **postulandum**.

251 commoveare = commovearis; second person singular present subjunctive passive.

252 temporibus rei publicae: *to the needs of the Republic.*

253 Neque enim is es . . . ut: *For you are not the* [sort of] *person that*; here **is** signals a result clause.

Chapter 23

255 Quam ob rem: *Wherefore, For this reason.* profiscere: imperative.

255–56 si mihi . . . invidiam: order for translation, si vis conflare invidiam mihi, tuo inimico, ut praedicas.

255–56 inimico . . . tuo: an **inimicus** was a personal enemy, as opposed to a **hostis**, an enemy of the state; **tuo inimico** is dative, in apposition with **mihi**.

256 ut praedicas: *as you say.* Catiline was apparently alleging that Cicero was motivated by personal animosity in urging him to go into exile. vis: second person singular present active indicative of **volo** (B130, G174). recta (adv.): *directly, by a straight route* (originally **recta via**). recta perge in exsilium: if Catiline goes into exile (and not to Manlius' camp) he will show that he is not in fact connected to the conspiracy. This, in turn, would bring strong public criticism of Cicero for harassing an innocent man.

258 iveris: second person singular future perfect indicative of **eo** (B132, G169.2).

259 mavis: second person singular present indicative of **malo** (B130, G174).

260 confer te ad Manlium: if Catiline joins Manlius' rebel forces at Faesulae, he will demonstrate that Cicero's accusations are correct.

261–62 ut . . . videaris: order for translation, ut videaris non eiectus a me isse ad alienos, sed [ut videaris] invitatus [isse] ad tuos [amicos]. Most likely a purpose clause; non may be used in a purpose clause when only a particular word (not the entire clause) is being negated (see B282.1c, G545R2).

Chapter 24

263 Quamquam: *And yet.* quid: *why?*

263–68 Quamquam . . . praemissam: this long PERIODIC SENTENCE is most easily translated by breaking it down into its constituent parts. Order for translation, Quamquam quid ego invitem te, a quo sciam [viros] iam esse praemissos, qui praestolarentur tibi, armati, ad Forum Aurelium? [Quid ego invitem te], cui sciam diem pactam [esse] et constitutam [esse] cum Manlio? [Quid ego invitem te], a quo sciam illam argenteam aquilam esse praemissam? [Illa aquila] quam confido

futuram [esse] perniciosam ac funestam tibi ac tuis omnibus [amicis]. [Illa aquila] cui sceleratum sacrarium constitutum fuit domi tuae.

263 **quid ego te invitem:** *why do I ask you?* (deliberative subjunctive). Cicero means: why do I bother to ask whether you are going into exile or to Manlius' army at Faesulae?

263–64 **a quo sciam [viros] iam esse praemissos:** *by whom I know that men have already been sent on ahead;* **sciam** is subjunctive in a relative clause of characteristic.

264 **qui tibi . . . praestolarentur armati:** *who would wait for you under arms* (i.e., *so that they would wait for you under arms*); a relative clause of purpose (B282.2, G630). **ad Forum Aurelium:** *near Forum Aurelium;* for the use of **ad** with the names of towns to mean *in the vicinity of,* see B182.3. **Forum Aurelium** was a small town in Etruria on the **Via Aurelia. cui:** *by whom;* dative of agent with a perfect passive verb (B189.2, G354).

265–66 **aquilam illam argenteam:** the silver eagle was the standard of the Roman legion. This particular eagle is said by Sallust (*BC* 59) to have belonged to Marius' army during the war against the Cimbri (101 B.C.) (see Historical Essay I.5).

267 **cui:** *for which* (the antecedent is the silver eagle). **sacrarium:** *a shrine.* Standards were kept in a special sacred area in the Roman camp. Cicero here charges that Catiline had made a special sacred area or shrine for the eagle in his own home. A legionary standard would certainly enhance Catiline's credibility with his troops, and he may also have felt that this particular standard, coming as it did from Marius' famous and successful campaign, would bring him good luck. **sacrarium sceleratum:** *an impious shrine;* oxymoron. The shrine would be impious because the silver eagle had been stolen; but the textual reading of **sceleratum** is uncertain.

267–68 **constitutum fuit = constitutum est.**

268 **Tu ut illa carere diutius possis:** *As if you would be able to be apart from it any*

longer! This is an exclamatory question with **ut** + the subjunctive (G558); cf. the note on exclamatory questions at lines 244–46 above.

269–70 **a cuius altaribus saepe istam impiam dexteram ad necem civium transtulisti:** *from whose altar you often used to move your impious right hand to the slaughter of citizens.*

Chapter 25

271 **Ibis:** second person singular future active indicative of **eo** (B132, G169.2). **quo** (adv.): *to where.*

271–72 **te iam pridem . . . rapiebat:** *now for a long time has been driving you* (B260.4, G234).

272 **haec res:** probably refers to Catiline's intention to leave Rome and fight against his country.

274 **natura . . . servavit:** this sentence exemplifies TRICOLON, ASYNDETON, and CLIMAX.

275 **non modo . . . sed ne . . . quidem:** *not only . . . but not even.*

276–77 **Nactus es . . . manum:** order for translation, **Nactus es manum improborum conflatam ex perditis [viris] atque derelictis non modo ab omni fortuna verum etiam [ab omni] spe.**

276 **ab:** ablative of personal agent; the abstract nouns here are PERSONIFICATIONS and thus are considered to be personal agents.

Chapter 26

278 **Hic:** *here,* (i.e., with this band of reprobates). **perfruere = perfrueris.** The alternative second person singular passive ending for **-ris** is **-re;** it is most frequently used with the future indicative, as here.

280 **quemquam:** *any* (i.e., *a single*). **Ad huius vitae studium:** *for the pursuit of this life* (i.e., of this depraved lifestyle).

281 **meditati . . . sunt:** *were practiced;* although **meditor** is usually deponent, it is

used passively here. **qui feruntur:** *which are reported.* Apparently Catiline was well known for his powers of endurance, which Cicero proceeds to enumerate; Cicero here criticizes Catiline for using these powers for disgraceful and wicked purposes.

281–83 iacere . . . vigilare: the infinitives are in apposition with **labores**; they can be translated into English either as infinitives (*to lie on the ground . . .*) or as gerunds (*lying on the ground . . .*).

281–82 non solum . . . verum etiam: *not only . . . but also.*

282 ad obsidendum stuprum: *to watch for adultery*; **ad** + accusative of gerund or gerundive shows purpose. **ad facinus obeundum:** *to engage in crime.*

284 Habes ubi ostentes: *You have the opportunity to show*; a relative clause of purpose (B282.2, G630). Literally, *You have [a place] where you might show*; a word such as **locum** is understood as the direct object of **habes** and antecedent of **ubi.**

285 quibus: *by which things*, i.e. hunger, cold and poverty.

Chapter 27

287 Tantum: *only so much.* **cum te a consulatu reppuli:** in the elections for the consulship of 63 B.C. Catiline had been defeated by Cicero; thus Cicero had "pushed Catiline out" of the consulship, and Cicero was now consul rather than Catiline.

287–88 ut exsul . . . posses: a substantive clause of result in apposition with **Tantum** (B297, G557). Order for translation, **ut posses temptare [rem publicam] exsul potius quam vexare rem publicam consul.** **potius . . . quam:** *rather than.*

287 exsul: *as an exile.*

288 consul: *as a consul.* The end-rhyme (**HOMOIOTELEUTON**) of the words **exsul** (line 287) and **consul** emphasizes the contrast between them.

288–90 ut id quod . . . nominaretur: another substantive clause of result, also in

apposition with **Tantum** (line 287). Order for translation, **ut id quod susceptum esset scelerate a te nominaretur latrocinium potius quam bellum.**

291–92 ut a me. . . detester ac deprecer: *in order that I may avert and plead against*; a purpose clause.

293 quae: *the things which*; the antecedent is expressed by the **ea** that follows.

294–95 multo . . . carior: *much dearer*; literally, *dearer by much*; **multo** is ablative of degree of difference, (B223, G403).

295 si omnis res publica loquatur: The Republic now speaks to Cicero; an example of **PERSONIFICATION. M. Tulli:** for the form of the vocative, see B25.1.

296–300 Tune eum quem . . . esse videatur?: a complex **PERIODIC SENTENCE** that is best translated by breaking it down into its constituent parts. Order for translation, **Tune patiere eum exire, quem comperisti esse hostem, quem vides futurum [esse] ducem belli, quem sentis exspectari imperatorem in castris hostium, [quem sentis esse] auctorem sceleris, [quem sentis esse] principem coniurationis, [quem sentis esse] evocatorem servorum et civium perditorum, ut videatur non emissus esse ex urbe abs te, sed [ut videatur] immissus [esse] in urbem [abs te]?**

297 imperatorem: *as a commander.*

298–99 evocatorem servorum et civium perditorum: Catiline steadfastly refused to bring slaves into the conspiracy (although his closest associates kept advising him to do it), but past rebellions against the government had included slaves, particularly the recent slave revolt lead by Spartacus (73–71 B.C.), which was no doubt still fresh in the senators' minds.

299 patiere = patieris; second person singular future indicative of a deponent.

299–300 ut . . . videatur: a purpose clause. **ut abs te non [videatur] emissus [esse] ex urbe, sed immissus in urbem esse [abs te] videatur:** *in order that he may seem not to* *have been sent out of the city by you, but sent against the city [by you].* Note the **HOMOIOTELEUTON** between **emissus** and **immissus**, emphasizing the contrast between them. If Cicero lets Catiline go, he might seem to be allowing him to attack the city at the head of an army; this is the complaint that Cicero is anticipating (**iustam patriae querimoniam,** lines 291–92). Cicero is really caught between two hostile groups: if he arrests Catiline without sufficient evidence he will be criticized by Catiline's supporters, but if he allows Catiline to leave the city he will be criticized by others for letting a dangerous man escape. Cicero explains his reasons for not arresting Catiline below (lines 315–39).

300–302 **Nonne . . . imperabis:** *Will you not command?* This sentence is an example of **TRICOLON, CLIMAX,** and **ANAPHORA.**

Chapter 28

303–304 **At persaepe . . . morte multarunt:** this is an exaggeration. Of the few examples that Cicero mentions at the beginning of this oration (Ti. Gracchus, C. Gracchus, L. Saturninus and two others, lines 17–35), only Ti. Gracchus was killed by a private citizen (he was actually killed by a mob led by a private citizen, Scipio Nasica), and this incident seems to have provoked a public outcry (see Historical Essay I.2).

304 **An leges:** *Or [are you concerned about] the laws?* Several laws had been passed protecting the rights of Roman citizens in capital cases; most recently C. Gracchus had passed the **lex Sempronia de capite civium** in 123 B.C., guaranteeing Roman citizens the right to a trial before the people in cases of capital punishment. The underlying issue (which Cicero does not wish to bring out) was the basic opposition between the **lex Sempronia** and the SCU (see Historical Essays I.4, II.3, and II.8).

304–305 **leges quae . . . rogatae sunt: legem rogare:** *to pass a law.*

305–306 **At numquam . . . tenuerunt:** this statement was not based on Roman legal

practice. A few weeks later, after five of the chief conspirators had been arrested, Cicero argued strongly for the death penalty, basing his case primarily on this argument (see *The Fourth Catilinarian Oration;* e.g., lines 128–32). Although Cicero prevailed at that time, his imposition of the death penalty on the conspirators was the main reason for his later banishment in 58 B.C. (see Historical Essay II.7 and II.8).

306–307 **Praeclaram . . . refers gratiam: gratiam referre:** *to return thanks, show gratitude.* Cicero is using **IRONY** here.

307–308 **hominem per te cognitum:** *a man known through your own efforts.* Cicero was a **novus homo,** a man who was not only the first in his family to be elected to the Senate but who was also elected consul (for a fuller description, see Historical Essay I.5).

308–309 **tam mature ad summum imperium:** Cicero was elected to the consulship in "his own year" (**suo anno;** i.e., in the earliest year in which he was legally eligible to do so); see the **cursus honorum** in Appendix A.

Chapter 29

311 **quis . . . metus = aliquis metus:** *any fear;* **aliquis** is used as an adjective here. **invidiae metus:** objective genitive (B200, G363.2).

311–12 **non est vehementius . . . pertimescenda:** order for translation, **invidia severitatis ac fortitudinis non est pertimescenda vehementius quam [invidia] inertiae ac nequitiae.** Cicero (speaking in the guise of the fatherland) is comparing two kinds of hatred and making the judgment that one kind should be feared more than the other; **severitatis, fortitudinis, inertiae,** and **nequitiae** are genitives of origin or source (B196).

313 **vexabuntur urbes, tecta ardebunt:** an example of **CHIASMUS** (reversed order).

313–14 **cum . . . tum:** *when . . . then.*

314 **conflagraturum = conflagraturum esse.**

315–16 vocibus ... mentibus: note the use of **HOMOIOTELEUTON** to accentuate the **ANTITHESIS** or contrast. Here **mentibus** means *sentiments* or *opinions*; both words are dative indirect objects of **respondebo.**

316–19 si ... iudicarem, ... non dedissem: a mixed present and past contrary-to-fact condition: *if I judged . . . I would not have given.*

316 hoc: *this*; explained by the infinitive phrase that follows: **multari Catilinam morte**.

317 optimum factu: *the best thing to do*; **factu** is a supine in the ablative (see B340.2, G436).

318 gladiatori isti: dative; a contemptuous term. **ad vivendum:** *for living*; **ad +** accusative of the gerund (or gerundive) shows purpose.

319 summi viri et clarissimi cives: summi viri refers to magistrates, such as L. Opimius and C. Marius, while **clarissimi cives** refers to private citizens, such as Scipio Nasica; see the notes to lines 17–35 and 303–305 above and Historical Essay I.2, I.4, and I.5.

319–20 Saturnini et Gracchorum et Flacci et superiorum complurium: subjective genitives with **sanguine** (B199, G363.1). Note that Cicero gives additional weight to these genitives by repeating the **et** after each one, a figure called **POLYSYNDETON**.

320 superiorum complurium: *of very many men of earlier times*; an exaggeration, as noted above (see the notes to lines 303–304).

320–21 non modo .... non ... sed etiam: *not only not ... but even ...*

321 contaminarunt ... honestarunt = contaminaverunt ... honestaverunt (syncopation). **sed etiam honestarunt: sed etiam [se] honestarunt.** This statement is also an exaggeration, as can be seen from the public outcry that followed these incidents (see Historical Essay I.2, I.4, and I.5).

321–22 verendum mihi non erat: an impersonal passive periphrastic.

322 hoc parricida civium interfecto: ablative absolute.

322–23 ne ... redundaret: a clause of fearing after **verendum** (line 321).

323 Quod si: *But if, But even if.*

323–24 si ... impenderet, tamen ... fui: this is a mixed condition of an unusual type; Cicero begins with a present contrary-to-fact condition but ends with an indicative statement; this break in the grammatical construction (**ANACOLUTHON**) reflects a break in thought.

324 hoc animo: ablative of description (B224, G400).

324–25 ut ... putarem: result clause following **hoc animo**.

324 invidiam virtute partam: *hatred acquired by courage*; **partam** is from **pario. gloriam:** *as glory*; predicate accusative (B177, G340).

Chapter 30

326 Quamquam: *And yet.* **non nulli:** *not none* (i.e., *some*); a common idiom. **hoc ordine:** i.e., the Senate.

326–27 qui aut ... non videant aut ... dissimulent: a relative clause of characteristic.

330–31 si ... animadvertissem, ... dicerent: a mixed past and present contrary-to-fact condition.

330 si in hunc animadvertissem: *if I had punished this man* (i.e., if I had put him to death).

331 regie: *tyrannically.* Since the Tarquins had been driven out of Rome in 509 B.C., the thought that any Roman would act like a king or tyrant was abhorrent to the Romans. Cicero was in fact later accused of acting tyrannically after he put five of the conspirators to death without a trial (see Plutarch *Cicero* 23.4 and Cicero *Pro Sulla* 21–22; see also Historical Essay II.8). **quo:** *to where, whither.*

331–32 si . . . pervenerit: subjunctive in a subordinate clause in indirect discourse (B314, G628).

332 in Manliana castra: *to Manlius' camp.* Catiline did in fact set out for Manlius' camp that very night (November 8), after Cicero gave this speech (see Historical Essay II.6). **fore = futurum esse.**

333 qui non videat: a relative clause of characteristic (B283) or result (B284.2).

334 qui non fateatur: a relative clause of characteristic (B283) or result (B284.2).

336 Quod si: *But if.* **eodem** (adv.): *to the same place.*

337 adgregarit = adgregaverit (syncopation or shortening).

338 non modo . . . verum etiam: *not only . . . but also.*

339 stirps ac semen malorum omnium: HYPERBOLE.

Chapter 31

340–41 iam diu . . . versamur: *for a long time we have been living.* With time expressions such as **iam diu**, the present is often used to designate an action beginning in the past and continuing in the present (B259.4).

340 in his periculis: *among these dangers.* In fact, however, there is no evidence that Catiline's conspiracy had lasted any longer than a few months (see Historical Essay II.4).

341 nescio quo pacto: *somehow or other;* literally, *I don't know in what way;* for the idiom, see B253.6, G467n.

343 latrocinio: here this word means *a band of robbers.*

343–44 si . . . tolletur, videbimur . . . esse relevati: a future-more-vivid condition, with future indicative in both clauses. For the nominative form of the infinitive with **videor,** see G528.

345–46 in venis atque in visceribus rei publicae: note the vivid METAPHOR; the comparison of the Republic to a person sick with fever continues as a SIMILE in the fol-

lowing sentence.

347 aestu febrique: *with the heat of fever;* literally, *with heat and fever;* HENDIADYS.

348 multo: ablative of degree of difference with a comparative (B223, G403).

349 relevatus: *although relieved.*

350 reliquis vivis: *if the rest remain alive;* an ablative absolute with conditional force (B227.2b).

Chapter 32

351 Qua re: *Wherefore.*

351–55 secernant, congregentur, secernantur, desinant, sit . . . inscriptum: jussive subjunctives (B275, G263.3).

352 quod: the antecedent is the clause **muro . . . secernantur a nobis** (lines 352–53).

353 desinant insidiari . . . consuli: insidior takes a dative object. Cicero refers to the attempt to assassinate him on November 6 (see Historical Essay II.5). **domi suae:** locative (B232, G411.4).

353–54 circumstare tribunal praetoris urbani: Cicero implies that Catiline had attempted to intimidate the court. The praetor's tribunal (located in or adjoining the Forum) was the platform from which he dispensed justice; the **praetor urbanus** presided over cases involving Roman citizens (see Appendix A).

354 obsidere cum gladiis curiam: the **curia,** or Senate house, was situated at the northern edge of the **comitium** (see Map 1). Cicero may be referring to the charge he made earlier (lines 159–61) that Catiline had been seen standing in the **comitium** with a weapon on December 29, 66 B.C.

355 sit . . . inscriptum: *let it be written upon.*

356 unius cuiusque: *of each and every one.* **quid . . . sentiat:** indirect question following **sit . . . inscriptum** (line 355). **hoc:** explained by what follows.

357 fore = futurum esse. in nobis con-

sulibus: *in ourselves the consuls.* Cicero may be referring to himself in the plural, or he may be referring to Antonius Hybrida, his consular colleague, along with himself (see Historical Essay II.3).

358 in vobis: i.e., in the Senate. in equitibus: *among the equestrians.*

359 in omnibus bonis: *in all good men.* Cicero has thus included all classes of citizens in the fight against Catiline's conspiracy. Cicero will expand this theme in his *Fourth Catilinarian Oration* (lines 199–235); he later created a plan for a permanent union of all good citizens (concordia ordinum), based on the fact that citizens from all walks of life came together to oppose Catiline's conspiracy (see the Historical Essay II.8).

359–61 ut ... videatis: result clause.

360 patefacta, inlustrata, oppressa, vindicata esse: the CLIMAX of these verbs is heightened by the use of ASYNDETON.

Chapter 33

362 Hisce = His: -ce is an enclitic particle used to intensify certain demonstrative pronouns. ominibus: from omen, -inis, n. Hisce ominibus: *with these omens;* ablative of attendant circumstance (B221). Cicero's promises that all citizens will work together against Catiline are (bad) omens for Catiline's plans. cum summa rei publicae

salute: *with the greatest advantage for the Republic.* Cicero means that the Republic will benefit from Catiline's departure.

364 proficiscere: imperative of proficiscor.

365 Tu, Iuppiter: Cicero is presumably addressing the statue of Jupiter Stator, in whose temple they were meeting.

365–6 Tu ... es constitutus: order for translation, Tu, Iuppiter, qui constitutus es isdem auspiciis, quibus haec urbs [constituta est] ab Romulo. This claim is not strictly true; Romulus was said to have vowed the temple during the war with the Sabines, but it was not actually built until 294 B.C.

366 Statorem: here Stator means *protector* or *guardian.*

367 hunc et huius socios: direct objects of arcebis (line 368).

369 homines bonorum inimicos: *men [who are] enemies of the good [men];* direct object of mactabis (line 371), as are hostis patriae and latrones Italiae.

370–71 aeternis suppliciis vivos mortuosque: Cicero's reference here to the punishment of wicked men after their deaths contrasts sharply with his rejection of such notions as mere fictions in the *Fourth Catilinarian Oration* (lines 105–109). Since both speeches were addressed to the Senate, this discrepancy cannot be explained by a difference in audience.

Cicero's *Second Catilinarian Oration*
Delivered November 9, 63 B.C. to the
Roman People in the Forum

Chapter 1

1 Tandem aliquando: *Finally, At last.* Quirites: *Citizens;* this term was the regular way of addressing the Roman people when speaking from the Rostra. L.: Lucium (accusative), but translate as nominative, *Lucius.*

3–4 vel ... vel ... vel ...: *either ... or ... or.* An example of ANAPHORA and TRICOLON. Cicero may give his listeners such a range of

choices because he does not yet feel confident enough to claim that he had driven Catiline out of Rome, yet he expresses his uncertainty with powerful rhetorical force.

4–5 Abiit, excessit, evasit, erupit: a dramatic CLIMAX, made even more powerful by ASYNDETON (lack of a connective word).

5 Nulla iam: *No longer.* pernicies: pernicies + dative: *destruction for.*

5–6 monstro . . . atque prodigio: HENDI-ADYS. Monstro suggests something unnatural, while **prodigio** implies supernatural influence; a bad omen or portent. Cicero may be foreshadowing his comparison of Catiline to a beast of prey (lines 19–20 below).

6 moenibus ipsis: datives with **pernicies**; *for our very walls*

8 sica illa: When **ille** follows the noun, it often means *that well known* or *that famous*. In this case, *that well known dagger* is a METAPHOR for Catiline himself. **Non . . . iam:** *No longer.*

8–9 Non . . . non . . . non . . . non . . . non: ANAPHORA.

9 campo: here, as often, **campus** refers to the Campus Martius, a grassy plain along the Tiber River where the Roman people assembled for the **comitia centuriata** (the assembly that elected the consuls). The Campus Martius was also used for games, exercise, and military drills (see Appendix A and Map 2). **foro:** *the Forum*. The Forum was the center of public life in Rome (see Map 1). **curia:** the Senate regularly met in the Curia or Senate house, situated on the northern edge of the Comitium, in the northwest area of the Forum (see Map 1).

9–10 intra domesticos parietes: *within the walls of our houses*. Cicero is probably referring to the attempt made against his life at his own home only two days before.

10 Loco ille motus est: *He was moved from his ground*; an expression taken from wrestling and gladiatorial combat. **Loco** is ablative of separation (B214, G390).

11 nullo impediente: *with no one interfering*, ablative absolute; **nullus** is frequently substituted for **nemo** in the ablative case. **bellum iustum:** here refers to an open war, as opposed to the struggle against the conspirators living in their midst.

Chapter 2

14 Quod vero: *Because* or *With regard to the fact that* (B299.2. G 538–542). **extulit:** from **effero.**

15 vivis nobis: ablative absolute; see note on **intra domesticos parietes** (lines 9–10) above. **ei:** dative of reference (B188, G350).

16 incolumis civis: accusative plural; **-is** is an alternate form for the accusative plural of third declension nouns and adjectives (instead of **-es**). It is used most frequently with i-stem nouns and adjectives.

16–17 quanto . . . maerore: ablative of means.

18 se: in indirect discourse, the use of a reflexive pronoun (like **se**) means that the subject of the direct statement is the same as the subject of the indirect statement. So in this sentence, **sentit se esse perculsum** means: *he perceives that he has been struck down.*

19–20 retorquet oculos . . . e suis faucibus ereptam: Cicero is comparing Catiline to a beast of prey.

20 quae: nominative singular; refers to the city (**hanc urbem**). **videtur: videre** frequently means *to seem* in the passive voice.

20–21 quod . . . evomuerit . . . proiecerit: Cicero uses the subjunctive because he is not giving his own reason but the reason he attributes to the (personified) city (B286, B541). An example of PERSONIFICATION.

Chapter 3

22 Ac si = Atque si: *But if.* **si quis = si aliquis:** *if anyone, if someone.* The Romans dropped the prefix **ali-** when **aliquis** or **aliquid** followed **si, nisi, num,** or **ne.** A helpful mnemonic device: "After **si, nisi, num,** and **ne** all the **ali-**'s go away." **talis . . . qualis:** *of such a sort, such as.* These correlatives often appear together. **talis qualis esse omnis oportebat:** *of such a sort, such as was fitting for everyone to be.* **omnis:** accusative plural. Note that **-is** is an alternate form of the accusative plural for third declension nouns, especially i-stems. **Ac si quis est talis (qualis esse omnis oportebat), qui . . . :** *But if there is anyone of such a sort (such as was fitting for everyone to be), who . . .* Cicero is trying to explain why he let Catiline go, instead of arresting him and putting him to death.

22–23 qui . . . accuset: order for translation, **qui accuset me vehementer in hoc ipso in quo mea oratio exsultat et triumphat. in hoc ipso:** *in this very thing (*i.e., Catiline's departure from the city).

23 accuset: subjunctive in a relative clause of characteristic (B283).

24 quod: *because.* When **quod** appears without a neuter antecedent, it usually introduces a causal clause. **quod . . . non comprehenderim:** Cicero uses the subjunctive because the reasoning is not his own, but another's (B286, G541).

25 temporum: *the fault of the times* (i.e., the circumstances; possessive genitive).

26 L.: Lucium (accusative), but translate as nominative, *Lucius.* **gravissimo supplicio adfectum:** *to have been punished by the most serious penalty* (i.e., death).

26–27 iam pridem: *long ago.*

27 oportebat + accusative person + infinitive: *it was fitting for accusative person to do infinitive* or *accusative person ought to have done infinitive.* **mos maiorum:** *the custom of our ancestors.* The Romans considered the **mos maiorum** to be an important standard of behavior and values.

27–28 huius imperi severitas et res republica: Cicero refers to the fact that he holds the office of **consul,** the chief executive office of the Republic, and that he now has an SCU (**senatus consultum ultimum**) against Catiline. See Historical Essays I.4 on the SCU and II.5 on the Senate's passing of the SCU against Catiline; see Appendix A on the consulship.

28 res publica: literally, *the public thing*; the usual term for the Republican government; translate as *republic.* **fuisse:** perfect active infinitive of **sum**; infinitive in indirect discourse after **putatis.**

28–29 quam multos fuisse putatis, qui quae ego deferrem non crederent: *how many [men] do you think there were who did not believe [the charges] which I was bringing.*

quae ego deferrem: *the charges which I was bringing*; literally, *the things with which I was charging him*; **quae:** neuter plural; **deferrem:** subjunctive in a subordinate clause in indirect discourse (B314, G650).

28–31 quam multos . . . quam multos . . . quam multos . . . quam multos: an example of ITERATIO.

29–30 qui . . . non crederent, . . . non putarent . . . etiam defenderent, etc.: Cicero did not arrest Catiline, because some men did not believe there was a conspiracy and others were sympathetic to Catiline.

31–32 si . . . iudicarem: the imperfect subjunctive is used in a contrary-to-fact condition. Translate: *But if I thought . . .*

31 illo sublato: ablative absolute; **sublato** is from **tollo.**

33 non modo . . . verum etiam: not only . . . but even. **invidiae meae . . . periculo:** *at the risk of my ill-will* (i.e., at the risk of ill-will toward me). **sustulissem:** *I would have taken away* (from **tollo**); pluperfect subjunctive in a mixed present/past contrary-to-fact condition.

Chapter 4

34–37 Sed cum viderem . . . videretis: this complex sentence can be broken down into parts. **Sed cum viderem**: *But when I saw*; this **cum**-clause introduces indirect discourse, explaining what Cicero saw.

34–35 ne vobis quidem omnibus etiam tum re probata: ablative absolute; *with the thing having been made clear not even to all of you at that time.*

35 si illum . . . multassem: order for translation, **si multassem illum morte (ut erat meritus)** . . . : *[that] if I punished him with death (as he deserved)* . . . This is the protasis of a future-less-vivid condition (should/would); ordinarily this would be in the perfect subjunctive, but here it is put in the pluperfect subjunctive because it is in indirect discourse (B320). **multassem:** shortened (syncopated) form; the full spelling is **multavissem,** pluperfect subjunctive, first person singular.

35–36 fore ut eius socios . . . persequi non possem: order for translation, **fore ut non possem persequi eius socios**: *I would not be able to pursue his allies*. **fore ut** (or **futurum esse ut**) + subjunctive is frequently used to express a future infinitive (B270.3). This is the apodosis of the condition; it is formed with a (future) infinitive because it is in indirect discourse.

36 rem huc deduxi ut . . . : *I drew out the affair to this point, so that . . . ;* this is the main clause of the sentence, followed by a result clause.

36–37 ut tum palam pugnare possetis cum hostem aperte videretis: *so that you could fight [Catiline] openly at that time when you clearly saw him as an enemy*; a result clause.

37 tum . . . cum: correlative adverbs, *at that time . . . when*. In this complex sentence, Cicero explains that he has brought the conspiracy into the open by forcing Catiline to leave the city and join his army at Faesulae.

37–38 Quem . . . hostem: literally, *which enemy*; translate: *and this enemy*. Latin writers often use a connective relative pronoun at the beginning of a sentence where English would use a conjunction and a demonstrative pronoun.

38 quam vehementer: *how strongly.*

39 putem: present subjunctive in indirect question, with **intellegatis** (B300, G467). **licet**: *it is permitted, it is possible*. **Licet** is an impersonal verb; it takes **ut** + the subjunctive; sometimes **ut** is omitted, as here (B295.6). **licet hinc intellegatis**: *it is permitted that you may understand from this;* or, more simply, *you may understand from this*. **quod**: *the fact that*; **hinc . . . quod**: *from this, the fact that* (B299.1a). **moleste fero**: *I take it badly, I am upset* (idiom). **illud moleste fero quod . . .** : *I am upset because of this, that . . . ;* **illud** (this) refers to the following clause, **quod . . . exierit** (lines 39–40).

40 parum comitatus: Catiline left the city *too little accompanied*. Cicero is upset that Catiline took so few of his co-conspirators with him.

40–41 Utinam . . . eduxisset: **utinam** with the imperfect or pluperfect subjunctive expresses a wish that cannot be realized (B279.2, G260–61). **omnis**: feminine accusative plural modifying **suas copias**.

41 mihi: dative of reference or interest (B188, G350–52). **in praetexta**: the **toga praetexta** was a toga with a purple edge or border worn by boys up to age sixteen (and also by curule magistrates). Thus the phrase, **in praetexta**, means *in his boyhood*. It was a common practice in Roman oratory to accuse one's opponent of moral turpitude, even if there was little or no evidence to support the charge.

41–42 Tongilium, Publicium, Minucium: nothing is known about these men, and that is part of the point. Cicero is saying that Catiline took his unimportant co-conspirators with him but left the powerful ones behind in Rome.

42 aes alienum: *debt.*

43 nullum rei publicae motum: the debts of these men were so insignificant that they posed no threat to the Republic.

44 quanto aere alieno: *men of how great a debt*; ablative of quality (also called ablative of description; B224, G400). **valentis, nobilis**: accusative plurals. **quam valentis, quam nobilis**: Cicero complains that the most dangerous conspirators are still in the city.

Chapter 5

45 illum exercitum: Catiline's army. **Gallicanis legionibus**: the Roman legions stationed in Cisalpine Gaul; these could easily be brought down from the north to Faesulae.

45–46 hoc dilectu: the soldiers recently recruited to protect the government; Quintus Metellus, the praetor, had drafted troops as soon as the Senate had learned of Manlius' movements at Faesulae (see Historical Essay II.5).

46 agro Piceno et Gallico: Picenum was located on the Adriatic Sea, east of Umbria. The **ager Gallicus** was adjacent to Picenum on the north (see Map 3).

46–47 his copiis: also dependent on **prae** (line 45).

48 conlectum: agrees with **illum exercitum** (Catiline's army, in line 45), in contrast to the Roman troops fighting in defense of the city. **senibus desperatis:** Cicero may be referring specifically to the veterans from Sulla's army, many of whom had joined Catiline's forces (see Historical Essay II.4). **agresti luxuria:** *country luxury.* Cicero means men who have been ruined by living beyond their means on their country estates. Extravagant living was strongly condemned by Roman public opinion of the time, though it was frequently practiced, especially among the wealthy.

48–49 rusticis decoctoribus: debt was a serious problem throughout rural Italy in the late Republic (see Historical Essay II.4).

49 vadimonium deserere: *to jump bail, leave town and forfeit one's bail* (an idiom); **vadimonia** is plural.

49–50 vadimonia deserere quam illum exercitum maluerunt: These men preferred to jump bail rather than desert Catiline's army.

50 quibus: indirect object of **ostendero** (line 51); translate as if it read **eis**: *to them.*

50–51 ego . . . concident: order for translation, **[Hi viri Catilinae] concident, non modo si [ostendero eis] aciem exercitus, verum etiam si ostendero edictum praetoris; concident:** future indicative. **non modo . . . verum etiam:** *not only . . . but even.*

51 edictum praetoris: the praetor's edict was the formal proclamation issued by the praetor soon after taking office, stating the principles according to which he would rule over the court during his term. Cicero suggests that the conspiracy would collapse if the courts took a strong stand against debt.

51–52 Hos quos video volitare in foro . . . : Cicero refers once again to Catiline's wealthy, powerful friends whom he has left in Rome.

52 ad curiam: *in front of the Senate house.*

53 nitent unguentis: the wealthy men are the ones who might oil their heads with costly perfumes (i.e., perfumed oil). **fulgent purpura:** senators and knights wore a vertical purple stripe on their togas. **mallem:** optative subjunctive (B279.2).

53–54 suos milites: *as his soldiers*; predicate accusative (B177, G340).

54 [ut] eduxisset: clause of wish or desire (B296.1a, G546 R2). **mementote:** future imperative of **memini** (B281.1a).

54–55 non tam . . . quam: *not so much . . . as much as.*

54–56 non tam exercitum illum . . . pertimescendos: some words have been left out. The full sentence would read: **non tam exercitum illum [pertimescendum esse nobis] quam hos . . . [esse] pertimescendos**; the construction is passive periphrastic with dative of agent (**nobis**); **esse** is in the infinitive because of indirect discourse after **mementote**.

55 hos qui exercitum deseruerunt: Cicero is referring to Catiline's powerful sympathizers who are still in Rome.

56 hoc: ablative of cause (B219, G408); **hoc . . . quod:** *for this reason . . . because.* **sunt timendi = hi sunt timendi:** passive periphrastic.

56–57 quod quid cogitent me scire sentiunt: order for translation, **quod sentiunt me scire quid cogitent:** *because they are aware that I know what they are planning.* **quid cogitent:** subjunctive in indirect question (B315, G467).

57 me scire: indirect discourse after **sentiunt.**

Chapter 6

58 cui: *to whom* (i.e., to which one of the conspirators).

58–60 sit, habeat, depoposcerit: subjunctives in indirect question.

60 **superioris noctis consilia:** Cicero is probably referring to the plans that the conspirators made at Laeca's house on the night of November 6 (see Historical Essay II.5 and *Cat.* 1.9).

61 **patefeci in senatu hesterno die:** Cicero is referring to what is now called his *First Catilinarian Oration*, delivered on November 8, 63 B.C.

62 **Ne:** intensive particle; *I assure you; surely, verily.*

64 **futuram = futuram esse.**

65 **Quod exspectavi:** *What I have been waiting for.*

65–66 **ut . . . videretis:** *that you should see*; a substantive clause, in apposition with the unexpressed object of **sum adsecutus**: *[that] I have obtained, [namely] that you should see* (B294, B297.1).

66–67 **si quis = si aliquis;** see note on **si quis** above, chapter 3, line 22. **nisi vero si quis est: si** is redundant after **nisi**; translate: *unless, indeed, there is anyone.* **nisi . . . quis est qui . . . non putet: putet** is subjunctive in a relative clause of characteristic, and it governs a clause in indirect statement.

67 **Catilinae similis:** *men similar to Catiline*; **similis** is accusative plural, and it is the subject of the indirect statement. **cum Catilina sentire:** *think with Catiline* (i.e., share his desire for revolution).

67–68 **Non . . . iam:** *No longer.*

69 **exeant, proficiscantur, patiantur:** jussive subjunctives (B275, G263.3).

69–70 **ne patiantur desiderio sui Catilinam miserum tabescere:** *let them not allow wretched Catiline to waste away with longing for themselves*; **sui** (genitive plural) refers to the subject of **patiantur.**

70 *Aurelia via*: ablative of means (B218, G401). The Aurelian way ran northwest from Rome (see Map 3). Catiline pretended that he was going to Marseilles, but he was really heading to Manlius' camp at Faesulae.

71 **ad vesperam:** *toward evening.*

Chapter 7

72 **fortunatam rem publicam:** accusative of exclamation (B183). **hanc sentinam:** Cicero compares Catiline's supporters in the city to bilge-water, the filthy water that collects in the bottom of a ship.

73 **me hercule:** by Hercules!; a common oath. **Catilina exhausto:** ablative absolute. Continuing with his METAPHOR, Cicero states that the Republic (the ship of state) has been lightened and refreshed since Catiline has been removed (**exhausto**: literally, *drained out*). If all the bilge-water of his supporters were removed as well, Cicero implies, the Republic would sail smoothly.

74 **mali, sceleris:** partitive genitives with **Quid**: *What evil or crime?* Also called genitive of the whole (B201.2, G369).

75 **Quis . . . veneficus:** here **quis** is used as an interrogative adjective, *what poisoner? what gladiator?* (etc). **tota Italia:** ablative of place where (B2281b, G388).

80 **hosce:** a more emphatic form of **hos** (see B87, footnote 1).

Chapter 8

82 **in ullo:** *in anyone.*

82–83 **tanta . . . quanta:** *so great . . . as great as.*

83 **alios . . . aliorum:** *some . . . of others.*

84 **aliis . . . aliis:** *to some . . . to others.* **fructum, mortem:** direct objects of **pollicebatur** (line 86).

85 **impellendo, adiuvando:** gerunds; ablative of means.

86 **quam subito:** *how suddenly.*

88 **non modo . . . sed ne . . . quidem:** *not only . . . but not even.* **Romae:** locative.

Chapter 9

91–92 **ut . . . possitis:** a parenthetical purpose clause, indicating Cicero's purpose in saying what follows (B282, G545R3).

91 **diversa studia in dissimili ratione:** *his various interests in a different connection;*

Cicero will now argue that Catiline is on intimate terms with two different types of corrupted people: bold and audacious gladiators and fickle, good-for-nothing actors.

92 ludo gladiatorio: in the gladiatorial schools, slaves and criminals who were forced to serve as gladiators received harsh training. **paulo . . . audacior:** i.e., a little bolder than the others.

93 nemo in scaena: actors in Rome were usually slaves or freedmen; their social position was very low.

93–94 levior et nequior: as with **audacior**, the implication is that these actors were more fickle and more untrustworthy than the average.

95–96 adsuefactus frigore et fame . . . perferendis: *having become accustomed to enduring cold and hunger,* etc.; this clause explains why Catiline was praised as courageous by his companions.

96 perferendis: this gerundive agrees grammatically with **vigiliis**, but in meaning it modifies **frigore, fame**, etc., as well. **ab istis:** *by Catiline's own followers*; **iste** frequently has a negative or pejorative connotation.

96–97 fortis . . . praedicabatur: Catiline was praised as brave and courageous by his followers, but Cicero implies that Catiline is not in fact praiseworthy because he developed his ability to endure hardships through debauchery.

97 cum: adversative; *although.*

97–98 industriae subsidia atque instrumenta virtutis . . . consumeret: Catiline wastes his natural abilities, which could be used to support hard work and military excellence, on the practice of lust and criminal activity.

Chapter 10

99 secuti erunt, exierint: future perfect indicatives.

100 o nos beatos: *O [how] happy we [shall be]!* This exclamation stands in place of the conclusion to this condition.

100–101 nos beatos, rem publicam, etc.: accusative of exclamation (B183, G343).

101–102 Non . . . iam: *No longer.*

101–103 Non enim iam sunt mediocres . . . audaciae: order for translation, **enim non iam libidines [horum] hominum sunt mediocres, non [iam libidines sunt] humanae et [non iam] audaciae tolerandae [sunt].**

103 nisi . . . nisi . . . nisi: ANAPHORA.

105 res: here, *money*; feminine singular, subject of **coepit** (there is a change of subject after **obligaverunt** in line 104). **iam pridem** (adv.): *long ago, for a long time now.* **fides:** here, *credit*; feminine singular, also subject of **coepit**.

106 [libido] quae erat [illis]: illis (understood) is dative of possession. **Quod si:** *But if.*

106–107 si . . . quaererent: present contrary-to-fact condition; they are <u>not</u> only seeking revels and prostitutes.

107–108 essent . . . desperandi: passive periphrastic; *they would have to be despaired of.*

108 essent ferendi: passive periphrastic; *they would have to be tolerated.* **hoc:** direct object of **ferre**, explained by the following clause; *who would be able to endure this, [the fact that] . . .* ; RHETORICAL QUESTION. **quis . . . possit:** *who would be able?* potential subjunctive (B280, G257).

109 inertis homines: masculine accusative plural, subject of **insidiari** in accusative/infinitive construction; this entire clause serves as an explanation of **hoc** (line 108). **fortissimis viris:** dative with **insidiari; insidior** + dative person: to plot against.

110 dormientis: masculine accusative plural. **mihi:** dative of reference (B188).

111 accubantes: the Romans usually ate dinner while reclining on low couches.

Chapter 11

115 improbitati, nequitiae, etc.: datives with **debitam**.

115–16 instare, appropinquare: infinitives in indirect discourse after **confido** (line 114); the subject is **poenam** (line 114).

117 sustulerit: future perfect of **tollo**: [*if my consulship*] *will have removed.* **nescio quod:** idiom; literally, *I know not what;* means *some;* cf. French: *je ne sais quoi.*

117–18 non breve nescio quod tempus sed multa saecula propagarit rei publicae: order for translation, [**meus consulatus**] **propagarit rei publicae non nescio quod breve tempus sed multa saecula**: [*my consulship*] *will have preserved the Republic not for some brief time, but for many ages.* **non nescio quod breve tempus sed multa saecula:** accusative of extent of time.

118 propagarit rei publicae: future perfect indicative; syncopated (shortened) form of **propagaverit;** here it takes the dative.

119 pertimescamus, possit: present subjunctives in two relative clauses of characteristic.

120 Omnia sunt externa . . . pacata: *All foreign things* (i.e., threats) *have been pacified.* **unius virtute:** i.e., Pompey, who had successfully fought wars against the pirates and Mithridates and was now "pacifying" the East. **terra marique: terra** refers to the battle against Mithridates, and **mari** refers to Pompey's earlier (67 B.C.) suppression of the pirates.

120–21 domesticum bellum: *civil war.*

121–22 intus . . . intus . . . intus: Cicero's use of ANAPHORA emphasizes the internal nature of these threats.

122–23 nobis . . . certandum est: bellum is the understood subject of this impersonal passive (B256.3, G208.2).

123 Huic . . . bello ducem: Cicero seems to be comparing himself to Pompey here.

124 quae sanari poterunt: this entire phrase is the object of **sanabo**(line 125): *the things which can be cured.*

125 quacumque ratione (adv.): *in whatever way [I can].*

125–26 ad perniciem: *for the destruction; ad* + accusative is occasionally used to show purpose.

126 exeant, quiescant: jussive subjunctives (B275, G263.3).

127 et in urbe et in eadem mente permanent: ZEUGMA (B374.2a).

Chapter 12

129 sunt qui dicant: relative clause of characteristic (B283, G631.2).

130 possem, eicerem: imperfect subjunctives in a present contrary-to-fact condition. **Quod:** *This* (i.e., throwing people out of the city); object of **adsequi. verbo:** *by means of a word* (i.e., by simply telling them).

131 Homo: refers to Catiline. **videlicet:** *clearly;* often has an ironical force, as here.

132 simul atque: *as soon as.*

133 Quin (conj.): *But indeed, In truth, But in fact.*

133–34 cum . . . paene interfectus essem: cum circumstantial clause. Cicero refers to an incident that had actually occurred two days earlier, on November 7 (see Cicero *Cat.* 1.9), when Catiline had sent out two Roman knights to kill Cicero at his home in the early morning hours; see Appendix B.

133 domi meae: locative.

134 senatum in aedem Iovis Statoris convocavi: this was Cicero's delivery of what is now called the *First Catilinarian Oration,* on November 8.

135 patres conscriptos: *senators.* **Quo:** *To which place,* as often. Cicero refers to Catiline's attendance at the Senate meeting.

136 quis . . . senator: *what senator?* **quis . . . quis . . . quis:** ANAPHORA.

136–37 ita . . . ut: *in such a way . . . as.*

137 ac non potius ut: *and not rather as.*

137–38 Quin etiam: *In fact even* (take closely with **reliquerunt** in line 139).

138 eius ordinis: *of that body* (i.e., the Senate).

Chapter 13

140 **Hic:** *At that point, Thereupon.* **vehemens ille consul:** a sarcastic reference to the criticisms made by Catiline's supporters. **civis:** accusative plural.

141–42 **[utrum] fuisset necne:** *whether he had been . . . or not*; a double indirect question, with **utrum** omitted (B300.4 a, G459).

141 **ad** (+ acc person): *at the house of.* **M.:** **Marcum** (accusative), but translate as nominative, *Marcus.*

143 **quid . . . egisset:** indirect question, dependent on **edocui** (line 145).

143–44 **in proximam [noctem]:** *for the following night.*

144 **quem ad modum:** *in what way, how.* **ei:** *by him*; dative of agent (B189, G354).

144–45 **quem ad modum . . . edocui:** order for translation, **edocui ad quem modum ratio totius belli descripta esset ei.**

145 **cum teneretur:** *when he was caught.* **quid:** *why?*; introduces indirect question.

146 **eo quo:** *to that place where.* **quo iam pridem pararet:** *where now for a long time he had been preparing [to go].*

146–49 **cum . . . scirem esse praemissam:** *since I knew that . . . had been sent on ahead*; **praemissam** agrees with the nearest subject but goes with all.

146–47 **arma, securis, fascis:** all accusative plural. Only magistrates with **imperium** (consul, praetor, dictator), who had the right to command a Roman army, also had the right to use the axes and fasces, which were symbols of authority. Catiline had no such office, but it seems that he had managed to secure some of these symbols and was using them to gain support for his conspiracy.

147–48 **aquilam illam argenteam:** *that silver eagle.* The silver eagle was the military standard of the Roman legion. According to Sallust (*BC* 59.3) Catiline had obtained a silver eagle that was said to have been used by Marius' army against the Cimbri. Cicero here repeats the charge made in his *First Catilinarian*

Oration (chapter 24) that Catiline possessed this eagle and had made a shrine for it in his own house.

148 **domi suae:** locative.

Chapter 14

150 **In exsilium eiciebam:** conative imperfect (B260.3, G233). **iam:** *already.*

151 **credo:** ironical here, as often.

152 **bellum . . . indixit: bellum indicere,** *to declare war.* **suo nomine:** *in his own name* (i.e., *on his own responsibility*): ablative of means; IRONY.

154 **Massiliam:** modern Marseilles, a sophisticated Greek colony and a favorite place for exiles (see Map 4).

155 **O condicionem miseram:** *O thankless task!*; accusative of exclamation; Cicero complains not only about the duties of governing the Republic (**administrandae rei publicae** in lines 155–56), but also of saving it (**conservandae rei publicae**) when he gets so little support from others.

156–63 **Nunc si . . . esse dicetur:** this is one long future-more-vivid condition; future perfect indicative in the protasis and future in the apodosis.

156 **L.:** *Lucius.*

158 **pertimuerit:** this and the following future perfects are all part of the protasis that ends at **converterit** (line 160).

160–63 **non ille a me spoliatus armis . . . esse dicetur:** this is the apodosis. For the nominative forms (**spoliatus esse** and others), see B332.

160–61 **non . . . non . . . non:** ANAPHORA.

163–65 **erunt qui illum . . . existimari velint:** relative clause of characteristic.

165 **velint:** third person plural present subjunctive of **volo.**

Chapter 15

166 **Est mihi tanti:** *It is worthwhile for me*; literally, *It is worth so great a value for me*; **tanti** is genitive of value (B203.3, G380).

167 **dum modo:** *if only, as long as, provided that.*

167–68 **dum modo . . . depellatur:** clause of proviso (B310, G573).

168 **Dicatur:** jussive subjunctive (B275, G263.3).

168–69 **dum modo eat:** clause of proviso (B310, G573).

169 **non est iturus:** *he does not intend to go*; more forceful than **non ibit.**

169–72 **Numquam . . . optabo . . . ut . . . audiatis:** indirect command (B296.1, G546).

172 **triduo:** *within a three-day period*; ablative of time when or within which. **multoque:** ablative of degree of difference (B223, G403). **illud:** *this, namely the fact that . . .* ; **illud** looks forward to the **quod** clause (lines 173–74) and explains what Cicero fears.

172–73 **multoque magis illud . . . aliquando, quod:** order for translation, **multoque magis timeo ne illud sit invidiosum mihi aliquando, quod . . .**

173 **invidiosum:** here, *a cause of hatred, a source of hatred*; **invidiosum** is neuter, agreeing with **illud** (line 172). **timeo ne . . . sit invidiosum:** clause of fearing (B296.2, G543.3); **aliquando:** *at some time in the future.*

173–74 **quod illum emiserim potius quam quod eiecerim:** *the fact that I let him go rather than that I drove him out.* Cicero is now being criticized for driving Catiline out of the city, but he fears that at some time in the future he may be criticized for allowing Catiline to leave the city unharmed.

174–75 **homines qui . . . dicant:** relative clause of characteristic.

175 **idem:** nominative plural, subject of **dicerent** (line 176).

175–76 **si interfectus esset, quid dicerent?:** *if he had been killed, what would they say?*

Chapter 16

177 **Quamquam:** *And yet.* **Massiliam = ad Massiliam. dictitant:** dictito, dictitare is a frequentative of **dicere** (B155.2).

177–78 **non tam . . . quam:** *not so much . . . as much as.*

179 **qui . . . non . . . malit:** relative clause of result (B284.2, G631). **Massiliensis:** see B152.3

180 **cogitasset = cogitavisset:** pluperfect subjunctive in a contrary-to-fact condition (B304). **me hercule:** *by Hercules!* an exclamation **hoc quod agit:** *this [thing] that he is doing* (i.e., his conspiracy against the government).

181–82 **Nunc vero:** *But as it is*; **nunc** is logical not temporal after a contrary-to-fact condition.

183 **nisi quod:** *except for the fact that.* **vivis nobis:** ablative absolute. **Roma:** ablative of separation. **optemus:** hortatory subjunctive.

183–84 **optemus potius ut eat in exsilium quam queramur:** *let us rather hope that he has gone into exile rather than complain [that he has gone].*

Chapter 17

186 **quod semper volui:** *something which I have always wanted*; the antecedent of **quod** is the situation described by **murus interest** (lines 186–87).

187 **qui dissimulant:** *those who pretend* (i.e., those who hide their real feelings of sympathy with Catiline). **Romae:** locative.

189 **possit:** impersonal; potential subjunctive (B280, G257). **non tam . . . quam:** *not so much . . . as much as.* **sanare sibi ipsos:** *to restore them to health for their own sakes.* Cicero implies that those who sympathize with Catiline are not in their right mind; **ipsos** is emphatic (*the men themselves*); **sibi** is dative of interest.

190–91 **Neque id qua re fieri non possit . . . intellego:** order for translation, **Neque intellego id non possit [ali]qua re fieri:** *nor do I think that this is not able to happen in some way* (i.e., *I do think that this can happen*; the two negatives cancel one another out).

190 **me audire:** *to listen to me* (i.e., to take my advice). **volent:** future indicative.

192 **singulis:** to each of the individual groups or types.

192–93 **medicinam consili atque orationis meae:** *a remedy consisting of my advice and speech*; genitive of material (B197); **consili atque orationis** is HENDIADYS: *the advice in my speech.*

193 **si quam = si aliquam medicinam.**

Chapter 18

194 **est eorum:** *consists of those.* **magno in aere alieno:** *(although) in great debt.*

qui, magno in aere alieno: participation in Roman politics required spending large sums of money, but the wealth of most senators was tied up in the form of houses and land. These men, therefore, frequently borrowed huge sums of money to finance their political careers and then ended up with very large debts.

195 **quarum:** the antecedent is **possessiones.**

197–99 **Tu . . . ornatus et copiosus sis, et dubites:** Cicero addresses an imaginary member of this class: *Are you abundantly furnished and well supplied . . . and do you hesitate . . . ?*; deliberative subjunctives (B277).

197–98 **Tu . . . tu . . . tu . . . tu . . . tu:** ANAPHORA.

199 **detrahere, adquirere:** ANTITHESIS, ASYNDETON.

199–200 **adquirere ad fidem:** *and [do you hesitate] to add to your credit* (i.e., by paying your debts).

200 **Quid ergo?:** *What then?* (i.e., what do you think will happen in a war?).

201 **futuras = futuras esse:** future infinitive in indirect discourse.

201–202 **tabulas novas:** the phrase **tabulae novae** meant *new account books* (i.e., *the cancellation of debt*). Catilinae had run for the consulship of 62 B.C. on a platform of canceling debts (see Sallust, *BC* 21.2), and he seems to have continued to make such

promises in order to gain support for his conspiracy.

202 **meo beneficio:** ablative of means.

203 **auctionariae [tabulae]: tabulae auctionariae** were *auctioneering placards*, listing the items to be auctioned. Cicero suggests that these wealthy men should get rid of their debt by putting some of their possessions up for auction.

204 **salvi:** this word has two meanings: *financially solvent* and *physically safe*, and Cicero may be being intentionally ambivalent here. His primary meaning is that the wealthy will never be free from debt until they sell some of their assets, but he also may be implying that, if Catiline's revolution should prove successful, the lives of wealthy men might be in danger. **Quod si: Quod** is a relative here; the antecedent is the main idea of the past two sentences (i.e., using part of their wealth to pay their debts).

204–205 **Quod si maturius facere voluissent:** *But if they had been willing to do this sooner.*

205 **neque . . . certare: voluissent** is used again; *and had not [wanted] to fight.*

205–206 **certare cum usuris fructibus praediorum:** literally, *to fight with the interest [on their debts] by means of the produce of their farms.* These men tried to pay the interest on their loans by means of the produce from their estates. Cicero suggests that they should have sold off their farms long ago. It should be noted, however, that this course of action would have deprived them of both their status and their means of livelihood.

205–207 **voluissent . . . uteremur:** mixed past/present contrary-to-fact condition; *if they had been willing . . . we would find.*

207 **uteremur: utor** usually means use or enjoy; here it means *find.* Cicero claims that if these men had been willing to sell off some of their land to pay their debts, we would find them to be wealthier and better citizens today. The correctness of this claim is not clear.

207 hosce = hos: the suffix **-ce** is emphatic. **minime:** i.e., *least of all*, among the six types of men who are followers of Catiline.

209 permanebunt: i.e., *if they remain fixed in the same intention.* **facturi = facturi esse:** *to be about to make, to be more likely to make;* future infinitive of **facio; facturi:** nominative masculine plural.

209–10 magis . . . vota facturi . . . quam arma laturi: *more likely to make vows . . . than to bear arms;* deprecatory. Notice Cicero's use of rhyme and rhythm to characterize these men as weak and ineffectual. **magis . . . quam:** *more . . . than.*

210 laturi = laturi esse: future infinitive of **fero.**

Chapter 19

212 rerum potiri: *to get control of the government;* an idiom.

213 honores: *the offices;* Roman magistracies (high offices) were frequently called **honores. quieta re publica:** ablative absolute. **perturbata [re publica]:** ablative absolute.

214–15 Quibus hoc praecipiendum [esse] [mihi] videtur . . . ut: *It seems to me that this should be considered ahead of time by them . . . that;* or, more smoothly, *I think that they should consider this ahead of time . . . that;* **praecipiendum [esse]** is an impersonal passive periphrastic conjugation; **Quibus** is dative of agent with the passive periphrastic. **unum scilicet et idem quod [praecipiendum est] reliquis omnibus:** *and to be sure the very same thing which [should be considered] by all the remaining groups.*

215–16 ut desperent id quod conantur se consequi posse: order for translation, **ut desperent se posse consequi id quod conantur:** *that they should stop hoping that they can obtain the thing which they are trying [to obtain]* (i.e., they should stop hoping that they will be able to get control of the government). The entire clause is an indirect command after **praecipiendum [esse]** (line 214).

216 primum omnium me ipsum vigilare: *first of all [they should know that] I myself am on my guard.* Cicero here gives, in indirect discourse, the reasons why they should give up hope of success; a verb of knowing, parallel to **praecipiendum [esse]** (line 214), is understood.

217 animos: *courage.*

218 ordinum: *of the orders.* This word has been added by Albert Clark, the editor of the Oxford Text; it is not in the manuscripts, but it is probably what Cicero intended to say. See Historical Essay II.8 for Cicero's plans for a harmony of the orders (**concordia ordinum**).

219 immortalis: masculine accusative plural, agreeing with **deos.**

219–21 deos denique . . . esse laturos: order for translation, **denique immortalis deos, praesentis, laturos esse auxilium huic invicto populo,** etc.

221 praesentis: *in person;* masculine accusative plural, agreeing with **deos** (line 219). **esse laturos:** future active infinitive in indirect discourse; **laturos** is from **fero. Quod si:** *But even if.*

221–22 si iam sint . . . adepti: *if they should now obtain;* potential subjunctive; the perfect subjunctive has the same force as the present subjunctive here.

222 num: *surely not?* **Num** expects a negative answer.

222–24 num illi . . . consules se . . . sperant futuros [esse]: order for translation, **num illi sperant se futuros [esse] consules:** *surely they do not hope that they will be consuls . . .*

223 quae: *things which;* referring to **cinere** and **sanguine** (line 222).

224–25 Non vident id se cupere quod: order for translation, **Non vident se cupere id quod:** *Do they not see that* (introducing indirect discourse) *they desire a thing* (i.e., supreme power in Rome) *which.*

225–26 si adepti sint . . . concedi sit necesse: *if they obtain it, it is necessary that it be granted to . . .*

225 **fugitivo . . . concedi:** if these men succeed in taking over Rome, any power they might attain would only be temporary; in a state of chaos, some slave or gladiator would soon usurp the reins of power.

Chapter 20

227 **aetate iam adfectum:** Manlius and the rest of the veterans had served in Sulla's army about twenty years before the time of Catiline's conspiracy.

228 **exercitatione:** *military training;* these were veterans of Sulla's army.

229–30 **ex eis coloniis quas Sulla constituit:** Sulla had settled his veterans on land in Etruria, displacing the previous owners, most of whom had been supporters of Marius.

230 **universas:** *in general, on the whole;* agrees with **quas [colonias]** (line 229).

231–33 **qui se insperatis ac repentinis pecuniis . . . iactarunt:** *who made a display by means of unexpected and sudden riches* (i.e., by means of the farms they had received from Sulla). **se . . . iactarunt:** *they made a display* (i.e., they showed off their wealth).

232 **sumptuosius insolentiusque:** comparatives often (as here) have the meaning of *too much, excessively.*

233 **tamquam beati:** *as though [they were] wealthy;* these men had only a small amount of property, but they acted as though they were wealthy.

234 **familiis magnis:** *large numbers of slaves.* **delectantur:** passive as middle; *they delighted themselves.*

235–36 **Sulla sit eis . . . excitandus:** Sulla had died in 78 B.C. (see Historical Essay I.8).

236 **non nullos:** literally, *not none;* an idiom meaning *some.*

236–37 **tenuis atque egentis:** along with **agrestis,** all masculine accusative plural, agreeing with **homines.**

237 **rapinarum veterum:** i.e., the plunder and wholesale confiscation of land, carried out many years earlier by Sulla and his men.

237–38 **Quos . . . utrosque:** *Both of whom.* Cicero had mentioned two different types within the third class: Sulla's veterans and others whom they had inspired with hopes of plunder.

239 **hoc:** *this;* explained by **desinant;** note that **moneo** takes two accusatives, one of the person, one of the thing. **desinant:** jussive subjunctive (B275, G263.3). **proscriptiones et dictaturas:** Sulla marched on Rome in 82 B.C. His subsequent reign of terror and dictatorship (including proscriptions) made an indelible impression upon all Romans, including those, such as Cicero, who may have shared Sulla's optimate political views (see Historical Essay I.8).

240 **inustus est:** from **inuro** + dative, *to burn in.*

240–42 **Tantus . . . dolor . . . ut . . . videantur:** result clause.

241 **ista:** *such things* (i.e., a repetition of such evils).

241–42 **non modo [non] . . . sed ne . . . quidem:** *not only [not] . . . but not even;* the second **non** is understood.

242 **passurae esse:** future active infinitive of **patior:** *willing to permit, endure;* the infinitive goes with both subjects (**homines** and **pecudes** in line 241) but agrees with the nearest subject, **pecudes.**

Chapter 21

244 **iam pridem:** *now for a long time;* when this phrase is combined with a verb in the present tense (as here), translate the verb as a present perfect. **premuntur:** i.e., oppressed by debt.

246–47 **vadimoniis, iudiciis, proscriptione bonorum:** the three stages in a lawsuit for debt: the giving of bail, the judgment, and the sale of property. **proscriptione bonorum:** *the sale or confiscation of property.*

248 **Hosce = Hos;** -ce is a particle that simply adds emphasis. **non tam . . . quam:** *not so much . . . as.*

249 lentos: that is, they are slow to pay their debts. **quam primum:** *as soon as possible*.

249–50 si stare non possunt: *if they cannot stand firm* (i.e., if they cannot pay their debts).

250 conruant: jussive subjunctive (B275). **sed ita ut:** *but [let them perish] in such a way that*; introduces a result clause.

250–51 non modo [non] ... sed ne quidem: *not only [not] ... but not even*; the second **non** is understood.

251 illud: *the following*; explained by the indirect questions that follow. **quam ob rem:** *on account of what reason; why*.

252 velint: present subjunctive of **volo**.

252–53 minore dolore: ablative of manner (B220.1).

253 perituros = perituros esse: future active infinitive in indirect discourse, dependent upon **arbitrentur**.

Chapter 22

255 neque- non.

256 pereant: jussive subjunctive.

257 carcer: the only prison in Rome was situated at the northwest corner of the Forum; under it was the Tullianum, or dungeon, reached through a hole in the floor. The Tullianum was used for execution, the Carcer for short-term detention. Long term imprisonment was not a usual punishment for Roman citizens (see Historical Essay II.7).

258–59 proprium Catilinae: *appropriate to Catiline*; **Catilinae** is dative.

259 de eius dilectu: *from his selection* (i.e., it is made up of his chosen companions). **immo vero:** *nay, rather indeed*.

260 pexo capillo: *with carefully combed hair*; **pexo** is from **pecto**; ablative of description (or quality; B224, G400). **nitidos:** this refers to the perfumed oils that they used on their hair. **imberbis:** accusative plural; *beardless* (i.e., effeminate). **bene barbatos:** *with full beards*, perhaps suggesting a dissolute life.

261 manicatis et talaribus tunicis: ablatives of description. During the late Republic it was fashionable for men to wear a short-sleeved tunic that fell only to the knees; a long-sleeved tunic or a tunic that reached the ankles was considered effeminate. **velis:** *with veils*; another insinuation that these men were effeminate.

262 vigilandi labor: *effort of staying awake*; these men stay up late, not to watch or guard others, but to attend all-night parties. Cicero (here and elsewhere in this speech) is using the time-honored Roman tradition of character assassination to convince his listeners to repudiate any connections they may have had with the conspirators; see May (1988: 51–55).

Chapter 23

264 gregibus: *gangs* (literally, *flocks*). Cicero implies that these men are hardly above the level of animals.

266 neque- et ne quidem. saltare et cantare: these activities would be contrary to the **dignitas** of a Roman citizen.

267 spargere venena: i.e., in the wine or food of someone that they wished to kill. **Qui nisi exeunt:** *And if they do not depart [from Rome]*; the present tense is used instead of the future tense here. **etiam si:** *even if*.

268 scitote: the future imperative of **scio** is more common than the present imperative. **seminarium Catilinarum:** *a breeding ground of Catilines* (i.e., of men like Catiline).

269 futurum = futurum esse. quid sibi ... volunt: *what do they want for themselves?*

269–70 num ... sunt ... ducturi: *surely they are not going to lead*.

270 Quem ad modum: *In what way? How?*

271 his praesertim iam noctibus: *especially during these present nights*; ablative of time when or within which. The date of this speech was November 9, but before Julius Caesar reformed it in 46 B.C. the Roman civic calendar was two to three months ahead of the real season of the year. Thus the time when Cicero was speaking would correspond to our late August. Since August nights are not usually cool in Italy, Cicero may have been anticipating the long cold nights that lay ahead.

271 Quo autem pacto: *But in what way? How?*

272 Appenninum: the Apennine mountains near Manlius' camp in Etruria; these mountains are always singular in Latin. **idcirco** (adv.): *for this reason*; the reason is given in the **quod** clause (lines 273–74).

273 toleraturos = toleraturos esse.

Chapter 24

275 O bellum magno opere pertimescendum: IRONY.

275–76 sit habiturus: periphrastic future subjunctive of **habeo** (B269.3, G247R2); translate as a normal future.

276 cohortem praetoriam: the **praetoria cohors** was the *praetorian guard*, the bodyguard of the praetor or general. Note the internal rhyme in **scortorum cohortem praetoriam**, which helps to emphasize the absurdity of the image.

278 gladiatori: Cicero is referring to Catiline. **confecto et saucio:** i.e., after being expelled from Rome.

279 consules: the consul was the highest public official of the Roman Republic (see Appendix A).

281 urbes coloniarum ac municipiorum: literally, *the cities of the colonies and towns.* If the text is sound (and some scholars have doubted this), Cicero means the *urban troops of the colonies and towns.* **coloniarium ac municipiorum: coloniae** were originally settlements of Roman citizens, while **municipia** were Italian towns. After the Social War (91–88 B.C.) both colonies and towns held Roman citizenship and the right of local self-government.

281–82 urbes coloniarum ac municipiorum respondebunt Catilinae tumulis silvestribus: *the urban troops of the colonies and towns will respond to Catiline's [troops*

situated in] the wooded hills [of Faesulae]. Cicero seems to be contrasting the urban (i.e., well-equipped and well-trained) Roman soldiers with Catiline's ill-equipped and untrained band, living in the woods and hills of Etruria.

284 conferre: *to compare.*

Chapter 25

285 omissis his rebus: ablative absolute. **quibus nos suppeditamur, eget ille:** *with which we are abundantly supplied [but which] he lacks;* ASYNDETON; **quibus** is ablative of means with **suppeditamur** but is ablative of separation with **eget.**

287–88 si . . . velimus: present subjunctive of **volo** in a potential subjunctive (B280.2).

288 ex eo ipso: *from the comparison itself.*

288–89 quam valde illi iaceant: *how utterly at a disadvantage they are.*

295 bona ratio cum perdita: *sound policy with reckless [policy].*

297 nonne: *would not?* (expects an affirmative answer).

298 deficiant, cogant: present subjunctives in a future-less-vivid condition (B303).

298–99 ab his praeclarissimis virtutibus: ab + ablative is personal agent, used here because the virtues are personified.

Chapter 26

300 Quae cum ita sint: *Since these things are so.*

300–301 quem ad modum iam antea dixi: Cicero may be referring generally to what he said about military preparedness; it is possible, however, that Cicero inadvertently omitted a specific passage directing the citizens to protect their homes when he revised the speech for publication.

301–303 mihi . . . consultum atque provisum est: *I have taken measures and provided;* literally, *it has been deliberated and provided for by me;* intransitive verbs (that do not take a direct object) are frequently used impersonally in the passive voice (B256.3, G217).

301 **mihi:** *by me*; the dative of personal agent is frequently used with passive verbs (B189.2, G354).

301–302 **ut urbi . . . satis esset praesidi:** order for translation, **ut esset satis praesidi urbi.** A result clause; **praesidi** is partitive genitive (genitive of the whole) with **satis** (B201.2); **urbi** is dative of possession.

303 **Coloni omnes municipesque vestri:** *Your fellow citizens in the colonies and towns.* For a description of colonies and towns, see the note to line 281.

303–304 **certiores a me facti:** *having been informed by me.*

304 **nocturna excursione:** referring to Catiline's departure the previous night.

305 **gladiatores:** gladiators (generally made up of slaves and criminals) were seen as a potential threat, especially after Spartacus' revolt of 73–71 B.C. **quam . . . manum:** *a force which.*

306 **fore = futuram esse. animo meliore sunt:** *they are of better disposition* (i.e., more favorable to the legitimate government); ablative of description (B224, G400). **quam pars patriciorum:** *than part [i.e., some] of the patricians*; an allusion to the fact that some of the leaders of the conspiracy (e.g., Catiline, Cethegus, Lentulus) were patricians.

307 **Q. : Quintus.**

308 **in agrum Gallicum Picenumque:** the praetor Quintus Metellus Celer was raising Roman troops in Picenum.

309–10 **Reliquis autem de rebus consitutendis, maturandis, agendis . . . :** order for translation, **de reliquis rebus constituendis, maturandis, agendis:** *concerning the remaining matters to be decided, hastened, accomplished . . .* **Constituendis, maturandis,** and **agendis** are gerundives modifying **rebus.**

309–11 **Reliquis autem de rebus constituendis . . . ad senatum referemus:** *But we [I] will report to the Senate concerning the remaining matters to be decided . . .*

311 **quem vocari videtis:** *[the Senate] which you see is being convened.* Perhaps messengers were passing through the Forum, summoning the senators to a meeting.

Chapter 27

313 **salutem:** goes with both **urbis** and **omnium vestrum.**

314 **monitos = monitos esse.**

315 **cui = aliqui.**

315–16 **hoc exspectavit:** *it [my gentleness] was waiting for this*; **hoc** is explained by the purpose clause that follows.

316 **Quod reliquum est:** *As for the future.*

316–17 **iam non:** *no longer.*

317–18 **horum, his:** *these men*; Cicero's loyal fellow citizens.

318 **mihi . . . vivendum aut . . . esse moriendum:** *I must either live with them or die for them*; literally, *it must either be lived by me*, etc.; an impersonal passive periphrastic. Cicero feels he must either save the citizens or die in the attempt.

319 **si qui = si aliqui** (plural).

320 **qui = si aliquis** (singular; B91.4). **vero:** *but.* **qui vero se in urbe commoverit:** **commoverit** is a future perfect indicative in a future-more-vivid condition, but it translates into English more naturally as a present.

320–21 **non modo . . . sed vel:** *not only . . . but even.*

323 **carcerem:** Cicero may actually be referring to the dungeon (**Tullianum**) below the prison (**Carcer**), where criminals were executed; this would explain his stipulation that the crime be clear.

324 **maiores:** *ancestors.*

Chapter 28

328 **post hominum memoriam:** *within the memory of men* (i.e., *within human memory*).

328–29 **me uno togato duce et imperatore:** ablative absolute. Cicero is highlighting his civilian status while stating his intention to put down the conspiracy without creating a public disturbance or bringing soldiers into the city. The fact that Cicero was actually able to accomplish this goal, particularly in a period when political violence was increasing, is a strong testament to his intelligence, foresight, and skill.

329 sedetur: goes with all the subjects in this clause but agrees with the nearest one, **bellum** (line 327); present subjunctive in a result clause. **Quod:** *This* (i.e., Cicero's goal of putting down the conspiracy).

333 de hac animi lenitate deduxerit: *will have led me away from this gentleness of spirit* (i.e., if Cicero must resort to using force). **illud:** *that*, explained by the result clause that follows.

333–34 quod . . . videtur: parenthetical; *a thing which seems scarcely to be hoped for in so great and so dangerous a war.*

334–35 ut neque bonus quisquam intereat: result clause.

335 poena: ablative of means.

Chapter 29

337 Quae: *These things;* direct object of **polliceor** (line 338).

338 fretus (+ abl.): *relying on;* **fretus** goes with **mea prudentia** (line 337), and **humanis consiliis** (lines 337–38), and also with **multis et non dubiis . . . significationibus** (lines 338–39).

339 quibus . . . ducibus: ablative absolute; *with the gods as leaders.*

339–40 hanc spem sententiamque: *this hope and purpose* (i.e., of bringing an end to the conspiracy).

340–41 ut quondam solebant: parenthetical, *as once they were accustomed [to do].*

343 Quos: i.e., **deos.**

343–46 implorare debetis ut . . . defendant: order for translation, **debetis implorare [deos] ut defendant hanc [urbem] a nefario scelere perditissimorum civium.**

344–46 ut . . . defendant: indirect command following **precari, venerari, implorare** (line 343).

344–45 quam urbem . . . esse voluerunt: parenthetical.

345–46 omnibus hostium copiis terra marique superatis: ablative absolute.

Cicero's *Third Catilinarian Oration*
Delivered December 3, 63 B.C., to the
Roman People in the Forum

Chapter 1

1 vestrum: genitive plural of **vos.**

4 hodierno die: ablative of time when.

6 ereptam, conservatam, restitutam [esse]: agree with their nearest subject (**urbem** in line 3), but understood to belong with the other subjects as well. **vobis:** dative of reference or interest (B188, G350-352).

Chapter 2

7 si non minus nobis iucundi . . . sunt ei dies: *if those days are no less pleasant for us;* LITOTES.

7–8 ei dies quibus conservamur: *those days on which we are saved;* **dies** is nomina-

tive masculine plural; **quibus** is ablative of time when.

8 quam illi [dies] quibus nascimur: *than those days on which we are born.* **quod:** *because;* Cicero now explains why the previous if-clause is true.

8–9 salutis certa laetitia est: order for translation, **laetitia salutis est certa:** *the happiness of our safety is assured.*

9 nascendi incerta condicio: order for translation; **condicio nascendi incerta [est]:** *our situation at birth is uncertain;* literally, *the situation of being born;* gerund (i.e., at the time of our birth our fate and fortunes are unclear). Note the ADVERSATIVE ASYNDETON between these two clauses. Cicero means: *the happiness of our safety is assured, but our situation at birth is unclear.*

10 **cum voluptate:** i.e., with conscious pleasure. Again, there is an adversative ASYNDETON between this and the previous clause. **profecto:** *then certainly*; the apodosis of the if-clause from the beginning of the chapter starts here.

10–11 **illum qui hanc urbem condidit:** Romulus was considered to be the founder of Rome.

11 **ad deos . . . sustulimus:** *we have raised to the gods.* The Romans worshipped Romulus as a god; **sustulimus** is from **tollo.**

12 **debebit:** *will deserve.*

12–13 **is qui . . . urbem . . . servavit:** Cicero is referring to himself, comparing himself to Romulus. **eandem hanc urbem conditam amplificatamque:** *this same city [after it has been] founded and extended.*

13–14 **toti urbi, templis, delubris, tectis, moenibus:** datives, with **subiectos** and **circumdatos** (lines 14–15).

13–15 **Nam toti urbi . . . restinximus:** order for translation, **Nam restinximus ignis prope iam subiectos et circumdatos toti urbi . . . :** *For we have extinguished the fires already almost brought to and placed around the entire city . . .*

14 **prope iam:** literally, *already almost* (i.e., *practically*). **ignis:** accusative plural, direct object of **restinximus** (line 15).

15 **idemque:** *and we also*; nominative plural masculine agreeing with **nos** (understood).

Chapter 3

18 **Quae quoniam:** *And since these things* (neuter plural; i.e., these dangers); a relative pronoun at the beginning of a sentence is usually best translated by a conjunction and a demonstrative pronoun.

19 **per me:** *through my efforts.*

19–21 **ut . . . vos . . . scire possitis:** purpose clause.

20 **qua ratione:** *in what manner.* **investigata et comprehensa sint:** subjunctives in indirect question, following **scire** (line 21).

21 **exspectatis:** *are waiting [to hear]*; Cicero will now explain the events that had just taken place in the Senate to the people, who have been waiting in the Forum to hear the news.

22 **ut:** *when.* **paucis ante diebus:** *a few days earlier.* Actually it was almost a month ago; it was now December 3, and Catiline had left Rome on November 8, after Cicero had delivered his *First Catilinarian Oration.*

22–24 **cum . . . reliquisset:** cum-circumstantial clause.

23 **huiusce = huius:** -ce is an intensive particle with demonstrative force; it need not be translated. **Romae:** locative.

24 **quem ad modum:** *in what manner, in what way, how?*

25 **tum cum:** *at the time when.*

26 **eiciebam:** conative imperfect (B260.3, G233).

26–27 **verbi invidiam:** *the hatred of this word* (i.e., the hatred arising from this word: **eiciebam**). Now that Cicero has solid proof that Catiline is involved in the conspiracy, he is no longer afraid that some Romans will blame him for forcing Catiline out of the city; contrast the beginning of his *Second Catilinarian Oration.*

27 **illa: illa [invidia]. quod:** *the fact that*; explains **illa [invidia]:** Cicero fears he will be hated because he let Catiline escape. **exierit:** subjunctive because the **quod**-clause introduces someone else's reason, not his own (B286.1).

29 **exituram [esse]:** indirect discourse after **putabam** (line 30). **eos qui restitissent:** *those who remained*; pluperfect subjunctive in a subordinate clause in indirect discourse (B314, G625R1). **debilis:** accusative plural.

30 **fore = futuros esse:** future active infinitive of **sum**, agreeing with **eos**; indirect discourse after **putabam.**

Chapter 4

31–32 quos . . . sciebam: parenthetical clause; the antecedent of **quos** is **eos**, on line 32. Cicero is referring to Catiline's chief co-conspirators.

32 in eo: *in this*; explained by the following purpose clause: **ut . . . sentirem ac viderem** (lines 33-34).

33 omnis: accusative plural. **quid agerent, quid molirentur:** indirect questions after **sentirem ac viderem** (line 34).

34–36 ut . . . rem ita comprehenderem: purpose clause. **quoniam . . . oratio mea:** causal clause (B286.1); parenthetical.

36–37 ut . . . provideretis: *so that, then at last, you would take precautions for your safety by means of your thoughts*; result clause (note **ita** in the previous clause). **tum demum . . . cum:** *then at last . . . when.*

36 animis: ablative of means; note the contrast with **oculis** (line 37) in the following clause.

37–42 Itaque ut comperi . . . litteras: this is a very long dependent clause, explaining the things that Cicero learned; the main clause begins with **facultatem** in line 42, and **putavi** is the main verb of the sentence.

38 comperi: according to Sallust (*BC* 41.5), Cicero learned this piece of information from Q. Fabius Sanga, the **patronus** (legal protector) of the Allobroges at Rome. **legatos Allobrogum:** the ambassadors of the Allobroges had come to Rome to ask the Senate for relief from the high taxes demanded by their Roman governors (cf. Sallust *BC* 40.3). **Allobrogum:** genitive plural of the **Allobroges**, a warlike tribe in Transalpine Gaul. **belli . . . et . . . tumultus: bellum** usually refers to a war outside of Italy, while **tumultus** means a rebellion either in Italy or in Cisalpine Gaul.

39 causa: causa in the ablative case functions as a preposition; it takes a preceding genitive and means *for the sake of*; **excitandi** is a gerundive in the genitive, agreeing with **tumultus Gallici** (line 38). **P. Lentulo:** Publius Cornelius Lentulus Sura had been a

consul in 71 B.C., but he had been expelled from the Senate in 70 B.C., supposedly for licentious behavior (see Historical Essay II.5). He had been elected praetor for 63 B.C., however, and had thus regained his seat in the Senate.

39–41 eosque in Galliam . . . esse missos: Cicero learned that the ambassadors of the Allobroges had been sent back home to Gaul.

40 civis: accusative plural. **eodemque itinere:** *and on the same journey.* On their way back from Gaul to Rome the ambassadors were supposed to meet with Catiline in his military camp at Faesulae in Etruria (see Map 4).

41 comitemque: in apposition with **T. Volturcium. T. Volturcium:** Titus Volturcius was one of Catiline's followers; he later became an important witness for the prosecution under promise of immunity (see Historical Essay II.6).

42 huic: i.e., to Volturcius. **facultatem mihi oblatam [esse] putavi:** this is the main clause of the sentence; **oblatam** is from **offero.**

43–45 ut . . . tota res . . . deprenderetur: a consecutive or result clause, explaining what kind of opportunity Cicero believed was being offered.

43 quod erat difficillimum: *a thing which was most difficult.* **ab dis:** *from the gods*; **dis** is ablative plural of **deus.**

Chapter 5

46 hesterno die: *on yesterday* (i.e., December 2). **praetores:** praetors in Rome served mainly as judges, but they also possessed military **imperium**, which allowed them to command troops (see Appendix A).

47 amantissimos rei publicae: *most loving of the Republic* (i.e., most patriotic); **rei publicae** is objective genitive (B200).

48 quid fieri placeret ostendi: *I showed what was pleasing [to me] to be done* (i.e., *I showed what I wanted done)*; **placeret** is used impersonally and is subjunctive in an indirect question; **fieri** is the infinitive of **fio.**

48–49 qui omnia de re publica praeclara atque egregia sentirent: *who felt all honorable and extraordinary things* (i.e., feelings) *toward the Republic*; **sentirent:** subjunctive in a relative clause of characteristic.

50 cum advesperasceret: note how Cicero's syntax becomes uncharacteristically simple here. The events themselves are so exciting that they have their most powerful effect by being told simply.

51 pontem Mulvium: the Mulvian Bridge, built across the Tiber in 109 B.C., is located about two miles north of Rome, on the Via Flaminia. Now known as the Ponte Milvio, it is still in use today as a pedestrian walkway and retains four of its ancient arches.

51–52 ita bipertito fuerunt: *were arranged in two parts in such a way.*

52 bipertito (adv.): *in two parts* (i.e., one at each end of the bridge). **ut . . . interesset:** order for translation, **ut Tiberis et pons interesset inter eos:** result clause; **interesset** is singular because **Tiberis et pons** forms a single unit. **Eodem** (adv.): *to the same place.*

53 fortis: accusative masculine plural.

54 praefectura Reatina: *the praefecture of Reate.* Reate was located about forty miles east of Rome (see Map 3). Praefectures were originally Italian towns, governed by a prefect from Rome. After 90 B.C. these towns gained independence, but the name remained. Cicero was the **patronus** (legal protector) of Reate and thus was able to organize the band of young men.

55 opera: *assistance*; ablative governed by **utor.**

Chapter 6

57 tertia fere vigilia exacta: *when the third watch was just about completed*; ablative of time when. The period between sunset and sunrise (about six P.M. to six A.M.) was divided into four watches (of about three hours each), so the end of the third watch would fall at about three o'clock in the morning. **cum iam:** *just when.*

58 magno comitatu: *accompanied by a large retinue*; the ablative of accompaniment usually takes **cum,** but **cum** may be omitted in military expressions when the noun is modified by an adjective (B222.1, G392R1). **unaque:** *and with them.*

59 ducuntur . . . gladii: *swords were drawn.*

60 Res: *The matter* (i.e., the reason for the attack). **Res praetoribus erat nota solis:** *The matter was known to the praetors alone.* We know from Sallust (*BC* 41–45) that the Allobroges told Cicero about the conspiracy through their **patronus,** Quintus Fabius Sanga; so even if the Allobroges did not know about the ambush ahead of time, they probably were not too surprised. The purpose of the ambush was to confiscate the compromising letters that they held (see Historical Essay II.6).

61 interventu: ablative of means. **Pomptini atque Flacci:** Pomptinus and Flaccus were the two praetors. **sedatur:** historical present (B259.3, G229). The attack was made against the Allobroges and Volturcius from both sides of the bridge, but the praetors soon stopped it. According to Sallust (*BC* 45), Volturcius resisted at first; but when he saw that the others had deserted him, he surrendered and begged that his life be saved.

62 Litterae quaecumque: *Whatever letters* (i.e., all the letters); the indefinite pronoun is used because at the time it was unknown exactly how many letters there were. **integris signis:** *with their seals intact.* The Romans wrote letters on hinged wooden writing tablets with a wax writing surface or on papyrus, which could be rolled up. In either case, the letter was tied with a linen thread that was then knotted. The knot was covered with wax and sealed with a signet-ring. The signet-ring often bore the image of the user or perhaps his father or grandfather. Because each person's signet-ring showed a different picture, an unbroken seal furnished proof that the writing inside was in fact written by that person.

63 ipsi: *the men themselves* (i.e., the Allobrogian ambassadors and Volturcius). **cum iam:** *just when.*

65 Cimbrum Gabinium: Sallust (*BC* 17.4) gives his name as P. Gabinius Capito, but Cicero refers to him as Cimber Gabinius. According to Bennett (1922: 232), Cicero occasionally reverses the order of a Roman's **nomen** and **cognomen**, especially if the **praenomen** (i.e., **Publius**) is omitted, as here. This explanation seems preferable to that of F. Münzer (*RE* 7.1, col. 431), who suggests that Cimber should not be understood as a **cognomen** but rather as a generic reference to the Gauls as the Romans' most savage enemies. (The Cimbri, a group of Gauls who had crushed a Roman army in 105 B.C. and threatened to sweep into northern Italy, were decisively defeated by Marius in 101 B.C.; see Historical Essay I.5.) Cicero seems to consider Gabinius the originator of the plan to compromise the Allobroges. Sallust (*BC* 40) agrees that Gabinius was involved, but he states that the idea originated with Lentulus. Both Cicero (*Cat.* 3.14) and Sallust (*BC* 40) agree that the freedman P. Umbrenus was the conspirator who made the first contact with the Allobroges. **dum:** (adv.): *still.*

66 L. Statilius: Lucius Statilius was a Roman knight and one of the conspirators.

67 Cethegus: Gaius Cornelius Cethegus was a senator of patrician birth and was one of Catiline's associates; like Gabinius, Statilius, and Lentulus, he was among those left behind at Rome when Catiline fled. **Lentulus:** Publius Cornelius Lentulus, Catiline's chief accomplice, was a member of a patrician family and was currently a **praetor** (see the note on line 39 above). When Catiline left Rome, Lentulus became the leader of the conspiracy in Rome. He had a reputation for laziness. **credo quod:** ironical; the letter (revealed later) was only four or five lines long.

67–68 in litteris dandis: *in writing the letter*; literally, *in the letter to be given*; gerundive.

68 vigilarat: a shortened (syncopated) form of the pluperfect: **vigilaverat.**

Chapter 7

69–71 Cum summis et clarissimis . . . viris . . . placeret: *Although it was pleasing to the very great and distinguished men*; **placeret** is impersonal with dative of person and infinitive.

69–70 viris (qui . . . frequentes ad me mane convenerant): *men (who gathered at my house in a crowd early in the morning).*

70-1 litteras . . . placeret: order for translation, **placeret litteras aperiri a me priusquam deferri ad senatum. prius . . . quam:** **priusquam**; the breaking up of a compound word into its constituent parts is called TMESIS (cutting).

71–72 ne . . . temere a me tantus tumultus iniectus civitati videretur: order for translation, **ne . . . tantus tumultus videretur iniectus [esse] civitati temere a me:** negative purpose clause.

72–73 negavi me esse facturum [ita]: introduces a result clause.

73–74 ut . . . non . . . deferrem: negative result clause; *that I would not bring forward the whole matter concerning a public danger to public deliberation.* Cicero refused to open the letters so that he could bring them before the Senate with their seals unbroken. Cicero's friends (the excellent and distinguished men who came to his house) wanted him to open the letters before he brought them to the Senate, so that if they contained no incriminating evidence he would not cause a public disturbance for no reason (**temere:** *unwisely* in line 72). Cicero, who knew what the letters were likely to contain, wanted to keep the seals intact so as to provide incontrovertible proof of the conspiracy. If the seals had been broken, the conspirators could claim that Cicero or his agents had tampered with the letters.

74 si = et si.

74–75 ea quae erant ad me delata: *those things which had been reported to me* (i.e., incriminating evidence against the conspirators).

75 reperta non essent: *had not been found* (i.e., in the letters).

76 nimiam diligentiam: *the charge of being overly careful.*

77 Senatum frequentem: *a full meeting of the Senate.* **Senatum . . . coegi:** Cicero had convened the Senate in the Temple of Concord, at the northwest corner of the Forum (see Map 1). **ut vidistis:** apparently the meeting of the Senate had just been dismissed.

Chapter 8

78–80 C. Sulpicium . . . misi qui . . . efferret: *I sent Gaius Sulpicius, who would bring out*; or, more smoothly, *I sent Gaius Sulpicius to bring out*; **qui** is a relative clause of purpose, used frequently after **mitto** (B282.2, G633).

79 ex aedibus Cethegi: aedes means *house* in the plural but *temple* in the singular.

79–80 si quid telorum esset: literally, *if anything of weapons were [there]*; more smoothly, *whatever weapons there were, if any*; **telorum** is a partitive genitive depending on **quid**; **quid** stands for **aliquid** after **si, nisi, num,** and **ne.**

80 ex quibus: i.e., **ex aedibus.**

82 Introduxi: i.e., to the meeting of the Senate. **Gallis:** the Allobroges. **fidem publicam:** *immunity from prosecution.*

83 ut . . . indicaret: indirect command after **hortatus sum** (B295, G553.2).

84 recreasset = recreavisset.

85 mandata et litteras: *verbal instructions and a letter.* **ut . . . uteretur:** indirect command, explaining what the instructions and the letter to Catiline were advising him to do. **servorum praesidio uteretur:** Although his advisors urged him to enlist slaves in the revolt, Catiline always hesitated to do so, perhaps fearing that this might alienate the bulk of his supporters, who were citizens (Sallust *BC* 56.5). But even the mention of including slaves was probably frightening to the senators, since they still had vivid memories of Spartacus' slave revolt (73–71 B.C.)

and the widespread destruction it had caused (see Historical Essay I.9).

85–86 ut . . . accederet: either a purpose clause or another indirect command.

86 quam primum: *as soon as possible.* **id:** refers to Catiline's arrival in Rome.

86–87 id autem [faceret] eo consilio: *furthermore, [let him do] it with this purpose.* **eo consilio:** *with this purpose*; ablative of manner (B220, G399); what this purpose was is explained by the **ut** (purpose) clause below.

87–89 cum urbem . . . incendissent caedemque . . . fecissent: cum-circumstantial clause (B288.1B, G585).

87 ex omnibus partibus: *from all sides*; according to Sallust (*BC* 43.2), Statilius and Gabinius had been ordered to set fire to the city in twelve places simultaneously.

87–89 ut . . . praesto esset ille: *so that he would be at hand*; this is the purpose clause that completes the meaning of **eo consilio,** above (lines 86–87).

89–90 qui et . . . exciperet et se . . . coniungeret: relative clause of purpose (B282.2, G630).

89 fugientis: accusative plural.

Chapter 9

91 Introducti . . Galli: *When the Gauls [Allobrogian envoys] had been brought in.*

91–92 ius iurandum [datum esse] sibi . . . dixerunt: *they said that an oath had been administered to them*; **ius iurandum dare:** *to take an oath.*

92 ad suam gentem: *for their own people* (the Allobroges). **datas esse:** agrees with its closest subject (**litteras** in line 91), but understood to go with **ius iurandum** as well. This is an example of ZEUGMA, since **dare** means *to take* an oath but *to give* an object.

93 ita sibi . . . esse praescriptum: *it had been directed to them thus* (i.e., *they had been ordered thus*); **praescriptum esse** is an impersonal construction, infinitive in indirect discourse; **ita** is explained by the following ut-clause (indirect command). **ab his:** i.e., by Lentulus, Cethegus, and Statilius. **L. Cassio:** Lucius Cassius Longinus was one of the conspirators. He was more cautious than the others and had refused to commit himself to the conspiracy in writing. Perhaps because he suspected a trap, he left town on December 2, the night before the Allobroges and Volturcius were arrested on the Mulvian Bridge (Sallust *BC* 44.2).

93–94 ut . . . mitterent: indirect command dependent on **esse praescriptum. equitatum:** *cavalry* (masculine accusative singular); the Gauls were famous for their fine horses and skilled cavalry.

94 pedestris . . . copias: *infantry*; **pedestris** is feminine accusative plural. **pedestris sibi copias non defuturas:** *[the Allobroges said they had been told that] infantry would not be lacking to them* (i.e., the conspirators). **sibi copias: sibi** refers to the conspirators.

95 Lentulum autem sibi confirmasse: *further [they said that] Lentulus had affirmed to them*. This **sibi** refers to the Allobrogian ambassadors. **ex fatis Sibyllinis:** *from the Sibylline prophecies*; the original Sibylline Books, containing prophecies in Greek, were said to have been brought to Tarquinius Superbus by the Sibyl of Cumae. They were placed in the Temple of Jupiter on the Capitoline Hill and were consulted in times of national emergency or crisis. After the Temple was burned in 83 B.C. a new collection of Sibylline prophecies was made. **haruspicum:** *of the haruspices*. The haruspices were originally Etruscan prophets who interpreted the will of the gods as expressed through lightning strikes and other portents and especially by examining the livers of sacrificial victims. By the late Republic the Romans had established a permanent board of haruspices.

96 se esse tertium illum Cornelium: *that he was third Cornelius* (i.e., the third member of the Cornelian clan); Lentulus' full name was Publius Cornelius Lentulus.

97 esset necesse: *it was necessary* (i.e., it was fated).

97–98 Cinnam . . . et Sullam: Lucius Cornelius Cinna and Lucius Cornelius Sulla. Cinna had been consul from 86 to 84 B.C. and ruled with almost sole authority. When Sulla marched on Rome in 82 B.C. after fighting against Mithridates, he overthrew Cinna's supporters and, in a brief but bloody civil war, established himself as dictator (see Historical Essay I.7–8).

98 Eundem: i.e., Lentulus; this sentence continues the indirect discourse governed by **Galli . . . dixerunt** (lines 91–92).

98–99 ad interitum: *for the destruction.*

99 qui esset annus decimus: *because it was the tenth year*; relative clause of characteristic showing cause (B283.3, G633).

99–100 post virginum absolutionem: this may refer to the acquittal in 73 B.C. of the Vestal Virgins Fabia and Licinia on charges of being compromised by Catiline and Crassus respectively (see Historical Essay II.1). The Vestal Virgins were six maidens from patrician families who served as priestesses of Vesta, goddess of the hearth. Their duties included maintaining the eternal flame in the Temple of Vesta in the Forum. The Vestal Virgins were bound by vows of chastity; a violation was considered a religious offense and the penalty was to be buried alive. After serving for thirty years a Vestal Virgin could retire and get married if she wished.

100 post Capitoli . . . incensionem: the first Temple of Jupiter on the Capitoline Hill had burned to the ground on July 6, 83 B.C., along with the statue of Jupiter Optimus Maximus and the Sibylline Books. After taking control of Rome in 82 B.C., Sulla sponsored the rebuilding of the Temple, which was dedicated in 69 B.C.

Chapter 10

101–102 autem . . . dixerunt: *[The Allobroges] also said that*; the remainder of this sentence is in indirect discourse governed by **dixerunt.**

101 Hanc . . . controversiam fuisse: *there had been this dispute.*

102 **quod:** *the fact that.*

102–103 **Lentulo et aliis . . . placeret:** order for translation, **placeret Lentulo et aliis caedem fieri atque urbem incendi Saturnalibus. placeret Lentulo et aliis:** *it was pleasing to Lentulus and the others.*

102 **Saturnalibus:** *on the Saturnalia*; the Saturnalia, a festival to the god Saturn, was held for several days (the precise number varied) beginning on December 17. During this time there was a joyful atmosphere of feasting and merry-making. Slaves mingled on equal terms with their masters, and many rich men kept open house. The unguarded atmosphere would provide a convenient opportunity for the conspirators to act.

103–104 **Ac ne longum sit:** *But in order that [the narration] not be long* (i.e., *to speak briefly*); negative purpose clause.

104 **tabellas:** *the tablets* (on which the letters were written; i.e., *the letters*). **Tabellae** were hinged writing tablets made of wood; inside, wax was smeared on a slightly depressed surface. The Romans would write on the wax with a sharp, pointed instrument called a **stylus**. The tablets were then closed and tied with a thread (**linum**) which was knotted and sealed with wax. As mentioned in the note to line 62 above, the wax was then stamped with the writer's seal (**signum**) to insure authenticity.

104–105 **quae a quoque dicebantur datae [esse]:** *[letters] which were said [to have been] given [to the Allobroges] by each [of the conspirators].*

106 **Erat scriptum:** *It had been written . . . that*; this clause introduces indirect discourse (beginning with **sese** in line 107). **ipsius manu:** *in his own hand*; the Romans often dictated letters to their slaves, but this was written in Cethegus' own hand.

106–107 **Allobrogum senatui et populo:** *to the Senate and people of the Allobroges.*

107 **confirmasset = confirmavisset** (syncopation).

107–108 **sese . . . facturum esse:** order for translation, **sese facturum esse [ea] quae confirmasset legatis eorum.**

108 **orare ut item illi facerent:** *[he said that] he prayed that they would do likewise;* the **ut**-clause is an indirect command following **orare. sibi:** *to himself* (i.e., Cethegus).

109–10 **qui . . . respondisset:** *although he had answered* (literally, *who had answered*); relative clause of characteristic showing opposition (B283.3, G634).

109 **aliquid:** *something or other*; direct object of **respondisset** (line 110). Cicero implies that Cethegus' excuse was not particularly credible. **paulo ante:** *a little while before*; **paulo** is ablative of degree of difference (B223). **tamen:** *nevertheless* (i.e., despite the evidence against him).

111 **bonorum ferramentorum studiosum:** *fond of fine iron implements.*

112 **conscientia:** ablative of means; *by consciousness of guilt, by a guilty conscience.*

113 **manum:** *handwriting.*

114 **in eandem fere sententiam:** *to about the same purpose* (i.e., it contained more or less the same contents).

115 **cognosceretne:** *whether he recognized*; in indirect questions, **-ne** is translated as *whether.*

116 **inquam:** *I said*; historical present. **imago avi tui:** *a likeness of your grandfather.* See the description of a signet-ring at the note to line 62 above. Lentulus' grandfather, Publius Cornelius Lentulus, had been consul in 162 B.C. In 121 B.C. he had opposed Gaius Gracchus and was wounded in the rioting during which Gracchus was killed (see Historical Essay I.4).

117 **civis:** masculine accusative plural. **quae:** refers to the **imago.**

117–18 **a tanto scelere:** *[back] from so great a crime.*

118 **etiam muta:** *although mute;* OXYMORON. **revocare debuit:** *ought to have called you back*; in English, the infinitive depending on **debeo** is translated as past when **debeo** refers to the past.

Chapter 11

119 **eadem ratione:** *along the same lines* (i.e., with about the same contents); ablative of description with **litterae** (line 120); cf. **in eandem sententiam** (line 114), above.

120 **Si quid = Si aliquid. Si . . . vellet:** *If he wished;* subjunctive in indirect command after **feci potestatem;** sometimes the **ut** is omitted, as here (B295.8).

122–23 **quid sibi esset cum eis:** *what they had to do with him;* literally, *what there was with them with regard to himself;* subjunctive in indirect question.

123 **quam ob rem:** *for what reason.* **domum suam:** accusative of motion toward (B182, G337).

125–26 **nihilne secum esset de fatis Sibyllinis locutus:** *whether he had said nothing to them about the Sibylline prophecies;* **-ne** means *whether* in an indirect question, **se** refers to the Allobroges. For the Sibylline Books, see the note on line 95 above.

126–27 **quanta conscientiae vis esset ostendit:** *he showed how great the force of conscience is.* Latin uses the imperfect subjunctive (**esset**) in this indirect question after the perfect indicative (**ostendit**) because of the sequence of tenses, but in English we would use the present tense, since the clause also states a general truth.

127 **posset infitiari:** *could have denied;* **posset** is subjunctive in a concessive **cum-**circumstantial clause (*although;* B288b, G603.6).

128 **opinionem:** *expectation.*

128–31 **Ita . . . defecit:** order for translation, **Ita non modo illud ingenium et exercitatio dicendi, qua semper valuit, defecit eum, sed etiam [illa] impudentia, qua superabat omnes [defecit eum], et improbitas [defecit eum] propter vim sceleris manifesti atque deprehensi.**

129 **qua semper valuit:** *by which he was always strong* (i.e., effective, persuasive).

131 **omnis = omnes.**

Chapter 12

133 **sibi:** Volturcius.

134 **perturbatus:** *although disturbed;* the concessive force of the participle is shown by **tamen** in the next clause.

135 **sine nomine:** *without a name.* Roman letters usually began with a formula stating the name of the sender as well as the addressee, which corresponded to our custom of putting a signature at the end of a letter. **Quis sim scies: sim** is subjunctive in indirect question.

135–36 **ex eo:** i.e., Volturcius.

136 **Cura ut vir sis:** *Take care that you be a man* (i.e., be brave); indirect command.

136–37 **cogita quem in locum sis progressus:** imperative and indirect question; *consider how far* (in the conspiracy) *you have advanced;* literally, *into what place you have advanced.*

137 **Vide ecquid tibi iam sit necesse:** *Consider whether anything is now necessary for you.*

137–38 **cura ut . . . adiungas:** indirect command.

138 **etiam infimorum:** *even [the assistance] of the lowest* (i.e., of slaves). Catiline steadfastly refused to enlist the help of slaves, although his top advisors urged him to do so.

139 **cum primo . . . coepisset:** *although at first he began;* concessive **cum-**circumstantial clause (B288b, G587). **ad extremum:** *at the end.*

Chapter 13

141–42 **cum . . . sceleris:** order for translation, **cum illa argumenta atque indicia sceleris visa sunt certissima. illa argumenta** is explained by **tabellae, signa,** etc.

141–43 **cum . . . tum:** *not only . . . but also.*

142 **tabellae:** *the letters* (literally, the writing tablets on which the letters were written).

143 **tum multo certiora illa:** order for translation, **tum illa [indicia sceleris visa sunt] multo certiora.**

144 **voltus:** *the [expressions on their] faces.*

144–45 **Sic . . . sic . . . sic:** ANAPHORA.

145 **non numquam:** literally, *not never* (i.e., *from time to time).* **inter sese aspiciebant:** *they cast glances at one another.* **non iam:** *no longer.*

145–46 **ut . . . viderentur:** result clause.

146 **indicare se ipsi viderentur:** note that both **se** and **ipsi** mean *themselves,* but **se** has no nominative forms and can never be the subject of a sentence, while **ipsi** (**ipse, ipsa, ipsum**) frequently serves as the subject.

147 **senatum consului:** at a meeting of the Senate, the presiding officer (usually the consul) would usually speak first and then ask the senators for their opinion, in order of importance. See Appendix A on the Republican constitution.

147–48 **de summa re publica:** *concerning the supreme welfare of the state.*

148 **quid fieri placeret:** *what was pleasing [to the Senate] to be done.*

149 **sine ulla varietate:** *without disagreement.*

150 **est secutus:** *adopted.*

Chapter 14

153 **aguntur:** the present tense is used because Cicero is reciting a resolution of the Senate. **verbis amplissimis:** *in most handsome terms.*

153–54 **quod . . . res publica . . . sit liberata:** the subjunctive is used because Cicero is giving the Senate's reasons for its action, not his own (B286.1, G539, and G541).

154 **maximis periculis:** ablative of separation.

155–56 **quod eorum opera forti fidelique usus essem:** *because I had used their strong and loyal assistance;* **utor** takes the ablative; **forti** and **fideli** are ablatives, agreeing with **opera.**

157 **conlegae meo:** Cicero's colleague in the consulship was C. Antonius Hybrida. Antonius had previously supported Catiline, but

Cicero had persuaded him to distance himself from his former ally by promising him the governorship of the rich province of Macedonia for the following year (see Historical Essay II.4). **impertitur** + dative: *is granted to.*

157–59 **eos . . . a suis et a rei publicae consiliis removisset:** *he had excluded these men from his personal deliberations and his deliberations concerning the Republic.*

159 **ita censuerunt ut:** *they decided thus, that . . . ;* indirect command; **censere** is the normal verb used to describe a senator's judgment or decree.

159–60 **cum se praetura abdicasset:** a Roman official could not be brought to trial while in office, but he could be forced to resign, as here.

160 **in custodiam:** we learn from Sallust (*BC* 47) that Lentulus and the others were placed into **liberam custodiam** (i.e., they were given to trustworthy persons who would be responsible for their safekeeping). **itemque uti:** itemque [censuerunt] ut; uti = ut.

161 **praesentes:** these men were all present in the Senate.

162 **idem hoc decretum est in L. Cassium:** *and the same thing was decreed against Lucius Cassius* (i.e., that he be handed over into custody). **L. Cassium:** Cassius, Ceparius, Furius, Chilo, and Umbrenus had fled from Rome. Only Ceparius was later caught and taken back to Rome (Sallust *BC* 44); he was later killed along with Lentulus, Cethegus, Statilius, and Gabinius.

163 **in M. Ceparium:** [idem hoc decretum est] in M. Ceparium.

163–64 **cui . . . indicatum:** order for translation, **erat indicatum Apuliam attributam esse cui ad sollicitandos pastores.**

164 **erat indicatum:** an impersonal passive that introduces indirect discourse: *it had been revealed that . . .*

165 **qui est ex eis colonis:** Sulla had settled large numbers of veterans on land in northern Italy and many of these, now disgruntled, had

joined Catiline's cause (see Historical Essay II.4). **Faesulas:** the town **Faesulae**; accusative of motion toward.

169 **constabat:** impersonal; *it was established.* **est usus:** *used* (i.e., *showed*).

169–72 **ut . . . arbitraretur:** probably a result clause, but the clause actually seems to give the reason for the Senate's leniency, rather than the result; literally, *the Senate showed such mildness that they thought that, with the Republic having been saved from so great a conspiracy and so great a number of domestic enemies by the punishment of the nine most desperate men, the minds of the rest could be restored to health*; **re publica conservata** is ablative absolute; **poena** is ablative of means, **novem** (nine) is indeclinable; **mentis** is accusative plural. What Cicero means is that the senators were lenient (i.e., they punished so few men) because they felt that the Republic would recover more quickly that way and that the rest of the conspirators could be persuaded to cut their ties with Catiline.

171 **novem hominum:** only five of the men were actually punished, but Cicero did not yet know this.

Chapter 15

173 **supplicatio:** *a public prayer of thanksgiving.* The Senate could decree such a prayer in honor of a victorious general or a savior of the state.

173–74 **pro . . . eorum merito:** order for translation, **pro . . . merito eorum:** *in return for their favor;* **eorum** refers to the gods.

174 **merito:** not the adverb, but the neuter noun, **meritum:** *kindness, favor;* **meo nomine:** *in my name* (i.e., *in my honor*).

174–75 **quod mihi primum . . . togato contigit:** *a thing which has happened first to me as a person wearing a toga* (i.e., *a civilian*) *since this city was founded.* Cicero is making the point that this honor had previously been granted only to generals for military achievements.

176 **civis:** accusative plural. **liberassem = liberavissem.** Cicero uses the subjunctive because he is giving another person's reason (i.e., the Senate's), not his own (B286).

177 **hoc interest:** *this difference exists.*

178 **quod:** *the fact that* (explains the **hoc** in line 177).

178–79 **ceterae . . . constituta est:** order for translation, **ceterae [supplicationes] [constitutae sunt] bene gesta [re publica], haec una constituta est conservata re publica. bene gesta [re publica]** and **conservata re publica** are ablative absolutes denoting cause (B227.2d). Cicero claims that all previous thanksgivings were decreed for managing the Republic well, but his alone was decreed for saving the Republic. One suspects that previous honorees might have disagreed.

179 **faciendum . . . fuit:** passive periphrastic, perfect tense (B115). **illud quod faciendum primum fuit:** what this was is explained by the next clause.

180–82 **quamquam . . . tamen:** *although . . . nevertheless.*

180–81 **indiciis, confessionibus:** ablatives of cause (B219, G408).

181 **iudicio:** ablative of respect (B226, G397); **iudicio senatus:** in the judgment of the Senate. **praetoris ius:** *the power of a praetor.*

182 **civis** (i.e., **civis ius**): *the rights of a citizen* (**civis** is genitive). Cicero's claim that Lentulus and the other conspirators have forfeited their rights as Roman citizens is a tendentious one. He will argue forcefully for this view in his *Fourth Catilinarian Oration.*

182–85 **ut . . . liberaremur:** a long and complex purpose clause. It is best to break it up into two separate clauses and translate the second one first, as follows: **ut . . . nos liberaremur ea religione in puniendo privato Publio Lentulo:** *in order that we might be free from that religious scruple in punishing Publius Lentulus as a private citizen.*

182–84 quae religio . . . occideret: order for translation, **quae religio non fuerat Gaio Mario, clarissimo viro, quo minus occideret praetorem, Gaium Glauciam . . .** literally, *which religious scruple was not present for Gaius Marius, that most illustrious man, by which the less he might kill the praetor, Gaius Glaucia* (i.e., the religious scruple did not prevent Marius from killing Glaucia). After verbs of preventing or hindering, **quo minus** + subjunctive (literally, *by which the less*) means *from* (B295.3, G549). In this case, the idea of hindering or preventing is implied in **religio . . . non fuerat. religio:** *religious scruple;* a magistrate, such as a praetor, could not be put on trial while in office; to do so would be to show disrespect for the office, which was backed by religious authority.

183–84 de quo nihil nominatim erat decretum: *[Gaius Glaucia] about whom nothing had been decreed by name.* In 100 B.C., when Marius was consul, Gaius Glaucia, a praetor, and Saturninus, a tribune, were thought to be threatening the safety of the Republic, and the Senate had passed an SCU against them. Although Marius shut them up in the Senate house, they were stoned to death by an angry crowd (see Historical Essay I.5). Cicero is stretching the point here, in claiming that Marius allowed Glaucia to be killed on the authority of the SCU alone (since the Senate had not passed a resolution against him by name). In fact, it is not clear that Marius had authorized or allowed the killing of Glaucia and Saturninus to take place.

Chapter 16
188–89 his depulsis . . . periculis: ablative absolute; **urbis:** objective genitive.

189 pellebam: conative imperfect (see B260.3).

190 remoto Catilina: ablative absolute.

191 somnum: *sleep* (i.e., *the laziness*). **adipes:** *fat* (i.e., *the corpulence*).

192 Ille: i.e., Catiline.

193 tam diu dum: *only as long as.*

194 norat = **noverat. omnium aditus tenebat:** *he held the approaches of all men* (i.e., he knew everyone's weakness and therefore knew how to approach them). **appellare, temptare, sollicitare:** CLIMAX.

195 poterat, audebat: he could do these things, and he also dared to do them; note the ASYNDETON. **Erat ei consilium: ei** is dative of possession.

195–96 consilio autem neque lingua neque manus deerat: *nor were tongue and hand lacking to his determination* (i.e., he had the practical ability to put his ideas into effect).

196–97 Iam ad certas res . . . habebat: order for translation, **Iam habebat certos homines delectos ac descriptos ad certas res conficiendas [esse].**

198 cum aliquid mandarat [=mandaverat]: *whenever he had ordered anything.*

198–99 quod non ipse obiret: *which he did not personally attend to.*

Chapter 17
201–204 Hunc . . . nisi . . . compulissem: *If I had not driven this man.*

203 in castrense latrocinium: *into his robber's camp.*

203–205 nisi . . . compulissem . . . non facile . . . depulissem: past contrary-to-fact condition, with pluperfect subjunctive in both clauses (B304, G597).

205–206 Non ille . . . constituisset: *He would not have decided upon the Saturnalia* (i.e. he would have chosen an earlier date). This is an apodosis to a past contrary-to-fact condition; a protasis, such as **si in urbe remansisset,** must be understood.

205 nobis: dative of reference.

206 tanto: ablative of degree of difference with **ante** (B223).

206–207 neque . . . denuntiavisset: order for translation, **neque denuntiavisset diem exiti ac fati rei publicae tanto ante.**

207 neque commisisset ut: *nor would he have acted in such a way that.*

207–208 ut . . . deprehenderentur: result clause.

208 testes: *as witnesses.* **Quae:** referring generally to all the conspirators' mistakes, mentioned above.

209–10 ut nullum . . . inventum: result clause; order for translation, **ut nullum furtum in privata domo umquam inventum sit tam palam**.

210 tam palam . . . quam: *so openly as.*

211 Quod si: *But if.*

212 quoad fuit: *as long as he was [in the city].*

212–13 quoad fuit . . . obstiti: a parenthetical clause; *as long as he was in the city, I opposed and hindered all his plans.*

213 ut levissime dicam: *in order that I may speak most lightly* (i.e., *to say the least*).

213–14 dimicandum nobis cum illo fuisset: *we would have had to fight with him;* impersonal passive; literally, *there would have had to have been a fighting with him for us.*

214–16 neque nos umquam . . . liberassemus: order for translation, **neque nos umquam liberassemus rem publicam tantis periculis (cum ille hostis esset in urbe) tanta pace, tanto otio, tanto silentio**. This is the apodosis of a past contrary-to-fact condition; the verb of the protasis is **remansisset** in line 212.

214–15 tantis periculis: ablative of separation.

215 tanta pace, etc: ablatives of manner.

Chapter 18

217 Quamquam: *And yet.*

218–19 gesta et provisa esse videantur: *they seem to have been accomplished and foreseen.*

219 Idque . . . consequi possumus: *And we are able to reach this conclusion.* **cum:** correlative with **tum** on line 221: *not only . . .*

but also. **coniectura:** *by reasoning, by inference.* **quod:** *because*; gives Cicero's grounds for making this inference.

219–20 quod . . . potuisse: order for translation, **quod gubernatio tantarum rerum vix videtur potuisse esse humani consili**.

220 humani consili: *[a matter of] human wisdom;* genitive of quality used predicatively (B203.5, G366).

221 ita praesentes his temporibus: *[the gods] so present at our time of need.*

222 ut . . . possimus: result clause. **ut illa omittam:** *if I may omit those things;* a type of purpose clause (B282.4, G545.3); **illa** refers to what follows (i.e., **faces, iactus,** etc.); an example of **PRAETERITIO**.

223 visas nocturno tempore ab occidente faces: these could be comets, meteors, or shooting stars. **ab occidente:** *from the West;* literally, *from the setting sun.* In Roman religion, the West was the unfavorable area of the sky for heavenly omens. The belief in omens and portents was quite strong in Cicero's time, especially among the common people, to whom Cicero was speaking. It is somewhat more difficult to determine the extent of belief in omens among the more educated.

223–24 ut fulminum iactus: order for translation, **ut [omittam] iactus fulminum; iactus** is accusative plural and **fulminum** is genitive plural.

224 terrae motus: *earthquakes.*

225 nobis consulibus: *during our consulship;* ablative absolute, referring to the present year.

225–26 ut . . . viderentur; result clause; order for translation, **ut di immortales viderentur canere haec quae nunc fiunt.**

226 canere: *to predict;* since oracular responses were usually delivered in verse, **canere** came to mean *to predict.*

226–27 hoc certe . . . quod sum dicturus: *this certainly . . . what I am about to say.* Cicero may omit a discussion of many of the omens and portents that have occurred during his consulship, but there are a few that are so important that he feels he must describe them.

Chapter 19

228 Cotta et Torquato consulibus: *when Cotta and Torquatus were consuls* (i.e., 65 B.C.)

229 Capitolio: the Capitoline Hill, a steep hill with two peaks, overlooking the Forum. On the southern peak, the **Capitolium** proper, stood the temple of Jupiter Optimus Maximus, dedicated to Jupiter, Juno, and Minerva (see Map 1). Lightning frequently struck the Capitoline Hill and damaged the temple. **de caelo esse percussas:** *were struck from the sky* (i.e., by lightning).

231 legum aera: literally, *the bronzes of the laws* (i.e., *the bronze tablets of laws*). Bronze tablets on which the laws were inscribed were kept in temples.

233 uberibus lupinis inhiantem: *his mouth open to the wolf's udders.* The famous bronze statue of a she-wolf suckling Romulus and Remus, known as the Capitoline Wolf, was for a long time identified with the statue that Cicero is referring to here. That identification is almost certainly false, however, in part because there is no evidence that the Capitoline Wolf ever had a gilded statue of Romulus associated with it. The Capitoline Wolf (without the twins) is very old, dating from the sixth or early fifth century B.C. The statue was well-known in the Middle Ages: by the late twelfth century it had been torn from its base and placed in the portico at the entrance to the pope's winter palace at the Lateran. In 1471 Pope Sixtus IV had the statue restored to its base and set up on the Capitoline Hill. The twins were added sometime before 1509, most likely because Renaissance scholars, who had read Cicero's *Third Catilinarian Oration*, mistakenly believed that the Capitoline Wolf was the statue that Cicero was describing. Since the hind legs and underbelly of the Capitoline Wolf seem to have been damaged by fire, it was easy to jump to

the conclusion that the damage must have been caused by the lightning strike that Cicero mentions. This romantic (but false) identification of the Capitoline Wolf with the Ciceronian statue is occasionally asserted even today, despite scholars' attempts to set the record straight. The Capitoline Wolf is still located on the Capitoline Hill (now called the Campidoglio), in the Palazzo dei Conservatori. (See Jones [1926: 56–58]; Haskell and Penny [1981: 335–37]; Bober and Rubenstein [1986: 218]; Albertoni et al. [2000: 7–18]; Macadam [2000: 80]; and Presicce [2000: 8–11].) **fuisse:** *stood;* the perfect tense indicates that the statue did not stand in the Capitol at the time when Cicero was speaking. **Quo . . . tempore:** *at that time* (i.e., when the statue of Romulus was struck).

234 haruspices: see the note on line 95 above. **caedis:** accusative plural.

236 appropinquare: infinitive in indirect discourse, following **dixerunt**; translate as present subjunctive: *would approach.*

236–37 nisi . . . flexissent: subjunctive in a dependent clause in indirect discourse. The pluperfect subjunctive is used according to the sequence of tenses, following **dixerunt** (B267, G509), but translate as simple past: *unless the gods turned aside.*

237 prope: *as it were, practically;* the idea that the gods might, under certain circumstances, be able to turn aside (or at least postpone) a terrible fate is as old as Homer (cf. *Iliad* 16.431–61, Herodotus 1.91.1–3).

Chapter 20

238 responsis: ablative of cause (B 219). **ludi:** Roman public games (consisting of chariot races, gladiator contests, etc.) were religious in origin and were often celebrated to appease hostile deities.

239 neque res ulla: *and not anything* (i.e., *and nothing*).

240 Idemque: *And they also* (i.e., the haruspices). **facere:** a subject, such as "the Roman people" or "the consuls," is understood.

maius: *larger* (than the previous statue). **simulacrum Iovis:** the statue of Jupiter Optimus Maximus stood on the Capitoline Hill. **in excelso:** *on high.*

241 **contra atque antea fuerat:** *opposite to the way it was before* (i.e., facing opposite to the way the previous statue faced); **atque** often means *as, than,* or *from* with words of likeness or difference. **ad orientem:** *toward the rising sun* (i.e., toward the East).

242 **signum:** *statue.* **quod videtis:** the new statue was on the Capitoline Hill and could be seen from the Forum, where Cicero was speaking (see Map 1).

243 **curiam:** the **Curia Hostilia** was the normal place for meetings of the Senate (see Map 1). **ea consilia quae clam essent inita:** *those plots which had been secretly formed.* Cicero is claiming that prophecies had been made two years earlier that predicted Catiline's conspiracy and its detection in the present manner. For a much earlier (and openly satirical) example of an earlier prophecy that purports to shed light on present circumstances, see Aristophanes, *Lysistrata,* lines 767–80.

243–44 **fore ut ea consilia . . . inlustrarentur:** *it would be the case that those plots . . . would be made clear;* **fore ut** (**futurum esse**) + subjunctive can be translated: *it would be the case that.* This construction was frequently used instead of the future passive infinitive (B270.3, G248).

244–45 **ut . . . possent:** result clause.

245–46 **illud signum conlocandum:** *for the placing of the statue;* after verbs expressing a decision or provision, the gerundive is frequently used to complete the thought of the verb (B337.8b2, G430).

246 **locaverunt:** *assigned a contract.* **consules illi:** those consuls were Cotta and Torquatus, consuls for 65 B.C. The censors were usually in charge of assigning public contracts; but the censors for that year had resigned, so the consuls fulfilled this task.

247 **nobis** (i.e., **nobis consulibus**): *during my consulship.* **ante hodiernum diem:**

Cicero states that the new statue of Jupiter had been placed on the Capitoline Hill that very day. This coincidence seems almost too good to be true, but it is also hard to see how Cicero could have planned it.

Chapter 21

250 **mente captus:** *captured in mind, impaired in mind, crazy.* **qui neget:** *so as to deny;* relative clause of characteristic expressing result (B284.2, G631.1).

250–51 **haec omnia quae videmus praecipueque hanc urbem:** *all these things which we see and especially this city.* The Epicureans believed that the gods did not participate in ruling the world; Cicero may be referring to them here in his insistence that the discovery of the conspiracy (and the omens that foretold it) proves that the gods do watch over human affairs and especially the affairs of Rome.

252 **ita:** *thus, as follows* (explained in indirect discourse). **caedis:** accusative plural.

252–53 **rei publicae:** dative with **comparari.**

253 **et ea per civis:** *and that these things [were being done] by citizens.*

254 **non nullis:** *to some people, to several;* an idiom.

256 **Illud vero nonne . . . est:** *Indeed is this not . . . ?* **Nonne** expects a "yes" answer. **Illud:** *this* (i.e., the following circumstances); explained by **ut . . . statueretur** (lines 257–59).

256–57 **ita praesens . . . ut . . . videatur:** *so providential that it seems;* result clause.

257–59 **ut . . . statueretur:** a substantive clause of result, explaining **Illud** (line 256) (B297.3, G557); translate **ut** as *the fact that.* **ut, cum . . . et coniurati et eorum indices in aedem Concordiae ducerentur, eo ipso tempore signum statueretur:** *the fact that, when . . . both the conspirators and their informers were being led into the Temple of Concord, at that very time the statue was being placed.*

257 per forum: Cicero's house was on the Palatine Hill, and the conspirators had been brought to him there at dawn. In the early morning he would have led them through the Forum to the Temple of Concord, where the Senate was going to meet.

258 aedem Concordiae: the Temple of Concord, goddess of harmony; Cicero had convened the Senate there earlier that day. It was located between the Forum and the Capitoline Hill (see Map 1).

259 eo ipso tempore: *at that very time.*

259–60 Quo conlocato . . . converso: ablative absolute.

260 et senatus et vos: both subjects of **vidistis** (line 261).

Chapter 22

262 Quo: *Wherefore.* **maiore . . . odio supplicioque:** ablatives with **digni.**

262–64 qui . . . sunt . . . inferre conati: *who tried to bring* accusative *to* dative.

264–65 si . . . dicam . . . sumam et non sim ferendus: present subjunctives in a future-less-vivid (should/would) condition.

265–67 ille, ille . . . ille . . . ille . . . ille . . . ille: ITERATIO and ANAPHORA.

265 restitisse: from **resisto** + dative: *to resist.*

267 salvos: modifies **Capitolium, templa** (line 266), and **urbem** as well as **vos** but grammatically agrees with its closest subject.

268 hanc mentem voluntatemque: *this purpose and desire* (i.e., his desire to expose the conspiracy and prevent it from being carried out).

269–73 Iam vero . . . esset ereptum: this sentence is a past contrary-to-fact condition (pluperfect subjunctive in both clauses), with the form: *x would not have happened if y had not occurred.*

269 Iam vero: *And furthermore.* **illa Allobrogum sollicitatio:** this subject is left hanging, and the sentence picks up with a new subject (**tantae res** in line 270) and a new

verb (**creditae . . . essent** in lines 271–72); **tantae res** is in loose apposition with **illa sollicitatio.**

269–71 iam ab Lentulo . . . et barbaris: order for translation, **tantae res [numquam] tam dementer creditae [essent] et ignotis et barbaris ab Lentulo ceterisque domesticis hostibus . . .**

272 essent: take with both **creditae** and **commissae** (line 271). **huic tantae audaciae:** the abstract concept is here used to refer to the men: *from this so-great boldness = from these so-greatly bold men;* the dative of separation is sometimes used, as here, with verbs of taking away (B188.2d, G345). **ab dis immortalibus:** the idea that the gods could influence people's minds (usually for worse) is as old as Homer (e.g., *Iliad* 16.684–91); cf. Herodotus 1.127.2: **theoblabes** *(god-harmed).*

273 consilium: *judgment.* **Quid vero? :** *And what is more.*

273–77 ut homines Galli . . . neglegerent vestramque salutem suis opibus anteponerent: *the fact that Gauls would disregard . . . and place your safety before their own interests;* a substantive clause of result, explaining **id** on line 277 (B297.2, G557).

274 male: here means *scarcely.* **quae gens una:** *the only people which.*

275 non nolle: *not unwilling;* LITOTES.

276 ultro: *voluntarily;* take with **oblatam** (from **offero**): *offered to them, without their seeking it.* **a patriciis hominibus:** Lentulus, Cethegus, and some of the others were members of the upper class; an offer coming from such men would be very persuasive.

277 divinitus (adv.): *by divine influence.*

277–78 id non divinitus esse factum putatis: this is the main clause in this sentence; the **ut**-clause in line 273 is dependent upon it; **id** refers to the Allobroges' refusal to participate in the conspiracy.

278–79 praesertim qui . . . potuerint: *especially since they would have been able . . . ;* relative clause of characteristic expressing cause (B283.3a). **tacendo:** i.e., by not informing anyone of the plot.

Chapter 23

280 Quam ob rem: *Wherefore, For this reason.*

281 supplicatio: during a **supplicatio** (public thanksgiving) a **lectisternium** (feast of the gods) was often held, during which statues of the gods were placed on couches (**pulvinaria**) and food was placed before them. **celebratote:** the future imperative is used when there is a clear reference to future time (B281.1a, G268.2).

285 togati: masculine nominative plural, agreeing with the subject of **vicistis**; *[you] wearing a toga* (i.e., *civilians*).

Chapter 24

287 recordamini: imperative. **omnis civilis:** accusative feminine plural with **dissensiones.**

288 audistis: *you have heard of.* **vosmet:** *you yourselves.*

289 vidistis: many in Cicero's audience would have been witnesses to the events that Cicero is about to describe. **L. Sulla P. Sulpicium oppressit:** in 88 B.C.; for a discussion of the events here described, see Historical Essay II.8 and Appendix B.

290 partim . . . partim: *partly . . . partly;* here means *some . . . others.*

292 omnis hic locus: the fight between Octavius and Cinna (87 B.C.) took place in the Forum.

294 Ultus est: from **ulciscor.**

295 ne dici quidem opus est: *indeed there is no need to say;* **opus est:** *there is need* (idiom); **dici**: passive infinitive.

295–96 quanta deminutione: *by how great a reduction;* **quanta** is ablative of degree of difference (B223, G403); the phrase as a whole is ablative of attendant circumstance (B 221), as is **quanta calamitate.**

296–97 M. Lepidus: for Lepidus' rebellion (78 B.C.), see Historical Essay I.9 and Appendix B.

297–98 order for translation, **interitus ipsius non attulit tam luctum rei publicae**

. . . quam [interitus] ceterorum [attulit luctum rei publicae]: *his own death did not bring sorrow to the Republic; as much as [the death] of others [brought sorrow to the Republic];* **non tam . . quam:** *not so much . . . as much as.*

298 ipsius: i.e., Lepidus. Lepidus was unpopular at Rome not only because he had greatly enriched himself during Sulla's proscriptions but also because he wanted to take land in Etruria away from Sulla's veterans and give it back to the peasants from whom it had been confiscated (see Historical Essay I.9). **ceterorum:** Cicero regrets the loss of Lepidus' followers, who were involved in his fall. In reminding his listeners of these recent incidents of civil bloodshed, Cicero is emphasizing the fact that he had managed to capture the leaders of Catiline's conspiracy without another outbreak of violence at Rome. Indeed, this was a great achievement.

Chapter 25

301–303 Non illi . . . voluerunt: order for translation, **illi non voluerunt nullam esse rem publicam, sed [voluerunt] se esse principes in ea [re publica] quae esset. illi non voluerunt nullam esse rem publicam:** *they did not want there to be no Republic.* **voluerunt se esse principes:** *they wanted themselves to be the leaders.*

301–302 se esse, se . . . florere: verbs of wanting or wishing (such as **volo, malo, nolo, cupio**) frequently take the infinitive to complete their meaning. When the subject of both the verb and the infinitive is the same, the reflexive pronoun is used as the subject of the infinitive; this usage of the reflexive pronoun is similar to that in indirect discourse (see B331 IVa, G532R2).

302 hanc urbem: the subject of **conflagrare.**

304–305 ut . . . diiudicatae sint: result clause; the perfect subjunctive sometimes follows a secondary tense in a result clause (B268.6, G513).

306 **post hominum memoriam:** *within human memory.*

307 **quale bellum:** *such a war as.* **nulla . . . barbaria: gens** or **natio** should be understood here.

308 **quo in bello**: in this war.

308–309 **lex haec fuit . . . constituta:** *this law was established.* Note that this was not an actual law; Cicero is simply representing the thinking of the conspirators.

309–10 **ut omnes qui salva urbe . . . ducerentur:** indirect command explaining the terms of the "law" (B295.4, G546.1).

309 **ut omnes qui salva urbe salvi esse possent:** *that all who could be solvent while the city was safe.* Cicero uses **salvus** in two different senses here.

310 **in hostium numero ducerentur:** *would be considered in the number of the enemy.* **ita me gessi:** *I acted* (literally, *I conducted myself*) *in such a way.* This is the main clause of the sentence.

310–11 **ut salvi omnes conservaremini:** result clause.

311 **tantum civium:** *only so many of the citizens.* **superfuturum = superfuturum esse.**

312 **quantum infinitae caedi restitisset:** *as many as resisted indiscriminate slaughter.* **tantum . . . urbis:** [*and when they thought that*] *only so much of the city* [*would remain*].

313 **quantum flamma obire non potuisset:** *as much as the fire was not able to envelop.*

Chapter 26

315 **Quibus pro tantis rebus:** *In return for such great deeds.*

320 **Nihil . . . mutum:** *nothing silent,* such as a statue or any permanent physical memorial.

321 **minus digni:** *less worthy men;* **minus** is an adverb. **Memoria vestra:** ablative of means.

322 **nostrae res [gestae]:** *my accomplishments.* Cicero refers to himself in the plural, as he does on line 225 above. **alentur, crescent,** etc.: future indicatives.

322–23 **litterarum monumentis:** i.e., through historical works.

323 **eandemque diem:** i.e., *the same length of time.*

323–25 **eandemque diem intellego, quam spero aeternam fore, propagatam esse et ad salutem urbis et ad memoriam consulatus mei:** *I know that the same length of time, which I hope will be eternal, has been established for the safety of the city and the memory of my consulship.* Cicero is saying that the memory of his consulship will last as long as the city, whose safety he has preserved, and that he hopes both will last forever.

324 **fore = futuram esse** (see B100, footnote 3). **propagatam esse:** *has been established, ordained.*

326 **exstitisse:** from **exsisto, exsistere, exstiti** = *to exist.* **finis:** accusative plural.

326–27 **alter . . . terminaret:** Pompey had recently defeated Sertorius and his forces in Spain, to the far west of Rome (72 B.C.), had cleared the pirates from the Mediterranean Sea (67 B.C.), and had finally conquered the seemingly indefatigable Mithridates, to the east (66 B.C.).

327–28 **alter . . . servaret:** Cicero himself; Cicero now clearly considers himself to be the equal of Pompey. Cicero's inflated sense of his own importance after exposing the Catilinarian conspiracy had a significant effect on his expectations for the future, expectations that (given Cicero's status as a **novus homo**) were bound to be unfulfilled. For a more detailed discussion, see Historical Essay II.8.

Chapter 27

329–30 **Sed quoniam earum rerum . . . externa bella gesserunt:** this is a complex comparison, made more complex by the fact that Cicero (perhaps deliberately) does not maintain a strict parallel between the two things being compared. The first element of the comparison is **fortuna atque condicio earum rerum quas ego gessi**: *the fortune and condition of the things which I have done.* What Cicero actually means here is: my own fortune and condition because of the things which I have done. **non eadem est . . . quae illorum qui externa bella gesserunt**: *is not the same [as the fortune and condition] of those who have waged foreign wars.*

331 **quod mihi . . . vivendum est**: an impersonal passive periphrastic; *because it is necessary for me to live.* **cum eis . . . quos vici ac subegi**: *with those whom I have conquered and suppressed.* **illi: [sed] illi**; refers to those Romans who have waged foreign wars. **hostis**: accusative plural.

332 **vestrum est**: *it is your duty*; genitive of possession (B198.2, G366.1).

332–33 **si ceteris facta sua recte prosunt**: *if their own deeds are rightly beneficial to others* (i.e., if Pompey's own deeds benefit Pompey, my deeds should not harm me); **sua** refers to **ceteris** here (B244.4, G309.2).

332–34 **vestrum est . . . providere**: *it is your duty to make sure* (B198.2, G366.1); order for translation, **vestrum est . . . providere ne mea [facta] [ali]quando obsint mihi**; an indirect command (B295.1, G546.2).

334–35 **Mentes . . . providi**: order for translation, **ego providi ne sceleratae ac nefariae mentes hominum audacissimorum possent nocere vobis.**

335–36 **ne . . . providere**: order for translation, **vestrum est providere ne [nefariae mentes hominum] noceant mihi**; indirect command (B295.1, G546.2).

336 **Quamquam**: *And yet.*

336–37 **mihi quidem ipsi . . . potest**: order for translation, **nihil potest noceri mihi ipsi ab istis. noceri potest** is used impersonally; **mihi ipsi** is a dative, governed by **noceri**; **nihil** is used adverbially (B187 IIb).

338–39 **magna . . . dignitas**: *a great authority.*

339 **magna vis conscientiae**: order for translation, **magna [est] vis conscientiae.**

340 **quam qui neglegunt = et eam qui neglegunt. volent, indicabunt**: future indicatives.

Chapter 28

341 **is animus**: *this determination* or *resolve;* explained by the result clause that follows. **nobis**: dative of possession. Cicero is probably referring to himself in the plural, as he does in lines 225 and 322 above.

341–42 **non modo . . . sed etiam**: *not only . . . but even.* **ut non modo nullius audaciae cedamus**: *that not only do I yield to the boldness of no one* (i.e., *I do not yield to anyone's boldness*); result clause.

342 **omnis**: masculine accusative plural.

343 **Quod si**: *But if.* **omnis impetus**: masculine nominative singular.

344 **se in me unum converterit: converterit** is future perfect indicative in a future-more-vivid condition, but it can be translated as present to conform to English idiom (G 595). **vobis erit videndum**: *it will have to be considered by you* (i.e., *you will have to consider*).

345 **qua condicione**: *in what condition* (i.e. whether you want them to be safe); ablative of quality. **velitis**: second person plural perfect subjunctive of **volo**; indirect question (B315, G467).

345–46 **qua condicione posthac eos esse velitis qui se pro salute vestra obtulerint invidiae periculisque omnibus**: *in what condition after this you want those men to be who have exposed themselves to hatred and all dangers on behalf of your safety.*

346 **obtulerint**: third person plural perfect subjunctive of **offero**; relative clause of characteristic (B283, G631.2). **ipsi**: dative with **mihi**.

347 **ad vitae fructum**: *to the enjoyment of life.* **adquiri**: *be added.*

348 **quicquam = quidquam**: *anything.*

348–49 **quicquam . . . altius**: *anything higher* (i.e., any greater height). Cicero is referring not only to his achievement of the consulship, the highest office in the Republic, but also to the fact that he has suppressed an attempted coup without any public disturbance.

349 quo mihi libeat ascendere: *to which it is pleasing to me to ascend* (i.e., *to which I desire to ascend*); relative clause of characteristic.

Chapter 29

350 Illud: explained by the result clause that follows. **perficiam:** future indicative.

350–51 ut . . . privatus tuear atque ornem: substantive clause of result (B297.1). Cicero means that he will continue to protect and preserve the Republic as a private citizen.

351–52 ut . . . laedat . . . [ut] valeat: purpose clause. **ut . . . laedat invidos:** *so that it* (the **invidia**) *may bring harm to the haters.* **ut . . . mihi valeat ad gloriam:** *so that it* (the fact that I saved the Republic) *may lead me to glory.*

353 me . . . tractabo: *I will conduct myself.* **meminerim:** since this verb occurs only in perfect forms, the perfect subjunctive is

equivalent in meaning to a present subjunctive (just as the perfect indicative, **memini**, is translated as a present indicative).

354 curemque ut ea . . . videantur: Cicero will act in the future so as to make it clear that his suppression of the conspiracy was due to his personal merit and not to chance.

355 Iovem, illum custodem: the new statue of Jupiter Optimus Maximus, referred to above.

356 vestrum: genitive of **vos. ea:** the direct object of **defendite** (line 358); refers to **tecta.**

357 aeque ac: *just as.*

357–58 custodiis vigiliisque: *by guards and watches.* Although some of the chief conspirators had been arrested, others—as well as Catiline and his army—were still at large.

358 diutius (comparative adv.): *for too long a time.*

358–59 Id ne vobis . . . providebo: order for translation, **providebo ne id vobis diutius faciendum sit atque ut possitis esse in perpetua pace.** For the subjunctive, see B295.5.

Cicero's *Fourth Catilinarian Oration*
Delivered December 5, 63 B.C. to the
Senate in the Temple of Concord

Chapter 1
2–3 video . . . sollicitos: order for translation, **video vos esse sollicitos non solum de vestro [periculo] ac [periculo] rei publicae verum etiam . . . de meo periculo.**

4 voluntas: *goodwill.*

5 eam: refers to **voluntas** (line 4); the direct object of the imperative **deponite. per deos immortalis:** *by the immortal gods* (an oath). **obliti salutis meae: obliviscor** regularly takes the genitive, as do most verbs of remembering and forgetting (B206.2, G376).

6–7 Mihi si haec condicio consulatus data est: *If this condition of the consul-*

ship were given to me (i.e., *if the consulship were given to me on these terms*).

7 ut . . . perferrem: an indirect command explaining **condicio** (line 6) (B295.1, G546.1).

8 dum modo: *provided that, as long as;* a clause of proviso (B310, G573).

Chapter 2
10–15 Ego sum ille consul . . . insidiis fuit: a long sentence, but not a terribly complex one; order for translation, **Ego sum ille consul, cui forum . . . campus . . . curia . . . domus . . . lectus . . . denique haec sedes honoris non umquam fuit vacua periculo atque insidiis mortis; vacua** goes with

forum, campus, curia, domus, and lectus, as well as with sedes, but it agrees grammatically with sedes, because that is its nearest subject; periculo and insidiis are ablatives of separation.

10–11 forum (in quo omnis aequitas continetur): the Forum was the center of public life in Rome, including the administration of justice; the law courts were located there (see Map 1).

11–12 campus (consularibus auspiciis consecratus): auspiciis is ablative of means. The comitia centuriata, the assembly that elected the consuls, met in the Campus Martius. Auspices (reading the future from the flight of birds) were taken before the comitia began its proceedings.

12 curia (summum auxilium omnium gentium): the Curia was the regular meeting place of the Senate. Because the Senate directed Roman policy toward the provinces and foreign nations, Cicero characterizes it as "the support of all nations." The embassy of the Allobroges reminds us, however, that the Senate did not always live up to this name.

13 domus, lectus: Cicero here refers to Catiline's attempts to murder him in his home at dawn; see The First Catilinarian Oration, chapters 9–10.

14 haec sedes honoris: the curule chair, the official seat of curule magistrates (consuls, praetors, censors, curule aediles).

15 Ego multa tacui: I have been silent about many things (i.e., I have endured many hardships in silence). multa concessi: I have yielded many things (i.e., I have made many concessions). Cicero had yielded his lucrative province of Macedonia to his consular colleague Gaius Antonius Hybrida, in return for Hybrida's support against Catiline. multa ... multa ... multa ... multa: ANAPHORA.

16 meo quodam dolore: ablative of attendant circumstance (B221). in vestro timore: in your time of fear. The citizens were in fear, but Cicero bore the pain.

16–17 Nunc si hunc exitum ... voluerunt: order for translation, Nunc si di immortales voluerunt hunc [esse] exitum consulatus mei. . . . In this sentence, hunc is used for hoc, attracted to the gender of the predicate noun, as often (B246.5, G211R5).

17–21 ut . . . eriperem: a purpose clause, explaining the gods' intentions.

21 quaecumque: feminine nominative singular, agreeing with fortuna.

22 subeatur: jussive subjunctive (B275, G260.3); Cicero is willing to undergo whatever fortune may come.

22-3 suum nomen ... fatale ad perniciem: Lentulus had been informed by soothsayers that he was destined to be the third Cornelius to rule Rome; see The Third Catilinarian Oration, chapter 9.

23 fore = futurum esse (B100n.3, G116); future infinitive in indirect discourse, dependent on putavit (line 24).

24 cur ego non laeter: why should I not rejoice?; deliberative subjunctive (B277, G465), which then introduces indirect discourse.

25 prope: almost, practically; Cicero hesitates to make the direct claim that his consulship was destined to save the Republic. exstitisse = fuisse.

Chapter 3

26 Qua re: For this reason, Wherefore.

29 omnis: masculine accusative plural.

30 pro eo mihi ac mereor relaturos esse gratiam: [the immortal gods] will show gratitude to me for this as I deserve (i.e., in accordance with my deserts); gratiam referre: to return thanks, show gratitude.

31 quid = aliquid. si quid obtigerit: if anything happens; future perfect indicative. This is a euphemism, as shown by moriar (future indicative). Notice the CONSONANCE between mereor (line 30) and moriar.

32–33 neque immatura consulari: neque immatura [mors potest accidere] consulari. Cicero is saying that if a man has reached the consulship he has attained the highest honor a Roman can strive for.

33 **sapienti:** *to a wise man or sage.* For the Stoics, the wise man or sage represented the ideal standard of behavior to which all others should aspire. Because the wise man always acts virtuously and according to reason, he would never allow himself to act in a way that would result in his dying a wretched or pitiful death (**misera mors**). **Nec . . . ferreus:** *Nevertheless I am not that iron person* (i.e., I am not so hard-hearted); **METAPHOR**.

33–34 **qui . . . non movear:** a relative clause of characteristic expressing result (B284.2a).

34 **fratris carissimi . . . praesentis:** Cicero's younger brother, Quintus, who was at that time praetor-elect and a member of the Senate.

35 **horumque omnium . . . circumsessum:** those senators who were sitting near Cicero to show their support. **lacrimis:** probably meant figuratively, but the Greeks and Romans were generally more open about demonstrating emotion than we are.

36 **Neque meam mentem non domum saepe revocat exanimata uxor:** *Nor does my terrified wife fail to recall my thoughts often toward home;* the two negatives (**neque** and **non**) make a positive. Terentia was a strong woman who provided much support for her husband in difficult times. They later quarreled, and Cicero divorced her in 48 B.C.; but there is no reason to doubt their closeness at this time.

37 **filia:** Cicero's daughter, Tullia, was now eighteen years old. When she died in childbirth eighteen years later (45 B.C.), Cicero was tremendously affected by her loss. **parvolus filius:** young Marcus was only two years old at this time.

39 **gener:** Tullia's husband, C. Calpurnius Piso. In 63 B.C. he was not yet a member of the Senate, but he may have been standing just outside the open door (**stat in conspectu meo**).

40 **sed in eam partem:** *but only to such an extent.* **uti = ut.**

41 **potius quam:** *rather than.* Cicero would prefer his family to be safe, along with the Senate and the Republic (even if he has to suffer the consequences), rather than do nothing and allow everyone to perish together.

42 **pereamus:** subjunctive in a result clause, parallel to **sint** (line 40); the two subjunctives are connected by **potius quam** (line 41), a coordinating conjunction.

Chapter 4

43 **Qua re:** *For this reason, Wherefore.* **incumbite:** *pay attention to;* literally, *bend to* (the oars); a nautical **METAPHOR**; the state is here (as often) being compared to a ship.

44 **circumspicite omnis procellas:** continuing with the nautical metaphor.

44–48 **Non Ti. Gracchus . . . adducitur:** Cicero stresses that Tiberius Gracchus and the others, whose crimes did not threaten the downfall of the Republic, are not being judged here; the conspirators intended to commit crimes that are far more serious. See Historical Essay I.2, I.4, and I.5 for discussions of the events to which Cicero is alluding.

47–48 **in discrimen aliquod atque in vestrae severitatis iudicium adducitur:** *is led into a certain decision and judgment of your strictness* (i.e., *is brought before your strict judgment and decision*).

48–50 **qui ad urbis incendium . . . restiterunt:** order for translation, **qui restiterunt Romae ad incendium urbis, ad vestram caedem omnium, ad Catilinam accipiendum; restiterunt:** stayed behind; **ad** + accusative shows purpose.

49 **ad vestram omnium caedem = ad caedem omnium vestrum.**

50–51 **litterae, signa, manus, confessio:** *letters, seals, handwriting, confession;* subjects of **tenentur**. For details about this evidence, see *The Third Catilinarian Oration*.

51 **servitia excitantur:** this is not strictly true. Catiline steadfastly refused to include slaves in the conspiracy, although he was urged to do so by Lentulus; see Cicero's

Third Catilinarian Oration, chapter 12, especially lines 136–38.

52 **id est initum consilium:** order for translation, **id consilium initum est**; **initum est** is from **ineo**.

52–54 **ut . . . nemo . . . relinquatur:** purpose clause, dependent upon **consilium**; the present subjunctive is used instead of the imperfect for greater vividness.

52–53 **ne . . . quidem:** *not even.*

53 **ad deplorandum . . . nomen: ad** + accusative showing purpose.

Chapter 5

55 **detulerunt:** from **defero**. **rei:** from **reus**.

55–56 **vos multis iam iudiciis iudicavistis:** *you have already made your judgment by means of numerous decisions.*

56 **quod:** *the fact that.* Cicero now goes on to list the numerous decisions of the Senate by which the Senators have (in Cicero's view) already determined their final judgment.

60 **iudicastis = iudicavistis. dandos = dandos esse. censuistis: censere** was the usual word for an individual senator's judgment or opinion on the question being proposed.

61–62 **honos . . . habitus . . . est: habere** here means *to grant or pay honor to a person.*

61 **togato:** *civil magistrate* (as opposed to a military commander).

62 **hesterno die:** December 4.

62–63 **praemia . . . amplissima:** these rewards probably consisted of large grants of money.

63–64 **Quae sunt omnia eius modi:** *All these things are of such a type.*

64–65 **ut . . . videantur:** result clause.

64 **qui in custodiam nominatim dati sunt:** Sallust (*BC* 47) supplies the names of those senators who were charged with guarding each of the conspirators: Lentulus was turned over to P. Lentulus Spinther; Cethegus to Quintus Cornificius; Statilius to Gaius Caesar;

Gabinius to Marcus Crassus; and Ceparius, after he was caught, to Gnaeus Terentius.

Chapter 6

66 **Sed ego institui referre ad vos:** a direct object of **referre**, such as **rem**, should be understood here.

66–67 **tamquam integrum:** *as if it were an open question* (i.e., not yet prejudged).

67 **et de facto quid iudicetis et de poena quid censeatis:** indirect questions; an introductory purpose clause, such as **ut dicatis**, should be understood. Order for translation: **[ut dicatis] quid iudicetis de facto et quid censeatis de poena.**

68 **quae sunt consulis:** *the things which are appropriate to* (i.e., *characteristic of*) *a consul*; a genitive of possession used predicatively (B198.2, G366).

70 **haberi:** *was being conducted.*

71 **quicquid est:** *whatever your decision is.*

72–73 **statuendum vobis . . . est:** impersonal passive periphrastic: *it must be decided by you* (i.e., *you must make a decision*).

72 **ante noctem:** a decree of the Senate had to be made before nightfall in order to be valid; the Senate could not continue its meeting after that time.

74 **adfinis:** masculine accusative plural. **Latius opinione:** *More widely than is thought.*

78 **quacumque ratione placet:** *in whatever way is pleasing [to you].*

Chapter 7

80 **adhuc** (adv.): *up to now, so far* (in the debate). **sententias:** *motions.* **D. Silani:** Decimus Junius Silanus was consul-elect and thus spoke first.

81–82 **C. Caesaris:** Gaius Julius Caesar. At the time of this speech Caesar had already served as a quaestor and aedile and had just been elected praetor for the year 62 B.C. He was already a recognized leader of the **populares**. Some of the optimates suspected him of secretly supporting Catiline's conspiracy, although there is no real evidence for this view. Caesar's speech is given in full by Sallust (*BC* 51). For a discussion of this Senate meeting, see Historical Essay II.7.

82–83 qui mortis poenam removet, ceterorum suppliciorum omnis acerbitates amplectitur. Note the ADVERSATIVE ASYNDETON between these two clauses. **omnis acerbitates:** *every harshness.*

83 Uterque: *Each [senator].* **pro sua dignitate:** *in accordance with his own dignity.*

84 in summa severitate versatur: *insists on* (literally, *is engaged in*) *the greatest severity.* **Alter:** i.e., Silanus.

84–87 Alter . . . oportere: order for translation, **Alter non putat oportere eos . . . frui vita et hoc communi spiritu punctum temporis**.

86–87 punctum temporis: *for a moment of time;* accusative of extent of time.

88–89 hoc genus poenae saepe . . . esse usurpatum: *this type of penalty has often been used.* This claim is not strictly true. Despite the predecents of Roman citizens who were killed when the Senate had passed an SCU against them, there was no provision in Roman law for the Senate to decide on the death penalty for a Roman citizen without the right of appeal to the people (see Historical Essays I.4 and II.3).

89 recordatur: *he calls to mind* (i.e., *he reminds us*).

91 quietem: *a respite.* Caesar seems to be arguing that the penalty of death should properly be determined by nature and the gods, rather than by the state.

92 oppetiverunt: goes with both clauses in this sentence.

92–94 Vincula . . . inventa sunt: i.e., in Caesar's view.

93 ad singularem poenam: long-term imprisonment was, in fact, extremely rare. A citizen could generally avoid the death penalty by going into exile, but if these conspirators were allowed to leave Rome they would simply join Catiline's camp in Faesulae. This would endanger the city, and it would certainly not punish the conspirators.

94 ista res: i.e., Caesar's plan to distribute the conspirators among the municipal towns.

94–95 Habere videtur ista res iniquitatem, si imperare velis, difficultatem, si rogare: *This plan seems to have unfairness if you wish to command [the towns to accept them], difficulty if you [wish to] ask them.* In other words, it would be unfair to <u>impose</u> such a burden on the towns, but it would be difficult to insure compliance otherwise.

Chapter 8

96 Decernatur: jussive subjunctive (B275, G263.3).

97–98 reperiam . . . recusare: order for translation, **reperiam [eos] qui non putent esse suae dignitatis recusare id quod statueritis causa salutis omnium.**

97 qui . . . non putent: relative clause of characteristic (B283.1, G631.2).

98 esse suae dignitatis recusare: *it is consistent with their dignity* (literally, *it is characteristic of their dignity*) *to refuse;* a genitive of possession used predicatively (B198.2).

99 horribilis: feminine accusative plural.

100 dignas scelere: *[guards] suitable for the crime.*

100–101 sancit . . . possit: order for translation, **sancit ne [ali]quis possit levare poenam eorum quos condemnat aut per senatum aut per populum. ne quis . . . possit:** indirect command (B295, G546.2).

104–105 quam si eripuisset . . . ademisset: pluperfect subjunctives in past contrary-to-fact condition (B304, G597). Order for translation, **si eripuisset quam [= vitam], ademisset multas miserias animi atque corporis et [ademisset] omnis poenas scelerum uno dolore. multas . . . ademisset:** Cicero is arguing that death would be a more merciful penalty because it would relieve them of all their suffering.

105 **omnis:** feminine accusative plural.

105–106 **ut aliqua in vita formido impro-bis esset proposita:** *in order that some fear might be placed before the wicked in life* (i.e., during their lifetimes); purpose clause; **improbis** is dative.

106–107 **apud inferos . . . voluerunt:** order for translation, **illi antiqui voluerunt quaedam supplicia eius modi constituta esse impiis apud inferos**.

106 **apud inferos:** *among the spirits of the dead* (i.e., in the afterlife).

106–107 **eius modi:** *of this type* (i.e., suffer-ings of the body and soul).

108 **his remotis:** ablative absolute, referring to the **supplicia** (line 107).

108–109 **non esse mortem ipsam per-timescendam:** Cicero here belittles the notion of punishment after death, but this contrasts sharply with the description of eternal punishments with which he closed his *First Catilinarian Oration* (chapter 33) and the long list of omens and portents that he gives in the *Third Oration* (chapters 18–20). Because Cicero generally uses arguments that will best support the point he is making at any given time, it is difficult to discern Cicero's own beliefs concerning these matters.

Chapter 9

110 **ego mea video quid intersit:** *I see what my interest is;* **interest** is an impersonal verb meaning *to be of interest to*. Instead of using a personal pronoun with **interest** to express the person whose interest is being described, the Romans used the possessive adjective (i.e., **meus, -a, -um**) in the feminine singular ablative (i.e., **mea**) (see B211.1a, G381).

111–12 **quoniam . . . secutus est:** order for translation, **quoniam is secutus est hanc viam in re publica quae habetur popularis.** Caesar generally followed a populist approach to politics. For a discussion of opti-mates and populares, see Historical Essay I.2.

112 **habetur:** Cicero uses **habetur** instead of **est**, perhaps implying that he does not con-sider the populares' policies to be really in the best interest of the people.

112–14 **fortasse . . . pertimescendi:** order for translation, **fortasse populares impetus pertimescendi erunt minus mihi hoc auc-tore et cognitore huiusce sententiae.** In other words, because Caesar usually speaks for the masses, they will be less likely to crit-icize a decree that he has sponsored.

112–13 **hoc auctore et cognitore:** ablative absolute.

114 **sin:** *but if* (see B306.3, G592). **illam alteram:** [eritis secuti] **illam alteram** [sen-tentiam], i.e., the death penalty. **nescio an:** *I don't know whether;* a polite way of saying *I rather think that*; for **nescio an** + a deliber-ative subjunctive, see B300.5, G457.2. **amplius . . . negoti:** *more trouble* (literally, *more of trouble*).

116 **vincat:** jussive subjunctive.

117 **maiorum eius amplitudo:** the Julian **gens** traced its origins back to Iulus, the son of Aeneas.

117–18 **tamquam obsidem . . . voluntatis:** Caesar's willingness to punish other popu-lares (such as Lentulus and Catiline) severely serves as a pledge of his continuing goodwill toward the Republic.

118–19 **Intellectum est quid interesset:** *It has been made clear what the difference is;* here **intersum** simply means *to be different*; note that **interesset** follows the normal sequence of tenses, even though Cicero is expressing a general truth; in English such general truths are usually put in the present.

119 **levitatem contionatorum:** a **contio** (from **conventio:** a coming together) was a public meeting, usually held in the Forum, in which a magistrate could discuss proposed legislation or any other issue of current importance. These meetings could be used to enhance a politician's standing with the crowd; hence the word **contionator** (one who addresses a **contio**) was frequently used to

mean demagogue or agitator, as here. **et animum vere popularem:** Cicero may have been flattering Caesar in the hopes of convincing him to change his mind (see also lines 127–33 below).

Chapter 10

121–22 **non neminem:** *not no one* (i.e., *someone*); LITOTES. Several of the **populares** (populist politicians) may have been absent from this meeting of the Senate, in order to avoid putting themselves on record as voting to punish the conspirators, but Cicero may be singling out Crassus here (see Taylor [1949: 124]).

122 **de capite:** *concerning the capital punishment.*

122–23 **ne . . . ferat:** negative purpose clause.

123 **nudius tertius:** *the day before yesterday* (i.e., Dec. 3). **Is et:** *But this man.* Cicero emphasizes the inconsistency of someone who would arrest the conspirators and reward the prosecutor and informers but is unwilling to punish the guilty.

124 **mihi:** *in my honor.*

125 **hoc nemini dubium est:** *this is doubtful to no one;* explained by the indirect question (**quid . . . iudicarit**) that follows (lines 126–27).

125–26 **qui . . . decrerit:** *a man who has decreed;* **decrerit** (a shortened form of **decreverit**) is subjunctive by attraction (B324, G629).

126 **quaesitori:** this word was generally used to describe the magistrate who presided at a criminal trial; here Cicero uses it of himself as the one who questioned the conspirators in the Senate on December 3 (cf. *The Third Catilinarian Oration*). Cicero's Senate inquiry was not the same as a trial, but Cicero wants to make it seem as if it were.

127 **Caesar intellegit:** *Caesar understands, Caesar recognizes.* Cicero here claims that Caesar agrees with his argument, but that is clearly not the case (see the note on 128–29

below). **legem Semproniam:** the Sempronian Law, put forward by Gaius Sempronius Gracchus in 123 B.C., decreed that a Roman citizen could not be put to death without a trial before the people (see Historical Essay I.3).

128–29 **qui autem rei publicae sit hostis eum civem esse nullo modo posse:** *[Caesar] also [recognizes that] a person who is an enemy to the Republic can in no way be a citizen;* **sit** is subjunctive in a dependent clause in indirect discourse (B314); **posse** is an infinitive in indirect discourse following **intellegit** (line 127). This is the main point that Cicero is trying to argue for, and he is on shaky legal ground. His argument is that a citizen who is proclaimed to be an enemy is no longer entitled to protection under the Sempronian Law. Not only is this point open to debate, but the five conspirators now under discussion were never declared enemies (**hostes**) by the Senate; only Catiline and Manlius had been declared enemies (see Habicht [1990: 36] and Lintott [1968: 169–71]). Thus Cicero's argument was weak on two counts, and it is quite disinguous of him to claim that Caesar agrees with it. In fact, Caesar's proposed alternative punishment of life imprisonment suggests very strongly that he did not agree with Cicero.

129–30 **ipsum latorem . . . dependisse:** order for translation, **ipsum latorem Semproniae legis dependisse poenas rei publicae iussu populi**. Gracchus was killed in 121 B.C. after the Senate passed an SCU against him (see Historical Essay I.4). Cicero here makes the highly dubious claim that C. Gracchus was killed **iussu populi**. Note the continuation of indirect discourse after **Caesar intellegit** (line 127). As Lintott notes (1968: 170); "This passage shows Cicero placing ideas in Caesar's mind."

130 **rei publicae:** dative. **Idem:** *The same man* (nominative) (i.e., Julius Caesar).

131 **ipsum Lentulum:** *Lentulus himself* (i.e., even Lentulus).

131–33 **cum . . . cogitarit:** a **cum-**circumstantial clause showing cause (B286.2, G586); **cogitarit** is short for **cogitaverit.**

133–4 **homo mitissimus atque lenissimus:** an ironic reference to Caesar .

135–37 **sancit . . . possit:** order for translation, **sancit ne [ali]quis possit se iactare levando supplicio huius et [sancit ne aliquis possit] esse popularis posthac in pernicie populi Romani.**

135–36 **huius supplicio levando:** *by lightening his punishment;* **levando** is a gerundive agreeing with **supplicio;** both are ablatives of means.

136 **in pernicie:** *to the destruction.*

137–39 **ut . . . consequatur:** result clause.

Chapter 11

140 **hoc:** Caesar's proposal. **comitem:** Cicero would probably announce the Senate's decision at a **contio** after the Senate's meeting. If Caesar's proposal was adopted, he would no doubt accompany the consul to the meeting. As a **popularis** politician, Caesar would naturally be welcome to the people.

140–44 **sive hoc statueritis . . . fuisse:** this is a long sentence, but not a difficult one. Order for translation, **sive statueritis hoc, dederitis mihi comitem ad contionem carum atque iucundum populo, sive malueritis sequi sententiam Silani, Romanus populus facile liberabit me atque vos [ex] vituperatione crudelitatis . . .**

140–42 **statueritis, dederitis, malueritis:** future perfects, but translate as present, future, and present respectively. Latin frequently uses the future perfect in a future-more-vivid condition (particularly in the protasis), but English prefers the present tense in the protasis and the future in the apodosis.

140–41 **ad contionem:** on the **contio,** see the note at line 119 above. **Contiones** had no authority to pass laws, but they did have a strong influence on public opinion. Cicero's *Third Catilinarian Oration* is an example of a

contio (the word is used both for the meeting and the speech given at such a meeting).

143–44 **atque obtinebo eam multo leniorem fuisse:** *and I will show that this* (Silanus' **sententia**) *is more lenient.*

144 **Quamquam** (conj.): *And yet.*

144–45 **quae potest . . . crudelitas:** order for translation, **quae potest esse crudelitas in punienda immanitate tanti sceleris?**

146 **liceat:** jussive subjunctive. **ita:** *so, thus.*

146–47 **ut . . . non atrocitate animi moveor:** *as I am not moved by cruelty of spirit;* **ut** does not introduce a result clause here (despite the **ita** in line 146) as the indicative, **moveor,** shows.

147 **quod:** *with regard to the fact that* (B299.2).

148 **me:** ablative of comparison.

149 **Videor enim mihi videre:** *for I seem to myself to see* (i.e., *I see in my imagination*).

151 **sepulta in patria: in sepulta patria; sepulta:** *ruined, destroyed.*

152 **insepultos:** *unburied.*

153 **bacchantis:** *as he exults;* agrees with **Cethegi.**

Chapter 12

154 **Cum vero mihi proposui:** *When, indeed, I propose to myself.* **regnantem:** *reigning as king.* Since the founding of the Republic, the Romans hated the thought that one of their fellow citizens might try to become king.

154–55 **ex fatis:** *from the fates;* cf. the prophecies referred to in *The Third Catilinarian Oration,* chapter 9.

155 **purpuratum:** *wearing purple.* In the eastern kingdoms, the high officials of the king's court wore purple; thus Cicero is suggesting that Lentulus intends to set up an eastern-style monarchy, with Gabinius as his top advisor. **huic:** *to* or *for him* (i.e., Lentulus, dative of reference).

156–58 **tum . . . perhorresco:** *then I shudder at . . . ;* **tum** (line 156) and **tum** (line 157) correlate with **cum** (lines 154 and 155) as follows: *When I imagine . . . then I shudder at . . .*

156–57 lamentationem, fugam, vexationem: all objects of **perhorresco** (line 158).

156 matrum familias: the **mater familias** was the lady or mistress of the household; **familias** is an archaic genitive (B21.2a, G29.R1).

159 misera atque miseranda: misera [esse] atque miseranda [esse].

160 si quis = si aliquis.

160–64 si . . . sumpserit, utrum . . . videatur: a mixed should/would condition, with perfect and present subjunctives (B303, G596).

160–62 si quis pater familias . . . sumpserit: order for translation, **si [ali]quis pater familias . . . non sumpserit supplicium quam acerbissimum de servis.**

161 pater familias: *father* or *master of the household;* for **familias**, see the note on **mater familias** above (line 156).

160–64 quaero . . . utrum . . . videatur: order for translation, **quaero . . . utrum is videatur esse clemens ac misericors an inhumanissimus et crudelissimus?**

161–62 liberis . . . domo: a succession of ablative absolutes.

162 supplicium de servis non quam acerbissimum sumpserit: *[if] he did not exact the harshest possible punishment from his slaves.* In English we say that we "inflict punishment on someone," while in Latin the idiom is to "exact punishment from someone." The "harshest possible punishment" in this case was likely to have been death. According to a decree of the Senate from the Augustan period (**SC Silanianum**), if a master had been killed, all the slaves who lived under the same roof could be tortured and eventually killed. The two situations are not exactly the same, of course, and the **SC Silanianum** dates from a slightly later period. But judging from this decree, it does seem likely that if a man's slaves killed his wife

and children and burned down his house, he would have had the right to punish them with torture and death.

163 utrum . . . an: *would . . . or?*

164 Mihi: i.e., **mihi videatur.**

164–65 qui non . . . lenierit: *who did not relieve;* relative clause of characteristic, with an underlying notion of cause (B283.3, G633). The ancients generally regarded the taking of revenge as completely justified, while today such actions are generally criticized as cruel and barbaric (although they often occur).

165–71 Sic nos . . . misericordes habebimur: this sentence has a short future-more-vivid-condition and a long dependent clause, set off by parentheses. The condition should be translated in the following order: **Sic nos habebimur misericordes in his hominibus . . . si fuerimus vehementissimi.** The dependent clause (characterizing these men) can be fit into the ellipses or placed at the end of the sentence.

165–66 in his hominibus: *in the case of these men.*

169 in vestigiis: *on the ruins.* Cicero is playing upon the Romans' fear of the Gauls, who had once invaded and destroyed Rome (387 B.C.).

171–72 summae . . . subeunda est: order for translation, **fama summae crudelitatis in pernicie patriae civiumque nobis subeunda est.**

172 in . . . pernicie: *with regard to the destruction.*

Chapter 13

173 Nisi vero: *Unless, indeed;* **nisi vero** usually implies that the supposition about to be introduced is ridiculous. **cuipiam:** from **quispiam. L. Caesar:** Lucius Julius Caesar (a cousin of Julius Caesar) had been consul the previous year.

174 nudius tertius: *the day before yesterday;* from **nunc dies [est] tertius:** *this [is] the third day;* Cicero is referring to the meeting of the Senate on December. 3.

174–75 sororis suae . . . virum: *the husband of his sister* (i.e., Publius Cornelius Lentulus, the conspirator).

176 iussu consulis interfectum: *killed by the order of the consul.* Cicero is referring to M. Fulvius Flaccus, who had been Lucius Caesar's maternal grandfather and a supporter of C. Gracchus. He was killed by order of the consul L. Opimius in 121 B.C. (see Historical Essay I.4).

177 filiumque eius impuberem legatum a patre missum: Flaccus sent his eighteen-year-old son to negotiate with Opimius, but Opimius put him in prison and later killed him.

178 Quorum quod simile factum: *What deed of those men* (i.e., Flaccus and his son) *was like [the deeds of the conspirators]?* **quod** is the interrogative adjective, agreeing with **factum.**

178–79 quod initum delendae rei publicae consilium: order for translation, **quod consilium delendae rei publicae initum [est]?** Cicero is arguing that the actions of Gracchus and Flaccus in 121 B.C. were far less threatening to the Republic than the deeds planned by the Catilinarian conspirators.

179 Largitionis voluntas: *A tendency for generosity* (i.e., to the poor). Cicero is trying to downplay the tensions in the Republic caused by C. Gracchus' measures to help the poor (see Historical Essay I.3-4).

180 versata est: *existed.* **partium quaedam contentio:** *a certain amount of factional strife;* literally, *a certain struggle of political factions;* again, this is a euphemism.

181 avus Lentuli: Lentulus' grandfather, P. Cornelius Lentulus, had been prominent in Roman politics as a strong supporter of the aristocracy.

182–83 ne quid de summa rei publicae minueretur: *in order that the highest welfare of the Republic might not be diminished;* literally, *in order that nothing concerned with the highest welfare of the Republic might be diminished;* a negative purpose clause.

183 hic: *this Lentulus,* the conspirator, contrasted with **ille** (the famous Lentulus, the grandfather) in line 182.

187–88 Vereamini minus, censeo, ne . . . videamini: vereamini is jussive subjunctive and introduces a negative clause of fearing; **censeo** is parenthetical (B275.2, B296.2).

188 aliquid severius: *something too harsh.*

188–89 multo magis est verendum . . . quam: *it is much more to be feared that . . . than [it is to be feared] that . . . ;* **quam** is used here as a conjunction (*than*) after the comparative **magis.**

189 ne . . . ne: each **ne** introduces a clause of fearing.

188–91 multo magis est verendum . . . videamur: order for translation, **multo magis est verendum ne remissione poenae videamur [fuisse] crudeles in patriam quam [verendum est] ne severitate animadversionis [videamur] fuisse nimis vehementes in acerbissimos hostis.**

190 hostis: accusative plural.

Chapter 14

193–94 voces . . . eorum qui: *the words of those [senators] who . . .* Apparently some of the senators had expressed doubts about Cicero's ability to carry out the proposed punishments for the chief conspirators.

194 ut habeam: *that I do not have;* a negative clause of fearing (B296.2, G550.2).

196–97 cum . . . tum . . . etiam: *not only . . . but also.* **mea summa cura atque diligentia:** ablative of means.

197–99 multo . . . maiore . . . voluntate: ablative of means.

199 omnium ordinum: there were three main orders of Roman citizens, the senatorial, equestrian, and plebian. For a discussion of Cicero's plan for a harmony of the orders (**concordia ordinum**), inspired by his success in unifying the Roman people against the Catilinarian conspiracy, see Historical Essay II.8.

201 **huius templi ac loci:** *of this temple and place* (i.e., the Temple of Concord); **HENDIADYS**.

202 **Causa . . . sola:** order for translation, **enim post urbem conditam haec causa sola inventa est.**

203–204 **cum sibi viderent esse pereundum:** order for translation, **cum viderent pereundum esse sibi:** literally, *when they saw that there must be a perishing for them;* more smoothly: *when they saw that they must perish.*

Chapter 15

205–207 **neque in improborum civium sed in acerbissimorum hostium numero habendos [esse] puto:** Cicero's claim—made quite clearly here—that the conspirators had forfeited their right to be considered citizens and thus should be considered enemies of the state, was one of his main arguments for supporting the death penalty against them (he also believed that the SCU allowed him to use the death penalty). By saying that he considers the conspirators to be enemies and not citizens, Cicero is arguing that the Sempronian Law **de capite civium**, which stipulated that no Roman citizen could be put to death without a trial, did not apply to them. For problems with this argument, see the note on lines 128–29 above; for a full discussion of these issues, see Historical Essays I.4 and II.7.

209 **hic:** adverb. **Quid . . . commemorem?:** *Why should I mention?* Deliberative subjunctive (B277, G265).

209–10 **qui vobis . . . concedunt:** the senators were primarily concerned with running the government, while the **equites** (equestrians) were mainly businessmen. Thus the equestrians yielded the supremacy in governing to the senators, but (Cicero is arguing) they rivaled the senators in their love for their country.

210 **summam ordinis consilique:** *the leadership of rank and deliberation.* **ita . . . ut:** a purpose clause (despite the **ita**), with the sense *in order that they might* or *on the condition that.*

211 **quos:** the **equites.**

211–13 **quos . . . coniungit:** order for translation, **hodiernus dies atque haec causa coniungit [eos] vobiscum, quos ex dissensione multorum annorum, revocatos [esse] ad societatem concordiamque huius ordinis.**

211 **ex multorum annorum dissensione:** order for translation, **ex dissensione multorum annorum.** This disagreement was mainly about the control of the courts.

212 **huius ordinis ad societatem concordiamque:** order for translation, **ad societatem concordiamque huius ordinis:** *to agreement and harmony with this order* (i.e., with the Senate). Cicero's claim of harmony between the two orders was wildly optimistic.

213–16 order for translation, **Quam conjunctionam in consulate meo, si tenuerimus [eam] perpetuam in re publica, confirmo vobis nullum civile ac domesticum malum venturum esse posthac ad ullam partem rei publicae.**

214–15 **confirmatam, confirmo:** note the two different meanings for this verb; **confirmatam:** *strengthened;* **confirmo:** *I assure.*

216–217 **Pari studio defendendae rei publicae:** *With equal eagerness for defending the Republic;* ablative of manner and a gerundive in the genitive.

217 **tribunos aerarios:** the tribunes of the treasury had originally been the paymasters of the army; they had a property qualification similar to that of the **equites**, or slightly below; for a discussion of Cicero's plan for a harmony of the orders (**concordia ordinum**) see Historical Essay II.8.

218 **scribas:** professional clerks who were career civil servants, the most important of whom were the **scribae quaestorii** who assisted the quaestors.

218–19 **cum casu hic dies ad aerarium frequentasset:** the public treasury (**aerarium**) was in the Temple of Saturn at the west end of the Forum, next to the Temple of Concord. Since the quaestors (treasury officials) took office on December 5, it is likely that this was also the day on which the **scribae** would come to the treasury and lots would be cast to determine which scribes would serve which quaestors (see Map 1).

Chapter 16

221 ingenuorum . . . multitudo: *crowd of free-born citizens;* these would be the poorer citizens who did not qualify for any of the higher property qualifications. It was from this portion of the citizenry that Catiline hoped to draw the bulk of his supporters (see Historical Essay II.4).

222–24 non . . . cum . . tum vero: *not only . . . but truly even.*

223 solum: *ground, soil.*

225 Operae pretium est: an idiom meaning *it is worthwhile;* literally, *it is [worth] the price of the effort* (G380).

226 sua virtute: *by their own merit;* slaves were frequently given the opportunity to earn their freedom. **fortunam huius civitatis:** i.e., the good fortune of citizenship at Rome.

227 quam: refers to **suam patriam**.

227–28 quidam hic nati: *certain people who have been born here* (i.e., the conspirators); most slaves were brought to Rome from conquered nations.

228 summo nati loco: *born from the highest rank;* ablative of source (B215, G395); some of the conspirators (including Lentulus and Catiline himself) were of patrician rank.

229–30 Sed quid ego hosce ordines . . . commemoro: the indicative is used instead of the subjunctive (as in line 209) because Cicero has, in fact, mentioned them.

232 excitavit: singular because it agrees with its closest subject.

232–33 qui modo . . . sit: *provided only that he be . . . ;* a relative clause of proviso (B310, G573 and 627). **tolerabili condicione:** ablative of quality or description (B224).

234 haec : i.e., the city and its institutions. **quantum audet et quantum potest:** *as much as he dares and as much as he can.* If a slave had a master who sympathized with the conspiracy, he would naturally be prevented from expressing his goodwill toward the state.

235 conferat: *contribute;* subjunctive in a relative clause of characteristic. **voluntatis** (i.e., **tantum voluntatis**); **tantum**, the correlative of **quantum**, is understood here; translate: *so much of goodwill.* **ad salutem:** i.e., **ad salutem rei publicae**.

Chapter 17

236 Qua re: *Wherefore, For this reason.* **quem vestrum** (i.e., **aliquem vestrum**); **vestrum** is the genitive plural of **vos**.

236–37 hoc quod auditum est: the rumor is explained in the indirect discourse that follows.

240 fortuna miseri: *wretched in circumstances.* Again, these citizens would have been the primary objects of Catiline's recruitment efforts (see Historical Essay II.4).

240–43 qui non . . . salvum esse velint: relative clause of characteristic.

240–41 illum ipsum . . . locum: order for translation, **illum ipsum locum sellae atque operis et quaestus cotidiani**. Cicero is describing small workshops and retail shops and their owners and employees. He is arguing that while these tradesmen and workers may be poor, they would much prefer the security of peace (since their places of business would remain safe) to the dangers and hazards of civil war.

243 Multo: ablative of degree of difference, with **maxima** (B223, G403).

243–44 immo vero: *nay rather even* (i.e., *to speak more correctly).*

244 id enim potius est dicendum: *for this rather should be said* (i.e., for this is closer to the truth).

245 omne instrumentum: *every tool* (i.e., the equipment of every worker).

246 frequentia civium sustentatur: frequentia is ablative of means.

247 occlusis tabernis: ablative absolute. **incensis** (i.e., **incensis tabernis**): ablative absolute, substituting for the protasis in a past contrary-to-fact condition.

247–48 quid . . . futurum [esse] fuit: *what would have happened?* This future periphrastic construction is a substitute for the pluperfect subjunctive in the apodosis of a past contrary-to-fact condition (B304.3b).

Chapter 18

249 Quae cum ita sint: *Since these things are so.*

250–51 vos ne . . . providete: order for translation, **providete ne vos videamini deesse Romano populo;** an indirect command (B295.5, G546.2).

254–55 Obsessa . . . communis: order for translation, **communis patria, obsessa facibus et telis impiae coniurationis, supplex, tendit manus vobis.**

255–59 vobis se . . . commendat: order for translation, **[communis patria] commendat se vobis, [commendat] vitam omnium civium vobis,** etc.; note the ANAPHORA.

256 arcem et Capitolium: *the citadel and Capitol.* The Capitoline Hill had two summits. The southern summit was the Capitolium proper; on it stood the temple of Jupiter, Juno, and Minerva (also called the temple of Jupiter Optimus Maximus). The northern summit was called the **arx**, or citadel; on it stood the temple of Juno Moneta (see Map 1).

256–57 aras Penatium: *the altars of the Penates.* In addition to the household **lares** and **penates** of each family, there were also **penates publici** of the city of Rome, considered as a greater family. These were supposedly brought from Troy by Aeneas. Originally the **lares** were the spirits of the ancestors, watching over and protecting the family, while the **penates** were guardians of the storeroom (**penus**) and were associated with the goddess Vesta; in time the **lares** and **penates** became almost indistinguishable as household gods.

257 illum ignem Vestae sempiternum: Vesta was the goddess of the hearth. Her temple, which held the eternal fire, was located in the center of the Forum, across from the Temple of Concord, in which Cicero was speaking (see Map 1).

261 iudicandum est: *a decision must be made;* a passive periphrastic in an impersonal passive construction.

Chapter 19

262 memorem vestri: *mindful of you;* objective genitive (B242.2).

262–63 quae . . . facultas: *a resource which;* refers to Cicero's claim that he is thinking only of his fellow citizens and is forgetful of his own advantage.

263 omnis ordines: the three main orders of citizens were the senatorial order, the equestrian order, and the common people, although Cicero has included other classes in the list he gave earlier in the speech (chapters 15–16), namely, the tribunes of the treasury, the scribes, the freeborn, freedmen, and slaves.

265–68 Cogitate . . . paene delerit: the syntax of this sentence is somewhat strained. Perhaps it is best to translate it something like this: *Consider with how great struggles the empire was established, with how great courage freedom was assured . . . [things which] one night almost destroyed.* **Una nox** is the subject of the sentence; **delerit** is short for **deleverit** (subjunctive in indirect question after **cogitate**); **imperium, libertatem,** and **fortunas** are all objects of **delerit**.

268–69 Id ne . . . hodierno die providendum est: order for translation, **hodierno die providendum est ne umquam posthac id possit non modo non confici sed ne quidem cogitari a civibus;** an impersonal passive, followed by an indirect command (B295.5, G546.2); **confici** and **cogitari** are passive infinitives. **non modo non . . . sed ne . . . quidem:** *not only not . . . but not even.*

270 **haec:** direct object of **locutus sum** (line 271). **ut . . . excitarem:** purpose clause. **qui mihi studio paene praecurritis:** *[you] who almost surpass me in eagerness.*

271–72 **ut mea vox . . . videretur:** purpose clause.

271 **mea vox, quae debet esse in re publica princeps:** the consul usually spoke first at a meeting of the Senate; he then called on other senators to speak in the order of their importance.

272 **officio . . . consulari:** ablative with **functa [esse].**

Chapter 20

273 **ad sententiam** (i.e., **ad sententiam rogandam**): after expressing his own views, the consul would ask other senators to state their opinion.

274 **quanta manus est coniuratorum:** *as great as the band of conspirators is.*

275 **tantam . . . inimicorum multitudinem:** *so great a number of enemies;* **quanta** (line 274) and **tantam** are correlatives.

276 **Quod si:** *But even if.*

277 **plus valuerit quam:** *will have become stronger than.* Cicero's fear came true in 58 B.C., when he was exiled for the actions he took at the end of this Senate meeting (i.e., putting the conspirators to death without a trial).

277–78 **vestra ac rei publicae dignitas:** *your authority and [the authority] of the Republic.*

278 **dignitas:** here **dignitas** is equivalent to **auctoritas.**

278–79 **me . . . meorum factorum atque consiliorum numquam . . . paenitebit:** *it will never cause regret to me for my deeds and plan* (i.e., *I will never regret my deeds and plans*).

279 **paenitebit:** from **paenitet** (*it causes regret*), an impersonal verb that takes an accusative of person and a genitive object (B 209).

280 **vitae:** note the strong position of this word; Cicero has just said that he does not fear death, because death is provided for all. Now he explains why he feels his life has been complete.

281 **honestastis = honestavistis.**

282 **bene gesta = re publica bene gesta:** an ablative absolute with causal force: *for managing the republic well;* literally, *for the republic having been managed well.* The distinction that Cicero is attempting to make (between saving the Republic and managing it well) is not an obvious one.

283 **gratulationem = supplicationem.**

Chapter 21

284 **Sit Scipio clarus ille: sit** is jussive subjunctive. Cicero here begins a list of Romans who have won great fame for their deeds on behalf of the state. While acknowledging their glory, Cicero also claims a place for himself among these men. **Scipio clarus ille:** this refers to Scipio Africanus the Elder, who conquered Hannibal at the Battle of Zama (202 B.C.), and brought an end to the Second Punic War.

285–86 **alter . . . Africanus:** this refers to Scipio Aemilianus Africanus the Younger. He was the son of Lucius Aemilius Paulus (referred to below, line 287), but he was adopted into the family of the elder Scipio Africanus, thus taking the name Scipio Aemilianus. The younger Scipio conquered Carthage in 146 B.C. (at the conclusion of the Third Punic War) and razed the city to the ground. Later, in 133 B.C., he conquered and destroyed the Spanish city of Numantia, thus securing Roman control of Spain.

287 **habeatur:** jussive subjunctive.

287–88 **Paulus ille:** Lucius Aemilius Paulus conquered King Perseus (or Perses) of Macedon in 168 B.C., successfully bringing the Third Macedonian War to a close.

288 **currum:** Perseus walked before Paulus' chariot in the triumphal procession.

289 **aeterna gloria:** ablative of description (or quality; B224, G400). **Marius:** Gaius Marius was consul seven times (107, 104, 103, 102, 101, 100, and 86 B.C.). He defeated the Teutones at Aquae Sextiae in 102 B.C. and the Cimbri near Vercellae in 101 B.C. **obsidione:** i.e., invasion.

290 **Pompeius:** Pompey had recently won victories over Sertorius in Spain (72 B.C.), the pirates in the Mediterranean (67 B.C.), and Mithridates in Asia (66 B.C.); he was currently engaged in winning new territories in the East. During the year following the Catilinarian conspiracy and the other events of his consulship (62 B.C.) Cicero was to write to Pompey, hoping that they could work closely together on Pompey's return, but Pompey apparently rebuffed him.

290–91 **res gestae:** *military achievements.*

290–92 **Pompeius . . . continentur:** order for translation, **Pompeius, cuius res gestae atque virtutes continentur isdem regionibus ac terminis quibus cursus solis [continentur].**

291–92 **regionibus ac terminis:** *boundaries and limits.*

291 **solis cursus:** *courses of the sun.* By his victories from Spain to Asia (west to east), Pompey has made conquests equal to the paths of the setting and rising sun. The Romans were not the first to make such claims (cf. Xerxes' boasts before the Persian Wars in Herodotus 7.8g.1–2); nor were they the last.

292 **aliquid loci:** *some place;* partitive genitive (genitive of the whole; B201.2, G369).

293 **nisi forte:** *unless perhaps;* implies that the supposition is false. **maius est:** *it is a greater thing.* **quo** (adv.): *to where.*

294 **curare ut . . . habeant:** a substantive clause with verbs of striving or effort (B295.5, G553). **quo:** i.e., **[aliquem locum] quo.**

Chapter 22

296 **Quamquam:** *And yet.* **uno loco:** *in one respect;* ablative of specification (respect; B226, G397).

297 **quod:** *the fact that.*

298 **recepti:** *accepted* (as allies). **beneficio se obligatos putant:** *they consider themselves put under obligation by the favor.* **qui autem:** *but those who* (**autem** is adversative rather than resumptive here). **ex numero:** *belonging to the class, from the class.*

299 **hostes patriae semel esse coeperunt:** order for translation, **semel coeperunt esse hostes patriae.**

300 **cum a pernicie rei publicae reppuleris:** *although you have driven [them] back from [posing] a danger to the Republic;* a **cum**-circumstantial (concessive) clause.

301 **possis:** potential subjunctive. **Qua re:** *Wherefore, For this reason.* **mihi:** *by me;* dative of agent with passive verb (B189.2, G354).

302 **Id:** refers to **bellum** (line 301).

302–305 **Id . . . confido:** order for translation, **Confido id posse facile propulsari a me atque a meis vestro [auxilio] et auxilio bonorum omnium,** etc.

303–305 **quae . . . haerebit:** order for translation, **quae [memoria] semper haerebit non modo in hoc populo qui servatus est, sed in sermonibus ac mentibus omnium gentium.**

305 **a me atque a meis:** ablative of separation.

306–308 **quae . . . possit:** relative clause of characteristic showing result (B284.2, G631.2).

306–307 **coniunctionem . . . conspirationem:** it is unclear whether such an alliance ever existed.

Chapter 23

309 **Quae cum ita sint:** *Since these things are so.* **pro imperio, pro exercitu, pro provincia,** etc. *in place of the chief command, in place of an army, in place of a province,* etc. Cicero describes the various privileges enjoyed by the governor of a province. The governor commanded an army (**exercitu**) and had supreme power (**imperio**); if he conducted a successful military

campaign he might receive a triumphal procession (**triumpho**) and other marks of honor (**ceteris laudis insignibus**).

310–11 quae sunt a me . . . repudiata: consuls generally governed a province during the year following their consulship. Cicero renounced his claim to the wealthy province of Macedonia in favor of his consular colleague, Antonius. Antonius was known to be sympathetic to Catiline; by this action Cicero was able to withdraw Antonius' support from the conspiracy. Later in the year Cicero also renounced his claim to the remaining province, Cisalpine Gaul.

311–12 pro clientelis hospitiisque provincialibus: a governor of a province would generally form valuable social connections, which could later yield social, political, and economic benefits.

312 quae tamen: *which things, nevertheless.* Cicero implies that he does have some ties of hospitality with provincial clients, despite the fact that he generally preferred to remain at Rome. Cicero's ties with families in Sicily had been instrumental to him in his prosecution of Verres in 70 B.C.

312–13 quae . . . comparo: *which I nevertheless maintain through my urban resources* (i.e., Cicero's influence in Rome) *with no less effort than [the effort by which] I acquire them.*

313–14 pro his igitur omnibus rebus: *therefore, in return for all those things.* Note that **pro** + ablative is used here and in the next two phrases in a slightly different sense from the way it is used above: *in return for* as opposed to *in place of.*

317 quae dum erit . . . fixa: *as long as this [memory] will be fixed* (B293.II, G569).

318 Quod si: *But if.*

318–19 fefellerit, superaverit: future perfect indicatives; **fefellerit** is from **fallo**.

319–20 cui profecto satis erit praesidi: *for whom, indeed, there will be sufficient protection;* **praesidi** is partitive genitive with **satis** (B201.2).

321–22 si . . . memineritis: order for translation, **si memineritis illum esse filium eius qui conservarit omnia haec suo solius periculo.**

321 conservarit = conservaverit. suo solius periculo: *with risk to himself alone;* **suo periculo** is ablative of attendant circumstance (B221); the genitive **solius** is used for emphasis (B243.3a, G321R2).

Chapter 24

323 Quapropter: *For this reason.* **de summa salute,** etc.: dependent upon **decernite** (imperative) in line 326.

326 ut instituistis: *as you have begun.* Debate in the Senate had already begun when Cicero delivered his speech.

327–28 qui . . . non dubitet: relative clause of characteristic.

327 parere: pareo takes a dative object; infinitive following **dubitet** (line 328).

328 quoad vivet: *as long as he lives* (B293.II, G 569).

329 praestare: *be responsible for* (carrying out).

Historical Essays and Appendices

From the Gracchi to Sulla

Background to the Conspiracy

The Catilinarian conspiracy—and the civil wars that followed—occurred within the context of a series of economic and social problems that had been plaguing Rome and Italy since the late second century B.C. These problems included the decline of the small farm, a shortage of men to serve in the army, deteriorating conditions of life for many Italian peasants, rising levels of debt, and the growth of the urban poor. Paradoxically, Rome's military successes abroad contributed to these difficulties, which continued to worsen in the years leading up to the Catilinarian conspiracy. The Republican government, however, proved unable (or unwilling) to solve these complex problems. Through a brief survey of the history of this period, this essay considers how these difficulties arose and why Rome's political structure failed to resolve them. The questions at the end of each section are meant to provoke discussion about some of the central points at issue.

1. The Agrarian and Military Crisis of the Late Second Century B.C.

Throughout the Republican period, the majority of people on the Italian peninsula had traditionally supported themselves by subsistence farming: they grew just enough to supply their family's needs, with a small surplus to sell or trade for necessities at the local market.[1] Most of these peasant farmers needed to supplement their income by gathering firewood, by grazing a few pigs or sheep on public land (*ager publicus*), or by hiring themselves out for seasonal work on larger farms. The size of these subsistence farms was generally between ten and thirty *iugera*.[2] Many peasant farmers lived on less than ten *iugera*, however, and we hear of some who managed to exist on as little as two.[3] The typical peasant lived a precarious, hand-to-mouth existence: his ability to provide for himself and his family depended on a delicately balanced system of farming, grazing, labor, and barter; any disruption to that system could easily result in a breakdown.

Unfortunately, the numerous foreign wars of the second century B.C. provided many such disruptions, not the least of which were frequent military conscriptions. Peasant farmers were the backbone of the Roman army. The main reason for this was that there was a minimum property qualification for military service; those who fell below this qualification were not considered fit to serve in the army because they could not even afford their own weapons. As long as a farmer owned a small plot of land, however, he was able to qualify for military service and could be drafted up to the age of forty-six. The required length of service changed in different periods, but even a relatively modest six-year tour of duty would be a very long time for a farmer to be away from his land. Rome's wars at this time were mainly foreign wars, so visits home were rare. With the prolonged absence of male family members, many peasant households fell into a permanent condition of debt. Eventually, many were forced to sell their farms. Once a peasant had lost his land, he was no longer required to serve in the army, of course; but as more peasants began to lose their land, the burden of conscription fell on fewer and fewer people. Many landless peasants drifted into Rome looking for work, while others remained in the countryside, working as tenant-farmers and depending on seasonal labor to eke out a meager existence. Unfortunately, the growth of large-scale farms and an abundance of slave labor to work them made even this source of income increasingly difficult to come by.

The foreign wars of the second century led to increased wealth for the Roman generals and their staffs, however, as well as lucrative business opportunities for those who could supply weapons to the Roman army or collect public taxes: "Immense profits were made by senators from booty, expense allowances and illicit exactions from Rome's subjects and by rich men outside the Senate, the Equites, from contracts for public works, army supplies, and the collection of provincial taxes."[4] As the newly rich began to invest their money in land, Rome's foreign conquests were opening up new markets for agricultural products. Large-scale farms began to develop, devoted to cash crops such as wine and olives, which could be sold for a profit in the capital or overseas. These large estates (or *latifundia*) could be as small as 100–240 *iugera* or as large as 350,000–400,000 *iugera*.[5] They were generally worked by slaves, of which Rome's foreign conquests were producing an abundant supply. The success of these *latifundia* came largely at the expense of traditional subsistence farming. As small farmers began to fall into debt, the owners of large-scale farms were eager to buy up their holdings.

A large labor force composed entirely of slaves could be a destabilizing influence. During this period there were two massive slave revolts in Sicily (138–132 and 104–101 B.C.). In each case the revolt was sparked by a particularly flagrant injustice on the part of the masters; in each case the slaves who originally started the rebellion were joined by thousands of fellow slaves (mainly herdsmen and agricultural slaves working on *latifundia*) and even the free poor. Both of these revolts dragged on for several years before they were finally put down, and both seem to have attracted runaway slaves from southern Italy. The conditions that sparked these revolts were not limited to Sicily; they reflected social and economic problems throughout the Italian peninsula.

Another factor in this complex situation was the semilegalized occupation of public land (*ager publicus*) by the owners of the *latifundia*. Rome had acquired large amounts of *ager publicus* in Italy from defeated enemies and rebellious allies, particularly after the Second Punic (Hannibalic) War (218–202 B.C.). Roman landowners could lease large tracts of *ager publicus* from the government for a nominal fee. The legal limit was 500 *iugera*, but many landowners had occupied much more than was strictly allowed. After working the land for a few generations, and in many cases improving the land with farm buildings and trees, most of these landowners considered this land to be their own. They stopped paying rent and simply absorbed the *ager publicus* into their private holdings. Small subsistence farmers, who may have used this public land for gathering firewood and for grazing a few pigs and cattle, were no longer able to do so.

All of these factors (increased conscription, rising debt, the increasing dependence on slave labor on the *latifundia* coupled with the decreasing availability of seasonal labor) combined to drive peasants off their land and into a state of permanent indebtedness. Farmers, recruited as soldiers, left their farms at risk of decline and vulnerable to being purchased by the wealthy owners of large-scale farms. Meanwhile, successful wars resulted in a flood of cheap slave labor to work those large-scale farms. After losing their land, debt-ridden peasants either stayed on as tenant farmers or drifted into Rome in the hope of finding work, although the abundance of slaves also reduced the ability of free men to find work. At the same time, successive military conscriptions on an ever-dwindling eligible population resulted in a serious recruitment problem for the Roman legions. These were the problems that Tiberius Gracchus (tribune of the plebs in 133 B.C.) and his younger brother Gaius attempted to address.

Discussion Questions

1. What were some of the economic and social pressures on Italy's rural and urban poor during the late second century B.C.?
2. Can you explain how these problems were related to one another as part of a larger process of economic and political change?

2. Tiberius Sempronius Gracchus

As a member of the Roman nobility—a small group of families (both patrician and plebeian) who dominated the high offices of the Republic—Tiberius Gracchus began his career with a great deal of support among the most powerful members of the Roman Senate.[6] His father, also named Tiberius Gracchus, had been consul twice and censor once; and his mother, Cornelia, was the daughter of the famous Scipio Africanus the Elder, who had conquered Hannibal. Tiberius' sister, Sempronia, was married to Scipio Aemilianus (destroyer of Carthage in 149 B.C.) and Tiberius himself had married into another noble family. Thus Tiberius Gracchus, as a member of the Roman *nobilitas*, had the right connections to ensure a successful political career.

But Tiberius wanted more than just a successful political career. Of course, he was eager to enhance his political influence, but he was also interested in addressing the economic and social problems confronting the Romans at that time. As a young man in 137 B.C., Tiberius was passing through northern Italy and saw the countryside devoid of its inhabitants, while foreign slaves were farming the land and tending the flocks. This first inspired him to find a way to bring disenfranchised peasants back to the land.

In 133 B.C. Tiberius Gracchus served as tribune of the plebs and in that capacity proposed a bill designed to address both the military recruitment problem and the condition of the Italian peasants through the reapportionment of public land. As mentioned above, many landowners had occupied far more than the legal limit of 500 *iugera* of public land, and most of them had stopped paying rent as well. Under Tiberius' bill, landowners who had annexed *ager publicus* would be limited to a base amount of 500 *iugera*, with an additional 250 *iugera* allowed for each child, up to a maximum of 1,500 *iugera* (about 1,000 acres) for a man with four children. Landowners would have to give back to the state any land in excess of that amount (including any improvements to the land that they might have made), but they would be able to keep the remaining land as their own, free of rent or encumbrances. According to Plutarch (*Tiberius Gracchus* 9.2), Tiberius' bill also provided for compensation for those who gave up land. The excess land would then be distributed in small lots (probably about 10 to 30 *iugera*) to peasant farmers who had lost their land. Those who received land would not be able to sell it; the land was to remain in the family as a source of support for future generations. Not only would peasants be able to return to the land, but they could also serve in the army, thus helping to alleviate the military shortage. Tiberius' land bill would not have completely solved Rome's agricultural and military crises, even if fully implemented, because it did nothing to address the underlying problems that had caused them in the first place. Nonetheless it was a first step toward solving these problems as well as a reasonable attempt to ameliorate their most pressing symptoms.

Tiberius' bill was certain to arouse resentment in the Senate, especially among those senators who would have to give up some land. Tiberius did have powerful connections among the senatorial elite, however. And even the senators could see that Rome's economic and social problems required decisive action. As D. L. Stockton notes (1979: 77): "Powerful and persuasive arguments could be adduced to show that some regeneration of the free peasantry, quite apart from reducing the risk of slave insurrections, would help to guarantee the security of Rome's empire, and thereby in the long term prove of benefit to all classes in the state." If Tiberius had made such arguments and had taken prudent steps to mollify the Senate, his bill might have passed through the Plebeian Council without serious challenge.[7] As it was, Tiberius made a series of decisions in the process of promulgating his bill that seemed almost calculated to incite the opposition.

Tiberius' first move was to take his bill directly to the Plebeian Council, without first submitting it to the Senate for approval, as was the custom. It was not strictly illegal for a plebeian tribune to bypass the Senate, but it was extremely rare, and, in view of the seriousness of Tiberius' proposal, clearly unwise; the Senate was certain to resent being ignored. When Tiberius brought the proposal to a vote in the Plebeian Council, he was in for a surprise: one of the other tribunes, M. Octavius, had been persuaded by senatorial interests to veto the bill. Plebeian tribunes had the right to veto any legislation, but they were not expected to use that power against the plebeians' own interests. Although it later became a common practice for senators to manipulate a tribune's veto, at this time it was an unusual, if not unprecedented, move.[8]

Tiberius responded to Octavius' veto by adjourning the Plebeian Council and postponing the vote, but at a second meeting Octavius persisted with his veto. In order to resolve the impasse, Tiberius belatedly agreed to seek the support of the Senate; but at this point the senators, perhaps sensing that they had the upper hand, refused to compromise. At the third meeting of the Plebeian Council, when Octavius again refused to rescind his veto, Tiberius proposed that a tribune should not be allowed to remain in office if he used his power to oppose the will of the people who had elected him. When Octavius remained unmoved, a majority of the plebeian tribes voted to unseat him from office. With Octavius deposed and a new tribune elected in his place, Tiberius' land reform bill was quickly voted into law. The extralegal means by which the bill had been passed, however, created an atmosphere of unease in the city.

The tension increased during the next few weeks when the Senate, led by the powerful Scipio Nasica, refused to grant the appropriations to support Tiberius' legislation. (Rumor had it that Nasica held a large tract of public land.) Tiberius' bill called for the creation of a three-member land commission that would have the power to review all holdings of *ager publicus* and make decisions on forfeiture and allotments. Because the commission would be unable to pursue its work without funding, the Senate's action threatened to obstruct the bill. But fortune intervened: King Attalus of Pergamum died at this time, and he bequeathed both his kingdom and his substantial treasury to the Roman people. Tiberius Gracchus announced that he intended to appropriate some of the money in Attalus' treasury to provide money for his land bill; he added that the Plebeian Council (under his direction, of course), and not the Senate, would make the arrangements for governing the Pergamene kingdom. This was a clear and direct challenge to the Senate, which had always taken charge of foreign affairs and public finance. Rumors began to circulate that Tiberius had received Attalus' royal diadem and purple robe and that he intended to crown himself the king of Rome! The charge, of course, was ridiculous, but the Senate may well have been correct in seeing Tiberius' pronouncements as part of a plan to challenge its authority. Several senators now began to openly charge that Tiberius had violated the law in having the Plebeian Council depose Octavian from the tribuneship; they promised to indict him as soon as he had completed his year in office.[9]

At this point Tiberius announced that he intended to seek reelection for a second term as tribune. Although there was no specific law against it, no one had ever held a second consecutive tribunate. It is important to remember that the Romans had always depended more on custom and the *mos maiorum* than on strict legality. "If Tiberius is willing to flout custom in this way," many Romans must have thought, "is there anything he wouldn't do?"

When the Plebeian Council met on the Capitoline Hill to elect the tribunes for 132 B.C., there was so much squabbling over the propriety of Tiberius' candidacy that the Council broke up and the election was postponed until the following day. During the night, Gracchus' supporters showed their strength by gathering en masse on the Capitoline Hill (see Map 2). The next day, as the voting was about to begin, some of Tiberius' opponents tried to stop it; consequently, a fight broke out. Meanwhile, the Senate was meeting at the nearby Temple of Fides (see Map 2), deliberating on what it should do in such a crisis. Most of the senators expressed the opinion that the consul, P. Mucius Scaevola, should protect the Republic by force of arms; but Scaevola quietly stated that he would not do anything by force.[10] At this point Scipio Nasica objected that the consul was destroying the Roman *imperium* through an excessive devotion to legal procedures. He covered his head with the edge of his toga and cried out: "Let those who wish to save the Republic follow me [*qui rem publicam salvam esse volunt me sequantur*]!"[11] A crowd of senators and their attendants, led by Scipio Nasica, marched to the area of the Capitoline Hill where the Plebeian Council was meeting. They carried clubs and, as they went, picked up stones and broken chairs left over from the council meeting. When they arrived, the senators and their attendants attacked Tiberius and his supporters. According to Plutarch, more than three hundred men were murdered by the senatorial mob, although many of these were probably trampled to death by the crowd. Tiberius himself was killed at or near the Temple of Jupiter Capitolinus. During the night, the bodies of Tiberius and hundreds of his followers were unceremoniously dumped into the Tiber.

When Scipio Nasica covered his head with his toga, he was imitating not only the sacrificial dress of the *pontifex maximus* or chief priest but also (and more pointedly) the dress used by the consul when making a formal declaration that the city of Rome was under attack from foreign invaders. That declaration, called a *tumultus*, empowered the consul to quickly arm the citizens in order to defend the state. In fact, the formula that the consul was supposed to use when calling the citizens to arms was precisely what Scipio Nasica had said: *qui rem publicam salvam esse vult, me sequatur*.[12] It is clear from this that Nasica believed the Republic was in grave danger and had to be protected by force, even if that meant that he, as a private citizen, would have to usurp the consul's power to arm the citizens and (taking even further liberties) lead them against fellow citizens. And Nasica was clearly not alone in his belief that force was necessary. The Roman aristocracy had traditionally believed that violence to defend one's rights was justified; they also believed that any politician who became too powerful might set himself up as a tyrant, which would jeopardize the rights of all the citizens. In their view, such an outcome should be prevented at all costs.

This attitude can clearly be seen in the remark made by Tiberius' own brother-in-law, Scipio Aemilianus. When told about Tiberius' death, Scipio Aemilianus is reported to have said that if Tiberius had intended to take over the Republic, he had been justly killed.[13] While there is no evidence that Tiberius had any intention of taking over the Republic, he did use his position as tribune to challenge the Senate's dominance in foreign and financial affairs. The Senate, of course, was bound to defend itself, though no one could have predicted that Nasica and his followers would react as violently as they did.

That violence was to bear bitter fruit. Ancient writers saw Tiberius' tribunate and death as a watershed event that divided the citizens into two opposing camps and initiated a prolonged period of civil unrest.[14] Modern historians, too, see the death of Tiberius and his followers as initiating a period of increasing divisiveness and escalating violence. As one scholar has noted:

We find in ancient Rome a society whose ethos supported violence . . . and which positively welcomed the use of force in defence of rights, and we also have two opposed visions of what was right. And it is this point that I would like to stress. It is true that in the late Republic there was much violence that was wilful, . . . but the problem with the great crises is that both sides had principles.[15]

Both the senatorial aristocracy and Gracchus and his followers believed that they were acting to defend their rights and to preserve the Republic; but the violence that ensued from this conflict set a dangerous precedent for the future. Those who committed violent acts against Tiberius and his followers were never punished, and the use of violence against him did open a kind of floodgate for future civic disruptions.

In the meantime, however, the Senate was firmly in control. Although Scipio Nasica was never formally tried for his actions, the Senate did send him on a mission to Asia, most likely to protect him from the wrath of an angry public. The Senate also commissioned Popillius Laenas, one of the consuls for 132 B.C., to conduct an investigation (*quaestio*) for the purpose of seeking out and punishing Gracchan sympathizers. Laenas' special tribunal was empowered to pass sentence against these men without the traditional trial before the *comitia centuriata*.[16] This process of investigation and trial, which was something of a witch hunt, continued for several months and resulted in numerous banishments and even executions. The Senate did allow the land commission to go forward with its work, however, at least for the next few years. Tiberius' reforms, when separated from his inflammatory methods, must have enjoyed at least some senatorial support.

Tiberius' reforms also changed the face of Roman politics. After Tiberius' tribunate, Roman politicians tended to fall into one of two categories. One group was called the *optimates* (the best men) or the *boni* (the good men). As these names indicate, such men tended to ally themselves with upper-class interests. They generally sought to maintain the status quo, from which the upper class derived considerable advantages. The other group, the *populares*, also was composed of members of the upper class, but they allied themselves politically with the lower classes. Following in Tiberius Gracchus' footsteps, the *populares* tended to seek the office of tribune of the plebs and to use that office as a counterweight to senatorial and aristocratic interests. Some *populares*, such as Tiberius and Gaius Gracchus, were genuinely interested in helping to alleviate the problems of the poor. Others simply used populist methods for their own political gain. And not even the Gracchi had completely selfless motives: *populares* politicians gained their power base by appealing to the equestrians and lower classes, and Gaius Gracchus was well aware of this (as we shall see). It should be stressed that both *optimates* and *populares*—like all political leaders in the Roman world—were members of the elite. The difference between the two was that, while the *optimates* appealed to the economic and political interests of their own class, the *populares* sought the support of the masses.

It is also important to note that neither the *optimates* nor the *populares* formed political parties in the modern sense. Roman politics tended to be more personal and more fluid than is the case with today's party politics; there was no "party allegiance," for example. Political alliances (*amicitiae*) varied with changing political fortunes and shifting marriage connections. Some Roman politicians (including Cicero himself) were not above using both optimate and populist rhetoric as it suited their changing political needs.

Discussion Questions

1. What were the measures Tiberius Gracchus proposed to help the poor and provide more men for the army?
2. Do you think that Tiberius' motives were entirely altruistic?
3. Were any of Tiberius Gracchus' actions counter-productive? What could he have done instead?
4. How did Tiberius Gracchus' actions lead to the split in Roman politics between *optimates* and *populares*?
5. In the long run, do you think that Tiberius' actions had a mostly positive or a mostly negative effect on Roman politics?

3. Gaius Sempronius Gracchus

Tiberius' program of reform was carried on by his brother, Gaius, who was ten years his junior.[17] Before discussing Gaius' political program and his legislative proposals, however, we must first briefly mention a few events that occurred between Tiberius' death in 132 B.C. and his younger brother's tribunate in 123, beginning with the work of the land commission, of which Gaius was a member. Although the land commission was allowed to proceed with its reforms after Tiberius' death, difficulties soon arose concerning the *ager publicus* that was held by Italian allies. At this time, only residents of Rome and a few other cities (such as Arpinum, where Cicero was born) were actually Roman citizens. Most residents of the Italian peninsula were allies of Rome. As such, they had to provide men to serve in the Roman army; in return they enjoyed some military protection, but they were not granted all the privileges of citizenship. One group, the Latin allies (originally composed of those who spoke Latin, but later extended to other close allies), did have the rights of intermarriage and commerce with the Romans; Latins could also become Roman citizens if they settled at Rome. But most Italians did not share even these privileges. They were not allowed to vote, for example; nor did they receive the full protection of Roman civil law. Of particular interest in the present context, Italian allies were not eligible to receive grants of *ager publicus* under Tiberius Gracchus' land reform bill.

The Italians were not eager to relinquish the public land that was located in their territory, especially since they were not eligible to receive any land grants themselves. In 129 B.C. Scipio Aemilianus (the general who had destroyed Carthage twenty years earlier) came forward as a spokesman for the disgruntled Italians, perhaps seeing the issue of Italian *ager publicus* as an opportunity to weaken the Gracchan land reforms without attacking them directly. Scipio succeeded in transferring the adjudication of Italian *ager publicus* from the land commission to the consuls; this in itself was a serious blow to the land commission's power. Furthermore, because the consuls took no action, the progress of land reform was significantly slowed if not completely halted.

A few years later (in 125 B.C.), the consul Fulvius Flaccus, who was also a member of the land commission, put forward a proposal granting full Roman citizenship to the Italian allies.[18] Flaccus' proposal seems to have been an attempt to win the Italians' cooperation for the land reform program, and it might well have succeeded: most of the allies wanted citizenship; and if they received it, they would then be eligible for land grants as well. But when the Senate (not yet ready to share citizenship rights with the allies) moved to block Flaccus' bill, the consul abandoned the attempt.

During the same year the Latin colony of Fregellae, on the border of Samnium (see Map 3), revolted against Roman rule. The causes of the revolt are unclear; we do not even know whether the revolt was connected to the failure of Flaccus' proposal or whether any other colonies participated in it.[19] The revolt was soon put down, and no other revolts from Latin or Italian colonies followed. When taken together with Italian displeasure over the issue of land reform, however, the revolt of Fregellae does seem to have been a sign that the Latin and Italian allies were ready for a greater share in the benefits of the Roman commonwealth. Thus when C. Gracchus became tribune in 123 B.C., land reform and citizenship for the Italian allies were two of the key items on the political agenda.

As a member of Tiberius' land commission, Gaius had already gotten a taste for Roman politics. By the time he became tribune in 123 B.C., Gaius was intent on reviving and expanding his brother's reforms. Gaius Gracchus was also an extraordinary speaker. Cicero, who was certainly no fan of Gaius' political views, believed that he would have become one of Rome's greatest orators if he had lived.[20] As tribune, Gaius used his oratorical skills—and the personal authority they brought him—to promote a wide-ranging program of reform. The scope of Gaius' political vision was vast, including "the condition of the urban commons, the food supply of Rome, agrarian and colonizing and construction projects, public finance, the legal system, the army, the government of provinces, the election and tenure of public officers, [and] the political status of Latins and Italians."[21] For the purposes of the present essay we must limit our discussion to those specific bills that seem especially relevant to the upheavals of the late Republic; but, even within these limitations, we need to discuss six different proposals.

One of the first bills that Gaius carried in the Plebeian Council was the *lex Sempronia de capite civium*, providing that no Roman citizen could be condemned on a capital charge without a trial before the people: *ne de capite civium iniussu populi iudicaretur.*[22] This trial generally took the form of an appeal before the *comitia centuriata*. The special inquiry (*quaestio*) of 132 B.C. by which the consul Popillius Laenas banished and even executed his brother's followers did not count as a trial before the people, however, and was, in fact, one of the bill's main targets. "Gaius' purpose was to attack the notion that a man could be treated as a *hostis*, bereft of citizen rights, although he had not been proved guilty of any crime recognized by the law."[23] Although a trial before the people in capital cases was consistent with ancient Roman customs, Gaius' bill was specifically aimed at preventing another witch hunt such as the Laenas tribunal. The *lex Sempronia* was also intended to bring Laenas himself to justice: it included a retroactive provision, stipulating that any magistrate who had banished or executed a citizen without a trial would himself be liable to prosecution. Popillius Laenas withdrew into voluntary exile rather than face a public trial under the law. The *lex Sempronia de capite civium* was a powerful protection of civil rights that would continue to be a source of controversy, as Cicero would one day discover.[24]

In the years just prior to 123 B.C. there had been a shortage of wheat and the prices had fluctuated wildly; a swarm of locusts in north Africa had severely damaged the crop, and wheat production in Sicily was probably still suffering from the Slave War of 138 to 132 B.C. Gaius Gracchus passed a *lex frumentaria*, the "first of its kind in Roman history," which provided for the regular, monthly sale of grain to citizens at Rome at a fixed, low price.[25] This bill was aimed at helping Rome's growing population of urban poor. By buying large quantities of wheat at the best prices possible, the government was able to provide it to the poor at a reasonable, fixed price despite market fluctuations. Gaius also had special storehouses built to house the grain. Of course, Gaius' bill also served to build up his own base of political support, and neither the senatorial class nor Gracchus himself would have been unaware of this.

Gaius' law on military recruitment (the *lex militaris*) provides an interesting insight into the continuing problems surrounding this issue. The law stipulated that a soldier's military clothing and equipment must be provided by the state, without any deduction from his pay; it also forbade the recruitment of any soldier under the age of seventeen. We can see from this law that the shortage of men available for the draft had not improved and that the Romans were apparently attempting to remedy the situation by drafting younger and poorer men. Gracchus' bill would certainly not reverse this trend, but it seems to have been an attempt to alleviate the situation.

Gaius also proposed to revive Tiberius' program of agrarian reform and to supplement it by establishing new colonies and building more roads. The details of Gaius' *lex agraria* are unclear, but he seems to have shifted the emphasis from distributing *ager publicus* in Italy (which had caused problems with the Italian allies) to founding new colonies on empty or abandoned sites both in Italy and abroad. Colonies were planned in Capua (which had been destroyed after the Hannibalic War), in Tuscany, and in the deserted areas of southern Italy (e.g., at Scyllacium and Tarentum).[26] These colonies were intended to alleviate the overcrowding in Rome, caused in part by the displaced peasants who had migrated there. The colonies also served to strengthen Rome's military control of these regions and boost economic development. To that end Gaius provided for roads to be built, which would provide the farmers with better access to markets and generally improve communication. Gaius also planned a Roman colony, with generous allotments (up to 100 *iugera*), on the former site of Carthage, despite Roman fears that this site was unlucky. This colony, called Junonia, would soon become the focus of considerable controversy.

The events of the year 122 B.C. are somewhat unclear. According to Plutarch (*C. Gracchus* 8.2), the people spontaneously elected Gaius to a second tribunate for that year, despite the fact that he was not an official candidate and had not sought the office. Although this scenario seems rather unlikely, it is possible that Gaius had not sought a second tribunate. He had ensured that one of his supporters, C. Fannius, would be elected consul; and his longtime ally Fulvius Flaccus had taken the unprecedented step of being elected to the tribunate after already having served as consul. Flaccus and Fannius would thus be in a good position to promote Gaius' legislative program. Moreover, Gaius was planning to spend a significant amount of time in North Africa, helping to establish the colony of Junonia, and tribunes were not allowed to be away from Rome for more than twenty-four hours without special permission. Thus Plutarch may have been at least partly right in stating that Gaius was reelected not because he sought the office but by popular acclaim. In any case, we should note that it was probably custom, not law, that had prevented previous tribunes from serving a second term. Gaius Gracchus' personal authority was far greater than his brother's and the force of his personality may simply have overridden the violent objections that had greeted his brother's attempt to seek a second tribunate.

Despite Gaius' reelection, however, it seems that by 122 B.C., his popularity had already begun to wane. Bad omens were reported to have occurred at the founding of Junonia, on the former site of Carthage. According to Plutarch (*C. Gracchus* 11.1), the standard at the head of the founding party was blown out of the standard-bearer's hands and ripped to pieces by the wind; the sacrifices were blown off the altars and scattered beyond the boundary markers of the colony, and the boundary markers themselves were torn up by wolves. It seems that Gaius' personal authority and prestige could not override the Romans' natural antipathy for the site of their former enemy. Gaius' enemies surely took note of this, but in 122 B.C. his support among the people was still so strong that he could not be attacked directly.

Meanwhile, Gaius put forward two important bills during his second year in office. At this time, provincial governors held almost absolute power within their provinces, but they were subject to a few restrictions. Among these was the rule, in force since 149 B.C., that if a governor extorted an excessive amount of money from his subjects—well beyond what was required for taxes and tribute—he could be tried for extortion (under the *quaestio de pecuniis repetundis* or extortion court) upon his return to Rome. In theory, the *quaestio de pecuniis repetundis* (literally, the "inquiry concerning money to be recovered") was an important safeguard against excessive rapacity and greed on the part of provincial governors. In practice, however, the *quaestio de repetundis* did not return a single conviction in the twenty-seven years from its inception in 149 B.C. down to 122 B.C., even when the illegal appropriations were considerable and quite well known.[27] One of the reasons for this failure was that the juries on the extortion court were composed solely of senators, senators who had either once served as provincial governors themselves or hoped one day to do so. These jurors could easily be persuaded to look the other way when considering extortion in return for receiving a similarly lenient treatment themselves. Gaius was determined to put an end to this situation of *manus manum lavat*. In his *lex de repetundis* of 122 B.C., Gaius stipulated that the juries for extortion trials would be drawn exclusively from those outside the senatorial class (i.e., the juries had to come from the *equites* or equestrian class).

The *equites* (literally, cavalrymen) or equestrian order had originally served as Rome's cavalry; they needed a high degree of wealth, as certified by the censors, to qualify for this rank; as members of this order, they played a leading role in the *comitia centuriata*. By the late Republic, however, Rome's cavalry was increasingly supplied by allied states, and the *equites Romani* came to denote a wealthy class of citizens who provided officers for the army and who were frequently involved in business and public contracts.[28] It was this group of well-to-do Roman citizens that Gaius tapped to be the jurors for the new *quaestio de repetundis*. The bill also raised the penalty from simple restitution to twice the amount of money that had been illegally taken. Successful prosecutors (usually men of prominence from the province that had been mistreated) were now granted citizenship or other privileges. Although it is clear that Gaius wanted to attract equestrian support with this bill, he also wanted to put an end to the rampant corruption that had characterized the *quaestio de repetundis*. And in this latter goal he seems to have been somewhat successful: after Gaius' law was enacted, about fifty percent of the *repetundae* cases resulted in a conviction.[29] The Senate (and particularly the inner circle of noble families who dominated it), however, regarded Gaius' judiciary legislation as a direct assault on its power. And the equestrians themselves, who previously had been focused mainly on pursuing their business interests, seem to have first gained political consciousness as a result of this bill.[30]

Gaius' final legislative proposal for 122 B.C. was a bill granting full citizenship to the Latin allies and limited voting privileges to the rest of the peoples of Italy. This moderate plan sought to fully assimilate only those allies already closely bound to Rome by ties of language and custom, but it also provided a sense of inclusion for the rest of the allies in Italy. Since 129 B.C. (when the allies had objected to relinquishing their *ager publicus* to Rome's urban poor), it had become increasingly clear that the Italian allies, who were subject to taxation and military recruitment, deserved a greater share in the rewards of the empire that they themselves were helping to build. The recent revolt of Fregellae might have been a warning of the sort of trouble that could result if the Romans were unwilling to be more inclusive in their policies. Nor could Rome continue to extend its power throughout the Mediterranean world without the solid support of Italian military manpower. Gaius' bill was a step toward resolving these issues. If the bill had become law in 122 B.C. it might have paved the way for the gradual absorption of the Italians into full citizenship.

But the Romans (who would later go to war to prevent their Italian allies from becoming citizens) were not yet willing to grant them even limited voting privileges in 122 B.C. Gaius refused to withdraw his bill, however; and by persisting with this unpopular proposal, he forfeited a great deal of the popular support he had always enjoyed. The consul Fannius, who had originally been one of Gaius' followers, was persuaded to attack the proposal in a powerful speech to the Roman people. In this speech, Fannius claimed that if the Latins were granted citizenship they would crowd out the ordinary citizens of Rome: "Do you think you will have a place at public meetings like the one you are now standing in? Do you think you will take part in games and festivals? Don't you realize that they will take over everything?"[31] We do not know whether Gaius' bill was abandoned or whether it was voted down by the plebs; but in any case, it did not become law.

Discussion Questions

1. Why did the Italian allies object to Tiberius' land reform bill and what was the result of their objection?
2. In what ways did Gaius' personality differ from that of his brother?
3. Discuss the provisions of C. Gracchus' *lex Sempronia de capite civium*. In what ways was it influenced by the events surrounding Tiberius Gracchus' death?
4. Could you argue that some of C. Gracchus' bills, such as the *lex frumentaria*, were primarily self-serving measures?
5. What sorts of fears was Fannius trying to arouse in his speech against Gaius' citizenship bill?
6. Why do you think that Gaius continued to persist with his unpopular proposals?

4. C. Sempronius Gracchus: Decline and Defeat

Although Gaius had easily won election to a second tribunate, his reputation had suffered from the bad omens connected with Junonia, the senators' resentment over jury reform, and the fiasco of his citizenship bill. At the same time, the Senate was finding new ways to erode Gaius' popularity. The senators authorized Livius Drusus, one of Gracchus' fellow tribunes, to upstage Gracchus' proposals with offers that were even more attractive to the plebs. For example, when Gaius proposed to found two colonies, Drusus proposed to establish twelve colonies, each with three thousand plots. While

Gaius' bill required his colonists to pay a small rent to the state, Drusus offered allotments rent free. Whereas Gaius offered citizenship to the Latin allies, Drusus offered them exemption from flogging even when serving in the army. There is no evidence that the Senate ever took any action on Drusus' bills, but his proposals did succeed in weakening Gracchus' support among the urban and rural poor.

While Gaius was away in Junonia, Livius Drusus also began to slander one of his most prominent followers, the tribune Fulvius Flaccus. Flaccus was apparently a wild and reckless character and a bit of a rabble-rouser, which made him an easy target. Drusus began to spread rumors that Flaccus was secretly inciting the Italian allies to revolt. These rumors were without foundation, as we learn from Plutarch (*C. Gracchus* 10.3–4), but Flaccus' reputation as a loose cannon made them sound plausible. And as the Romans' fear and suspicion of Flaccus increased, they began to project those feelings onto Gaius Gracchus.

By 121 B.C. there was an open attempt to repeal some parts of Gaius' legislation, particularly the bill establishing the colony of Junonia, which had always been unpopular. A public meeting was held in the Forum to discuss the repeal of this bill, and Gaius and Flaccus, now private citizens, were present, accompanied by a crowd of supporters. The mood was tense. According to Plutarch (*C. Gracchus* 13.3), Quintus Antyllius (one of the consuls' attendants) pushed his way through the crowd of Gaius' supporters and shouted out: "Make way for honest citizens, you riffraff." As he said this, he raised his naked arm in an insulting gesture. Gaius' supporters, already enraged at the attempt to disestablish Junonia, fell on Antyllius and stabbed him to death with their writing styluses. The mêlée that developed was fortunately interrupted by a sudden shower of rain, but the act of murder could not be undone. The next morning, the consul, Lucius Opimius, arranged for Antyllius' naked body to be paraded on a bier through the Forum, surrounded by grieving senators. A meeting of the Senate was called, and the senators formally voted that Opimius, as consul, should "see to it that the Republic take no harm." The formula of this decree is recorded by Cicero in his *First Catilinarian Oration* (1.4): *Decrevit . . . senatus uti L. Opimius consul videret ne quid res publica detrimenti caperet.*[32] This is the first use of this type of senatorial decree, later known as the *senatus consultum ultimum* or SCU,[33] which the Senate would use again and again in the late Republic as a means of imposing martial law in a time of emergency. Because the Senate's use of the SCU—and its ambiguous legal status—played an important role in the Catilinarian conspiracy, a few words should be said about it here.

The consul's power was ordinarily limited by a variety of legal restrictions, such as Gaius' own *lex de capite civium*, providing that no Roman citizen could be put to death without a trial before the Roman people. In a time of emergency, however, the consuls needed to take quick, decisive action, perhaps overstepping the legal boundaries, in order to avert a catastrophe. How could the Senate provide for strong leadership during a crisis while protecting the rights of citizens? The solution discovered by the senators in 121 B.C.— officially declaring an emergency and empowering the consul to use any means necessary to defend the state—proved to be so successful (at least from the Senate's point of view) that they were to resort to it ten more times during the crises of the late Republic.[34] Three of these uses of the SCU are particularly relevant to our topic: an SCU was passed against L. Saturninus and C. Glaucia in 100 B.C.; against M. Lepidus in 77 B.C.; and against Catiline in 63 B.C. The wording of the decree became somewhat formulaic, with the senators addressing those magistrates whom they wished to take action: *consules [praetores] viderent ne quid res publica detrimenti caperet*. But the Senate felt free to vary the wording, at least to some extent, to suit the occasion at hand.[35]

Because the *senatus consultum ultimum* was so broad in its wording, it was never clear exactly how far the magistrate was allowed to go in imposing martial law. Each time the SCU was used (particularly when it resulted in the deaths of prominent citizens) there was a strong public reaction after the event, directed against the magistrates who had been responsible. The Roman people wanted to know whether the state of emergency had been real and whether the degree of force and the extent of extralegal measures had been justified. The answers to these questions were not always satisfactory. Furthermore, it was not even clear whether the Senate had the legal authority to grant to the magistrates the extralegal powers implicit in the SCU. According to the (unwritten) Roman constitution, only the people had the authority to establish laws, through their regularly constituted voting assemblies (see Appendix A, on the Roman constitution). The Senate, despite its great influence and power, was only supposed to act as an advisory board to the magistrates. It was precisely because the SCU did not provide a clear basis for action that Cicero called for a debate in the Senate concerning the fate of the Catilinarian conspirators in 63 B.C. (he later published his own part in this debate as the *Fourth Catilinarian Oration*). The ambiguous results of that debate helped to provide the grounds for Cicero's banishment five years later.

In 121 B.C., however, this was all in the future: the Senate, in a state of panic after the murder of Antyllius, decreed that the consul Opimius should use any means necessary to reestablish order and ensure the safety of the Republic. By using this formula, the Senate was, in effect, authorizing the consul to override Gaius' own *lex de capite civium*. It is ironic (but not, perhaps, entirely accidental) that the very first use of the SCU was directed against Gaius himself.

Backed by the senatorial decree, Opimius ordered the senators and *equites*, along with their servants, to appear under arms in the Forum the next day.[36] Rome at that time had no police force, but Opimius was able to support his impromptu militia with a force of Cretan archers who happened to be available.[37] As the news of the senators' actions spread, C. Gracchus, along with Flaccus and a crowd of supporters, occupied the Aventine Hill (a place traditionally associated with the plebeians) and waited for dawn. When day broke, Flaccus sent his youngest son to the Forum to negotiate with the senators and *equites* who were assembled there; but Opimius sent him back to the Aventine with orders that Gaius and Flaccus should present themselves to be tried for the murder of Antyllius. Although Gaius was willing to do this, his supporters refused to allow it; so Flaccus sent his son back to the Forum once more. This time Opimius had the boy arrested and began to lead his forces against Gaius Gracchus and his supporters on the Aventine Hill.

After an initial struggle, the Cretan archers proved decisive, and Gaius' supporters fled. In the rout, Flaccus and his elder son were killed (his younger son, who had tried to arrange a truce, was killed after the battle). Gaius Gracchus either was killed while attempting to flee across the Tiber or he committed suicide. According to Plutarch (*C. Gracchus* 17.5), the bodies of Gaius, Flaccus, and hundreds of their supporters were thrown into the Tiber River. During the next few days Opimius held an inquiry (*quaestio*) of Gracchan sympathizers; a great many people were imprisoned and put to death, though any state of emergency had surely passed. According to Plutarch, by the time the affair was over, three thousand of Gracchus' followers had been killed.

A few months later, Opimius was brought to trial on the charge that he had executed Roman citizens without a trial before the people, although his use of armed men against unarmed civilians was also an underlying issue.

Opimius successfully defended himself, however, by stating that he had acted "for the sake of the Republic after he had called the citizens to arms on the authority of a decree of the Senate."[38] This argument shows that Opimius specifically invoked the authority of the SCU in justifying his actions. The fact that Opimius was acquitted in this case gave strength to subsequent uses of this decree and allowed it to develop into a quasi-institution, though it was never formally granted any legal status and continued to be quite controversial.

Discussion Questions

1. Why were Livius Drusus' proposals so popular?
2. Why did the consul L. Opimius make such a public display of mourning over the death of Q. Antyllius, who was only an attendant?
3. What were the characteristics of the SCU that made it so controversial?
4. In your opinion, what was the main cause of C. Gracchus' decline in popularity and defeat?

5. Marius and Saturninus

In the decade following the assassination of Gaius Gracchus and his followers, the senatorial aristocracy ruled without serious opposition, although much of Gaius Gracchus' legislation was retained.[39] Meanwhile, one of the problems that both of the Gracchi brothers had failed to ameliorate—the shortage of men for the military—was finally solved by a newcomer, Gaius Marius. In 111 B.C. the Romans declared war against Jugurtha, the renegade king of Numidia, who had driven his brother out of the country and had massacred scores of Italian residents in the process (see Map 4). The war against Jugurtha dragged on for three years with only limited success, due in part to senatorial corruption (Sallust, *BJ* 15–16 *et passim*), but also due to a lack of training and discipline among the troops and an acute military shortage. In 108 B.C. Gaius Marius, a deputy-general serving in Numidia, was elected to the consulship for 107 B.C. based on his promise of a quick and successful conclusion to the war.

Because no one from Marius' family had ever been a consul before, Marius was considered an outsider or new man (*novus homo*). The term *novus homo* is used by different authors in different ways, so it is worthwhile to take some time to explain it. The Romans seemed to have used the term *novus homo* in both a narrow and a broader sense. In its strictest sense, a *novus homo* was a man from a nonsenatorial family (i.e., an equestrian family that had not yet produced a senator) who was not only the first person in his family to become a senator but was further elected to the office of consul. Once a Roman attained the consulship, his descendants were no longer considered outsiders but were members of the *nobilitas*, the ruling inner circle.[40] The term *novus homo* also seems to have been used in a broader sense, however, to refer to someone who was simply the first man in his family to become a senator. It was not unusual for an equestrian to become a new man in this broader sense, but the advancement of an equestrian all the way to the consulship (i.e., a new man in the strict sense) was extremely rare.

The Roman nobility (*nobilitas*) used all of its wealth and influence to try to prevent *novi homines* from being elected consul. As Sallust states (*BJ* 63.6–7): "The *nobilitas* handed down the consulship from hand to hand amongst themselves. No matter how famous a new man was through his own outstanding deeds, he was still considered unworthy of that office and almost unclean." Cicero concurs: "[T]he nobility held the consulship strengthened by a garrison and fortified in every way" against the incursions of new men (*De lege agraria* 2.3). According to M. Gelzer (1969: 50–52), in the 303 years from 366 B.C. (the first year that plebeians were eligible for the consulship) to 63 B.C. (the year of Cicero's consulship), only fifteen new men served as consul. Cicero, who in 63 B.C. became the first *novus homo* to be elected consul in over thirty years, did not hesitate to speak publicly about the extraordinary nature of his achievement.[41]

Because it was so unusual for a *novus homo* to attain the consulship, Marius' election indicates just how frustrated the Romans had become over the lack of progress in the war against Jugurtha. As soon as he was elected, Marius addressed the military crisis by abolishing the minimum property qualification required for military service. The property qualification had already been lowered so that farmers owning even a small amount of land could qualify. Furthermore, those landless men who did not meet the property qualification, the *proletarii*, had been recruited into military service during periods of crisis. But Marius made a significant change by abolishing the property qualification altogether and opening up the legions to *proletarii* on a grand scale. With this one move, Marius cut the Gordian knot of the military recruitment problem: hundreds of new volunteers flocked to the legions, which from then on were composed of an increasingly large proportion of men without property. But Marius' reforms had serious consequences that he could not have foreseen. The soldiers, who were now volunteering in large numbers, were motivated to enlist by the wages they would receive while serving in the army and by the prospect of an allotment of land after they retired. Because the Senate never regularized the process of land grants to veterans, preferring to leave this responsibility to the individual generals, the soldiers became increasingly attached to their commanders as the main source of their economic stability. This situation tended to undermine the soldiers' loyalty to the Senate and the Roman people, as Sulla's actions in 87 B.C. soon made clear (see Historical Essay I.7 below). But Marius himself could not have foreseen this turn of events when he signed up large numbers of *proletarii* in 107 B.C. to fight against Jugurtha.

Marius brought his newly enlisted troops to Africa and put them through a rigorous training. Within two years (105 B.C.) he had defeated Jugurtha's forces, and, thanks to the high-stakes negotiations of his quaestor, Cornelius Sulla, he had captured the wily king himself and had him brought to Rome in chains (Sallust *BJ* 102–13). While Marius was finding great success in Africa, however, the Romans had turned their attention to a new and more dangerous military threat. The Cimbri and Teutones, two Germanic tribes driven from their homes in northern Germany and southern Denmark, were moving into southern Gaul and northern Italy. In October of 105 B.C. (shortly after Marius' defeat of Jugurtha), a combined force of Cimbri and Teutones defeated two Roman armies near Arausio in southern Gaul (modern Orange; see Map 4). This was a disastrous defeat for the Romans; estimates of Roman casualties run as high as 80,000. The road to Italy now stood open to the foreign invaders.

In a panic, the Roman people turned to a proven and incorruptible general, electing Marius to five successive consulships (for the years 104, 103, 102, 101, and 100 B.C.), despite the fact that a ten year interval was supposed to be required between successive consulships.[42] While the Germanic tribes turned their attention elsewhere for the next few years, Marius used the time to recruit and train another proletarian army. He introduced several tactical reforms, so that the legions became better armed, better trained, and easier to maneuver in battle. He also introduced a new legionary standard, the silver eagle, to enhance the soldiers' pride in their legions.

In 102 B.C. the Teutones and the Cimbri, joined by a related tribe, the Tigurini, made a coordinated attack against Rome. Marius engaged the Teutones near Aquae Sextiae (modern Aix; see Map 4), using Hannibal-style tactics to lure the enemy into a narrow valley and surround them. The rout was complete, and 300,000 Teutones were killed or captured. The next year (101 B.C.)

Marius also handed a crushing defeat to the Cimbri at Vercellae (just north of the Po River; see Map 3) while the Tigurini retreated to their homes in Switzerland. Thus by 101 B.C. the serious threat of invasion from the north had been averted. Marius had saved the state and was hailed as the third founder of Rome, after Romulus and Camillus.[43]

In 100 B.C., with the wars against the Germanic invaders concluded, Marius asked L. Appuleius Saturninus, a tribune of the plebs in the Gracchan mold, to help provide land for his veterans. Although the stories of Saturninus' resentment against the nobility are probably exaggerated, it is clear that Saturninus had a rougher, more confrontational style than either of the Gracchi. During his first tribunate in 103 B.C., Saturninus had carried a bill granting land allotments of 100 *iugera* in north Africa to Marius' veterans from the Jugurthine War. The passage of this bill had been marked by violence: when one of the other tribunes attempted to veto the bill, Saturninus' men drove him away with a shower of stones, and the bill was passed.

Now in his second tribunate (100 B.C.), Saturninus proposed a bill granting land in southern Gaul to Marius' veterans of the recent wars against the Cimbri and Teutones; another bill provided for veterans' colonies in Sicily, Achaea, and Macedonia. Land in these colonies was to be granted not only to those veterans who were Roman citizens but also to the Latins and Italians, who had provided the bulk of the soldiers for Marius' army. These allies who had fought for Rome certainly deserved the land grants, but this idea did not sit well with Rome's urban plebs, who had previously been Saturninus' allies. When Saturninus proposed his bill at the Plebeian Council, some of the plebeians tried to break up the meeting on the grounds that thunder had been heard. Public business could not be conducted in the presence of evil omens, but the presiding magistrate was responsible for deciding whether to recognize reports of such omens. On this occasion Saturninus ignored the reports of thunder and proceeded with the voting.[44] The urban plebs then attempted to block the bill by force, using broken chairs and wooden clubs to drive its supporters away. Marius' veterans, who had been brought into the Forum by Saturninus, overpowered the Roman mob. In this way, the bill was passed, although not without violence on both sides.

But Saturninus also had to deal with senatorial opposition to his bill providing land for Marius' veterans. To counter this opposition, Saturninus had included a provision in the bill requiring each senator to swear an oath of obedience to its provisions within five days of its passage by the Plebeian Council, on pain of expulsion from the Senate. The senators were not amused.

The consul C. Marius, who was Saturninus' ally and the beneficiary of his bill, must have felt torn; how could he condone this attempt to hijack the Senate's power? In the end, the consul found a clever compromise: he advised the senators to swear the oath with the proviso that it would only be in force if the bill itself were found to be legal. At the same time Marius assured them that the bill could not possibly be valid, because it had been carried by force and in the presence of bad omens. All the senators agreed to Marius' compromise and swore the oath, with the exception of Metellus Numidicus (Marius' personal enemy), who withdrew into exile. Thus Saturninus, having outsmarted both the Senate and the urban plebs, succeeded in having his land bill passed into law. But Saturninus' brazen attempt to manipulate the Senate only increased its hostility to him.

During the consular elections that year (100 B.C.), Servilius Glaucia, one of Saturninus' allies, had presented himself as a candidate for the consulship, even though, as a current praetor, he was barred from seeking the consulship for at least two years.[45] On election day Glaucia's candidacy was rejected. A brawl ensued, during which one of the other candidates, C. Memmius, was clubbed to death by a mob of Saturninus' men (see Cicero, *Cat.* 4.4). The voting assembly broke up in confusion. The next day a crowd assembled to attack Glaucia and Saturninus; but these men, along with their supporters, had already seized the Capitoline Hill. Meanwhile, the Senate, for the second time in its history, passed the *senatus consultum ultimum*, requesting the consuls to defend the Republic. Marius was once again caught in a conflict of loyalties: Saturninus was Marius' political ally, but he was also fomenting violence. Marius armed the citizens in accordance with the SCU, formed a militia, and besieged Saturninus and his allies on the Capitoline Hill. After the water supply to the Capitol was cut off, the besieged party surrendered, hoping for leniency from Marius. Marius accepted their surrender and shut them up in the Senate house, intending to take legal action against them. But the angry crowd demanded immediate action; it surged forward. Many of the men climbed onto the Senate house, tore off the roof, and stoned the captives to death with roof tiles. Saturninus and Glaucia, along with several other prominent Romans, were among the dead. There was no judicial inquiry into the events surrounding the deaths of these men, even though the crowd had taken matters into its own hands, killing Saturninus and Glaucia against the wishes of the consul.

Thirty-seven years later (in 63 B.C.), Julius Caesar would charge a man named C. Rabirius with treason for his role in these events, as a way to challenge the legitimacy of the SCU (see Historical Essay II.3). Meanwhile, the legal status of Saturninus' land bill for Marius' veterans remained unclear. It was never formally repealed, but some of its provisions were never enacted. Numismatic evidence suggests, however, that at least some of the veterans' colonies in Cisalpine Gaul were actually founded. Marius, who seems to have alienated both sides in this affair, retired to Asia and temporary obscurity.

Looking back over the years from 133 to 100 B.C., we can see several emerging trends. Perhaps the most important of these is the growing realization by the tribunes that they could challenge the traditional leadership and dominance of the Senate. The Gracchi brothers and Saturninus—each more stridently than the last—used the power of tribunate to pass legislation and provide benefits for the poor while building up a power base for themselves. The Senate reacted against this challenge with more violence than strategy; as a result, violence was more and more frequently used to resolve political conflict. By the time of Saturninus (100 B.C.), the urban plebs, the Italian allies, and even senators and veterans had all contributed to this alarming trend.

Marius' admission of the proletariat into the army solved the recruitment problem but caused a new and perhaps more serious difficulty: individual generals were now responsible for finding land for their veterans. As a result, the soldiers began to feel a special allegiance to their commanders. The generals' constant need for land increased the tension between the urban poor and the Italian allies, an animosity that soon exploded into war.

Discussion Questions

1. What is a *novus homo*? What does the existence of such a term tell you about electoral politics at Rome?
2. Looking ahead, what are some possible effects of Marius' solution to the military recruitment problem?
3. What are the pros and cons of the SCU? Was it a necessary tool for keeping order in a state that lacked a police force? Was it an unnecessary infringement on the Romans' civil rights?

6. The Italian or Social War

The Senate dominated the political scene throughout the next decade, but the Italians continued their push for citizenship.[46] Every year the allies supplied the Roman legions with both infantry and cavalry, and yet they could not enjoy citizenship rights in the state whose fortunes they were helping to build. The contentiousness of this issue in Roman politics can be seen in the *lex Licinia Mucia* of 95 B.C., providing for the expulsion from the city of any Italians whose claims to Roman citizenship were determined to be invalid. The Italians, of course, were incensed by the bill. According to Asconius (67–68), this law was "perhaps the greatest cause of the Italian War."

As a result of the mounting tensions, M. Livius Drusus, one of the tribunes for 91 B.C. (and the son of Gaius Gracchus' nemesis of the same name), proposed a bill granting Roman citizenship to the Italian allies so that they could be, in Appian's words (1.35), "co-rulers instead of subjects." The bill was not well received at Rome, and Drusus was assassinated before it could be voted on. Drusus' death made it clear to the allies that the Romans were not ready to grant them the citizenship they desired; toward the end of that year a group of Italian states withdrew from their alliance with Rome and declared war on their former ally. They named their new federation Italia and minted their own coins, including one that showed the Italian bull (*vitulus*) goring the Roman wolf. The revolt soon spread to central and southern Italy, and it came to be called the Italian or the Social War (from the Latin word *socius*, meaning "ally").

The Romans were very powerful, of course, even without the Italians; in addition to their own citizen-soldiers, they could also rely on those allies who did remain loyal (particularly the Latins, who had always held a privileged position) and their foreign allies, such as Numidia, Spain, Sicily, and Cisalpine Gaul. But the Italians, too, possessed great military resources. The Italian cavalry and infantry, whose military skill and tactical expertise had previously been placed in the service of Rome, were now arrayed against their former ally. During the first year of the war, the Romans lost battle after battle. A series of Roman losses in the north was partially reversed by Marius, who came back on the scene and won battles against the Marsi and Marrucini. In the south, however, the rebels won important victories around the Bay of Naples. By 90 B.C. it became clear to the Romans that they could not win on military terms alone; they also realized that it was pointless to continue a war against men who would really rather be their allies. The *lex Julia* was passed in late 90 B.C., granting full Roman citizenship to all Italian communities that had remained loyal. The *lex Plautia Papiria* was passed a few months later (early in 89 B.C.), granting citizenship to those cities and individuals who had rebelled but who were willing to lay down their arms within a reasonable period of time.

Having gained the chief object for which they were fighting, the rebellious allies began to rejoin the fold, and the rebellion began to lose steam. It was now clear that the Romans would eventually prevail. L. Cornelius Sulla, who had first gained fame in the Jugurthine War by engineering the capture of the Numidian king, won significant victories in Campania against the Samnites and recaptured the cities around the Bay of Naples. By 89 B.C. the war was essentially over, although a few rebellious tribes, such as the Samnites and Lucanians, remained in Campania and southern Italy.[47] Sulla left his army, which was stationed in Campania, and traveled to Rome, where he was elected consul for the following year.

In retrospect it is clear that the Italian War was an unnecessary conflict.[48] Rome could not win the war without granting the allies what they wanted, while the allies should not have had to fight for the rights and privileges that they had clearly earned. The war was particularly devastating because, with no clear boundaries between Roman and Italian territories, neighbor had been fighting against neighbor on land that was common to all. Aside from the senseless loss of life and destruction of territory, the Italian War had estranged Rome from its natural allies in Italy—allies that Rome would need if it wanted to expand its empire. The war also gave Mithridates VI the opportunity to initiate a revolt.

7. Marius, Cinna, and Sulla

In 89 B.C. Mithridates VI, the dynamic king of Pontus (see Map 4), had taken advantage of Rome's preoccupation with the Italian War to invade neighboring Bithynia (ousting King Nicomedes, a Roman client). Then, turning south, he had taken over the Roman province of Asia, winning over the loyalty of Asian towns by promising them a five-year relief from taxation. After taking control of the Roman province of Asia, Mithridates ordered the local leaders (many of whom were Greek) to kill all Roman and Italian residents (mainly businessmen) along with their wives and children and to leave their corpses unburied. As many as 80,000 Romans and Italians were said to have been killed in the massacre that followed. The enthusiasm with which Mithridates' orders were carried out is a striking indication of how strongly Roman rule was resented, although the Asians' fear of Mithridates was probably also a contributing factor.

Now that Rome was free from the distraction of the Social War, it was free to take action against this dangerous foe. When Sulla became consul in 88

B.C., the Senate granted him the command against Mithridates and authorized him to pick up the army he had left at Campania (this was the army
that he had commanded during the Social War) and take these troops to
Asia. But Marius, too, was eager for the wealth and glory that the campaign
against Mithridates seemed likely to provide. The rivalry between Marius
and Sulla had been growing since Sulla had negotiated the capture of
Jugurtha in 105 B.C., and Marius did not want to see his former lieutenant
take this plum assignment.[49] Sulpicius Rufus, one of the tribunes for that
year, put forward a series of bills that, among other measures, would trans-
fer the command against Mithridates from Sulla to Marius. In supporting
Marius against Sulla, Sulpicius also reawakened the struggle between the
Senate and the tribunes over the conduct of foreign affairs. The Senate, seeing
Sulpicius' bill as a challenge to its authority, tried to prevent the Plebeian
Council from voting on it by having the consuls proclaim a *iustitium* (a sus-
pension of public business), traditionally used only in moments of great crisis.
In response, Sulpicius (the tribune) surrounded himself with a bodyguard
and led a mob of armed supporters into the Forum demanding that the *iustitium*
be lifted. When the consuls refused, a violent fight broke out, during which
several prominent Romans were killed. Realizing that his life was in danger,
Sulla (the consul) fled to the nearest house he could find. The nearest house
happened to be that of his archrival Marius, which was conveniently located
right next to the Forum. Marius was now in the unusual position of having
complete power over a man who had become his personal enemy. After a
hasty meeting, Marius agreed to shield Sulla from the crowd, on the condition that he would lift the *iustitium* and allow Sulpicius' measures to be
voted into law. Thus Sulla would be allowed to keep his consulship (and his
life), but the command against Mithridates would be transferred to Marius.

Sulpicius' bill was duly passed, but Sulla did not allow the law to stand in
his way. Although the six legions in Campania had been legally transferred
to Marius' command, they had served under Sulla in the Social War; he
could still depend on their personal allegiance to him as their paymaster and
general. He quickly joined them in Campania and, after explaining how he
had been tricked out of a command that was rightfully his, invited them to
follow him to Rome. His soldiers responded enthusiastically (except for the
senior officers, who withdrew) and thus—for the first time in history (though
by no means the last)—a Roman general, leading Roman troops, marched
against the city of Rome.[50] Sulla's soldiers supported him partly because of
his personal charm, and partly because the command had been taken away

from him unjustly, but also because, thanks to Marius' army reforms, they now depended on Sulla not only for their pay and a share in the spoils of war, but also for land grants after their service was over. Thus the unwelcome consequences of Marius' army reforms were felt for the first time by Marius himself.

As Sulla and his forces entered the city, the Roman people offered a fierce resistance. They climbed onto the roof-tops and showered Sulla's soldiers with stones and roof tiles, slowing down their progress. But Sulla ordered his men to set fire to the houses, and they pressed on. Marius and Sulpicius met Sulla's army on the Esquiline Hill with a small, hastily armed force, and thus ensued the first battle between armed combatants in the city of Rome.[51] But the citizen militia was no match for Sulla's troops; in the end, Marius and Sulpicius were forced to flee. With Sulla's troops stationed throughout the city, a cowed Senate declared Marius and Sulpicius public enemies. (Sulla had no intention of repeating Marius' mistake of protecting his rival.) Sulpicius was caught and killed, while Marius narrowly escaped and fled to Africa, where many of his former soldiers were now settled. Over the next few weeks Marius was joined in Africa by many of his partisans who had fled from Rome.

Sulla, now in control of Rome, passed several emergency measures designed to strengthen the Senate and confirm its supremacy over the other institutions of the state. As an optimate, Sulla sought to reverse the encroachments against the Senate's authority that had been made by the Gracchi and the other *popularis* politicians who had succeeded them. Sulla also reinstated his own command against Mithridates. Then, after overseeing the consular elections and forcing the new consuls to swear an oath of loyalty to the current political arrangement, he gathered up his legions and set off against Mithridates, who by this time (87 B.C.) had taken control of Athens and most of central and southern Greece as well.

But Sulla's march on Rome had forever altered the political landscape, and his rivals could not be prevented from following his example. As soon as Sulla had gone, one of the consuls, L. Cornelius Cinna, reneged on his oath to Sulla and (against the wishes of the other consul, Cn. Octavius) reintroduced Sulpicius' legislation. A riot ensued; Cinna, forced to flee from Rome, traveled through Latium and Campania, gathering military forces for a march on Rome. As he marched with his soldiers back to the city, Cinna joined forces with Marius, who had recruited an army from his own *clientelae*, including his veterans from Africa, newly enfranchised citizens from the Italian countryside, and slaves recruited from *latifundia*.

This second march on Rome was accompanied by the wholesale murder of leading members of the senatorial class. Marius and Cinna allowed their soldiers to go on a rampage for weeks, killing and pillaging without restraint. Marius and Cinna were then declared consuls for 86 B.C.; but Marius (now seventy-one years old), died soon afterward, after serving only a few days of his seventh consulship. Sulla's march on Rome had now been matched by an even more vicious attack from the opposite camp.[52]

During the next three years (86–84 B.C.), Rome remained relatively calm. Cinna reappointed himself consul each year and selected his own colleague, but (despite this undemocratic means of acquiring the consulship) he seems to have governed with moderation and restraint. Many leading Romans must have felt ambivalent about the current state of affairs: they probably resented Cinna's virtual dictatorship but were glad for the calm after two successive military attacks against Rome. Some of Sulla's fellow optimates, such as M. Crassus, chose to leave the city; others, such as Gnaeus Pompey, decided to stay. But the calm could only be a temporary one: Sulla, though officially declared an outlaw, was now in the East, commanding a Roman army against Mithridates. Sooner or later he would reappear at Rome to challenge the legitimacy of Cinna's rule.

Discussion Question

The essay says that "Sulla's march on Rome had forever altered the political landscape." Explain the meaning of this statement and state whether or not you agree with it. Give evidence to support your conclusion.

8. L. Cornelius Sulla Felix

When Sulla left Rome in 87 B.C., he went directly to Greece, which had gone over to Mithridates. After a series of successful battles against Mithridates' forces in Greece (86 B.C.), Sulla marched up through Macedonia and crossed the Dardanelles into Asia, driving Mithridates out of that Roman province. Instead of pursuing Mithridates further, however, Sulla made a generous peace treaty with the rebellious king. Mithridates had to withdraw to the borders of Pontus and pay a fine, but he would be recognized by Rome as the king of Pontus. Sulla wanted to make a quick end to the war with Mithridates in order to focus all his energies on making a return to Rome.

After concluding his peace treaty with Mithridates, Sulla landed at Brundisium (see Map 3) in 83 B.C., along with the legions he had led against Mithridates. Prominent Romans (including M. Licinius Crassus and a young Gnaeus Pompey) now flocked to his camp, bringing with them additional forces raised through their own wealth and influence. The consuls also raised a large force to attack the invading general (perhaps as many as 100,000 men), but these troops were relatively untrained and generally unwilling to fight against their fellow citizens.[53]

Sulla marched unopposed as far as Campania (see Map 3), where he encountered two government armies. The first of these was badly beaten, and the second defected to Sulla, after peace negotiations had broken down.[54] When fighting continued in the spring of 82 B.C., Sulla marched along the Via Latina toward Praeneste and surrounded the city, trapping Marius' son (who was one of the consuls) inside. Crassus and Pompey, now in northern Italy, marched south toward Rome along the Via Flaminia. With Sulla's armies closing in on Rome and government soldiers continuing to desert, the second consul, Gnaeus Papirius Carbo, lost his nerve and fled from Italy.

Sulla then marched north from Praeneste to Rome, and the Battle of the Colline Gate (at the southern entrance to the city) became the decisive battle of this war. In this battle, which continued through the night, the government army (largely composed of Samnites) made a valiant effort to defeat the invading forces; they succeeded in forcing Sulla's soldiers, stationed on the left wing, to retreat.[55] Sulla would have lost the battle if Crassus' soldiers had not been victorious on the right flank and then come to Sulla's rescue. Almost all the Samnite warriors died on the battlefield. The next day, those Samnites who had survived were butchered in the Circus Flaminius by Sulla's forces, along with several thousand other captives. The senators, meeting with Sulla in the nearby Temple of Bellona (see Map 2), could hear the victims' anguished cries. Sulla calmly told the senators to listen to what he was saying and to ignore the noise outside, for it was only some criminals who were being punished by his orders.[56] After establishing his control of Rome, Sulla returned to Praeneste to force the surrender of that city. The younger Marius was either killed or committed suicide. Sulla, who had always held an almost mystical belief in his own good fortune (hence his nickname, Felix), must have felt that Fortuna was certainly smiling on him now.

Sulla now began to take revenge against his enemies on a scale that dwarfed the reprisals of Marius and Cinna. After the indiscriminate killing had provoked protests even from his supporters, Sulla began to organize his murders in a process known as "the proscriptions." Under the proscriptions, the names of those men whom Sulla wished to eliminate would be "written up" (from the Latin *proscribere*) and posted in the Forum. The men thus proscribed were now officially branded as enemies of the state: they could be hunted down and killed with impunity, and a reward would be granted to their executioners. Furthermore, a penalty would be imposed on anyone who tried to shelter them. The rewards were taken from the victims' estates, which, of course, were confiscated by the government. Not only were Sulla's political enemies eliminated by this method, but Sulla's followers pursued private vendettas as well. Lucius Sergius Catilina, for example, tortured and killed Marius Gratidianus (a nephew of the elder Marius) because of a personal grudge (see Historical Essay II.1). Eventually men were targeted simply because of their wealth, and the proscriptions became a source of enrichment for Sulla and his friends. Estimates vary as to the number of senators and *equites* who were proscribed, but the total was very likely more than 2,000.[57]

After he had pacified Rome, Sulla took vengeance on those areas of Italy that had opposed him, especially Etruria and northern Italy. Sulla drove out the inhabitants and used the land to settle his veterans. According to some accounts, as many as twenty-three legions were settled in these areas. These settlements later became a destabilizing factor in Roman society. Not all of the veterans made good farmers; some of them quickly fell into debt, while others sold their land. Furthermore, the original inhabitants who had been driven from their land, many of whom remained in the area as tenants or laborers, continued to be a source of discontent.

Once he had settled scores with his enemies and rewarded his friends, Sulla arranged to have himself appointed dictator for the purpose of restoring order and reorganizing the state. This office was to last for an unspecified length of time and would have unlimited powers: "Any measure he might take was ratified in advance; whether or not he submitted his proposals to the people for formal validation was entirely up to him. In particular he was to have the right to condemn citizens to death without trial."[58] With his power legally established, Sulla passed a series of reforms aimed at bringing the Senate back to the position of dominance it had held before the Gracchi had begun to challenge it. As an optimate, Sulla seems to have genuinely believed that, if the Senate were restored to its former position of preeminence, the Republic's problems would be solved. Sulla began by building up the Senate (which had been depleted through the proscriptions) to its normal strength of about three hundred; he then doubled its membership to about six hundred, nominating suitable (i.e., pro-Sullan) members of the equestrian class. Sulla moved to vitiate the tribunate, which, since the Gracchi, had become a powerful platform for political leadership. Tribunes were no longer allowed to introduce legislation and were deprived of the right to hold any higher office.[59] With the first measure Sulla rendered the tribunate harmless, and with the second he made it undesirable. In the words of Velleius Paterculus (2.30.4), Sulla left the tribunate an image without substance: *imaginem sine re*. Sulla also reversed other *popularis* legislation: juries were now to be composed entirely of senators, and the monthly subsidized distributions of wheat to the poor were discontinued. Finally, Sulla moved to prevent another general from using his legions to wield undue power: henceforth a provincial governor could not leave his province or take his army outside its boundaries. With these measures, Sulla did his best to try to prevent another Sulla.

To his credit, Sulla was aware that the Republic had been experiencing great upheavals during the past fifty years, and he made a genuine attempt to ameliorate the situation. But Sulla did not understand that Rome's economic and social problems could not be solved by political reorganization alone. Moreover, Sulla's insistence on giving the Senate disproportionate powers made his political solution unpopular in post-Gracchan Rome. The Roman people, through their tribunes, demanded a greater share of power; whether they would use that power well is, of course, another question. Within twelve years all of Sulla's measures had been reversed, with the exception of some practical, administrative reforms.[60]

Sulla himself faded from the scene far more quickly than anyone could have imagined. He resigned his dictatorship at the end of 81 B.C. and held one of the two consulships for 80 B.C. The fact that Sulla held the regularly constituted office of consul was probably meant to be a signal that the governmental crisis was over and that life could now return to normal. At the end of his year as consul, Sulla retired to his villa in Campania; but two years later he was dead, probably from a massive hemorrhage.[61] The lurid tale found in Plutarch, that Sulla died from the spontaneous eruption of worms from inside his body, is probably a fiction, resulting from a general desire for some kind of justice to be visited upon him.[62]

Discussion Questions

1. Sulla's march on Rome in 82 B.C. was not the first time a Roman general had attacked his own city, but in some ways it was precedent-setting. How would you say that this march on Rome differed from the two previous ones?
2. What were the proscriptions? What were some of their immediate effects? What kind of long-term effects do you think they were likely to have?
3. Why did Sulla need to provide land for his veterans? Why did he choose some areas in Etruria to settle his veterans in? What does it mean to refer to these settlements as a "destabilizing factor in Roman society"?
4. What were some of Sulla's political reforms? What do you think may have motivated him to establish such reforms?

9. Postscript:
Lepidus, Sertorius, and Spartacus

The events of the half-century from the Gracchi to Sulla have amply illustrated the nexus of problems that were threatening the Roman social fabric, as well as the range of attempts—all, unfortunately, inadequate—to solve them.[63] The Gracchi tried to solve the agrarian crisis through a series of measures promoting land reform, grain subsidies to the poor, the building of new roads, and the founding of new colonies both in Italy and abroad. While these measures certainly had a substantial positive effect, they also served to increase the power of Gracchi themselves, precipitating a protracted struggle between the Senate and a series of *popularis* tribunes. Both the SCU and Sulla's attempt to weaken the tribunate emerged as by-products of that struggle. The military crisis was finally solved by Marius, who opened up military service to the proletariat. This action, however, led to the formation of client armies whose welfare (and therefore allegiance) became closely linked to their generals. Sulla's first march on Rome in 88 B.C. and the subsequent marches by Cinna and Marius in 87, and by Sulla again in 82, were a direct (though unintended) result of Marius' reforms. Sulla's successful takeover of the government was, in turn, clearly a model for Catiline. Through it all, Romans became inured to the use of mob violence and assassination as a normal part of the political process. And the level of political violence continued to rise.

While it would be useful to narrate a connected history of the 70s B.C., that task is far outside the present topic. But a brief mention should be made of three revolts against Roman authority that occurred during the decade, because they do shed light on some aspects of the widespread discontent that helped to spark the Catilinarian conspiracy.

M. Aemilius Lepidus

Lepidus was a member of the Roman *nobilitas* and the father of the future member of the Second Triumvirate. He had served as one of Sulla's officers and had made significant profits through that association. He was elected consul for 78 B.C., however, on a platform that was openly hostile to Sulla's constitution. Sulla did not conceal his displeasure at Lepidus' candidacy but presented no serious opposition. Soon after Sulla's death, Lepidus brought forward a series of anti-Sullan proposals, which included the resumption of the sale of cheap grain to the poor and the restitution of land to the dispossessed Italians in Etruria. Lepidus also proposed (either at this time or a little later) that the tribunate be restored to its former powers, a measure that would surely be popular with the masses.

At Faesulae in Etruria some of the dispossessed Italians, perhaps anticipating the success of Lepidus' proposals to reinstate them, attacked the Sullan settlers and drove them from their allotments. Sulla's veterans had not forgotten how to use their weapons, however, and a small battle ensued, in which several men were killed. Both consuls were sent north to Faesulae with troops to prevent the spread of violence; but in Lepidus' case, this assignment was rather like asking the fox to guard the hen house. Lepidus made common cause with the rebels and proceeded to enlist them as soldiers into his own, private army. When the nervous Senate finally summoned the renegade general home in 77 B.C., Lepidus marched on Rome at the head of his army. The Senate immediately passed the SCU and raised its own army, under the direction of the proconsul, Q. Lutatius Catulus. Sulla's veterans gladly enlisted to fight against those who had taken their land. As Lepidus marched south to Rome on the Via Flaminia, he was defeated by Catulus and his army on the Mulvian Bridge, just north of the city (see Map 3).[64] Lepidus escaped to Sardinia with some of his soldiers, although he soon fell ill and died. After Lepidus' death, the remains of his army (under the direction of his general, M. Perperna) joined the forces of Sertorius in Spain.

Though not significant in itself, Lepidus' rebellion was an important precedent for Catiline's revolt. Using Sulla's coup as a model, Lepidus tried to ride the wave of discontent that was spreading through northern Italy, where so many peasants had been expelled from their land. The Senate, perhaps still stunned by Sulla's depredations, had reacted quite lamely, although Lepidus was finally defeated. As Stockton notes (1971: 16): "Lepidus was beaten, but nothing had been cured. Etruria was to provide the main strength of Catiline's following in 63, and the discontents of Rome and Italy were to prove highly combustible fuel."

Quintus Sertorius

Q. Sertorius was an equestrian who had served under Marius in the Cimbric and Italian Wars. He participated in Marius and Cinna's march on Rome in 87 B.C. and probably served as a praetor two years later. During Sulla's march on Rome in 82 B.C., Sertorius was sent to Spain to hold the peninsula against Sulla's forces. After Sulla had successfully established his power in Rome, he proscribed Sertorius; and in 81 he sent his general, C. Annius Luscus, with two legions to recapture the province. Defeated in battle, Sertorius fled south with a few loyal followers to Mauritania in North Africa (see Plutarch *Sertorius* 7). The following year Sertorius and his men were invited back to Spain by the native Lusitanians to lead them in a revolt against Rome.

For most of the decade (80–72) Sertorius governed the Spaniards as an independent ruler. He organized the native Lusitanians and Celtiberians into a powerful fighting force that remained undefeated in any general engagement. He made treaties with Mithridates and the Cilician pirates like a Hellenistic king and (probably after Perperna's arrival) formed a senate on the Roman model, with three hundred senators chosen from his Roman followers. He also established a school for the sons of the Spanish chieftains, where they were educated in Latin. In 77 B.C. M. Perperna, Lepidus' erstwhile general, joined Sertorius' forces, bringing with him some 20,000 infantry and 1,500 cavalry. The Senate was frightened and began to think of Sertorius as a second Hannibal, threatening to cross over the Alps and march on Rome. In late 77 the Senate sent the young Gnaeus Pompey to Spain, along with heavy reinforcements, to support Metellus Pius, who was then commanding the forces against Sertorius.

Throughout the next few years of fighting, Sertorius remained undefeated, although his lieutenants (including M. Perperna) suffered their fair share of losses. When Pompey sent out a desperate plea to the Senate for additional support in 74 B.C., the Senate responded by sending two additional legions as well as money and supplies. These reinforcements turned the tide of war, and Sertorius was now on the defensive. Perperna eventually formed a plot against his leader (perhaps with encouragement from Metellus Pius) and murdered him. Once Sertorius was gone, Pompey easily defeated the hapless Perperna, and the long war was over. Pompey returned to Rome in 71 B.C. and celebrated a triumph for his victory in Spain. Even after his death, the colorful Sertorius continued to capture the hopes and dreams of those who felt trampled by Roman imperial power.

Spartacus

So far we have discussed the uprisings of two groups of disaffected people: the dispossessed peasants of Etruria, led by M. Lepidus, and the native Spaniards who resented Roman rule, led by Q. Sertorius. We now turn to the rebellion of another discontented population, the slaves, who were led by Spartacus. Spartacus was a gladiator of Thracian origin who had also served in the Roman auxiliary forces. In 73 B.C. he escaped from a gladiatorial school at Capua, along with seventy-four fellow gladiators, and began an insurrection. At first he was joined mainly by Thracian and Celtic fighters; but as his reputation grew, his ranks were joined by thousands of runaway slaves from the *latifundia* of southern Italy and by a large number of free peasants as well. They looted and plundered the rich country estates of southern Italy and formed their base camp in the crater of Mt. Vesuvius. Estimates of the number of Spartacus' forces (at their height) range from 70,000 to 120,000 men.

In 73 B.C., Spartacus' men easily defeated a small praetorian force that had attempted to blockade them on Vesuvius. In the following year they beat off several praetorian and two consular armies. Spartacus then took his followers north, where they defeated an army led by the governor of Cisalpine Gaul. Spartacus had hoped that his men would disperse to their homes across the Alps; but, having defeated every Roman army that had yet been sent against them, they preferred to remain in Italy. So Spartacus and his army again turned south, gaining more recruits and plunder as they went. Spartacus seems to have formulated a plan to sail to Sicily (with ships provided by the Cilician pirates) in the hopes of reviving another Sicilian slave revolt (see Historical Essay I.1), but negotiations with the pirates fell through.

Meanwhile, Sulla's former lieutenant, M. Crassus (now a propraetor), had taken over the defeated consuls' forces and recruited six new legions, which he subjected to rigorous training. In 71 B.C. he marched against Spartacus, but at first he made little headway against him. Pompey, who had just returned from Spain, was authorized to take his army south and provide support to Crassus. Crassus finally engaged Spartacus' forces in a full scale battle in Apulia (see Map 3), in which the slave leader was killed. His body was never found. Six thousand captured slaves were displayed on crosses set up along the length of the Appian Way, from Capua to Rome. Pompey arrived in time to help Crassus round up the last surviving fugitives; he later used this action to claim some of the credit for Spartacus' defeat, a move that did not endear him to Crassus.

Conclusions

The fact that three major revolts occurred within a single decade shows that the Republic was faced with significant economic problems that remained long-term sources of instability. The agrarian crisis had been exacerbated by the seizure of land for Sulla's veterans; the administration of the provinces was generally characterized by corruption and over-taxation, while at home the lot of slaves and peasants remained deplorable. These revolts were all internal rebellions by men who were so desperate that they preferred violence (with a high risk of death) to accepting the status quo. Although the men who revolted were among the most marginalized members of Roman society (dispossessed peasants, provincials, and slaves), the rebellious peasants were Roman citizens, and Spartacus' slave revolt attracted many impoverished free men as well. The participation of large numbers of citizens in these revolts is another indication of widespread social and economic problems. Finally, it is important to note that two of these insurrections were led by members of Rome's ruling class: M. Aemilius Lepidus and Q. Sertorius. These men attempted to use the discontented masses for their own political advantage. By the time of Catiline's conspiracy, the question was not whether another Roman general would try to seize control of the government as Sulla had done, but who would do so and when.

The Catilinarian Conspiracy in Context

1. Lucius Sergius Catilina

Lucius Sergius Catilina was born into an old patrician and noble family, but no one from his family had achieved the consulship in quite some time. Catiline was determined to revive his family's fortunes. He was born in 108 B.C. or perhaps a few years earlier. By all accounts, he was a handsome, charismatic young man who led a wild and licentious lifestyle. Both Cicero (in the *Catilinarian Orations*) and Sallust (*BC* 5 and 14) characterize him as cunning and ambitious, with a tendency toward sexual excess and depravity. Catiline was also famous for being able to endure hunger, cold, and other physical hardships. Cicero castigates Catiline for using his powers of endurance for disgraceful ends: "lying on the ground not only to wait for debauchery, but also to seek out crime; staying awake not only to plot against the sleep of husbands, but also against the goods of peaceful citizens."[1] Later, in the *Pro Caelio* (12–14), Cicero puts a more positive spin on Catiline's lifestyle, praising his excellence in war, legendary endurance, generosity to friends, and extraordinary charisma.

During the Italian War, Catiline served in the northern front under Pompeius Strabo, the father of Pompey the Great. The young Cicero also served under Strabo, so it is likely that Cicero got to know Catiline at this time.[2] Catiline served as a legate (lieutenant-general) under Sulla, and participated in Sulla's proscriptions of 82–81 B.C., killing several members of the equestrian order, including, perhaps, his own brother-in-law.[3] He also is said to have tortured and killed Marius' adopted nephew, Marius Gratidianus, on the tomb of Q. Lutatius Catulus, as a favor to his friend Q. Lutatius Catulus the younger. Gratidianus had prosecuted the elder Catulus, who had committed suicide rather than face conviction, and so the murder of Gratidianus seems to have been a revenge killing.[4] Many years later (in 64 B.C.), Catiline was tried on charges of having committed these murders, but was acquitted. Catiline presumably argued, as had others before him, that he had simply been carrying out Sulla's orders.[5] In 73 B.C. a Vestal Virgin named Fabia was charged with being unchaste, and Catiline was implicated in her crime.[6] The details of the case are unclear, but the prosecutor eventually withdrew the case against Fabia; Catiline's name was cleared as well, with the help of his friend Quintus Lutatius Catulus, who testified in his favor.

Cicero and Sallust further suggest that at various times during the next few years Catiline committed several acts of adultery, incest and murder. In his *First Catilinarian Oration* (chapter 14), for example, Cicero accuses Catiline of murdering his first wife in order to marry his second; elsewhere he charges that Catiline's second wife was also his daughter through an adulterous relationship. Sallust claims that Catiline murdered his stepson to make way for his second wife.[7] It is noteworthy that the stories of Catiline's familial crimes change with each telling; furthermore, the names of the alleged victims are not given, and these charges are not corroborated by any independent accounts. In order to evaluate such accusations, we need to understand that the Romans did not hesitate to exaggerate or even fabricate charges against a political competitor or personal enemy; such allegations were considered part of the genre of political invective.[8] Catiline was already known for his loose morals and high living and was Cicero's chief rival for the consulship in the elections of 64 B.C., so we should not wonder that Cicero (and Sallust, following him) should charge the man with adultery, incest, and various familial murders on little or no evidence. Thus it seems best to take these particular accusations with a healthy grain of salt.

In 68 B.C. Catiline served a term as a praetor. This elective office was the second highest in the Republic and was seen as a stepping-stone to the consulship (see Appendix A). After his praetorship, Catiline served for two years as governor of the Roman province of Africa (see Map 4). The competition for the highest offices—especially the consulship—had recently become more intense with the increase in the number of citizens after the Italian War. Furthermore, the competition was especially fierce in the mid-60s B.C. The censors for 70 B.C. had expelled sixty-four senators from the Senate; these men were all seeking reelection to those offices (quaestor, praetor, and consul) that would allow them to become members of the Senate once more.[9] Because of the increased competition for higher offices, high levels of spending during the elections (otherwise known as electoral bribery) were considered necessary. For many politicians, the governorship of a province was an important source of funds. Governors had to walk a fine line between collecting whatever funds they might need for their future careers and extorting so much money out of their provinces that they would be put on trial for extortion when they returned. A Roman governor and his staff were expected to leave their province far wealthier than they had been when they arrived (cf. Catullus' Poem 10); but if a governor's greed was excessive, an embassy from his province could come to Rome and complain to the Senate. If the Senate found the information credible, the governor would be tried for extortion (*pecuniae repetundae*; see, for example, the case of C. Verres, discussed below). In Catiline's case, a delegation from Africa came to Rome and presented their evidence to the Senate before the governor had even returned from his province.[10] By the time Catiline had arrived back in Rome in the summer of 66 B.C., it was clear that he would be tried for extortion.

Meanwhile, the consular elections of 66 B.C. (to elect the consuls for 65) were embroiled in scandal. The winners of the election, Autronius Paetus and P. Cornelius Sulla (the dictator's nephew), had been charged with electoral bribery (*ambitus*) by the two defeated candidates, L. Torquatus and L. Cotta.[11] Both Autronius and Sulla were convicted, and a new election was held. Catiline, who had just arrived from Africa, put himself forward as a candidate for this second election. The presiding consul, Lucius Volcacius Tullus, after seeking the advice from leading men of the state, rejected Catiline's candidacy, either because of his upcoming trial for extortion or because he had not announced his candidacy within the specified period.[12] Although it is impossible to tell for sure which of these reasons is more correct, the impending extortion trial makes the most sense. A person about to be charged on a criminal offense was not automatically barred from seeking a public office, but it did not look good for the Republic; this may explain why Volcacius Tullus felt the need to seek advice before making his decision. As T. P. Wiseman notes (1994: 340): "If he [Catiline] were elected, or even allowed to stand, it would be a deplorable victory for corruption over the rule of law." Catiline would have no reason to announce a late candidacy, however, since there would be no chance of its being accepted.[13] At any rate, Catiline was not allowed to run for the consulship; L. Torquatus and L. Cotta, who had lost the first election, were declared the winners of the second.

What happened next is extremely unclear. Both Cicero and Sallust report vague rumors about a conspiracy in which the two ousted consuls, Autronius and Sulla, planned to murder the winners of the second election, Cotta and Torquatus, on their first day in office (January 1, 65 B.C.) and install themselves as consuls in their stead. In some of these rumors, Catiline was implicated in the plot, which was also supposed to involve the slaughter of men from the upper class and the murder of many senators.[14] Because of Catiline's alleged involvement, this scheme has been dubbed "The First Catilinarian Conspiracy," but it is now widely agreed that, if there was such a plot, Catiline had nothing to do with it.[15] Nothing actually happened on January 1, 65 B.C.,[16] and the rumors themselves are extremely vague. According to Cicero (*Cat.* 1.15), Catiline was seen in the Forum on December 29, 66 B.C., armed with a weapon (*cum telo*). Cicero accuses Catiline of planning to "kill the consuls and the leaders of the state"; but, as R. Seager (1964: 339) notes, this accusation makes no sense: "Those who would do murder on New Year's Day do not conduct dress-rehearsals on the last day of December." There are any number of reasons why Catiline might have been carrying a weapon on December 29.[17] Furthermore, while Autronius and Sulla may have had a motive for ousting the consuls who had replaced them, Catiline had none; he had not yet made even a single run for the consulship. It was only after Catiline had lost two consular elections that he had any reason to turn to violence. Finally, M. Torquatus, one of the intended victims, defended Catiline in his extortion trial later that year. Torquatus would not have testified in Catiline's favor if he thought that Catiline had been involved in a plot to murder him.[18]

So what can we conclude about the existence or nonexistence of a plot to kill the consuls on January 1, 65 B.C.? The fact that the Senate voted bodyguards to L. Torquatus and L. Cotta points to the likelihood that someone was plotting against the new consuls. The evidence seems to suggest, however, that—if there was a conspiracy to murder Torquatus and Cotta—Catiline had no part in it: he simply had no reason to do so. So much time has been devoted to discussing this nonevent, partly because the so-called First Catilinarian Conspiracy does make a prominent appearance in many older accounts of this period.[19] But this discussion also shows how easy it was to spread false rumors in ancient Rome, especially about a man who later became as hated as Catiline, and how well such rumors could stick. It is only by subjecting the available evidence to a critical examination that scholars can have any hope of gaining accurate knowledge about the ancient world.

In 65 B.C. Catiline was finally tried on charges that he had extorted an excessive amount of money from the province of Africa. If acquitted, Catiline was expected to run in 64 B.C. for the consulship of 63; but if found guilty, he would be constitutionally debarred from running.[20] The previous year, when the embassy from Africa presented its evidence to the Senate, his guilt had seemed abundantly clear.[21] But Catiline had powerful friends. Cicero, speculating about the elections of 64, wrote to his friend Atticus: "Catiline will certainly compete, as long as the jury decides that the sun does not shine at noon."[22] Just as Cicero had predicted, Catiline was acquitted. There were persistent rumors that the prosecutor, P. Clodius, had colluded with the defense in the matter of jury selection. Furthermore, as mentioned above, L. Torquatus, the consul, had spoken in Catiline's defense. Bribery had also clearly been involved; the wealth that Catiline had acquired in Africa must have stood him in good stead. As one wag put it, Catiline "left that trial as impoverished as some of his jurors had been when they entered it."[23] The combination of ready money and powerful friends was hard to beat. Even Cicero had briefly considered defending him. He wrote to Atticus shortly before the trial: "At this time I am thinking about defending my fellow-candidate, Catiline. We have got the jurors we wanted, along with the greatest goodwill of the prosecutor. I hope that, if he is acquitted, he will collaborate with me in the election campaign."[24] In the event, Cicero did not speak in Catiline's defense, and the prospective collaboration did not materialize (as we shall see, Catiline collaborated with another candidate *against* Cicero). But the fact that so many prominent citizens were rushing to his side shows that in 65 B.C. Catiline was still very much a member of the Roman political establishment.[25]

By the summer of 64 B.C., Catiline had been acquitted of all charges, and he was finally free to run for the consulship. He had six competitors, but only two of them presented any serious competition: C. Antonius Hybrida, who came from a noble but plebeian family, and the *novus homo* M. Tullius Cicero. Catiline, who was both a noble and a patrician, decided to form a partnership with Antonius in the hopes of preventing Cicero's election.[26] At this point Catiline's story merges with that of Cicero, and it is to Cicero's life that we now must turn.

Discussion Questions

1. How do you think Catiline's family background and personal character might have led him to expect to have the opportunity to serve as consul?
2. Catiline was accused by Cicero, Sallust, and others of having committed several murders as well as acts of incest and adultery. Which (if any) of these accusations do you find credible and why?
3. What general information about provincial administration in the late Republic can you ascertain from the story of Catiline's trial and acquittal on charges of extortion from the province of Africa?

4. What is the evidence for and against the conclusion that there was a plot to kill the newly elected consuls on January 1, 65 B.C.? Do you think that such a plot existed?

2. Marcus Tullius Cicero:
Youth and Early Political Career

Youth

M. Tullius Cicero was born in 106 B.C. in the town of Arpinum, about sixty miles south-east of Rome (see Map 3).[27] The residents of Arpinum had been granted Roman citizenship in 188 B.C., so by Cicero's time they considered themselves thoroughly Roman. Cicero's family was prominent in local politics; but, of course, that was small-town stuff compared to the power and prestige of the political life at Rome. To be sure, the distinguished patrician Aemilius Scaurus had complimented Cicero's grandfather by telling him that he should have exercised his talents on the larger stage of Roman politics, but no one in his family had ever done so. Cicero's father was determined that his sons would have this opportunity. At an early age Cicero and his younger brother, Quintus, were brought to Rome to pursue their education in Roman law, Greek rhetoric and philosophy, and, of course, Roman politics.

In 91 B.C., at the outbreak of the Italian War, Cicero served on the staff of Pompeius Strabo, the father of Pompey the Great. Cicero certainly met Pompey (who was the same age as himself) at that time, and he probably met Catiline there as well, since Catiline had also served with Strabo (see Historical Essay II.1). Perhaps it was because of that early connection that Cicero had considered defending Catiline at his extortion trial in 65 B.C. and forming an electoral alliance with him.

After serving in the Italian War, Cicero remained in Rome during the civil wars of 87–82 B.C., completing his education and keeping a low profile. Cicero's family seems also to have remained unscathed by the proscriptions that followed.[28] Cicero began his legal career in 81 B.C., and he had the opportunity to argue an important case in the following year when he defended Sextus Roscius on a charge of parricide (*Pro Roscio Amerino*). The trial took place during Sulla's consulship (80 B.C.), against the backdrop of the proscriptions, and it gives us a rare insight into the sordid machinations of this period. Sextus Roscius Senior, a well-to-do citizen of the town of Ameria (and, according to Cicero, a partisan of Sulla), was killed one night while on a visit to Rome. His murderers (probably his neighbors and kinsmen who had a grudge against him) had the victim's name illegally added to the proscription lists after his death with the help of Chrysogonus, Sulla's freedman and personal assistant, even though the proscription lists had officially been closed since June 1, 81 B.C. Because proscribed men forfeited their property to the state, Chrysogonus was able to acquire the dead man's considerable wealth and property at a very low price; the murderers received their share from Chrysogonus. When Roscius' son complained that he had been illegally deprived of his patrimony, he was promptly charged with his father's murder.

The defense of the younger Roscius was politically risky, because it involved an attack on the powerful Chrysogonus, but it was a risk worth taking for a young, ambitious orator like Cicero. Cicero revealed the facts of the case and criticized Chrysogonus' involvement, while making it clear that Sulla could not be expected to know about his subordinate's actions and therefore could not be held responsible for them. Cicero's balancing act paid off. Roscius was acquitted, and Cicero's reputation was made; other clients now sought his services.[29]

Cicero left Rome the following year—perhaps to improve his health or perhaps to remove himself from the watchful eye of Sulla—and spent the next two years traveling abroad.[30] He spent six months studying philosophy and oratory in Athens and also visited Rhodes, where he heard the famous Stoic philosopher Poseidonius.[31] Shortly after his return to Rome (after Sulla's death), Cicero won election as a quaestor for 75 B.C., an office that would gain him membership in the Senate.

Early Political Career

Cicero served his term as quaestor in western Sicily. Sicily was an important source of wheat, which was scarce in Rome at that time. Cicero was able to send a particularly large amount of grain back to Rome, while at the same time holding down the cost to the Sicilians by suppressing the usual extortions of his subordinates. Cicero thus gained the trust and goodwill of the people of Sicily, and they honored him greatly.[32]

In 70 B.C. Cicero ran for the post of plebeian aedile for the following year.[33] Only a few days after his election Cicero led a successful prosecution against Gaius Verres, who had governed Sicily from 73 to 71 B.C. Verres was charged with extortion during his term as governor. This case is interesting partly because of Cicero's role in it; his astonishing success under adverse conditions gave a substantial boost to his career. But the case is also interesting because of the role that Cicero's speech may have played in promoting jury reform. Verres' depredations against the wealthy island of Sicily had been carried out on a very grand scale, far beyond the limits of most provincial governors, a group not noted for their moderation or self-restraint. The Sicilians, remembering Cicero's fairness during his quaestorship, requested the orator's help in prosecuting Verres. Cicero's task was made especially difficult because Verres had powerful friends. Hortensius, the leading orator of the day, was speaking for the defense; Hortensius also happened to be one of the consuls-elect for the following year (69 B.C.). The other consul-elect was Q. Metellus, a close ally of Verres.[34] M. Metellus, Quintus' brother, was praetor-elect and would have jurisdiction over the extortion court in 69 B.C. Verres' plan for securing his acquittal was simply to stall long enough so that his trial would be held over until 69 B.C. (when his supporters would be in office), and his strategy looked like a good one. One of his friends had already openly congratulated him on his victory.[35] But Cicero worked with lightning speed, gathering evidence in Sicily in half the allotted time and outmaneuvering the defense in pretrial motions, thus forcing the trial to be held in 70 B.C. In his speeches against Verres (particularly the first speech, which we know was actually given), Cicero refers again and again to the corruption in the extortion courts.[36] The juries for these courts had been composed entirely of senators since Sulla's reforms of 82 B.C. At the time of Verres' trial (August of 70 B.C.), a bill had been proposed to hand the juries back to the equestrian class.[37] Cicero made Verres' case a referendum on the senatorial jury. He exhorted the senators to convict C. Verres, reminding them that if they acquitted a man whose depredations were so painfully clear, they would prove to the world that senators could not be trusted to regulate themselves.[38]

The evidence against Verres was so damning, and Cicero's first speech against him was so effective, that a guilty verdict became inevitable. Verres withdrew from Rome and went into exile at Marseilles before the trial was completed (taking a large amount of silver with him), and he was condemned by default. Cicero had won a case against Hortensius, Rome's leading advocate, and he could now claim that title as his own. Later that year the praetor L. Aurelius Cotta passed a compromise jury bill, in which the juries on the extortion courts were drawn equally from the senators, equestrians, and *tribunii aerarii*, an order that had a property qualification similar to that of the equestrians, or perhaps slightly lower.[39] This compromise was apparently satisfactory, since it remained in force for the rest of the Republican period. Of course, this compromise did not prevent jury tampering; Catiline's acquittal in 65 B.C. is evidence of that. But the balanced juries were at least some check to rampant bribery and corruption.

Cotta's jury reform was part of a group of measures enacted during the years 75–70 B.C. that marked the final breakdown of Sulla's reforms. In 75 B.C. a law had been passed restoring the ability of tribunes to hold higher offices, thus removing a powerful disincentive for holding this office. In 72 B.C. the distribution of grain to the poor at a reduced price was resumed, and in 70 B.C. tribunes were once again granted the right to introduce legislation. With the restored power of the tribunate, the Senate's post-Sullan period of domination was over, and *popularis* politicians became active once more.[40] As noted above (Historical Essay I.2), the term *popularis* refers more to the tactic of appealing to the people than to any political agenda. But, in practice, populist measures such as land reform, justice for provincials, grain distribution to the poor, civil rights, and debt relief were favored by this group. As the reform movement gained momentum during the following decade (69–60 B.C.), the tribunes began to claim new powers for themselves, including the right to assign commanders to Roman armies and to dispense funds, powers that had traditionally belonged to the Senate alone.[41] Cicero, whose natural inclination was oriented toward order and stability, eventually began to align himself more and more with the Senate and those who wanted to maintain the status quo.[42] These shifts in political alignments took several years to develop, however. In the early years of his political career, Cicero allied himself with Pompey, and both considered themselves part of the movement away from senatorial control.

Cicero gave his first important speech outside the courtroom as praetor, in 66 B.C. The *Pro lege Manilia* signaled Cicero's readiness to play a role in shaping public policy. In 67 B.C. Pompey had been sent to the eastern Mediterranean to fight against the pirates, who had been harassing merchants and kidnapping Roman citizens for ransom. Pompey was given a three-year command and unlimited power throughout the Mediterranean, along with vast supplies of money, ships, and men. Now in 66, after Pompey had conquered the pirates with lightning speed, a tribune named Gaius Manilius proposed that the command against the redoubtable Mithridates should be transferred to Pompey, along with the powers and forces that he currently held. In his speech, Cicero stressed Pompey's honesty and freedom from corruption, and the need to restore a safe environment for Roman business interests.[43] The *Pro lege Manilia* was a success; the Manilian Law was passed and Pompey received broad powers to make settlements in the East.

Discussion Questions

1. What character traits do you see displayed in the way Cicero handled his duties as quaestor in western Sicily?
2. What character traits do you see in the way Cicero gathered evidence against C. Verres? In his prosecution of Verres, why do you think Cicero chose to make the arguments that he did? What do you think his motives were in taking the case?

3. The Consular Elections of 64 B.C. and Cicero's Consulship

The Consular Elections

In 64 B.C. Cicero was one of seven candidates for the consulship of 63; and of these, he was the only *novus homo*:[44] two of his rivals were patricians (one of whom was Catiline), two (including C. Antonius Hybrida) came from noble plebeian families, and two had a senatorial (though not noble) background.[45] To make matters worse, Catiline and Antonius had formed a political alliance to jointly promote their candidacies.[46] As an outsider, Cicero faced considerable disadvantages: not only did he lack the inherited political connections enjoyed by members of the *nobilitas*, but as a newcomer he also had to endure the distrust and even disdain of those who were well connected. According to Sallust (*BC* 23.6), "the nobility believed that the consulship was, in a sense, polluted if a *novus homo* should attain it, no matter how outstanding he might be." Not only was Cicero a *novus homo*, but his family was not even from Rome. Sallust reports (*BC* 31.7) that, after Cicero had delivered his *First Catilinarian Oration* to the Senate (November 8, 63 B.C.), Catiline stood up and asked the senators whether it made any sense that a patrician such as himself would try to overthrow the government while an immigrant (*inquilinus*) like Cicero would try to save it. These passages from Sallust illustrate the deep-seated prejudices that bound the members of the ruling class to one another and tended to exclude anyone from the outside.[47]

Cicero did have a strong constituency, of course. He had won important friends through his courtroom oratory, and he could draw on the powerful support of the equestrian order, from whose ranks he had come and whose interests he had championed. Cicero also had a good reputation in the Italian towns, and he was also popular at Rome.[48] Finally, Cicero had worked hard to gain the backing of Pompey and his followers. But Cicero needed stronger support among the upper class if he had any hope of beating Catiline and Antonius.

An electioneering manual, the *Commentariolum petitionis*, purportedly written to Cicero by his younger brother, Quintus, gives Cicero advice about how to manage his election campaign. This work has been handed down in the manuscripts of Cicero's *Letters to His Friends*. There are questions about its authenticity: why would Cicero need the advice of his younger brother, who had far less political experience than he did? Furthermore, some of the most brilliant passages in it seem to have been lifted from Cicero's own speeches. Because of these questions, we cannot be sure that the document was actually written by Cicero's brother. But whether it was written by Q. Cicero or not, the writer has an exceptional grasp of Roman electoral politics, and the pamphlet is a valuable resource in helping us understand Cicero's strategy for winning the election.

In the *Commentariolum petitionis* (51–53), Cicero is told that he must work hard to keep the broad range of support that he has already gained but that he must acquire in addition the goodwill of the most illustrious men, the *nobiles* or *boni*. In order to do this, Cicero should let it be known that the hope of a strong future for the Republic, as well as the good opinion of honorable men, rests with him. Furthermore, Cicero is advised not to undertake any serious public business during the campaign, whether in the Senate or in a public assembly. Rather, he should act so that the Senate will consider him a defender of its authority, the equestrians and the upper class will consider him to be devoted to peace and maintaining the status quo, and the masses will consider him not opposed to their interests. Cicero is also encouraged to spread scandalous rumors about his competitors' crimes, their passions, and their bribery, appropriately adapted to their characters.

Such advice, while fairly cynical, fits in well with Roman electoral politics. And Cicero was given a golden opportunity to slander his fellow candidates shortly before the election. According to Asconius (83), the incidence of electoral bribery (*ambitus*), while always high, had increased substantially during this campaign, much of it due to the lavish spending of Antonius and Catiline. The Senate had promoted a new law against *ambitus* with increased penalties; but one of the tribunes, Q. Mucius Orestinus (allegedly acting on behalf of Catiline), had vetoed the bill. Mucius had also publicly stated that Cicero was not worthy to hold the consulship (Asconius 86). Mucius was apparently casting aspersions on Cicero's status as a *novus homo*, in comparison with the nobility of Antonius and Catiline.

At a meeting of the Senate on the day after Mucius' speech, the senators expressed their outrage at his veto of the bill on electoral bribery. Then Cicero was asked to give his opinion concerning Mucius' actions. This was Cicero's chance to garner support from the upper class only a few days before the election, and he did so by attacking Catiline and Antonius. He stood up and gave an impromptu speech, lambasting the immorality and wickedness of his political opponents, just as the *Commentariolum* had advised him to do. Although the speech itself (entitled *In toga candida*, because candidates for office would wear a white toga) has been lost, fragments have been preserved in a commentary by Q. Asconius Pedianus, who lived during the first century A.D. In this speech, Cicero mixes well-known facts about Catiline's career with unsubstantiated charges, in the tradition of Roman invective. Catiline's well-known actions during the Sullan proscriptions are described in great detail, and his recent acquittal on bribery charges is mentioned again and again. Cicero also makes unsubstantiated charges that Catiline committed incest and murder (see Historical Essay II.1) and hints that Catiline was involved in a plot to murder the consuls of the previous year (the so-called First Catilinarian Conspiracy). As discussed above, Cicero provides few details about these charges of incest and murder, and scholars today generally dismiss them; but these inflammatory accusations, leveled only a few days before the election, were enough to provoke suspicions in the minds of Catiline's upper-class supporters. Cicero was able to portray Catiline as immoral, violent, and unrestrained, while promoting himself as the candidate of trustworthiness and integrity. As Stockton (1971: 83) notes, Cicero "put aside the rapier in favor of the hatchet. Conservative opinion swung decisively behind the man who promised unflinching and unremitting opposition to any serious attack on the *status quo*."

Asconius (93–94) reports that "Catiline and Antonius replied insolently to Cicero's speech and . . . attacked his low birth [*novitas*]." But the damage had already been done. By a brilliant piece of invective, Cicero was able to gain the upper-class support he had previously lacked, and he was elected by a unanimous vote of all the centuries.[49] Antonius came in second, and Catiline came in third, losing the consulship to the "immigrant" from Arpinum.

Cicero's Consulship

Even before Catiline's conspiracy, Cicero's consulship was fraught with controversy. One of the challenges that Cicero faced at the beginning of his consulship was the land reform bill brought by P. Servilius Rullus. Rullus, one of the tribunes in 63 B.C., seems to have put forward two major proposals. The first one, which would have abolished all debts, seems to have been set aside. High levels of debt were becoming endemic to all levels of society, and some alleviation of this problem was needed. Not enough information is known about Rullus' proposal, however, to be able to give the reasons why it was discarded. Rullus' second proposal was a land bill, which garnered a great deal of popular support. Unlike previous land bills, which sought to confiscate *ager publicus* from those who had illegally acquired it, this bill proposed to purchase private land—on generous terms—from those who were willing to sell. Potential sellers included those who had gained land during the Sullan proscriptions or who had received allotments of public land and no longer wished to farm it. The vast and fertile *ager publicus* in the region of Campania (which had never been divided into allotments) would also be distributed.[50] The funding for this massive government project would come from Pompey's conquests in the East, which, although not yet completed, were certain to bring in huge revenues in the form of tribute and plunder.[51] The Rullan bill provided for new colonies to be founded with the purchased land, giving a fresh start to both the urban and the rural poor.[52] A board of ten men would administer the program, with broad powers to make decisions on land titles and plenty of money at their disposal. The need for such a land bill was clear: "the desperation of many of Catiline's supporters in 63 finds much of its explanation in a deep hunger for land."[53] The Rullan land bill, however, seems to have combined needed economic reforms with unabashed political cronyism.

Antonius supported Rullus' bill, but Cicero opposed it. In his three speeches *De lege agraria*, delivered both to the Senate and to the people, Cicero argued that he was not opposed to land reform *per se*, but he feared that this bill would drain the public treasury and wreak havoc with the real estate market, while providing no real benefit to the poor.[54] Cicero may have been correct in his assessment of this bill, although it is also true that Cicero, like many other senators, "always encountered difficulty in favoring specific proposals . . . where in theory he recognized that something needed to be done."[55] Cicero spoke out so forcefully against the bill that Rullus withdrew it before it could be voted on. While the Rullan bill was certainly flawed, its failure only inflamed the resentment among Italy's poor and dispossessed—resentment that could prove useful to *populoris* politicians.[56]

Meanwhile, the *populares* were active on other fronts. They put forward a proposal to restore civil rights to the sons of the men who had been proscribed by Sulla, allowing them to run for political office. This proposal was defeated by Cicero, on the grounds that these men were so full of anger and resentment that, if they were elected, they would be likely to overthrow the Republic (*si essent magistratus adepti, rei publicae statum convolsuri viderentur; In Pisonem* 4). The defeat of this bill, however, may actually have contributed to the instability of the Republic, because it almost certainly drove some of these men to join Catiline.[57]

At around this time, an aged senator named Gaius Rabirius was tried on an antiquated charge of treason (*perduellio*) for having participated in the lynching murder of Saturninus some thirty-seven years earlier. As discussed above (Historical Essay I.5), the Senate had passed the SCU against Saturninus in 100 B.C., after violence had broken out during the consular elections and Saturninus and his supporters had seized the Capitoline Hill. Marius, who was consul at the time, had accepted the surrender of Saturninus and his men, but the crowd, relying on the protection afforded by the SCU, had stoned Saturninus to death, along with many of his followers. Although the event had occurred many years earlier, one of the tribunes for 63 B.C., T. Labienus, acting in conjunction with the young Julius Caesar, brought Rabirius to trial as a way of reopening debate about the SCU. The SCU had never been intended to provide a cover for mob violence; it granted unusual powers only to the magistrates named in the declaration, and it granted those powers only for the purpose of preventing imminent harm to the state. In 100 B.C., however, the mob had acted not only in defiance of the consul's orders but also after Saturninus and his followers had already been arrested, and so any threat to the state had surely passed. Thus Labienus' aim in conducting this trial was to establish the precise extent of the SCU: to whom did it authorize extralegal powers and to what extent did it authorize them?[58] Furthermore, the legality of the SCU had never been fully established: it was not clear that the Senate had the legal right to abrogate Gaius Gracchus' *lex Sempronia de capite civium*, according to which a Roman citizen could not be put to death without a trial before the people.[59] Rabirius' trial was not simply an opportunity for public debate about the SCU, however; it was also a warning to the Senate that the *popularis* politicians were once more in a position to challenge its authority.

Because Rabirius was charged with treason (*perduellio*), his case would be heard by two judges selected by lot, not by a jury composed of senators, equestrians, and *tribuni aerarii*, who would certainly have acquitted him. To no one's surprise, the lot fell upon Julius Caesar and his cousin, Lucius Caesar (consul in 64 B.C.). When the judges pronounced him guilty, Rabirius appealed, claiming (quite reasonably) that the judges had not been impartial. Then, in conformity with Roman law, Rabirius was tried before the Roman people, in the *comitia centuriata*. As consul, Cicero spoke for the defense, arguing passionately that Rabirius, along with many others, had been acting in accordance with the SCU (*Pro Rabirio* 19–20). The SCU, Cicero continued, is a necessary and legitimate weapon, which the Senate uses in times of crisis to reestablish the rule of law:

> What would I do if T. Labienus had made a slaughter of citizens, as L. Saturninus did . . . if he had occupied the Capitoline Hill with armed men? I would do the same thing that Gaius Marius did, I would submit a proposal to the Senate [requesting the SCU], I would exhort you to defend the Republic, I myself would take up arms, and, along with you, I would take a stand against an armed opponent. (*Pro Rabirio* 35)

Cicero was making a valid point: without a standing army or even a police force, the government needed a legal means of imposing martial law in times of crisis. But the opponents of the SCU had a valid point as well. The SCU was an ad hoc measure that had never been voted into law by a popular assembly; its legal standing was based only on precedent and thus had never been fully established. As such, the SCU was "a decree urging unconstitutional measures, which overrode laws passed by the popular assemblies," such as C. Gracchus' *lex de capite civium*; thus it "could always be represented as an infringement of popular sovereignty."[60] Finally, the SCU was open to abuse; it could be used to support a partisan political agenda or provide a cover of legitimacy for what was essentially mob rule. Unfortunately, this important debate was never resolved. Rabirius' trial was broken off abruptly: the praetor lowered a red flag on the Janiculan Hill, an ancient signal that the city of Rome was under attack from the Etruscans.[61] The tribune Labienus, following ancient custom, duly broke up the *comitia centuriata*, and the trial was never completed. The entire scenario was probably orchestrated according to a prearranged agreement with the praetor. The *populares* had successfully challenged the SCU; henceforth it would be used with greater caution.[62] But the Roman people still had not made a formal judgment about the SCU; thus the question of its legal standing remained unresolved.

Discussion Questions

1. Cicero was an outsider in more ways than one. Not only was he a *novus homo*, but his family came from outside of Rome. What challenges did Cicero face as a result of his status as an outsider? Do you think this difficult position may have given him some advantages as well?
2. What do you think of the political advice contained in the *Commentariolum petitionis*? Does it remind you in any way of political strategy in the United States today?
3. As consul, Cicero argued successfully against the Rullan land bill and against a proposal to restore civil rights to the sons of the proscribed. What were Cicero's main arguments in each case? What were the long-term consequences of these policies? In terms of Roman politics, do you see Cicero as more supportive of optimate or *popularis* views at this point in his career? Why do you think that Cicero took the positions that he did?
4. What were the main issues involved in the trial of C. Rabirius? Briefly set forth the two opposing arguments about the SCU. Which views make more sense to you and why?

4. The Consular Elections of 63 B.C.

One of Cicero's responsibilities as consul was to oversee the consular elections, and Catiline was once again a candidate. Decimus Junius Silanus was favored to win the first consulship, and Catiline and Lucius Licinius Murena were the top two candidates for the second. Murena had served as a legate under the general Lucullus, who could be counted on to bring his veterans to the elections to support his former lieutenant. And Murena's lavish spending was also sure to win him many votes. But Catiline, too, was putting a lot of effort into his campaign, well aware that this election would be his last chance to win a consulship and the prestige it would bring. The Romans did not like to back a loser, so a candidate who had been twice rejected at the polls rarely tried again.[63]

Since Catiline had lost the backing of much (though not all) of the nobility during the previous election, he now turned to the people for support. Catiline campaigned on a platform that featured the cancellation of debts, or *novae tabulae* (literally, new account-books), as its major focus. Levels of debt had been steadily increasing among all classes of Roman society since the time of the Gracchi; but recently Roman indebtedness had reached dangerous levels, particularly since the rates of interest were unusually high.

Roman indebtedness can be divided into three main categories: rural, provincial, and urban.[64] Rural debt went hand in hand with the continuing agricultural crisis. As peasants fell into debt through poor harvests or their rich neighbors' machinations, they either lost their land completely or became tenant-farmers on the land they had formerly owned. Even as tenant-farmers they would sometimes have to borrow money to pay the rent on their land; they would thus fall even deeper into debt to the man who was both landowner and moneylender. A similar situation existed in the provinces, where the local population was frequently forced to borrow money at a high rate of interest (in at least one instance, as high as 48 percent) to pay their taxes.[65] Unfortunately, they would usually have to borrow the money from the private tax-collectors (*publicani*) themselves, who thus made a double profit on the taxes they collected. The Allobroges, a tribe living in Transalpine Gaul, were particularly hard hit by this problem, "overwhelmed" as Sallust says (*BC* 40.1), "by public and private debt."

The third type of debt, urban debt, also took several forms. Plebeians, shopkeepers, merchants, and artisans had to borrow money to pay the rent on their shops, workshops, and *tabernae*. Even more prosperous merchants had to borrow money to cover the destruction caused by violence, pirates, bad sailing weather, and other unforeseen difficulties. Surprisingly enough, many aristocrats borrowed large sums of money as well. Senators needed large amounts of money to finance their election campaigns and provincial administrations and to provide entertainment for the poor. They also frequently borrowed money to pay for the expensive villas that had become a standard part of their lifestyle. Although these men owned land, they were generally unwilling to sell it to pay off their debts, since these were the properties that enabled them to belong to the highest property classification (see Cicero, *Cat.* 2.18). Such men borrowed freely, hoping to repay their loans with lucrative provincial assignments. These positions did not always provide the expected amount of revenue, however (see Catullus Poem 10), so high levels of debt remained a common problem even among the highest social classes.

Because indebtedness was so widespread, Catiline hoped to capture broad support with his promises of *novae tabulae*, but he concentrated his efforts on three specific groups of debtors: Sulla's veterans, the sons of the men who had lost their land during Sulla's proscriptions, and the urban proletariat. Sulla's veterans had been given substantial plots of land, mainly in Etruria and Apulia, but many of them were not as good at farming as they had been at fighting. As Wiseman (1994: 347) points out: "Fifteen years on, some of the veteran settlers were as desperate as the peasants they had dispossessed, with the added resentment of disappointed hopes." Being an old Sullan officer himself, it was natural that Catiline would turn to those disaffected veterans for support. But, following in Lepidus' footsteps (see Historical Essay I.9), Catiline also gained adherents among the sons of those peasants who had been driven off their land by Sulla's veterans. These two groups made strange bedfellows, but Catiline's charismatic leadership and populist rhetoric held them under his sway. He also sought support among the urban proletariat, especially those workmen and urban shopkeepers who were staggering under a crushing burden of debt. By tapping into a vast reservoir of discontent, Catiline managed to secure a large following among the poor.

Catiline also enjoyed the support of at least some prominent *popularis* politicians. Gaius Antonius Hybrida, Cicero's colleague in the consulship, had formed a political partnership with Catiline in the previous election, and he seems to have given his former ally certain promises of help.[66] Cicero, who had been Catiline's political enemy since his speech *In toga candida*, persuaded Antonius to withdraw his support for Catiline by making an exchange of provinces. Consuls generally governed a province after their year in office, and these provinces were awarded by lot. Cicero had drawn the potentially lucrative province of Macedonia, while Antonius had received the less wealthy Cisalpine Gaul. Cicero now volunteered to yield Macedonia to Antonius in return for his neutrality toward Catiline.[67]

There are also persistent rumors that M. Licinius Crassus and C. Julius Caesar, both *populares*, supported Catiline's political aspirations. The most important evidence comes from Cicero's commentator, Q. Asconius Pedianus. In his commentary to Cicero's *In toga candida*, Asconius states flatly (83) that Crassus and Caesar strongly supported Catiline's bid for the consulship. But can Asconius be trusted on this matter? As several scholars have noted, Asconius may have based his claim on an exposé, written by Cicero to be published after his death, that was intended to blacken the reputations of Caesar and Crassus.[68] This so-called Secret Memoir no longer exists, and we do not know for sure whether Asconius had seen it or whether he had access to more reliable sources. It would certainly make political sense for Caesar and Crassus to support a populist such as Catiline, but we will never know for certain whether they did so. It is important to emphasize, however, that—even if they did back Catiline's candidacy—Caesar and Crassus certainly withdrew their support when Catiline began to veer into extremism, shortly before the 63 B.C. consular elections.[69]

Catiline did heighten his rhetoric as the elections drew near, a sign, according to Cicero, that he felt confident of his election.[70] Catiline's opponents may also have feared that his populist strategy would succeed. A possible sign of that fear is the fact that M. Porcius Cato, a stern upholder of the status quo, threatened to slap Catiline with a lawsuit, probably for electoral bribery. Catiline replied that if any fire were kindled against his fortunes, he would extinguish it "not with water but with catastrophe."[71] There is no reason to suspect that Catiline was actively plotting a revolution at this time (he had no need to turn to violence as long as he had hopes of winning a consular election); but, as this threat makes clear, he was already considering violence as an option if his legitimate bid for power did not prove successful.

The day before the election, Catiline made a speech to his followers that was widely reported. According to Cicero (*Pro Murena* 50), Catiline told his supporters:

The only trustworthy defender of the wretched [*miserorum*] is a man who is wretched [*miserus*] himself; those who are wounded and beaten down [*miseros*] should not trust promises made by men who are fortunate and untouched by hardship. For this reason, anyone who wants to replenish what has been lost and recover what has been snatched away should consider how much Catiline himself owes, how little he possesses, what he would dare. A man who intends to be the leader and standard-bearer of the wretched [*calamitosorum*] should be afraid of nothing and should himself be thoroughly wretched [*calamitosum*].

After hearing about this inflammatory speech, Cicero postponed the elections and called an emergency meeting of the Senate. At the Senate meeting, Cicero called on Catiline to explain his words of the previous day. Catiline boldly replied that the Republic was composed of two bodies. One was feeble and had a weak head (by this he meant the Senate). The other was strong, but it had no head at all (this was the Roman people). If the people treated him well, Catiline declared, they would never lack a head as long as he was alive. A collective groan arose from the Senate, but the senators refused to take any direct action.[72] There was no hard evidence that Catiline was actually planning any violence. Besides, Catiline was a patrician and a member of the nobility, as well as a man of great personal charm, while Cicero was only a newcomer and (the senators probably reasoned) surely an alarmist one at that.[73] When the Senate refused to postpone the elections any longer, Cicero organized them, as he was told.

On election day, Cicero appeared at the Campus Martius surrounded by a personal bodyguard, with his breastplate conspicuously peeking out from under his toga.[74] Cicero took these precautions, not for actual protection, as he later explained, but in order that "all good men would notice and, when they saw their consul in such fear and danger, they would run to his defense and protection."[75] Was the consul—or the Republic—in any real danger at this election? Consular elections had been known to erupt into violence (e.g., the election of 100 B.C.), but there is no reason to suspect that Catiline had planned any violent action at this time. Cicero's famous breastplate was more melodrama than judicious precaution; but as melodrama it was successful. The fears of violence inspired by Cicero's armor and his bodyguard turned enough votes away from Catiline to give Murena the victory, along with Decimus Junius Silanus. As Cicero himself later explained (*Pro Murena* 53): "In a consular election, a sudden change of opinion is important, especially when it inclines toward a good man whose candidacy is supplied with many other advantages." Thus Cicero's histrionics succeeded in providing for his chosen candidate, Murena, the same kind of last-minute swing of opinion that he had gained for himself with his speech *In toga candida* the previous year.

For Cicero, with his equestrian background, Catiline's talk of land reform and remission of debt threatened the rule of law and the right of private property, upon which Cicero believed that Roman society was built. While such views were no doubt at least partially correct, Cicero and other *optimates* seriously underestimated the depth of economic discontent that gripped much of Italy, particularly Etruria, where Sulla's land confiscations had caused serious economic damage. As Plutarch notes (*Cicero* 10): "Rome was in an extremely unstable condition and ready to fall into revolution on account of the great disparity of wealth . . . so that affairs needed only a slight movement to upset the balance, and it was in the power of any bold adventurer to overturn the government, which was itself diseased at its core."

With the loss of this election, Catiline had exhausted all legitimate avenues for seeking the position he craved. During his two runs for the consulship, he had gained a large following, including not only many desperate men, who were willing to resort to violence to obtain a better way of life, but also a few wealthy individuals like himself who hoped to gain power through the masses. As a member of the Roman nobility, Catiline believed he had a right to Rome's highest office; and he was determined to acquire that office by any means necessary. Furthermore, Catiline might have gained some confidence in the thought that he would not be the first Roman to march on Rome at the head of an army. He may well have felt the same way that Pompey supposedly did, some fourteen years later, on the eve of civil war: "Sulla potuit, ego non potero?"[76]

Discussion Questions

1. How did it happen that men from widely divergent socioeconomic backgrounds were burdened by debt?
2. How did Catiline use the problem of widespread debt for his own political advantage?
3. What conclusions can you draw about Catiline's political persona from the rhetoric of his speech at a preelection rally? From his response to Cato's threatened lawsuit? From his metaphor of the Republic's two bodies?
4. Do you see any similarities between the strategy of Cicero's speech *In toga candida*, by which he helped secure his own election, and his actions at the 63 B.C. consular elections?

5. The Early Stages of the Conspiracy

Immediately after the consular elections, Catiline began to set his plans for a violent insurrection into motion.[77] Catiline's conspiracy included men from all walks of life: senators, equestrians, ordinary citizens, and even freedmen swelled his ranks. Because the conspiracy ultimately did not succeed, many of the conspirators never revealed their identities. Of those who were known, seven of the most important conspirators will be briefly mentioned here: the five who were eventually executed (Lentulus, Cethegus, Statilius, Gabinius, and Ceparius), one key conspirator who escaped (L. Cassius), and one (Q. Curius) who played an important role in uncovering the conspiracy.

The most prestigious member of the conspiracy was the praetor Publius Cornelius Lentulus Sura. He had been consul in 71 B.C., but had been expelled from the Senate the following year, along with sixty-three others. According to Plutarch (*Cicero* 17), Lentulus was expelled for his licentious behavior. By 69 B.C. he was again climbing the *cursus honorum,* and in 63 he had reached the rank of praetor. The conspirators undoubtedly hoped that Lentulus' high office would lend some legitimacy to their scheme. Cicero does not speak highly of Lentulus' intelligence, however. In his *Third Catilinarian Oration,* Cicero derides Lentulus' torpor (*somnum; Cat.* 3.16); and in the *Brutus* (a dialogue on oratory, published in 46 B.C.), he claims that Lentulus used to hide the slowness of his thinking by the dignity of his manner, the elegant movement of his body, and his sonorous voice (*Brutus* 235). Lentulus' actions as deputy chief of the conspiracy in Rome after Catiline's departure (on November 8; see below) seem to bear out Cicero's assessment.

Lucius Cassius Longinus had been a praetor in 66 B.C. with Cicero and Antonius and was also a candidate with them for the consulship of 63 B.C. According to Asconius (82), as a consular candidate, Cassius "seemed to be stupid rather than wicked, but a few months later he showed up in Catiline's conspiracy as a promoter of the cruelest and most bloodthirsty proposals." Cicero claims that Cassius had asked to be put in charge of the plot to set fires throughout Rome (*Cat.* 3.14). Cassius was also noted for his corpulence (*Cat.* 3.16). Cassius left town the night of December 2 and was never caught.

Another senatorial member of the conspiracy, C. Cornelius Cethegus, was known for his crazy recklessness (*furiosam temeritatem; Cat.* 3.16). According to Sallust (*BC* 43), Cethegus "constantly complained that the other conspirators were dragging their feet, affirming that by their hesitation and delay they were wasting great opportunities." A large cache of weapons was eventually recovered from Cethegus' house (Cicero *Cat.* 3.8).

Lucius Statilius was of equestrian rank (Sallust *BC* 17). A key player in the conspiracy, Statilius was part of the plot to set fires around the city in order to create confusion (Sallust *BC* 43). Statilius wrote one of the incriminating letters to the Allobroges (see below) and was eventually executed for his role in the conspiracy. P. Gabinius Capito, another equestrian, was also a leading member of the conspiracy. He was implicated in the plot to set fires in Rome and played an important role in negotiations with the Allobroges (Cicero *Cat.* 3.14). M. Ceparius, a native of Terracina, had been assigned the task of stirring up a slave revolt in Apulia (Sallust *BC* 46; Cicero *Cat.* 3.14). Last, but not least, Q. Curius deserves to be mentioned. A former senator,

Curius had also been expelled from the Senate in 70 B.C. because of his vices; he was apparently a notorious gambler (Asconius 93). According to Sallust (*BC* 23), "his fickleness was matched by his boldness; he could not keep quiet about what he had heard, nor did he even bother to conceal his own crimes. He was utterly thoughtless of what he said and did."

Quintus' curious lack of discretion seems to have been the key to the unraveling of the conspiracy. Sallust informs us that Curius was having an affair with an upper-class woman named Fulvia. After a while, as his funds began to run out and his gifts to her became less lavish, Fulvia began to lose interest in the relationship. But suddenly he began to make extravagant promises to his mistress, telling her that "the sky was the limit" and that he would soon be able to buy her whatever her heart desired.[78] After a few questions, Fulvia discovered the reason behind her lover's braggadocio: he was planning to get rich quick by helping to overthrow the government. As soon as Fulvia learned of the plot, she told several people about it, including Cicero; and she continued to keep Cicero informed as the plot unfolded.[79]

Curius' extravagant promises to Fulvia also help us understand why so many men of senatorial rank would be willing to take part in Catiline's hare-brained scheme. While discontented peasants and urban poor were hoping for a redistribution of land and an end to crushing debt, men like Lentulus, Curius, and the others discussed above were hoping to lead the disaffected masses into battle and to attain, through them, the abundant wealth and power that had so far eluded their grasp. As Sallust explains (*BC* 17.5), the upper-class conspirators were "motivated more by the hope of supremacy [*spes dominationis*] than by poverty or other distress."

In late July or early August of 63 B.C. Catiline sent Gaius Manlius, an ex-centurion from Sulla's army, to Faesulae in northern Etruria (see Map 3) to organize an army. Manlius easily recruited followers among the poor and desperate peasantry, many of whom had lost their land during Sulla's proscriptions. Manlius also found followers among Sulla's veterans who had not been successful at farming, and he even recruited some local outlaws (Sallust *BC* 28.4). While Manlius was in Etruria raising troops, a smaller force was being organized in Picenum (see Map 3), and a slave revolt was planned for Apulia (Sallust *BC* 27.1). Catiline himself stayed in Rome to orchestrate the movements of his followers.

Some letters were mysteriously left outside of Crassus' door one night in mid-October. One was addressed to Crassus, the rest to other leading senators. Upon opening the letter addressed to him, Crassus found an unsigned warning to leave the city, as Catiline was planning a massacre. Crassus hurried to Cicero's house that same night, bringing the rest of the letters with him. The next day Cicero called a meeting of the Senate, at which the rest of the letters were opened and read. When they were found to contain similar warnings, the Senate declared a state of disorder (*tumultus*) and instituted a search for more information.[80]

Within a few days, Cicero had acquired more definite information about the conspirators' plans, probably through Fulvia. He called a meeting of the Senate for October 21, at which he informed them that Manlius and his followers were set to begin their march against Rome on October 27. A coordinated massacre of leading citizens was to take place in Rome on October 28, and an uprising in the Sullan colony of Praeneste (see Map 3) was planned for November 1 (*Cat.* 1.7–8). The Senate now passed the SCU against Catiline: *Decrevit . . . senatus uti . . . consul videret ne quid res publica detrimenti caperet* (Cicero *Cat.* 1.4).[81] This was the first time that the Senate had passed the SCU since Lepidus' rebellion in 78 B.C. In addition to passing the SCU, the Senate raised several armies. Q. Marcius Rex and Metellus Creticus were sent as proconsuls with armed forces to Faesulae and Apulia, respectively. The praetor Q. Pompeius Rufus was sent to Capua, and his colleague Metellus Celer was sent to Picenum, with emergency powers to levy troops (Sallust *BC* 30). Cicero fortified Praeneste with guards and a military garrison (*Cat.* 1.8) and ordered night watches to be set up in all districts of Rome. The city was gripped by panic. A few days later, on November 1 or 2, a senator named L. Saenius read a letter to the Senate from Faesulae reporting that Manlius had in fact taken up arms on October 27. Slave revolts were also reported in Capua and Apulia.

As Q. Marcius was leading his army toward Faesulae, Manlius sent an embassy to him with a letter in which the rebels begged for debt relief, and explained the reason for their armed rebellion. According to Sallust (*BC* 33), the letter read as follows:

> We call upon the gods and men as witnesses, commander, that we have not taken up arms against our fatherland, nor do we wish to place others in danger, but we act to protect our bodies and keep them safe from harm. We are the wretched [*miseri*]. Most have been driven from our fatherland through violence and the cruelty of moneylenders; all of us have been deprived of fame and fortune.

Marcius listened to the ambassadors' words and then advised the rebels to put down their weapons and make their petition before the Senate in Rome: "The Senate of the Roman people has always been so full of compassion and mercy that no one has ever sought its help in vain" (Sallust *BC* 34). The ambassadors, however, returned to Manlius' camp, apparently unwilling to take their chances with the Senate's compassion.

Meanwhile, Catiline, who was still at Rome, was formally charged with public violence under the *lex Plautia de vi*.[82] Catiline knew that there was not sufficient evidence to tie him to the conspiracy, so he offered to place himself in the custody of various senators, who would then be able to vouch for his innocence. Each senator Catiline approached, however (including Cicero himself), refused to take responsibility for him (Cicero *Cat.* 1.19). As it turned out, Catiline left Rome before he could be brought to trial. But Catiline's bold offer reveals Cicero's difficult position: Cicero did not have enough evidence against Catiline to actually arrest him; if he waited until he had undeniable proof of Catiline's guilt, however, the safety of Rome could be put into jeopardy.

October 28 came and went without incident. With no clear proof that Catiline was involved in the conspiracy, Cicero was not in a position to take any action beyond the defensive measures that he had already set in motion. The Senate was reluctant to move against one of its own, and Cicero knew this. Although the Senate as a whole had passed the SCU, many individual senators remained unconvinced that Catiline himself was involved (*Cat.* 1.30). And while Cicero's own measures had prevented the attack on October 28, the very fact that nothing happened made him seem an alarmist. Cicero decided to take no further action until he had solid evidence.

Some evidence was soon forthcoming. On the night of November 6, the leading conspirators in Rome met at the house of M. Porcius Laeca (a senator and a member of Catiline's inner circle; Sallust *BC* 17), to revise their plan of attack. Commanders were assigned to various regions of Italy: Apulia, Etruria, Picenum, and Cisalpine Gaul. Others were to remain in Rome and coordinate plans for arson and murder in the city in conjunction with a planned attack by Manlius' troops at Faesulae. Catiline himself had decided to join Manlius' camp so that he could lead the troops in their march on Rome. The conspirators also realized that the consul Cicero posed a serious threat to their plans. Antonius, the other consul, had been closely allied with Catiline during the elections, and his neutrality (if not support) could be counted upon, but Cicero was taking an active role in attempting to obstruct the conspiracy. Consequently, the decision was made to remove Cicero as soon as possible. Gaius Cornelius, an equestrian, and Lucius Vargunteius, who was either an equestrian or a senator, volunteered to visit Cicero early the next morning.[83] They planned to assassinate him at his house, under the pretext of making a ceremonial call.[84] Cicero learned of the danger as soon as the meeting had broken up; apparently Curius was now playing the role of a double agent and was reporting events to Cicero through Fulvia. By the time Cornelius and Vargunteius showed up, Cicero had set guards around his house and barred the doors. The assassination had been prevented.

On November 8, Cicero called a meeting of the Senate in the temple of Jupiter Stator (see Map 1), which was more easily defensible than the Curia (the Senate house), to discuss the danger that Catiline posed to the city. Catiline himself brazenly attended the meeting, however, which Cicero surely did not expect. It is likely that Catiline had originally intended to leave Rome for Etruria on the night of November 7 and that Cicero had heard about his plans from Fulvia and Curius. Cicero may have called the Senate meeting for November 8 with the intention of using Catiline's departure from Rome as a way to prove his involvement in the conspiracy. But Catiline did not leave Rome as he had planned, perhaps because his plans to eliminate Cicero had been thwarted. With Catiline present at the Senate meeting, denying any involvement in the conspiracy, Cicero's hands were tied: without clear proof of Catiline's involvement, the consul could not take direct action against him.[85]

Cicero turned the stalemate into an opportunity for a rhetorical *tour de force*. He delivered perhaps his most famous speech, now known as the *First Catilinarian Oration*, in which he openly baited Catiline—flaunting his knowledge of Catiline's plans and urging him to leave the city while he was still free to do so. In the speech, Cicero attempts to frighten Catiline into leaving the city voluntarily, while at the same time trying to solidify the Senate's opposition against him. Cicero claims that, because of the SCU, he has the authority to execute Catiline, but says that he hesitates to do so until he is sure of the Senate's support (*Cat.* 1.1-6). Senatorial support remained elusive, however. Later in the speech, when Cicero raises the question of Catiline's banishment, the senators "respond" with only a wary silence (*Cat.* 1.21). Why did the senators remain silent? Some senators no doubt secretly supported the conspiracy, while others would not favor direct action against

Catiline without definite proof of his involvement. And Cicero's own status as a *novus homo* tended to diminish his political clout.

According to Sallust (*BC* 31.7), after Cicero had finished speaking, Catiline stood up and (with downcast eyes and a respectful voice) begged the senators not to believe Cicero's allegations. Catiline reminded them that a patrician like himself, whose ancestors had provided many benefits to the Roman people, would have no need to destroy the Republic. He also questioned whether a man like Marcus Tullius, who was only an immigrant (*inquilinus*) to Rome, would be likely to save it. Catiline had attacked Cicero at his most vulnerable point; many senators would not trust the word of a *novus homo* against that of a patrician and noble like themselves.

Discussion Questions

1. With regard to the short biographies of some of the chief conspirators, do you find certain character traits that might link them together? What do you think were their main motivations for joining the conspiracy?
2. The conspirators' letter, brought to the Roman general Q. Marcius, sets forth the rationale for the rebellion. What sentiments and complaints does the letter convey? What is your assessment of Marcius' reply?
3. What was Cicero trying to accomplish with his speech to the Senate on November 8, 63 B.C.? Did he succeed? What does Sallust's account of that meeting add to the information we can get from Cicero's *First Catilinarian Oration*?

6. The Conspirators and the Allobroges

That night Catiline did leave the city, just as Cicero had hoped, but not before sending letters to some of Rome's leading senators. In the letters, Catiline explained that he was going into exile at Massilia (modern Marseilles; see Map 4) in order to spare the Republic from being disturbed by his personal struggle. One of the letters was given to his good friend Quintus Lutatius Catulus, who read it aloud in the Senate. Sallust includes what may be a genuine copy of this letter in his *Bellum Catilinae* (35).[86] In the letter, Catiline protests that he had taken up the cause of the poor and wretched (*publicam miserorum causam . . . suscepi*) not because he could not pay his own debts but because—through no fault of his own—he had been denied a position of honor, while he saw unworthy men raised to high office (*non dignos homines honore honestatos videbam*). This letter, full of wounded dignity and pride, may give an accurate portrait of a man who believed that the consulship was his birthright and who felt no qualms about destroying the commonwealth to obtain it.

The next day (November 9), Cicero, pleased with the fact that he had driven Catiline out of Rome, delivered his *Second Catilinarian Oration* to the people. Acknowledging that many Romans were not convinced of Catiline's involvement in the conspiracy, Cicero predicted (*Cat.* 2.14–15) that the fugitive would not go into exile as he had claimed, but would go directly to Manlius' camp at Faesulae (thus confirming his connection to the conspirators). By mid-November it was reported at Rome that Catiline had indeed showed up at Manlius' camp; now there was no doubt about his intentions. The Senate immediately declared Catiline and Manlius public enemies and set a date by which Catiline's followers could lay down their arms and receive amnesty. The Senate also authorized the consuls to raise troops. It was decided that Antonius would march with the army against Catiline while Cicero would remain at Rome to provide for the protection of the city (Sallust *BC* 36). In the next few weeks, Roman generals fought unsuccessfully against the rebels in the Apennine regions, Capua, and Cisalpine Gaul. But, in Etruria, Catiline (who had managed to raise the number of his troops to 10,000) continued to evade Antonius' forces and thus avoided a battle.[87]

Meanwhile, the leading conspirators at Rome were finalizing their plans. Once Catiline had finished gathering his forces, he was expected to lead them within a single day's march from Rome. Then Lucius Bestia, a tribune, would call a public meeting (*contio*) at which he would accuse Cicero of causing a dangerous war. That would be the signal for the rest of the conspirators to take action. The following night, Statilius and Gabinius, leading an armed gang, would set fires in twelve key parts of the city; Cethegus was to kill Cicero at his home, while other conspirators were to murder other leading citizens. In the midst of the resulting confusion, the conspirators would break out of the city and join forces with Catiline, who would then march on Rome.[88] The conspirators disagreed, however, as to precisely when this attack should take place. Lentulus and the others thought they should carry it out on the Saturnalia, which was held in mid-December, in order to take advantage of the general confusion of the day.[89] But Cethegus, living up to his reputation as a violent and impetuous man, was eager to act as soon as possible.[90]

For all his lack of restraint, Cethegus may have been correct in his assessment. For while the conspirators were taking the time to coordinate their plans, they made a crucial mistake in judgment, which Cicero used to his full advantage. The Allobroges, a tribe of southern Gaul (see Map 4) that had been made subject to Rome in 121 B.C., had been extremely hard pressed not only by the high levels of taxation but also by the high rate of interest on the money that they had to borrow to pay the taxes. They were staggering under their debts (both public and private) and were chafing under the greed of Roman officials (*avaritia magistratuum*; Sallust *BC* 40). They sent two members of their tribe as ambassadors to Rome to beg the Senate for some relief (Plutarch *Cicero* 18.4), but the senators refused to act on their requests. Because the Allobroges were so desperate, Lentulus thought that they might be interested in joining the conspiracy. He approached the two envoys through a middleman named P. Umbrenus, a freedman who had done business in Gaul and was personally acquainted with several Gallic leaders (Cicero *Cat.* 3.14; Sallust *BC* 40). Umbrenus, accompanied by Publius Gabinius Capito, an equestrian and one of the leading conspirators, met with the Allobrogian envoys and disclosed the entire plot.[91] Umbrenus and Gabinius promised the Allobrogian people relief from debt as well as other rewards if they would send cavalry into Italy to support Catiline's foot soldiers in battle (Sallust *BC* 40; Cicero *Cat.* 3.9).

The Allobrogian envoys must have been excited by the promises that had been made to them, but perhaps they doubted whether the conspirators could actually deliver on those promises. At any rate, they did not immediately accept the conspirators' proposal, but sought the advice of Quintus Fabius Sanga, who served as the principal patron of their tribe.[92] Sanga immediately told Cicero that the Allobroges had been approached by the conspirators; Cicero, realizing that this was a golden opportunity to get irrefutable evidence against them, asked the Allobroges to help save the Republic. The Allobrogian ambassadors were told to continue their negotiations with the conspirators as if they were genuinely interested, but to ask the conspirators to put their promises in writing (Sallust *BC* 41).

The Allobroges requested letters from Lentulus, Cethegus, Statilius, and Cassius. They used the excuse that, since their people were being asked to furnish cavalry for the conspiracy, they needed written proof of the conspirators' goodwill. In an amazing display of arrogance and stupidity, Lentulus, Cethegus, and Statilius wrote self-incriminating letters and gave them to the two envoys. Cassius, sensing a trap, declined to write a letter and quickly left town (Sallust *BC* 41). Lentulus then asked Titus Volturcius, apparently a man of relatively low status and perhaps even one of his own clients, to accompany the Allobroges as they carried the letters back to Gaul. Volturcius later claimed that he had been told of the conspiracy only a few days before the journey (Sallust *BC* 47). Volturcius and the Allobroges planned to travel to Gaul to convince the Allobrogian people to support the conspiracy. On their way back to Rome they planned to stop off at Faesulae and meet with Catiline to confirm the alliance. Lentulus also gave Volturcius a letter for Catiline and some additional verbal instructions (Sallust *BC* 44; Cicero *Cat.* 3.8 and 3.12).

Cicero was, of course, informed of all these plans through the Allobrogian ambassadors. The story of how he was able to apprehend Volturcius and the Allobroges just north of Rome as they were crossing the Mulvian Bridge in the early morning hours of December 3 is brilliantly told in his *Third Catilinarian Oration* (*Cat.* 3.5–6). Once he had possession of the letters, Cicero arrested the three letter writers (Lentulus, Cethegus, and Statilius) as well as Gabinius, who had helped to facilitate the meeting with the Allobroges. Cicero also tried to arrest M. Ceparius, who had been assigned the task of stirring up a slave revolt in Apulia (Sallust *BC* 46; Cicero *Cat.* 3.14). But Ceparius had left Rome during the night (presumably for Apulia), and so, for the moment, he was able to escape. He was soon caught, however, and brought back to Rome. Cicero then called a meeting of the Senate at the Temple of Concord (see Map 1). In his *Third Catilinarian Oration*, delivered to the people immediately after the Senate meeting, Cicero describes how he confronted the conspirators in the Senate and forced them to confess (*Cat.* 3.7–13). The five conspirators (Lentulus, Cethegus, Statilius, and Gabinius as well as Ceparius, who had just been caught) were taken into the custody of individual senators (the prison at Rome was not used for this purpose). Officers were sent to arrest four other key conspirators (L. Cassius, P. Furius, Q. Annius Chilo, and P. Umbrenus), but there is no record that any of these men were ever caught (Sallust *BC* 47; Cicero *Cat.* 3.14). Volturcius was granted immunity from prosecution in return for the evidence he had given.

It is clear from this speech that Cicero was extremely proud of himself; and, in fact, he had every reason to be. He had finally found the evidence that was needed to convict the conspirators. Plans to burn the city, massacre leading citizens and invite Gallic cavalry into Italy had been revealed—and forestalled—without any bloodshed. A grateful Senate, finally convinced that Cicero had in fact saved the city from widespread anarchy and slaughter, decreed a *supplicatio* (a formal thanksgiving to the gods) in Cicero's name (*Cat.* 3.15). It was at this meeting, or perhaps a few days later, that Q. Catulus, the leader of the Senate (*princeps senatus*), named Cicero the father of his country (*parens patriae*) for his outstanding service in preserving Rome from destruction (Cicero *In Pisonem* 6).

The events of the following day (December 4) indicate that a hysterical atmosphere now prevailed at Rome. Some of Lentulus' freedmen and clients apparently circulated around the poorer sections of Rome, inciting the residents to rise up and free their patron from confinement. Cethegus, too, was caught sending messengers to his freedmen and slaves, in the hopes of effecting his escape (Sallust *BC* 50; Cicero *Cat.* 4.17). Meanwhile, others were attempting to exploit the chaotic situation for their own political advantage. A man named L. Tarquinius, allegedly caught on his way to Faesulae, informed the Senate that Crassus was a member of the conspiracy; he claimed to have been sent to Faesulae by Crassus with verbal instructions for Catiline, urging him not to lose hope. But, as Tarquinius was unable to give any new information beyond what Volturcius had revealed the previous day, the senators decided that his testimony was not credible. Under Cicero's leadership, the Senate decreed that Tarquinius should be kept under guard until he revealed who had urged him to give false information to the Senate. The Senate also voted handsome rewards (*praemia amplissima*) to Volturcius and the Allobrogian envoys (Cicero *Cat.* 4.5). Meanwhile, two of Caesar's political enemies asked Cicero to bring a false allegation of complicity against Caesar. When Cicero refused, the two men spread such wicked gossip against the young senator that he was mobbed as he tried to leave the Senate.[93]

Discussion Questions

1. What conclusions about Catiline's motives can we draw from his letter to Catulus? Does this fit well with his outburst in the Senate after Cicero's *First Catilinarian Oration*?
2. Why was it important to the Senate to find out for certain whether Catiline had gone to Massilia or Faesulae?
3. What was the conspirators' coordinated plan for attacking Rome from both inside and outside the city?
4. In your opinion, why did the conspirators agree to write self-incriminating letters and give them to the Allobrogian envoys?

7. The Fate of the Conspirators and the End of the Conspiracy

The Fate of the Conspirators

With rumors flying throughout the city and conspirators doing their best to break out of confinement, it was clear that order needed to be restored to the city as soon as possible. Catiline and Manlius had an army of some 10,000 men in Faesulae, and the government needed to stabilize the situation in Rome in order to focus on this external threat. Cicero called a meeting of the Senate for December 5 to decide on the fate of the five arrested conspirators.[94] There were serious issues for the senators to discuss. In Cicero's view, the conspirators had to be killed in order to restore calm to the city. The execution of the conspirators might seem to be a straightforward matter; after all, they had confessed to conspiring to overthrow the government. But these men had not actually carried out their plans for murder and mayhem; they had simply conspired to do so. Furthermore, the *lex Sempronia de capite civium*, passed in 122 B.C. by Gaius Gracchus in response to the summary execution of his brother's followers (see Historical Essay I.3), provided that no Roman citizen could be put to death without a trial before the people. Any Roman magistrate who did so would himself be liable to a capital charge. In this case, however, the safety of the Republic could be seriously compromised while the trials were taking place. Furthermore, there was really no way to tell how many conspirators and their sympathizers remained in the city. Could the people be trusted to impose an appropriately harsh penalty? Finally, the conspirators had already shown that they would make use of any delay to try to bring about their escape. Could the government afford to take the chance of an escape when Catiline and his army were still preparing to attack?

These were the issues weighing on Cicero's mind when he convened a meeting of the Senate at the Temple of Concord (see Map 1) on December 5 under tight security (Sallust *BC* 50.3; Cicero *Cat.* 4.14–15). Cicero began the debate by proposing that the five conspirators in custody should be killed, as well as four others who were then being sought.[95] Junius Silanus, the senior consul-elect, agreed, as did Lucius Murena, his colleague, and fourteen other senators of consular rank.[96] But when Julius Caesar, a praetor-elect, was asked his opinion, he sounded a note of caution. In the version of his speech presented by Sallust, Caesar agreed that the conspirators were guilty of treasonous intent and that they deserved a serious punishment. But

Caesar also argued that the laws protecting Roman citizens, such as Gracchus' *de capite civium*, must be respected (*BC* 51.15–25).[97] Caesar recalled that Sulla had begun his reign of terror by executing criminals and assassins. Everyone praised Sulla when he was killing these men, even though what he was doing was actually illegal. Sulla had established a precedent, however, and when he later began to murder innocent men, it was too late to stop him. Using Sulla as an example, Caesar argued that the Senate, too, would be establishing a terrible precedent if it now abandoned the rule of law (Sallust *BC* 51.35–36):

> I do not fear that M. Tullius [would do] these things or that [they will happen] at this time; but in a great state there are many and varied characters. Perhaps at another time, when another consul has command of the army, a false [accusation] will be believed as true. If some future consul, using our deed as an example, draws his sword in accordance with the Senate's decree, who will impose a limit or restrain him?

As an alternative to the death penalty, Caesar proposed that the conspirators be sentenced to life imprisonment in various Italian rural towns (*ipsos in vinculis habendos per municipia*) and that their property be confiscated.[98]

Caesar's speech was a powerful argument against the legality of the SCU and in favor of the rule of law; his arguments were also consistent with his prosecution of Gaius Rabirius a few months earlier. Caesar later abandoned this high-minded position, of course; but in 63 B.C. he seems to have been perfectly sincere in his arguments in favor of the rule of law. But Caesar's suggestion of life imprisonment, while not unprecedented, was distinctly unusual and highly impractical.[99] Roman prisons were not designed to hold lifetime (or even long-term) inmates. The public prison was generally used only for the short-term custody of convicted criminals awaiting execution. Respectable criminals were usually allowed to flee quietly into exile (consider the fate of Gaius Verres or Catiline's own pretense of fleeing to Massalia). In the present case, however, exile was not a viable option; if sent into exile, the conspirators would simply join the rebel army at Faesulae, as Catiline himself had done (Sallust *BC* 51.43).

Although Caesar's proposal was impractical (Cicero *Cat.* 4.7), his speech did cause several of the senators to question the wisdom of putting the conspirators to death, and other solutions were now proposed. Tiberius Claudius Nero (an ex-praetor and the grandfather of the future emperor) proposed that the conspirators be kept under guard and that a decision on their fate be postponed until Catiline and his army had been beaten and more accurate information could be obtained (Appian 2.5). Tiberius' proposal received much support; even Junius Silanus changed his mind, saying he would now favor imprisonment rather than death (Plutarch *Cicero* 21). When the tribunes-elect were asked for their opinion, however, Marcus Porcius Cato stood up and spoke powerfully in favor of the death penalty. Cato pointed out that, because Catiline and his army were still at large, the conspirators now in custody posed a serious threat to the city. He noted that in Caesar's proposal the conspirators were to be imprisoned outside the city, presumably through fear that if they were held at Rome they would be set free. But nothing would prevent the conspirators from being rescued by their friends no matter where in Italy they were being held. Cato urged his fellow senators to send a strong message to Catiline by punishing the conspirators quickly and severely: because they had confessed to planning murder, arson, and other terrible crimes, they should be punished with death, just as if they had been caught in the actual commission of those crimes (Sallust *BC* 52). When Cato had finished speaking, the Senate burst into applause.

As consul, Cicero was probably the last to speak, and he came out strongly for the death penalty. In his speech, which he later published as the *Fourth Catilinarian Oration*, Cicero claims that by their treasonous actions the conspirators had given up their right to be treated as citizens. Because the conspirators had acted as enemies to the state, they should be treated as enemies; hence the provisions of the *lex Sempronia* should not apply to them.[100] The problem with this argument is that the conspirators' guilt and their consequent forfeiture of citizenship rights were precisely the points at issue; the purpose of a trial would be to formally establish the validity of those charges.[101] Cicero's argument assumed that the charge that the conspirators were *hostes* had already been proved.[102] Furthermore, the conspirators had simply plotted to burn the city and overthrow the government; thanks to Cicero's own actions they had not carried out their plans; could they be executed for acts that they did not actually commit?

In his speech, Cicero also implied that the Senate had already given him the authority to impose the death penalty by passing the SCU (*Cat.* 4.5–6). But the Senate did not have that authority to give. The legality of the SCU had never been established; no law had ever been passed to ratify its provisions, and only the popular assemblies had the authority to pass such a law.

In fact, the legality of the SCU had recently been challenged through the trial of Gaius Rabirius (see Historical Essay II.3). Cicero's reliance on the SCU put him in a weak position, and he was well aware of this. The very fact that Cicero was unwilling to execute the prisoners without a formal vote in the Senate suggests that he did not believe the SCU had given him sufficient authority to do so.[103] Nonetheless, Cicero's desire for the death penalty was consistent with the position he had taken in his defense of Gaius Rabirius. And he was certainly correct in his view that, as long as Catiline's army remained undefeated, the conspirators posed a serious danger to the state.

In the final paragraphs of his speech, Cicero reveals his fears for the future. He notes that—if the conspirators are killed—he will be hated by those who are sympathetic to Catiline; and he characterizes himself as the man "who preserved everything at a danger to himself alone" (*Cat.* 4.23). Although his words are characteristically melodramatic, they indicate Cicero's awareness of his own dilemma: if he should take the decisive action he believed to be necessary, he would be making himself vulnerable to the charge of having put Roman citizens to death without a trial.

The senators, moved primarily by Cato's speech (a fact which Cicero found annoying, *ad Att.* 12.21.1), voted overwhelmingly for the death penalty. Cicero did not waste any time; the prisoners had already demonstrated their eagerness to escape. The Roman state prison (*carcer*) was located in the northwest corner of the Forum (see Map 1).[104] The upper chamber was used to hold prisoners awaiting trial or execution. The lower, subterranean, chamber, called the Tullianum, was used to carry out executions and was accessible only through a hole in the floor of the prison above.[105] As Sallust notes, the appearance of the Tullianum was terrifying, "on account of neglect, darkness, and its foul stench" (*BC* 55.4). Cicero personally led Lentulus through the Forum and into the Carcer then handed him down to the executioners in the Tullianum below, where he was strangled. One by one, the praetors brought the other four conspirators into the Carcer and passed them down to the executioners. When it was over, Cicero reappeared in the Forum and announced to the waiting crowd that the conspirators' lives were over: *vixerunt* (they have completed their lives). The grateful crowd cheered Cicero, calling him the savior and founder of his country. Some of Rome's most prominent citizens accompanied Cicero to his home, and many people placed lamps and torches at their doors and rooftops to honor the man who had saved Rome from chaos and murder without any violence or bloodshed (Plutarch *Cicero* 22.3–7).

The End of the Conspiracy

Cicero had almost single-handedly saved Rome from a violent uprising. But the backlash that Cicero had feared did not take long to materialize. When the new tribunes took office on December 10, one tribune, Quintus Metellus Nepos, declared at a *contio* (public meeting) that anyone who had executed a citizen without a trial should not be allowed to address the people (Cicero, *ad Fam.* 5.2.7). When Cicero was about to make his customary speech to the people on the last day of his consulship (December 31), Nepos prevented him from doing so, allowing him only to swear the usual oath that he had faithfully performed his duties. Cicero outsmarted the tribune, however, by swearing instead that he alone had saved both the city and the Republic. Cicero's oath was greeted with a roar of approval from the crowd, who, with a single voice, confirmed his oath and escorted their hero home.[106]

Sometime during the first few days of January of 62 B.C., Nepos attacked Cicero in the Senate on the grounds that he had illegally condemned citizens to death without a vote of the people. The Senate, however, responded by passing a decree of immunity for all those who had managed the affairs of state during the conspiracy. A few days later Nepos introduced a bill in the *concilium plebis* to recall Pompey with his army back to Rome from the East (where he was now finishing up his conquests) so that he could bring order to the state.[107] This was clearly an attempt by Nepos (who had just returned from serving with Pompey's army) to give preeminence to Pompey, and perhaps to secure for him the command against Catiline and his army.[108] Nepos' bill, however, was successfully vetoed (although not without some violence) by Cato, who was also one of the tribunes for 62 B.C. Cato then extolled Cicero's consulship; the people responded by addressing Cicero as the father of his country (*pater patriae*), just as Q. Catulus had done in the Senate a few weeks before.[109] The failure of Nepos' attempts to vilify Cicero (he had even referred to Cicero's consulship as a tyranny) showed how much support Cicero had from both the people and the Senate, but Cicero's vulnerability had been made painfully clear.[110]

Meanwhile, when the news of the executions at Rome reached Faesulae, Catiline's followers began to slip away.[111] Catiline had managed to enlist almost ten thousand men in his army; but, after the news of the executions came from Rome, his forces dwindled down to three or four thousand.[112] Since an attack on Rome was now out of the question, Catiline led his remaining forces north into the mountains by back country roads, intending to escape into

Transalpine Gaul. The praetor Q. Metellus Celer, who was stationed with three legions in Picenum (see Map 3), got word of Catiline's intentions from deserters, however, and was able to intercept him (Sallust *BC* 57–58). Catiline, caught between the armies of Celer and Antonius Hybrida, realized that he would have to fight. He decided to take his chances with Antonius, his former ally, in the hopes of receiving lenient treatment. But as the day for battle drew near, Antonius suffered a convenient foot ailment and handed the command of his army to his legate (chief lieutenant), M. Petreius, an experienced military commander.[113]

The battle was fought near Pistoria (modern Pistoia), about twenty-five miles northwest of Florence (see Map 3). Just before the two armies came together, Catiline and his officers sent away their horses, so that all of their soldiers would face an equal danger. It was a long and bloody battle, with Catiline's troops putting up a much stronger fight than anyone had anticipated. Finally Petreius sent his best troops, his praetorian cohort, against the enemy's center. This threw Catiline's men into confusion and they began to give ground. When Petreius then attacked his weakened opponents on both wings, resistance collapsed.

According to Sallust, when Catiline realized that his men had been conquered and all hope was lost, "mindful of his noble birth and former dignity he ran into the enemy where they were most crowded and he died there fighting, stabbed through and through" (Sallust *BC* 60). All Catiline's remaining soldiers died in that battle; none of them fled or were taken alive. Catiline himself was found amidst the corpses of his enemies, with a fierce and defiant expression on his face.

Over the course of the next few months, several high-ranking conspirators (including M. Porcius Laeca, at whose house the conspirators had met, and Gaius Cornelius, one of the *equites* who had tried to assassinate Cicero on November 7) were prosecuted for inciting public violence under the *lex Plautia de vi*. They were all convicted.[114]

But while these conspirators got what they deserved, the Allobrogian people most certainly did not. As mentioned above, the Senate gave generous rewards to the Allobrogian envoys, who had proved their loyalty to their Roman captors. The Senate did not soften its stance against the Allobrogian people, however, who had requested some relief from their double burden of taxation and debt. In 61 B.C. the Allobroges felt that they had no choice but rebellion. Their uprising was successful at first, but in 60 B.C. the revolt was put down by the governor, C. Pomptinus; the Senate voted him a public thanksgiving.

Discussion Questions

1. What were the main arguments for and against executing the five conspir-ators? What were the arguments for and against Caesar's proposal of life imprisonment? Which punishment would you have voted for and why?
2. What actions did the tribune Q. Nepos take against Cicero on December 10 and December 31 of 63, and in early January of 62 B.C.? What do you think were his motivations for those actions?
3. The information about Catiline's final battle comes mainly from Sallust. Assuming this information is correct, what character traits do you see revealed in Catiline's actions? Do any of Catiline's actions surprise you?

8. Cicero's Exile and Return

As consul, Cicero had uncovered and foiled a plot to massacre leading citi-zens and overthrow the government, and he had managed to do so without any eruption of violence in the city. Only five leading conspirators had been killed; no other civilian blood had been shed. Catiline and his followers had died in armed combat far from Rome; they never had the chance to march on Rome as they had planned. Cicero had been hailed as the "father of his country" by both the people and the Senate (Plutarch *Cicero* 23.6; Cicero *In Pisonem* 3.6). There had been public criticism from Nepos and those whose interests he represented; but in the competitive atmosphere of the late Republic, these challenges were no more than what any prominent leader would expect. In fact, Cicero's achievement in putting down the Catilinarian conspiracy had significantly raised his expectations for the future.

As a senator from an equestrian family (a *novus homo*), Cicero's highest ambition had been to achieve the consulship, which would raise his family to noble status. But after having almost single-handedly saved the Republic, Cicero began to think of himself as one of the few really great men who had the power to shape Roman policy.[115] Cicero's inflated sense of his own importance can already be seen in his *Fourth Catilinarian Oration* (4.21), in which he compares his suppression of the conspiracy with the military achievements of Scipio Africanus, Marius, and Pompey.[116] In a letter written to Pompey in the spring of 62 B.C. (Pompey was still wrapping up affairs in the East), Cicero cast himself in the role of Pompey's sage advisor. Cicero hinted that Pompey and Cicero together—the great general and wise civic leader—could some day join forces and save the Roman Republic (Cicero *ad Fam.* 5.7.3). The reality, unfortunately, proved to be quite different. Pompey did not respond warmly to Cicero's letter; perhaps he resented the fact that Cicero had done such a good job of suppressing the conspiracy that there was no need for Pompey himself to return and restore order.[117] And in fact Cicero's suppression of Catiline's conspiracy turned out to be the high point of his career; he was never again to wield the influence over public affairs that he had achieved during his consulship.

The reasons why Cicero failed to achieve political preeminence are varied and complex. Surely his own flawed political judgment, always clouded by an inflated sense of his own importance, must have played a role. But Cicero's failure was also due to his insistence on working within the institutions of the Republic, at a time when those institutions were beginning to crumble. Some insight into the fragility of the governmental structures and the fierce competitiveness that the resulting power vacuum unleashed can be gained by examining Cicero's ideal of the *concordia ordinum* (harmony of the orders). The *concordia ordinum* was Cicero's optimistic plan to bring all classes of the Roman people together and breathe new life into the Republic. In the middle of his *Fourth Catilinarian Oration*, Cicero directs the senators' attention outside the Temple of Concord, where they were meeting, to the great crowd of citizens who have gathered in the Forum to show their support. Perhaps inspired by the symbolism of the temple's name, Cicero declares:

> Everyone is present, men of every order, of every class, and finally of every age; the Forum is full, the temples surrounding the Forum are full, the entrances and grounds of this temple are full. Since the founding of the city, this is the only occasion that has been found in which everyone feels one and the same thing. (Cat. 4.14)

Cicero then goes on to enumerate the various orders or classes who have come to the Forum to support the Senate: the *tribunii aerarii*, the scribes, the freeborn, the freedmen, and even the slaves (*Cat.* 4.15–16). Cicero was clearly elated by the spontaneous encouragement from people of all walks of life who came together, under his leadership, to support the Senate and save the Republic. In the early months of 62 B.C., after the threat from Catiline had passed, Cicero tried to develop the idea of a union of responsible citizens from all classes (but especially from the senators and equestrians) who would work together to discourage irresponsible elements and breathe new life into the Republican institutions. As Cicero states in his *Fourth*

Catilinarian Oration: "This union [of orders] that has been established in my consulship—if we maintain it forever in the Republic, I guarantee to you that in the future no civil or domestic harm will ever come to any part of the Republic" (*Cat.* 4.15; cf. 4.22).

The problem with Cicero's *concordia ordinum* was that he did not offer the other orders any reason why they should follow the Senate's lead. Specifically, he did not initiate any economic policies that might lead the equestrians to identify their own interests with those of the senators. Nor did he attempt to provide a solution for the serious economic and social problems (such as a shortage of farmland, excessive debt, and the high price of food and shelter) that had been placing a stranglehold on the poor for many years. Catiline's conspiracy had presented an immediate threat to the well-being of the city, and its suppression may well have produced a sincere outpouring of goodwill from all classes of citizens. But such an immediate reaction is difficult to maintain once a crisis has passed; and Cicero's idealism, however well-intentioned, could not be a substitute for policy.

In fact, during the next few months it became clear that the various factions in the state were motivated primarily by their own self-interest. One incident that occurred in December of 62 B.C., the infamous Bona Dea scandal, is an excellent illustration of this tendency. The rites of the Bona Dea (the Good Goddess), which were open only to women, were being celebrated in the house of the *pontifex maximus*, Julius Caesar. Although it was a sacrilege for men to attend the ritual, a prominent young man named P. Clodius Pulcher dressed up as a woman and joined the festivities, ostensibly to keep a tryst with Caesar's wife, Pompeia.[118] Clodius was caught by the maidservants sneaking around Caesar's house, and he was duly tried for religious impurity (*incestum*). Caesar, who had divorced his wife without admitting her guilt (since Caesar's wife must be above suspicion), refused to testify against Clodius, recognizing his value as a client and political ally. Rumor had it that enormous sums were being spent on the fifty-six jurors who would try the case, and that the jurors also received various gifts, promises, and other attentions from Clodius' influential friends.[119] Cicero, however, bluntly disproved Clodius' alibi and humiliated him with taunts about paid-off jurors. Cicero did this even though there had been no previous personal enmity between them.[120] Clodius was acquitted by a vote of thirty-one to twenty-five, and (predictably) from that day on, he hated Cicero with a deep, abiding passion. Meanwhile, the Senate, shocked at the equestrian jurors who had acquitted an obviously guilty man, attempted to investigate the jury. Cicero blocked the investigation (even though he knew that the jurors had accepted bribes), in the name of the *concordia ordinum*.

The strange tale of the Bona Dea scandal is fascinating in its own right, but it also serves to indicate the deteriorating health of the Republic and its institutions. Caesar was not concerned about the religious sacrilege that had occurred or about the viability of his marriage; he saw only a valuable political connection that could be exploited. Even the attempt to investigate the jury for corruption had been blocked for political reasons. Clodius, too, was clearly unconcerned with the niceties of marital vows, religious sanctity, or judicial honesty; he had been caught red-handed while playing an adolescent prank and was fighting for his political life. Cicero's own motives for exposing Clodius' guilt were probably also mixed. Although he claimed to have destroyed Clodius' alibi in order to curtail licentiousness and restore the Republic to health (*ad Att.* 1.18.2), Clodius' trial had become a contest between popular and senatorial interests. Cicero (who had come to represent senatorial authority after his execution of the Catilinarian conspirators) may well have acted to bolster the Senate's influence.[121] But Cicero's actions— whether from political naiveté or loyalty to the Senate, or both—turned out to be quite self-destructive. The widespread support for Clodius after the Bona Dea scandal clearly demonstrated that partisan politics were now the only thing that mattered; the *concordia ordinum,* if it had ever existed, had been shattered long ago. In such a context of self-interest, Cicero's insistence on disproving Clodius' alibi was a costly and foolish political mistake.

Toward the end of 60 B.C. Caesar struck a death blow to the already fragile Republic by forming the secret partnership with Pompey and Crassus that is now known as the First Triumvirate. The events leading up to this watershed agreement can be quickly summarized. In June of that year, Caesar had returned from his governorship of Further Spain, ready to run for the consulship. While in Spain he had conducted a successful military campaign for which he had been voted a triumph (a triumphal procession through the center of the city). In order to receive his triumph, a general had to remain with his army, outside the city walls, until the triumph could be celebrated. But in order to run for the consulship, the candidate had to present himself in person, inside the city walls. Since he obviously could not be in two places at once, Caesar requested permission to run for the consulship *in absentia*, an exception that had previously been granted to others in similar circumstances. But the Senate, led by the indomitable M. Porcius Cato, refused his request, fearing that Caesar might become too powerful. Caesar, always sensitive to the realities of power, decided to give up his triumph in order to stand for election. Meanwhile, the Senate, in anticipation of Caesar's success at the polls, had already assigned to the consuls of 59 B.C. very unattractive provinces: the forests and cattle-paths of Italy.

In attempting to prevent the future dictator from becoming too powerful, the Senate was using the same obstructionist tactics on Caesar that it had used on Pompey and Crassus. Pompey had returned from the East almost two years earlier, but the Senate still had not ratified the settlements he had made for the region or granted land allotments to his veterans. These were both reasonable requests that should have been handled expeditiously. The Senate had also prevented Crassus from helping the tax-farmers. These *publicani* had bid too high a price for the taxes in Asia and had asked to negotiate a lower price. Crassus, who represented their interests, had argued in favor of the request, and Cicero, too, had supported it. But the Senate, again following Cato's lead, had refused to allow it. The Senate had chosen obstructionism over a positive political strategy.

In its ill-considered attempt to prevent any one of these three men from becoming too powerful, the Senate drove them into an alliance, an alliance that they would certainly never have entered on their own. Caesar first approached Pompey and then enlisted Crassus, Pompey's political rival (see Historical Essay I.9). Together they swore a solemn promise to use their official government posts to promote one another's interests (Suetonius *Divus Julius* 19.2). Cicero, too, seems to have been invited to join the alliance. Caesar's agent visited Cicero in December of 60 B.C. and promised him the backing of both Pompey and Crassus if he would agree to support the legislative program that Caesar would promulgate during his upcoming consulship (*ad Att.* 2.3.3; *De provinciis consularibus* 41). Caesar greatly admired Cicero's skill as an orator, and he valued Cicero's influence with the equestrians and Italian aristocrats. But Cicero declined the invitation. This was no ordinary political alliance, as Cicero correctly saw; this secret agreement would undermine the Republic. Aptly quoting Hector, who had died fighting for Troy, Cicero wrote to his friend Atticus: "One omen is best, to fight in defense of the fatherland" (*ad Att.* 2.3.3–4; *Iliad* 12.243). Cicero was right, of course: if Roman magistrates were primarily serving one another's interests, they could no longer be working for the Roman people; as consuls, praetors, and senators, their primary allegiance should be to the Republic, not to themselves. But the Republic that Cicero fought so hard to protect had reached such a state of paralysis that it could no longer perform its most basic functions.

Backed by Pompey and Crassus, Caesar, as consul in 59 B.C., was able to break up the logjam of government. With Pompey's veterans present under arms, Caesar forced a bill through the Plebeian Council granting their land allotments. When Bibulus, Caesar's consular colleague, tried to object, his fasces were smashed. Bibulus himself was forced to flee for his safety. Caesar also got the Plebeian Council to reduce the Asian tax-farmers' contracts by one-third and to ratify Pompey's eastern settlements. For himself, Caesar procured the provinces of Cisalpine Gaul, Transalpine Gaul, and Illyricum with four legions and a five-year command; he was not going to settle for the forests or cattle-paths of Italy.

In December of 60 B.C., Caesar had invited Cicero to join his political alliance because he valued the orator's ability to sway public opinion. A year later, after the Triumvirate had achieved its goals and its existence was no longer a secret, Caesar began to be concerned that Cicero might use those same abilities to stir up popular sentiment against the alliance.[122] Meanwhile, P. Clodius Pulcher, Cicero's enemy since the Bona Dea scandal, was elected with Caesar's help as a tribune of the plebs for the following year. Clodius now began to threaten Cicero because of his actions as consul in executing the Catilinarian conspirators without a trial (*ad Att.* 2.19.1). Caesar offered Cicero a position on his staff in Gaul, which would have protected him from any attack by Clodius; but Cicero declined. A few months later, Caesar offered Cicero a place on his land commission and renewed his offer of a staff appointment (*ad Att.* 2.18.3). As Stockton notes (1971: 180): "It looks as if Caesar . . . was planning either to get Cicero on his side or silence him through fear." But Cicero did not relish the thought of accepting favors from a political rival, and he naively believed that his own authority and personal connections would be enough to shield him from an unsavory character such as Clodius. In a letter to his brother, Quintus, written during November of 59, Cicero is full of confidence:

If Clodius takes me to court, all Italy will run to my defense, so that my glory will end up being greatly enhanced. But if he tries to attack me by force, I hope to be able to resist him with force, helped not only by my friends, but even by outsiders. Everyone is generously promising his help, his friends, his clients, freedmen, slaves and even his money. My old band of tried-and-true followers is burning with eagerness and devotion . . . Pompey promises his complete support and Caesar does as well. (*ad Quintum* 1.2.16)

Bolstered by his characteristic self-confidence, Cicero maintained his independence and refused to rein in his rhetoric.

But events soon proved that Cicero had seriously underestimated Clodius' threat, just as he had overestimated his own influence and power. As soon as Clodius took office as tribune, he passed a bill legalizing the formation of clubs and associations (*collegia*), a practice that had recently been abolished, and then organized an armed band of thugs under the guise of a *collegium*.[123] In February Clodius proposed two further bills, one (*de capite civis Romani*) banishing anyone who had put Roman citizens to death without a trial.[124] This bill was directed against Cicero, although he was not specifically named. The other bill guaranteed attractive provinces for the two current consuls, thus insuring that they would not object to Clodius' plans. Nor did Caesar or Pompey or any of Cicero's other friends come through with their promised support. During the next few weeks, Clodius and his *collegium* made it clear that violence would ensue if anyone attempted to come to Cicero's aid. At last, on March 20 of 58 B.C., Cicero yielded to pressure and quietly left Rome, just before Clodius' bill was passed. As soon as Cicero had gone, however, Clodius passed a second bill that specifically named him and sent him into exile; Cicero was banished to a distance of about 400 miles from Rome, and harsh penalties were imposed on anyone who harbored him. Furthermore, Cicero's property was confiscated, and his expensive house on the Palatine was destroyed. Cicero (now forced to leave Italy because of Clodius' second bill) spent the next few months in Thessalonica and Dyrrhacium in northwest Greece (see Map 4).[125]

Cicero was devastated by exile; all his illusions about the *concordia ordinum* and the legacy of his consulship had been shattered. Although his friends were able to effect his return only a year and a half later (he made a triumphant return to Rome on September 4, 57 B.C.) and he was eventually allowed to rebuild his house on the Palatine, Cicero's independence was gone. After his return, Cicero made a public declaration of his support for Caesar and his policies (*ad Att* 4.5.2–3; cf. *De provinciis consularibus*) and bent his will to the new political reality.

Only a few years earlier (in the spring of 60 B.C.), Cicero had published a collection of his consular speeches, including his *Catilinarian Orations*, "in an attempt to remind people of his great deeds, and of a period, as he saw it, of concord and unity."[126] Cicero's hard-won goal of preserving the Republic, expressed so hopefully and so forcefully in the *Catilinarian Orations*, was already the subject of nostalgia.

Discussion Questions

1. Explain Cicero's concept of the *concordia ordinum*. Give at least two reasons why it never became a reality.
2. What was the Bona Dea scandal? What was Cicero's role in the aftermath of the affair? What do Cicero's actions reveal about his political acumen (or lack thereof)?
3. Describe the political alliance known as the First Triumvirate. What events precipitated its formation? Why did Cicero decline the invitation to join?
4. How was Clodius able to orchestrate Cicero's exile? What information can you gather from those events about the viability of the Republic and its institutions?

9. Conclusions

Catiline's attempt at revolution makes exciting reading, with a secret plot to murder the consul at dawn, Gallic double agents, and an ambush at 3 A.M. on the Mulvian Bridge. But the conspiracy is also interesting because it occurred at a historically significant time, when the Roman Republic was still a viable government, but was already rapidly disintegrating. By 63 B.C., the Republic was ripe for a coup d'état. The cumbersome, inefficient Republican government, designed to provide self-rule for a city-state of moderate size, was overwhelmed with the responsibilities of administering a vast, overseas empire. The influx of wealth from foreign wars and the resulting economic expansion had produced a continuing agrarian crisis, which a series of narrowly focused agrarian bills had done little or nothing to solve. Wealth and property were increasingly concentrated in the hands of a few; levels of debt were high among all classes of society, while displaced peasants continued to flock to Rome. And all these events took place within an atmosphere of increasing political violence. Faced with these complex problems, the Senate preferred to look out for its own interests rather than risk losing some of its power and prestige to try to solve them. Meanwhile, large, private armies had elevated individual generals to positions of unprecedented power. Sulla had already demonstrated that the right man could march on Rome at the head of an army and take the reins of power into his own hands. Catiline, however, was not the right man.

Sometimes a failure is more revealing than a success, which, because it changes what comes after it, tends to obscure its own development. Through

Catiline's failed attempt at revolution, his goals and motivations are revealed. Catiline's lineage had led him to believe that the consulship was rightfully his; he was determined to win that position and the prestige that went with it, even if it meant destroying the Republic in the process. In using the discontented masses (the *miseri*) to gain political power, Catiline and his co-conspirators were only doing what elite Roman politicians had always done. The fact that they aimed at overthrowing the established government (rather than merely manipulating it) might have seemed to them only a matter of degree—a question of means, fully justified by the ends. The rewards of power had become too great to give up, and the political institutions had become too weak to pose a serious threat. The fact that large numbers of Roman citizens were willing to participate in an armed revolt against their own government reveals how poor and desperate they had become.

Because of the rapidly deteriorating condition of the Republican government, it was only a matter of time before another, more capable general would succeed where Catiline had failed. Caesar was a much smarter politician than Catiline and one of the finest generals the world had ever seen. But in 63 B.C. even Caesar did not realize that the Republic had already ceased to function as an effective government. Cicero's heroic efforts to salvage its crumbling institutions—and his dream of a *concordia ordinum*—are certainly deserving of praise and admiration. But although he succeeded in outwitting Catiline and his accomplices, in the long run Cicero's efforts at reviving the Republic were doomed to failure. With the prizes of empire hanging in the balance, Cicero's exhortations to adhere to the traditional virtues of nobility and justice sounded hollow and old-fashioned, and just a little naive. Cicero's four *Catilinarian Orations* provide a snapshot of the Republic at a time when it was teetering on the brink of destruction, but no one yet knew how or when or even if it was going to fall.

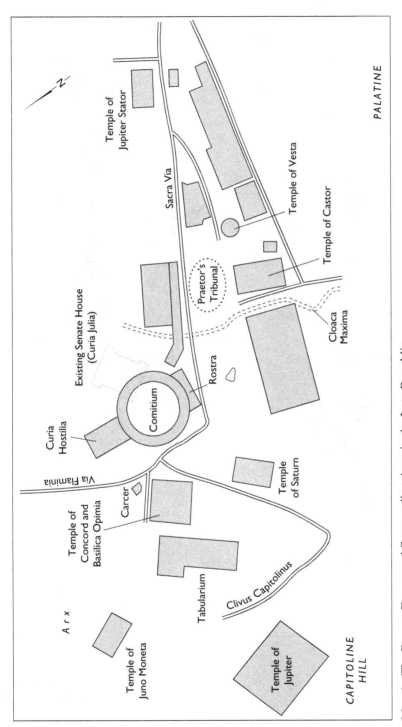

Map 1. The Roman Forum and Surrounding Area in the Late Republic

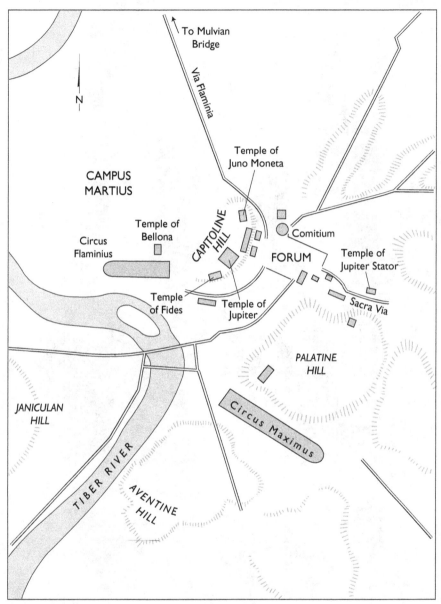

Map 2. Rome

Map 3. Italy

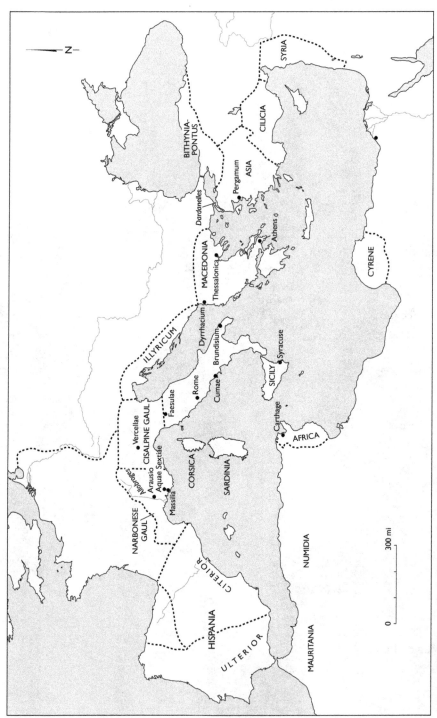

Map 4. The Roman World in the Time of Cicero

The Roman Republican Constitution

> Politics in the Republic were a game played according to complex rules. Without knowledge of these it is hard to grasp the behavior of the contestants.
>
> A. W. Lintott, *The Constitution of the Roman Republic*

The Roman Republic did not have a written constitution, although some important aspects of government, such as the laws, were written down.[1] As such, the Roman constitution can be said to be a combination of three separate entities: tradition (the *mos maiorum*), written laws, and political institutions.[2] As one might expect, these three different elements did not combine to form a coherent, unified government in anything like the modern sense. As one scholar puts it, the Republican constitution "exhibited a remarkable degree of incoherence and built-in friction, or opposition of powers, in which voting bodies that were structured in quite different ways elected annual magistrates whose respective rights were not fully defined and who in no sense formed a unified government or administration."[3] Furthermore, the most powerful men of the late Republic were skilled at manipulating these inconsistencies to their own political advantage. As a result, it is extremely difficult for a modern reader to understand the complex actions of men like Pompey and Caesar, and even Cicero and Catiline, without at least a basic understanding of the political system within which they operated. The following outline of the governmental structure in Cicero's time is intended to help provide that context.

The institutions of the Republican government can be conveniently divided into the assemblies of citizens (voting assemblies), the Senate, and the magistracies, or higher offices. Short notes have also been included on the standing criminal courts (*quaestiones perpetuae*) and the sequence of magistracies (*cursus honorum*). While this description of the Republican government is extremely simplified, it should provide some assistance to students attempting to understand the rules by which the power games of the late Republic were played.

The Roman Voting Assemblies

There were four voting assemblies in the Roman Republic. Of these, the *comitia curiata* had lost most of its importance by the late Republic and existed only in vestigial form. We will therefore concentrate on the other three.

Comitia Centuriata

The *comitia centuriata* was an assembly of all male citizens, supposedly first organized by Servius Tullius to provide men for the army. It was said to have become a voting assembly when it voted for the first consuls in 509 B.C. It was convened by a consul or praetor and met just outside the city in the Campus Martius (see Map 2). It had electoral, legislative, and judicial functions. Its most important duties were to elect the consuls and praetors every year (these were the magistrates who possessed *imperium*, the right to command an army) and the censors every five years; these elections were carried out under the supervision of the consul. The *comitia centuriata* had originally been the primary law-making body in Rome, but by the late Republic this function had largely passed to the two other legislative bodies, the *comitia tributa* and the *concilium plebis*. The *comitia centuriata* did retain its authority to declare war, to ratify treaties, and to confirm the census, however. And it was this body that passed the law in 57 B.C. recalling Cicero from exile.

The *comitia centuriata* had also originally served as a court of law for capital cases, but its judicial functions had also largely been taken over by other institutions by the late Republic, in this case the permanent courts (*quaestiones perpetuae*; see below). On occasion, the *comitia centuriata* did continue to serve as a court of appeal for capital cases involving a Roman citizen, as it did in the trial of Gaius Rabirius for *perduellio* (treason) in 63 B.C.

Since it had originally been established to organize men for military service, the *comitia centuriata* was organized by centuries (groups responsible for providing 100 soldiers for the army) according to property classes. After 241 B.C. the *comitia centuriata* had 193 centuries: 18 centuries of *equites* (cavalry), the highest property class, limited to those whose property was worth at least 400,000 sesterces; 170 centuries of *pedites* (infantry), divided into five descending property classes; and 5 centuries of men who could not afford their own weapons. Because the voting began with those in the highest property classes and continued only until a majority was reached, the *equites* and the highest property classes of *pedites* had the greatest influence over its decisions. The principle behind this uneven distribution of power was that, since the wealthier citizens had greater military responsibilities, they should be granted greater power as well. In practice, however, it is not always clear exactly how much influence the wealthy actually had.[4]

Comitia Tributa

The *comitia tributa* was an assembly of all Roman citizens divided according to their tribes or districts. This concept needs a little explanation. All Roman citizens were divided into tribes (*tribus*). Since the word *tribus* meant a district, the concept originally referred to the area where the citizen lived and did not imply kinship. When a young man became a citizen he was enrolled into his father's tribe. If a family moved, however, its members stayed in their original tribe, so eventually a citizen's tribe might have little to do with where he lived. After 241 B.C. there were four urban tribes (or districts), and thirty-one rural tribes, bringing the total to thirty-five. After the Italian (or Social) War, when practically all Italians became Roman citizens, the new citizens were distributed into the existing thirty-five tribes, further weakening the connection between tribe and place of residence.

The *comitia tributa* was usually presided over by a consul or praetor, but it could be convened by any curule magistrate (a consul, praetor, curule aedile, or censor), and it could meet in a variety of places, depending on the function of that particular meeting. For legislation and judgments, the *comitia tributa* usually met in the Forum or on the Capitoline Hill. For elections (at least in the late Republic) it met in the Campus Martius.

The *comitia tributa* elected quaestors, curule aediles, military tribunes, and some other lower officers. It also passed legislation and served as a court of law for noncapital crimes against the state (i.e., those punishable by exile or a fine). When the *comitia tributa* functioned as a court of law, it was convened and presided over by a curule aedile. In the late Republic its judicial functions were not often exercised, however; by this time most trials were brought before the *quaestiones perpetuae*, or standing courts.

Concilium Plebis

The *concilium plebis* (Plebeian Council) was the formal assembly of all plebeian citizens, and it was also organized according to tribes. The chief difference between the *comitia tributa* and the *concilium plebis* was that the *concilium plebis* was open only to plebeians (patricians were excluded), while the *comitia tributa* was open to all (male) citizens. The *concilium plebis* was usually convened and presided over by a plebeian tribune. This body elected tribunes and plebeian aediles; it also passed resolutions (called *plebiscita*) and conducted some trials. At first these *plebiscita* were binding only upon the plebeians, but in 287 b.c. the *lex Hortensia* made *plebiscita* equivalent to laws (*leges*), and thus binding on all citizens. From that time on, most legislation at Rome was proposed by tribunes and passed in the *concilium plebis*. It was Tiberius Gracchus, however, who first understood the potential of the *concilium plebis* as an independent political agent that could challenge the Senate's power.

When the *concilium plebis* served as a court of law it could be convened by a plebeian aedile (as well as by a tribune), and, like the *comitia tributa*, it was restricted to judging non-capital cases (i.e., those involving exile or a fine). As with the two other assemblies that had judicial functions (the *comitia centuriata* and the *comitia tributa*), most judicial functions of the *concilium plebis* began to be transferred to the standing courts (*quaestiones perpetuae*) after the Gracchan period. Like the *comitia tributa*, the *concilium plebis* could meet in the Forum or on the Capitoline Hill for legislation and judgments, but for elections its members assembled in the Campus Martius.

The Senate

For much of the Republican period, the Senate was the most powerful governing body. Although it had only advisory powers (it did not pass laws as the voting assemblies did), it used its enormous prestige to control (or attempt to control) many aspects of government. The reasons for the Senate's influence were twofold. First, since the magistrates (consul, praetor, tribune, quaestor, etc.) were elected for only one-year terms, they could not hope to attain the knowledge and experience possessed by the senators, who served for life and were all ex-magistrates. The senators' collective knowledge and experience gave them tremendous power and authority. Second, since the Romans did not have a written constitution, the Senate was able to claim substantial authority over almost all areas of government, including foreign and domestic policy, the army, finance, and religion. Much of the Senate's power was thus based on custom (*mos maiorum*). For this reason, when populist challenges to the Senate's authority, initiated by the Gracchi brothers, began to gain strength in the late Republic, the Senate had few means, other than violence, to defend its prerogatives. This struggle precipitated the crises that led to the downfall of the Republic.

To be eligible to serve in the Senate, citizens had to qualify for membership in the equestrian order, which meant that they had to own landed property worth at least 400,000 sesterces. After the time of Sulla, the Senate consisted of 600 members, and anyone who had been elected to the office of quaestor automatically became a member of the Senate. Senators served for life, although the censors could expel senators who were guilty of serious misconduct or immoral behavior. As a mark of their rank and dignity, senators wore a broad purple vertical stripe (*latus clavus*) on the front of their tunic, a gold ring, and special red leather shoes. They had reserved seats at religious ceremonies and games. Membership in the Senate was always easier to obtain if one's father was a senator, but the Senate seems to have always contained at least a few new men (*novi homines*; i.e., first-generation senators). It was unusual, however, for a *novus homo* to rise to the highest offices.[5]

At first the right of summoning the Senate was possessed only by consuls and praetors—those officers who held *imperium* (the right to command an army). By the late Republic, however, tribunes were also empowered to convene senatorial meetings. The Senate regularly met in the Senate House (the Curia Hostilia; see Map 1), but any building that was both public and sacred (e.g., a temple) could be used. Thus Cicero delivered his *First Catilinarian Oration* in the Temple of Jupiter Stator and the *Fourth* in the Temple of Concord. Only senators were admitted to the meetings, though the doors were kept open so that others might listen to the proceedings (see *Cat.* 4.3).

At the opening of the meeting, the presiding magistrate outlined the matter for discussion and called upon individual senators in turn to express their opinions (*sententiae*) about the matter at hand. The consuls designate were called on first, then the consulars (ex-consuls) in the order of their seniority. Praetors designate were then asked for their opinion, followed by the praetors and ex-praetors and tribunes, aediles, and quaestors in turn. Each senator could speak for as long or as short a time as he wished. As a result of these two factors (the strict order of speaking and the lack of a preset time limit), the senators of humbler rank would rarely get to voice their opinions. At any point the presiding magistrate could take the floor and express his own opinion, which usually signaled the end of the debate. After the debate was concluded, a formal vote was taken. The result of such a vote was called a *senatus consultum* (decree of the Senate). To be valid, a *senatus consultum* had to be approved by the presiding magistrate and had to be passed before sunset. The formal purpose of a *senatus consultum* was to give advice to the consuls and praetors. Although it did not have the force of law, a *senatus consultum* did carry considerable weight, since it was backed by the Senate's full authority.

In addition to passing senatorial decrees, the Senate also claimed a broad range of powers on the basis of custom (*mos maiorum*). It controlled all state revenues and appropriations, although the actual bookkeeping was done by the quaestors. The Senate controlled the raising of military forces and the assigning of military commands, the conduct of foreign affairs, and the maintenance of law and order in both Italy and Rome. The Senate also granted triumphs (triumphal processions) to victorious generals. The people, through the *comitia centuriata*, had the right to declare peace or war and to ratify treaties. In practice, however, it is clear that the *comitia centuriata* simply gave formal approval to the resolutions that were presented to it by the Senate. The Senate similarly expected to be given the opportunity to approve in advance any bills that a magistrate might bring before the legislative assemblies. In addition, the Senate exercised an informal control over Rome's religious activities, since most of the places on the priestly colleges (or boards) were held by senators. The Senate also reserved the right to call for a vote of thanksgiving to the gods (*supplicatio*) and to consult the soothsayers or the Sibylline books on behalf of the state in times of danger.

The Magistracies (Executive Offices)

The Consuls

The consulship was the highest office of the Republic. Two consuls were elected annually by the *comitia centuriata*. Elections usually took place in July and the new consuls began their term of office on January 1. The consul's most important rights were to command an army (*imperium*) and to summon the Senate and the Roman people (in the form of the *comitia centuriata* and the *comitia tributa*). The consuls usually acted together, and although it was possible for one consul to block the actions of another (*intercessio*), this rarely occurred.[6] The consul's *imperium* was symbolized by the twelve fasces (bundles of rods) carried before him at all times by attendants known as lictors. When the consul was commanding his forces on the field, a single-headed ax was added to the fasces, symbolizing the consul's power of life and death over noncitizens. Inside the city, the ax was removed from the fasces, symbolizing the citizens' right of *provocatio* or appeal to the Roman people against the coercion of a magistrate.

After his year in office, a consul generally served as the governor of a province. His official title in that capacity was proconsul (meaning "in place of a consul"). A proconsul generally governed his province for one year, but occasionally he would serve for a longer period. Julius Caesar, for example, managed to procure a five-year command in Gaul after his consulship in 59 B.C.

The Praetors

The office of praetor was originally a military command (the word *praetor* comes from *praeire*, to lead the way in battle), and the praetor did hold *imperium* (the right to command an army), although a praetor's *imperium* was less than that of a consul. As a mark of his *imperium*, the praetor was preceded by six lictors, each holding the fasces. The praetor could perform almost all the activities of the consul; and when the consuls were away from the city, the praetor served as the chief magistrate at Rome.

By the late Republic, however, the praetors mainly served as judges. Sulla raised the number of praetors to eight and established a system whereby all eight praetors would remain in Rome during their year in office to fulfill their judicial functions. One praetor, designated as *praetor urbanus*, was the judge in civil suits between citizens. Another served as *praetor inter peregrinos*, presiding over cases in which at least one party was a foreign resident at Rome. The remaining six praetors presided over the standing criminal courts (*quaestiones perpetuae*) established for trying particular types of crimes (see below).

After his year in office, a praetor usually served as the governor of a province, with the official title of *propraetor*. In most cases a *propraetor* governed his province for a year, but (as with consular provinces) there were exceptions. Catiline governed the province of Africa as a *propraetor* from 67 to 66 B.C.[7]

The Censors

Every five years the *comitia centuriata* elected two censors, who held their office for a period of eighteen months. The office of censor possessed considerable authority and prestige (though not *imperium*) and was usually held by ex-consuls. The censors' primary functions were to make and maintain the official list of Roman citizens (the *census*) and to assign citizens to the appropriate property classes for voting in the *comitia centuriata*. The censors could also remove members from the Senate (by making a mark of censure against the senator's name) for immoral conduct or otherwise reprehensible behavior. In 70 B.C. the censors removed sixty-four senators from the Senate, including some who later joined Catiline's conspiracy. Once censored, a senator could gain reentry into the Senate by being elected to the quaestorship or other higher office. Because of their ability to control the membership of the Senate, the censors came to be seen as exercising a general supervision over public morals.

The censors also held some important financial responsibilities. They assigned contracts to private tax-collecting companies to collect provincial taxes and harbor dues. The censors negotiated the leases for private companies to farm public lands, cut timber on public forests, and work public mines. They also assigned the contracts for public works (such as the construction of roads, bridges, and temples) and supervised the work. The allocation of funds for these projects, however, was the responsibility of the Senate.

The Tribunes

The tribunes were plebeian officials, originally charged with protecting the persons and property of plebeians against the arbitrary actions of the patrician magistrates (*ius auxilii*). The office of tribune was created sometime between 500 and 450 B.C. (the date of the first secession of the plebs). The tribunes' power originally derived from their *sacrosanctitas* or inviolability, which the plebeians took an oath to protect.

By the later Republic there were ten tribunes, elected annually by the *concilium plebis* (Plebeian Council). Tribunes could convene the Plebeian Council and bring resolutions (*plebiscita*) before it. After 287 B.C. *plebiscita* passed by the Plebeian Council had the force of law for all citizens. Tribunes also presided over the *concilium plebis* when it held elections for tribunes and plebeian aediles. By the late Republic, tribunes could introduce bills before the Senate and the *comitia tributa* as well.

The tribunes' most powerful right was the *veto* (literally, "I forbid"). With the veto, a tribune had the power to block the action of any other magistrate (even a consul) as well as elections (except plebeian elections), laws (passed by any legislative assembly), and decrees of the Senate. The tribunes' veto power was based on their personal inviolability (*sacrosanctitas*), since (in theory, at least) they needed to have the power to physically prevent a magistrate from harming any plebeian. The plebeians, in turn, were bound to protect their tribunes. The power of the tribunate was not fully utilized during much of the Republican period; Tiberius and Gaius Gracchus recognized the revolutionary potential of this office, however, and used the tribunate to challenge the Senate's power.

The Aediles

There were originally two plebeian aediles, elected annually by the *concilium plebis*. The aediles assisted the tribunes and cared for the plebeians' temple (*aedes*) and cults (the cults of Diana and Ceres on the Aventine Hill). In 367 B.C. two curule aediles were added, elected by the *comitia tributa* under the leadership of a consul. The curule aediles, along with the consuls, praetors, and censors, were classed as curule magistrates. This classification allowed them to sit on a curule chair (a square chair without a back or armrests whose legs were made of ivory) and wear the *toga praetexta* (a white toga with a purple border) when performing their official duties. Despite the honor of being elected to a curule magistracy, however, the duties of curule aediles were essentially the same as those of the plebeian aediles.

By the late Republic, the main duties of all four aediles were the care of the city (*cura urbis*), the care of the grain supply (*cura annonae*), and the supervision of public games (*cura ludorum*). Under the *cura urbis*, the aediles were charged with the supervision of the streets of Rome, the control of the public water supply, and the maintenance of public order. For these purposes, the city was divided into four districts, and each aedile was in charge of one of them. Under the *cura annonis*, the aediles had to supervise the public markets and were responsible for maintaining an adequate supply of grain in the city. The aediles' most exciting responsibility was the production and supervision of public games (*cura ludorum*). Activities at the games included chariot racing, theatrical performances, and gladiatorial contests.

Although the aedileship was not an official part of the *cursus honorum* (see below), by the late Republic the office of aedile had become an important step on the road to higher office. As a result, even though the Senate appropriated funds for the games, the aediles (driven by the desire to gain public recognition) tended to spend increasingly larger amounts of their own money in order to stage more lavish games than those of the previous year. Thus, while the games of the late Republic became more and more lavish, the aediles' debts became heavier and heavier. A successful aedile could hope to recoup his losses when, after rising to the office of praetor or consul, he would have the opportunity to serve as the governor of a province. If he was unable to achieve those higher offices, however, an aedile might well be unable to pay off the debts he had accrued.

The Quaestors

The quaestors were the financial officers of the state. They were elected annually by the *comitia tributa*. Originally there were four, but after Sulla's reforms there were twenty. Sulla also established the rule that quaestors automatically became members of the Senate.

Two quaestors were chosen as *quaestores urbani*. They were in charge of the state treasury (housed in the Temple of Saturn, see Map 1), and they kept various public documents, such as the census lists, public building contracts, and copies of senatorial decrees. The remaining eighteen quaestors were assigned to the staffs of the provincial governors, where they helped the governor manage the fiscal affairs of the province.

Dictator

The office of dictator was a short-term magistracy, used only in times of crisis. The dictator held the highest *imperium* (symbolized by twenty-four fasces, carried by lictors), which gave him supreme (if not absolute) power. Nominated in public (usually by a consul) after authorization by the Senate, the dictator was usually asked to command the army against a foreign enemy (such as Hannibal), although he was occasionally requested to perform a specific task (such as quelling an internal revolt). The dictator was expected to resign after completing his task, but in any case he was not to remain in office for longer than six months.

After the Second Punic War (when the dictator Fabius Maximus Cunctator famously wore down Hannibal by refusing to fight an organized battle), the office of dictator fell into disuse. In 122 b.c. the Senate passed the SCU (*Senatus Consultum Ultimum*) against Gaius Gracchus and Fulvius Flaccus, thus empowering the consul L. Opimius to use force against them. After Opimius was acquitted of the charges arising from his actions, the use of the SCU became more common and was used instead of the dictatorship to put down internal revolts. (For a discussion of the SCU see Historical Essay I.4.) In the late Republic, however, first Sulla and then Caesar had themselves appointed dictator in order to lend the appearance of legality to their usurpation of power. In each case they justified their office by stating that their purpose in holding it was to restore the constitution. Sulla's dictatorship was not given a preset time limit, although he resigned from office after little more than a year. Caesar was eventually made *dictator in perpetuo*, thus destroying the original concept of the dictatorship as a temporary office held only in times of crisis.

Quaestiones Perpetuae

The *quaestiones perpetuae* were permanent criminal courts, presided over by a praetor, established for trying particular types of crimes. If a praetor was not available, a *iudex quaestionis* would be appointed, usually an ex-aedile. The verdict in each case was given by a jury. The juries, at first composed of senators, were made equestrian by Gaius Gracchus, and brought back to senatorial control by Sulla. A compromise was struck in 70 b.c., according to which the juries were composed equally of senators, equestrians, and the *tribunii aerarii*, a group with a property qualification similar to that of the equestrians.

The first *quaestio perpetua* was established in 149 B.C. for trying cases of extortion from the provinces by a provincial governor and his staff (the *quaestio de pecuniis repetundis* or *de repetundae*). Other *quaestiones perpetuae* developed over the years; Sulla brought the total up to at least seven, including a court for electoral bribery (*quaestio de ambitu*), one for public violence (*de vi*), one for assassins and poisoners (*de sicariis et veneficiis*), and one for crimes of treason (*de maiestate minuta populi Romani*).[8] Because these courts had a more stream-lined procedure, they gradually took over many of the cases traditionally brought before the *comitia centuriata*, although the *comitia* never completely lost its judicial function.

The Cursus Honorum

The *cursus honorum* (sequence of offices) was at first simply a generally accepted career path, according to which a Roman would usually hold the lower magistracies before running for the higher ones. After 197 B.C. a definite order was established: the office of quaestor had to be held before the praetorship, and the praetorship had to be held before a Roman could become a consul. Although the offices of tribune, aedile, and censor were not part of the official *cursus honorum*, the tribunate and/or aedileship were usually held after the quaestorship (but before the praetorship), and the office of censor was usually reserved for ex-consuls.

The *lex Villia Annalis* of 180 B.C. set minimum ages for each of the curule magistracies (curule aedile, praetor, consul, and censor), and stipulated a minimum two-year interval between offices. This requirement was sometimes waived. Marius, for example, was elected to five successive consulships (104–101 B.C.) because of the threat of barbarian invasions. Sulla added an age limit for the quaestorship, thirty-seven, and made the quaestorship a requirement for holding higher office. If the quaestorship was held at thirty-seven, the praetorship could be held at forty, and the consulship at forty-three, allowing for a two-year interval between each office. When a Roman promised to run for the tribunate or aedileship after the quaestorship, however, he could be allowed to hold the quaestorship at the age of thirty. Cicero held the quaestorship at thirty and prided himself on that fact that he was always elected to the next highest office in his own year (*suo anno*), that is, the earliest year in which he was eligible.

Appendix B

Timeline

(Note: all dates B.C.)

133 Tiberius Gracchus as tribune passes agrarian laws and establishes a land commission; he is clubbed to death by a mob of angry senators while attempting to be elected tribune for a second time.

123 C. Gracchus as tribune passes laws: *de capite civium, agraria, frumentaria,* and more.

122 C. Gracchus is tribune for the second time; continuation of his legislation.

121 Senate passes the SCU against C. Gracchus; first use of SCU. Death of Gracchus.

108 Probable date for birth of Catiline.

107 C. Marius elected consul; army reforms.

106 Jan 3: birth of Cicero at Arpinum.

104 C. Marius is elected consul for the second time; further army reforms.

103 Third consulship of C. Marius.

102 Fourth consulship of C. Marius; Marius conquers the Teutones at Aquae Sextiae.

101 Fifth consulship of C. Marius; Marius conquers the Cimbri at Vercellae.

100 Sixth consulship of C. Marius; Saturninus is tribune; **Senate passes the SCU against Glaucia and Saturninus,** who are besieged on the Capitol by Marius and subsequently stoned to death by a mob. Birth of C. Julius Caesar.

91–89 The Social War.

88 L. Cornelius Sulla is consul. P. Sulpicius, a tribune, proposes a bill to give the command against Mithridates to Marius; Sulla seizes Rome; **First March on Rome**; Marius flees to Africa.

87 Cn. Octavius and L. Cornelius Cinna are consuls. Sulla leaves to fight Mithridates in the East. Cinna opposes Sulla's legislation, is declared an enemy, and flees. Cinna and Marius march on Rome; **Second March on Rome**. Siege and taking of Rome. Octavius is killed.

86 Cinna and Marius are consuls (Cinna's second and Marius' seventh consulship). Marius dies on Jan. 13.

86–84 Cinna elected consul each year; Sulla in the East.

84 Distribution of the new citizens among all the tribes is ordered by a decree of the Senate.

83 Sulla lands in Italy and begins to march toward Rome; the praetor Sertorius flees to Spain.

82 Battle of the Colline Gate (Nov. 1); Sulla enters Rome; **Third March on Rome**; proscriptions; Sulla is appointed dictator for the purpose of reorganizing the constitution.

81 Sulla's principal measures as dictator: expansion of the Senate to 600 members; curbing of *tribunicia potestas*; systemization of the *quaestiones perpetuae*. Sulla resigns his dictatorship.

80 Sulla serves as consul. Cicero defends Sextus Roscius on a charge of parricide (*Pro Roscio Amerino*).

78 Sulla dies. M. Aemilius Lepidus, the consul, gathers forces in Cisalpine Gaul and marches on Rome at the head of his makeshift army; **Fourth March on Rome**. **Senate passes the SCU.** Lepidus is defeated by Q. Lutatius Catulus at the Mulvian Bridge. Lepidus flees to Sardinia.

77 Lepidus dies in Sardinia; M. Perperna takes his remaining forces and joins Sertorius, who is now in control of Spain.

75 The *lex Aurelia* is passed, restoring the right of tribunes to hold further office. Cicero serves as quaestor in western Sicily.

73–71 Spartacus' slave revolt.

72 Assassination of Sertorius; M. Perperna is defeated and killed by Pompey.

71 Crassus defeats Spartacus.

70 Pompey and Crassus are consuls; the *lex Pompeia Licinea* restores all powers back to the tribunes. Censors expel sixty-four senators, including Lentulus Sura (the future Catilinarian conspirator) and C. Antonius (later Cicero's colleague in the consulship). Cicero prosecutes Verres for extortion (*In Verrem*).

69 Cicero serves as aedile.

68 Catiline is praetor.

67 Pompey is given special powers against the pirates and clears them from the Mediterranean. Catiline is governor of Africa as propraetor.

66 Pompey is given command against Mithridates. Pompey defeats Mithridates and continues his campaign in the East (66 to 62 B.C.). Cicero is praetor. The consuls-designate, P. Cornelius Sulla and P. Autronius Paetus, are convicted of bribery and thus forfeit their consulship. Catiline returns from Africa during the summer but is unable to run in the special election for the consulship. Cicero is praetor.

65 Jan 1: The First Catilinarian Conspiracy, if it existed, does not take place. Catiline is acquitted of *repetundae*, but not in time to run for the consulship of 64 BC. C. Julius Caesar is aedile.

64 The censors abdicate; Catiline, Antonius Hybrida, M. Tullius Cicero, and four other candidates run for the consulship of 63 B.C. Cicero delivers the speech *In toga candida* to the Senate. Cicero and Antonius are elected consuls.

63 Cicero and Antonius Hybrida are consuls. Julius Caesar is elected *pontifex maximus*. **The Catilinarian Conspiracy**.

July Catiline is a candidate for the consulship of 62 B.C., running on a platform of *novae tabulae* (debt relief). He makes vague threats, implying that if he does not win the consulship he will resort to violence. Cicero, who as consul is required to supervise the consular elections, asks that the July elections be postponed; he also requests a bodyguard. The Senate postpones the elections for only a few days and refuses to provide Cicero with a bodyguard. On voting day, Cicero appears at the Campus Martius with a bodyguard of his own and wearing a breastplate that is visible under his toga, stressing the danger of violence that Catiline poses. While it is impossible to gauge the effect of Cicero's actions on the voting centuries, Catiline did lose the election.

July–Oct. After his second loss at the polls, Catiline puts his plans for violence into action. It is probably at this time that Catiline sends Manlius (along with money and weapons) to Faesulae in Etruria to set up an armed camp, and begins to form a nucleus of conspirators around himself at Rome.

Oct. 18 (approximately) In the evening, several letters are mysteriously left outside of Crassus' door. One is addressed to Crassus, the others to leading men of the Senate. Crassus opens the one addressed to him; it contains an anonymous warning to leave the city because Catiline is planning a massacre in Rome. Crassus, accompanied by two senior senators, brings the letters to Cicero the same night.

Oct. 19 Cicero calls a meeting of the Senate, at which the other letters are opened and read; they contain identical warnings. The Senate decrees a state of disorder and orders the consul to begin an investigation.

Oct. 21 Cicero now has more definite information about Catiline's planned massacre in Rome and about Manlius' actions in Etruria. He calls a meeting of the Senate and informs them that Manlius and his followers are set to take up arms and march against Rome on October 27, and that a massacre in Rome is planned for October 28 (*Cat.* 1.7). **The Senate now passes the SCU against Catiline**, the first time the Senate has passed an SCU since Lepidus' rebellion in 78 B.C. At this time the Senate sends Q. Marcius Rex with an army to Faesulae against Manlius. Metellus Creticus is sent to Apulia. The praetor Q. Pompeius Rufus is sent to Capua, and his colleague Q. Metellus Celer is sent to Picenum to raise an army. At the same time, the town of Praeneste (about twenty miles southeast of Rome) is put under guard, as Cicero has information that the conspirators are planning to attack it on Nov. 1. Cicero now orders that night-watches be kept throughout the city.

Nov. 1 (approximately) At a meeting of the Senate, L. Saenius reads a letter brought to him from Faesulae, informing him that Manlius had in fact taken up arms on Oct. 27 with a large force. Slave revolts are also reported in Capua and Apulia.

Nov. 6 Catiline meets at night with the leaders of the conspiracy at the house of M. Porcius Laeca (a senator and one of the leading conspirators), in the Street of the Scythe-makers. At this meeting Catiline states his intention to go to Etruria to raise troops and prepare for the march on Rome. The conspirators at Rome are to arrange for the massacre of leading citizens in their houses and for fires to be set at strategic points throughout the city. The massacre and arson at Rome are to be timed to coincide with Catiline's march on Rome with his troops from Etruria. Catiline requests that Cicero be killed before he leaves. Two equites, Cornelius and Vargunteius, arrange to kill Cicero at his home before dawn, under the pretext of making a ceremonial call.

Nov. 7 Cicero, informed of the plot against his life, prevents the would-be assassins from entering his house.

Nov. 8 Cicero calls a meeting of the Senate at the Temple of Jupiter Stator, which is easily defensible. He no doubt plans to inform the Senate of the events of the past few days, including the attempt on his life; but seeing that Catiline himself has come to the meeting, Cicero delivers what later became known as the *First Catilinarian Oration*, exposing Catiline's plans and urging him to leave the city at once. Catiline does leave Rome that night, although he claims to be going into exile at Massilia.

Nov. 9 Cicero, clearly relieved that Catiline has left the city, delivers the *Second Catilinarian Oration* to the people, explaining the events of the past few days.

mid-Nov. (The precise sequence of events is unclear.) Catiline does not in fact go to Massilia. He goes to join Manlius and his troops in Faesulae. When this news reaches Rome, the Senate declares Catiline and Manlius public enemies. Antonius, the other consul, is sent against them with an army. Catiline continues to raise troops in Etruria, although they are now prevented from marching on Rome by the Roman legions in the area. Also during Nov. the conspirators at Rome decide to enlist the help of some envoys of the Gallic tribe, the Allobroges, who had come to Rome to ask the Senate for relief from the avarice of their Roman governors. The Allobroges have been denied the requested help, but are still in Rome, when they are approached by the conspirators. The conspirators offer them relief from financial burdens (and perhaps much more) if they can convince the Allobrogian people to give cavalry support to Catiline's troops in their planned march on Rome. Unsure of what to do, the Allobroges consult their patron, Fabius Sanga, who goes straight to Cicero. Cicero asks the Allobroges to continue their negotiations with the conspirators (now as double agents) and to try to obtain conclusive proof of the conspiracy.

Dec. 2 About midnight, the envoys of the Allobroges, accompanied by a messenger, a certain T. Volturcius of Crotona, leave Rome and travel north along the Via Flaminia. They carry letters to the Allobrogian people from three of the conspirators, Lentulus Sura, C. Cethegus, and L. Statilius, urging them to rise up in rebellion and to use their cavalry to assist Catiline's infantry. Volturcius also carries both a letter and a verbal message from Lentulus to Catiline.

Dec. 3 The Allobrogian envoys and Volturcius are arrested about 3 A.M. as they cross the Mulvian Bridge by the praetors L. Flaccus and C. Pomptinus, along with a small band of armed men, who had been sent by Cicero. The entire party is brought back to Rome. At dawn, Cicero summons the Senate to meet at the Temple of Concord and orders the arrest of Lentulus, Cethegus, Gabinius, and Statilius. At the Senate meeting, Volturcius and the Allobroges give incriminating evidence about the conspiracy; then the conspirators' letters are opened and read. All four conspirators eventually confess. At the end of the meeting, the Senate formally decrees a vote of thanks to Cicero and hands over the five conspirators (the four already mentioned plus M. Ceparius; see Sallust *BC* 47) to individual senators for safekeeping. In the afternoon, Cicero delivers the *Third Catilinarian Oration* to the people, giving them a full account of the events that have taken place.

Dec. 4 The Senate votes monetary rewards to Volturcius and the envoys of the Allobroges. In an atmosphere of increasing tension, attempts are made to incriminate Crassus and Caesar in the Catilinarian conspiracy. Meanwhile, the freedmen and clients of Lentulus and Cethegus attempt to release them from custody.

Dec. 5 Cicero convenes the Senate in the Temple of Concord to decide the fate of the prisoners. After a heated debate (Cicero later published his speech as the *Fourth Catilinarian Oration*; Caesar's and Cato's speeches are given by Sallust in *BC* 51–52), the Senate decides that the conspirators have forfeited their rights as citizens and condemns them to death without a trial. Cicero leads the five prisoners to the prison, where they are strangled.

Dec. 10 Q. Metellus Nepos takes office as tribune.

mid-Dec. The execution of the conspirators polarizes political opinion. Cicero's supporters hail him as the founder of his country, while his opponents call him a tyrant. When news of the execution of the prisoners in Rome reaches Etruria, Catiline's supporters begin to desert in large numbers. Catiline attempts to flee northward into Gaul, but he is trapped by Metellus Celer and his army to the north and by Antonius to the south.

Dec. 31 Q. Metellus Nepos, the tribune, forbids Cicero from making the customary address to the people as he steps down from office and orders him to make only the required oath that he has obeyed all the laws. Cicero agrees to this but (to the cheers of his supporters) adds an additional oath that the Republic has been saved by him alone.

62

Jan. 2–3 (approximately) Metellus Nepos attacks Cicero in the Senate (accusing him of the unlawful execution of Lentulus and the other conspirators), but the Senate passes a decree of indemnity for all those involved in the recent executions. Nepos then proposes a bill to the *concilium plebis* requesting the recall of Pompey from the East to deal with the situation in Rome. Cato vetoes the proposal, however, and the people address Cicero as the "father of his country." Caesar is praetor.

early Jan. Catiline, with an army of roughly 4,000 followers, hemmed in by Metellus Celer to the north, turns south to fight against Antonius and his army at Pistoria. Antonius delegates his command to his legate, M. Petreius. After a long and bloody battle, Catiline and all of his supporters are killed.

Publius Autronius Paetus, L. Vargunteius, and other leading conspirators (including

M. Porcius Laeca and G. Cornelius) are prosecuted under the *lex Plautia de vi* and condemned. In Dec. Pompey returns to Rome.

60–61 The Allobroges in Transalpine Gaul, angry at the extortion of their Roman governors, stage a revolt. The revolt is crushed by the governor, C. Pomptinus.

60 "The First Triumvirate" of Pompey, Crassus, and Caesar.

59 Caesar is consul.

58–50 Caesar in Gaul.

58 Cicero is exiled.

57 Cicero returns (Sept.).

56 Conference at Luca (Apr.).

55 Crassus and Pompey are consuls (second consulship for both).

53 Defeat and death of Crassus at Carrhae.

52 Pompey is sole consul until Aug.

50 The consul C. Claudius Marcellus urges Pompey to "save the state" (Nov.).

49 The Senate passes the SCU against Caesar (Jan. 7). Caesar crosses the Rubicon (Jan. 10); **Fifth March on Rome.**

49–45 Civil War; Caesar is nominated dictator by the Senate.

44 Caesar assumes the title of dictator for life; he is also elected consul. Murder of Caesar (Mar. 15).

43 Octavian marches on Rome (Aug.); **Sixth March on Rome.** Octavian is made consul. Second Triumvirate: Octavian, Antony, and Lepidus (Nov.). **Cicero is murdered (Dec. 7).**

Appendix C

Glossary of Key Rhetorical Terms

Anacoluthon (Greek "not following"): a grammatical inconsistency, such that a grammatical construction in the beginning of a sentence is not carried out and the sentence ends with a different construction. Example: in *Cat.* 1.15 (lines 163–66) Cicero begins his sentence in such a way that we expect a list of Catiline's minor crimes, but he interrupts his sentence with a parenthetical explanation and completes it with an exclamation *about* Catiline's crimes, rather than a list. We understand very well what Cicero means, but the grammatical construction has changed.

Anaphora (Greek "carrying back"): repetition of the same word at the beginning of successive clauses for emphasis. Example: the repetition of **nihil** in *Cat.* 1.1 (lines 3–5).

Antithesis: contrasting ideas put in close proximity. Example: **vocibus . . . mentibus** in *Cat.* 1.29 (lines 315–16).

Asyndeton (Greek "lack of connection"): omission of connective words (such as **et** or **atque**) between coordinated elements. Example: **meis praesidiis, custodiis, vigiliis** in *Cat.* 1.8 (line 81). **Adversative asyndeton** occurs when the connecting word to be supplied is **sed, autem,** or another conjunction of opposition.

Chiasmus (Greek "diagonal arrangement," from the Greek letter X): crosswise arrangement of two pairs of words by arranging the second pair in reverse order, to form the pattern *ABBA*. Example: **vexabuntur urbes, tecta ardebunt** in *Cat.* 1.29 (line 313).

Climax (Greek "ladder"): a style in which words or phrases are arranged in order of increasing intensity; frequently used with TRICOLON. Example: **Nihil agis, nihil moliris, nihil cogitas** in *Cat.* 1.8 (line 82); here used with TRICOLON and ANAPHORA.

Colon (Greek "limb, member"): a grammatically independent clause that depends on the rest of the sentence for its meaning.

Consonance resemblance of stressed consonant sounds in two or more words, where the corresponding vowels differ. Example: **mereor** and **moriar** in *Cat.* 4.3 (lines 30–31).

Hendiadys (Greek "one through two"): expression of an idea by two words connected connect by "and" rather than by a noun and its modifier. Example: **vim et manus** for the *force of hands* in *Cat.* 1.21 (line 235). Frequently it makes sense to translate HENDIADYS according to the intended sense rather than the literal meaning.

Homoioteleuton (Greek "similar ending"): the use of words with similar endings to produce an effect. Example: **exsul . . . consul** in *Cat.* 1.27 (lines 287–88). In this example the similar ending of the two words emphasizes the contrast between them.

Hyperbaton (Greek "transposition"): separation of words (frequently a noun and an adjective) that belong together grammatically. Such displacement usually gives emphasis to the first of the two separated words but sometimes to the second as well. Example: **Magna . . . gratia** in *Cat.* 1.11 (lines 116–17).

Hyperbole (Greek "overshooting"): an exaggerated or extravagant statement used for rhetorical effect and not intended to be taken literally.

Irony (Greek "dissimulation"): the use of words to suggest the opposite of their literal or surface meaning. Example: Cicero uses **virum optimum** ironically to imply that a man is not well regarded, *Cat.* 1.19 (line 217).

Iteratio (Latin "repetition"): repetition of a word or words for emphasis or fullness. Example: **Fuit, fuit** in *Cat.* 1.3 (line 22).

Litotes (Greek "plainness, simplicity"): an understatement that intensifies; in particular, a strong affirmation expressed by denying the opposite. Example: when Cicero says in *Cat.* 3.2 (lines 7–8) that "the days on which we are saved are no less pleasant than the days on which we are born," he means that the days on which we are saved are far *more* pleasant than the days on which we are born.

Metaphor (Greek "transference"): a type of comparison in which one thing or concept is identified with another. A metaphor differs from a simile in that, in a metaphor, one thing is actually said to be another. A well-placed metaphor can add vividness. Example: in *Cat.* 1.4 (lines 36–38) Cicero says that the senators have allowed the edge of their authority to grow dull, thus comparing the unused SCU against Catiline to an unused sword that has grown dull.

Oxymoron (Greek "cleverly foolish"): a condensed paradox. Example: in *Cat.* 1.18 (line 197) Cicero says that the fatherland speaks in a certain way, although it is silent (**quodam modo tacita loquitur**).

Periodic Sentence: a long, complex sentence consisting of several distinct parts that are set in a clear syntactical relationship to one another. The periodic sentence is intellectually stimulating and creates suspense in the reader or listener, who must keep all parts of the sentence in play while waiting until the very end to get the full meaning.

Personification: occurs when an animal or inanimate object is represented as having human attributes and is addressed or made to speak as if it were human. Example: in *Cat.* 1.18 the fatherland is personified as a real parent and speaks to Catiline.

Polysyndeton (Greek "many connections"): the use of a conjunction between each of several words or phrases; the opposite of ASYNDETON. Example: **Saturnini et Gracchorum et Flacci et superiorum complurium** in *Cat.* 1.29 (lines 319–20).

Praeteritio (Latin "a passing over"): a rhetorical device by which a speaker emphasizes something by claiming to pass over it. Example: in *Cat.* 1.3 (lines 20–22) Cicero states that he will "pass over" (**praetereo**) a relevant historical example because it is too ancient, but he proceeds to mention it anyway.

Rhetorical: speech that is adorned or manipulated in some way to produce an effect.

Rhetorical Question: a question asked not for the purpose of obtaining information (in fact, a specific answer is usually implied), but to produce an effect. The entire first chapter of *Cat.* 1 consists of rhetorical questions.

Simile (Latin "like"): a comparison in which one thing is likened to another by the use of a word such as "like" or "as." Example: in *Cat.* 1.31 (lines 346–50) Catiline and his followers are likened to a sickness in the body of the Republic (**Ut saepe . . .**).

Tmesis (Greek "cutting"): the interposition of a word or phrase between two parts of a compound word and the resultant separation of the compound into its two component parts. Example: **litteras a me prius aperiri quam ad senatum deferri placeret** (*Cat.* 3.7, lines 70–71).

Tricolon (Greek "having three limbs or members"): grouping three words or phrases into a unit for emphasis. Example:

Nihil agis, nihil moliris, nihil cogitas in *Cat.* 1.8 (line 82).

Zeugma (Greek "junction, yoke"): a word, usually a verb, that governs two or more objects in such a way that each object elicits a slightly different meaning from the governing word. Example: in *Cat.* 2.11 (line 127) Cicero warns the conspirators that he will destroy them "if they remain in the city and in the same purpose."

Notes

Historical Essay I

1. This section is based on the following sources: Appian 1.7–8; Gelzer (1969: 20–21); Lintott (1994: 25–27 and 40–59); Frayn (1979: 15–29); Brunt (1971a: 194, 296, and 399–426); Brunt (1971b: 14–41); White (1970: 387); Evans (1981: 441); Gabba (1976: 5–6); and Stockton (1979: 6–19 and 206–16).

2. A Roman *iugerum* is about two-thirds of an acre.

3. Brunt (1971b: 35); Frayn (1979: 15).

4. Brunt (1971b: 17).

5. Ibid., 34–35.

6. The primary sources used in this section are Plutarch's *Tiberius Gracchus*, especially sections 8–21, and *Gaius Gracchus*; Appian 1.11–17; Sallust *BJ*, sections 31 and 42; Velleius Paterculus 2.1–4; and Cicero *De republica* 1.31. Among secondary sources, I have relied most heavily on Stockton (1979: 28–91) and Lintott (1994: 62–73); see also Gelzer (1969: 27–49); Stockton (1971); Astin (1967); and various articles in *OCD* 3.

7. For a discussion of the *concilium plebis*, see Appendix A.

8. Lintott (1994: 66).

9. Roman magistrates were immune from prosecution as long as they were in office; but once they returned to private life, they could be prosecuted for crimes allegedly committed while in office.

10. Valerius Maximus 3.2.17: *Scaevola negavit se quicquam vi esse acturum.*

11. Ibid. Cf. Plutarch *Ti. Gracchus* 19.3.

12. Lintott (1968: 91 and 183).

13. Velleius Paterculus 2.4.4: *si is occupandae rei publicae animum habuisset, iure caesum.*

14. As Cicero states: *mors Tiberii Gracchi . . . divisit populum unum in duas partis (De republica* 1.31).

15. Lintott (1968 [2nd ed.]: xviii); see also the discussion in Habicht (1990: 9–15).

16. Lintott (1968: 162–63).

17. Throughout these two sections on Gaius Gracchus I have relied heavily on Lintott (1994: 76–85) and Stockton (1979: 99–105 and 114–97), as well as Appian 1.19–23 and Plutarch *C. Gracchus*. On events prior to Gracchus' tribunate see Astin (1967: 239–40), Brunt (1971b: 4–5), and Hall (1977: 284–85).

18. If a community did not wish to lose its separate identity (which would occur if it accepted Roman citizenship) it could opt for the right of *provocatio* instead. This was the right of appeal to the plebeian tribune for protection against the summary justice of a Roman magistrate. For more on *provocatio*, see Lintott (1972).

19. Lintott (1994: 76).

20. Cicero *Brutus* 125–26.

21. Stockton (1979: 99).

22. The wording comes from Cicero *Rab. perd.* 12, which, however, reads *vestro* for *populi* since Cicero is actually addressing the *comitia centuriata* in this speech. For a complete discussion of the *lex Sempronia de capite civium*, see Lintott (1972: 259–62, 1968: 162–67).

23. Lintott (1972: 260). See also Lintott (1994: 45, 1968: 163).

24. For Cicero's banishment in 58 B.C., see Historical Essay II.8.

25. Stockton (1979; 126).

26. On the lack of population in southern Italy, see Brunt (1971a: 353–75).

27. Lintott (1994: 77).

28. For more detailed discussions on the equestrian class see Taylor (1949: 17 and 37); Gelzer (1969: 4–18); Stockton (1971: 33–35); and Lintott (1994: 90–91).

29. Lintott (1994: 82).

30. Habicht (1990: 10).

31. For the text, see Stockton (1979: 238–89).

32. See also Sallust *BC* 29.3. On the SCU, see Stockton (1971: 92–96, 133–40, and 198n49) and Stockton (1979: 198–200).

33. This name was first used by Caesar *Bellum Civile* 1.5.3, in reference to the Senate's imposition of the SCU against him in 49 B.C.

34. Lintott (1996).

35. Lintott (1968: 151–52). The Senate appealed to different magistrates at different times; see Mitchell (1971: 50*n*17).

36. Plutarch *C. Gracchus* 14.4.

37. Stockton (1979: 197) suggests that Opimius may have intentionally imported these troops to Rome.

38. Cicero *De oratore* 2.132; cf. 2.106.

39. I have consulted Last and Gardner (1932: 139–50); Lintott (1994: 86–103); and Gabba (1994: 110) for the events in this section, as well as Plutarch, *Marius*; Sallust *BJ;* and Appian 1.29–33. On the term *novus homo*, see Taylor (1949: 3); Gelzer (1969: 34–35); Syme (1939: 11); Brunt (1982); and Marshall (1985: 281–82). On the pre-Marian army and Marius' army reforms, see Brunt (1971a: 298–408) and Gabba (1976: 1–20).

40. The *nobilitas* consisted of patricians and those from plebeian families whose ancestors had held the consulship.

41. Cicero *De lege agraria* 2.3–4 and *Pro Murena* 17. For a different view of the number of new men who became consul, see Wiseman (1971: 203 and 108–109).

42. Seager (1994: 201).

43. Plutarch, *Marius* 17–27. Camillus was the legendary hero who saved Rome from the Gallic invasion of 387 B.C.

44. This seems to have been the first example of a practice that later became quite common: the cynical reporting of evil omens for the purpose of disrupting a legislative assembly; see Lintott (1994: 100) and Taylor (1949: chapter 4).

45. Lintott (1999: 145); cf. Astin (1958: 9).

46. Gabba (1994) is the main source for this section, along with Velleius Paterculus 2.15; Asconius 67–68C; and Appian 1.35. See also Sherwin-White (1973: 134–49).

47. The Samnites never surrendered; though they were later granted citizenship by Marius and Cinna, they always remained hostile to Sulla (see below).

48. Brunt (1971b: 6).

49. Plutarch *Sulla* 4.

50. Plutarch *Sulla* 9; Appian 1.56–57.

51. Appian 1.58.

52. Ibid., 1.71–74.

53. Cinna had been murdered the previous year while raising an army against Sulla; the mutinous soldiers were angry at the prospect of fighting other Romans; Appian 1.78.

54. Seager (1994: 189–90).

55. The Samnites were a fierce, central Italian tribe who had not surrendered at the end of the Italian War. Because Sulla had tried to conquer them during the Italian War, and because he never recognized their citizenship (granted by Marius and Cinna in 87 B.C.), they gladly fought against him.

56. Plutarch *Sulla* 30.3.

57. Appian (1.95) estimates 1,600 *equites* and several hundred senators. Florus (*Epitome* 2.9.25) puts the total of *equites* and senators at about 2,000. Orosius (*Histories* 5.21) places the total as high as 9,000.

58. Seager (1994: 199).

59. Ibid., 201; Millar (1998: 53–55).

60. For more on Sulla's reforms, see Seager (1994: 200–205); for a different view, see Gruen (1974: 6–46).

61. Seager (1994: 205–207).

62. See Plutarch, *Sulla* and Africa (1982).

63. The references for this section include Cary and Scullard (1975: 239–242); Last (1932: 313–322); Stockton (1971: 15–16); Seager (1994: 208–223); and the relevant articles in *OCD3*.

64. This bridge was also the site where several of Catiline's co-conspirators would be captured some fourteen years later; see Cicero's *Third Catilinarian Oration* and Historical Essay II.6.

Historical Essay II

1. Cicero, *Cat.* 3.16; cf. *Cat.* 1.26.

2. *RE*, vol. 2 pt. A2, col. 1693; Stockton (1971: 7).

3. *Comm pet.* 9; cf. *In toga candida apud* Asconius 84.6 and Marshall (1985: 289).

4. *Comm pet.* 9–10; Asconius 83; cf. 90–91; Sallust *Hist.* 1.44; Valerius Maximus 9.2.1; Plutarch *Sulla* 32.2.

5. Gruen (1974: 277); Asconius 90–91; Marshall (1985: 307–308). The court (*quaestio de sicariis*) was set up in 64 B.C. to investigate the murders that had been carried out during the proscriptions.

6. Asconius 91; Sallust *BC* 15.1, Cicero *Cat.* 3.9; Gruen (1974: 271); Marshall (1985: 309–310). According to Marshall, the case of Crassus and

Licinia, the Vestal Virgin (Plutarch *Crassus* 1.2), should probably be connected with this one, especially since Cicero refers to an acquittal of the virgins that occurred in 73 B.C. (*Cat.* 3.9, line 100), implying that more than one Vestal Virgin was prosecuted.

7. Cicero, *In toga candida, apud* Asconius 91–92; Sallust *BC* 15.2; cf. Valerius Maximus 9.1.9 and Appian 2.2.

8. Syme (1939: 83); Crawford (1994: 167); see also Historical Essay II.3 on *In toga candida*.

9. C. Antonius Hybrida (who would later be Catiline's ally in the 64 B.C. elections) and P. Lentulus Sura (a future leader in Catiline's conspiracy) were both among those expelled from the Senate in 70 B.C.

10. According to Asconius (85), the senators were shocked by Catiline's actions: *multaeque graves sententiae in senatu de eo dictae sunt.*

11. Actually, Torquatus' son (also named L. Torquatus) prosecuted Sulla on his father's behalf; see Cicero *De fin.* 2.62.

12. Asconius 89 and Sallust *BC* 18.

13. Marshall (1985: 304–305); for a different view, see Seager (1964: 338–39); and Stockton (1971: 74n19).

14. Cicero, *In toga candida apud* Asconius 92; Sallust *BC* 18.7.

15. See, for example, Seager (1964); Marshall (1985: 288); Stockton (1971: 74–78).

16. The Senate, however, did vote to give the new consuls an official bodyguard on January 1 (Cassius Dio 36.44.4), so it is likely that someone was plotting against them. But Catiline's alleged involvement is probably nothing more than slander.

17. Seager (1964: 344) argues that Catiline was participating in a political riot in support of Gaius Manilius, who was being tried for extortion on that day. This sounds reasonable; it is certainly true that by this time violent demonstrations had become a normal part of political life in Rome.

18. Cicero *Pro Sulla* 81; Stockton (1971: 74).

19. See, for example, Cary (1932: 476–78).

20. Catiline could not run in 65 B.C. because he had been formally charged with extortion, but the trial had not yet taken place. See Asconius 76 and Crawford (1994: 168–69).

21. Cicero, *ad Att.* 1.1.1; Asconius 85, 89.

22. Cicero, *ad Att.* 1.1.1 (July, 65 B.C.): *Catilina, si iudicatum erit meridie non lucere, certus erit competitor.*

23. *Comm. Pet.* 10.

24. Cicero, *ad Att.* 1.2.1.

25. Ungern-Sternberg, von (1997: col. 1030).

26. Asconius 83.

27. Recent biographies of Cicero include Stockton (1971), Rawson (1983), Mitchell (1979 and 1991), Habicht (1990), and Fuhrmann (1992). See now May (2002a) for a brief, helpful summary of Cicero's life. Everitt (2001) is a fast-paced, exciting narrative of Cicero's life and times that is, unfortunately, marred by several inaccuracies.

28. Rawson (1983: 17).

29. Cicero *Brutus* 312; cf. *Orator* 107.

30. See Plutarch *Cicero* 3.6; Cicero says he left for health reasons: *Brutus* 313–15.

31. Cicero *De natura deorum* 1.6; *Brutus* 9.1; Plutarch *Cicero* 4.4.

32. Fuhrmann (1992: 36–37); Cicero *ad Att.* 6.1.2; and Plutarch *Cicero* 6.1.

33. Taylor (1949: 102).

34. This is a different Q. Metellus from the one mentioned by Cicero in *Cat.* 1.19; the Q. Metellus mentioned in *Cat.* 1.19 was praetor in 63 B.C. and consul in 60.

35. Cicero *In Verrem* 1.18–19.

36. Verres himself was reported to have remarked that the money he had extorted during his first year in Sicily was for himself, but the money from his second and third years had been set aside for his attorneys and his jurors (*In Verrem* 1.1.40).

37. Cicero, *In Verrem* 2.5.177.

38. Ibid., 1.47 and 2.1.5–6 See also Stockton (1971: 43).

39. The *tribunii aerarii* had probably once been the paymasters of the army, although they no longer performed this function. See Taylor (1949: 201n13); and Seager (1994: 225).

40. Millar (1998: 72).

41. Ibid., 77.

42. Murray (1966: 297).

43. Cicero *Pro lege Manilia* 36–46 and 15–19.

44. In the broadest sense of the term, a *novus homo* (new man) was a man who was the first member of his family to be elected to the Senate. For a more detailed discussion of the term see Historical Essay I.5.

45. Asconius 82; See Gelzer (1969: 27–40). The Roman nobility (*nobilitas*) consisted of patricians and those from plebeian families who could boast a consul among their number.

46. Asconius 83.

47. Taylor (1949: 106).

48. *Comm. pet.* 3.

49. See Wiseman (1994: 349) for sources.

50. Cicero, *De lege agraria*. 2.68–70 and 2.80–83.

51. Wiseman (1994: 350).

52. Cicero, *De lege agraria* 2.79–83.

53. Stockton (1971: 87).

54. Cicero, *De lege agraria* 2.10–12.

55. Stockton (1971: 85–86).

56. Wiseman (1994: 352).

57. Ibid., 353.

58. Lintott (1968: 169).

59. Wiseman (1994: 352); Stockton (1971: 92–96).

60. Lintott (1968: 173).

61. Millar (1998: 16).

62. Habicht (1990: 31).

63. Ibid., 25.

64. See especially Wiseman (1994: 347–48) and Nicolet (1994: 641–42).

65. Brunt (1971b: 21).

66. Cicero *Pro Murena* 49.

67. I follow Stockton (1971: 101) in preferring Sallust's account of this exchange (*BC* 26) to that of Plutarch (*Cicero* 12).

68. Brunt (1957: 193–95); Gruen (1994: 138); Seager (1964).

69. Stockton (1971: 100).

70. Cicero *Pro Murena* 49.

71. Ibid., 51: *non aqua sed ruina*.

72. Ibid.

73. Stockton (1971: 106).

74. These elections probably took place in July, the normal time for consular elections. See Stockton (1971: 336–337); Benson (1986).

75. Cicero *Pro Murena* 52; cf. Plutarch *Cicero* 14.

76. Cicero *ad Att.* 9.10.2

77. The sequence of events followed here is taken largely from Sallust, *BC* and Cicero's *Catilinarian Orations*, which were delivered in November and December of 63 B.C. and published in June of 60 B.C. (*ad Att.* 2.1.3). I have been greatly helped by Stockton's narrative of the Catilinarian conspiracy (1971: 110–42 and 339), supplemented at various points by Hardy's detailed reconstruction (1924: 49–97) and Wiseman (1994: 347–58).

78. Sallust *BC* 23: *repente glorians maria montisque polliceri coepit*.

79. Sallust *BC* 23 and 26. As R. Syme has shown (1939: 75–77), Sallust placed the beginning of the conspiracy too early, in June of 64 rather than July or August of 63. But, as Stockton rightly notes (1971: 113n8), that fact "need not invalidate his [Sallust's] narrative of Curius and Fulvia; it merely requires that we move his story up some months later." In fact, once the dating problem has been dealt with, Sallust provides valuable information about the conspiracy that Cicero omits (Syme [1939: 81–82]).

80. Plutarch *Cicero* 15; Hardy (1924: 55); cf. Cassius Dio 37.71.

81. Cf. Sallust *BC* 29: *senatus decrevit . . . darent operam consules ne quid res publica detrimenti caperet*.

82. For more on the laws against public violence and the trials of those who were charged, see Lintott (1968: 107–24 and 217–20).

83. Sallust states that Vargunteius was a senator, but Cicero refers to both of his would-be assassins as equestrians. J. Linderski (1963) argues that Vargunteius had once been a senator but that he had been convicted of electoral bribery (*de ambitu*) and expelled from the Senate in 66 B.C., which would have made him an equestrian at the time when he tried to assassinate Cicero.

84. The clients and close friends of a distinguished Roman would go to his house at dawn to greet him and/or escort him to the Forum; this was called the *salutatio* (ceremonial call). On the events of November 6–7, see Sallust *BC* 27–28; Cicero, *Cat.* 1.8–10, 2.6; *Pro Sulla* 18 and 52.

85. Stockton (1971: 118).

86. Syme (1939: 72): "Here speaks the authentic Catilina."

87. Sallust *BC* 56; Stockton (1971: 125).

88. Sallust *BC* 43; Stockton (1971: 121 and note 32); cf. Cicero *Cat.* 3.8.

89. See Scullard (1981: 205–207); Beard et al. (1998: 451).

90. Sallust *BC* 43; cf. Cicero *Cat.* 3.10.

91. Cicero refers to this man as Cimber Gabinius (*Cat.* 3.6), but the full name is reported by Sallust (*BC* 17.4); see the commentary on *Cat.* 3.6, line 65.

92. A patron would protect the interests of a foreign people at Rome. This task was generally undertaken by the nation's conquering general, who would pass it on to his sons. Sanga had thus inherited the patronage of the Allobroges from his father, Quintus Fabius Maximus Allobrogius, who had conquered the tribe in 121 B.C.

93. Sallust *BC* 48–49; According to Stockton (1971: 132), Caesar's difficulties outside the Senate probably occurred on December 5.

94. Lentulus, Cethegus, Statilius, Gabinius, and Ceparius.

95. L. Cassius, P. Furius, Q. Annius Chilo, and P. Umbrenus.

96. Cicero, *ad Att.* 12.21.1; Cassius Dio 37.36.

97. *Eis utendum censeo quae legibus comparata sunt* (Sallust *BC* 51.8).

98. Sallust *BC* 51.43; cf. Cicero *Cat.* 4.7–8.

99. Lintott (1968: 169).

100. Cicero, *Cat.* 4.10; cf. Lintott (1968: 171).

101. Habicht (1990: 37).

102. Cicero's comment that one senator's absence from the meeting was probably due to his reluctance to vote on the death of Roman citizens (*ne de capite videlicet civium Romanorum sententiam ferat*; *Cat.* 4.10) seems to be an acknowledgment that the vote was in fact a violation of the *lex Sempronia*.

103. For a discussion of this issue, see Lintott (1968: 165–166 and 166*n*1. For a different view, see Mitchell (1971).

104. See Richardson (1992: 72) and Platner and Ashby (1929: 99–100). Since the *carcer* was later used to execute Christian martyrs, it was turned into a Christian shrine; it is now preserved underneath the church of San Giuseppe dei Falegnami. The modern name for the *carcer* is the Mamertine Prison.

105. The name Tullianum probably came from its original use as a spring-house (*tullius* is an old Latin word for spring), although the Romans believed that it was named after Servius Tullius, who was supposed to have built it.

106. Plutarch *Cicero* 23.1–3; Cicero *In Pisonem* 6–7; *Pro Sulla* 33–34; *ad Fam.* 5.2.7.

107. Cicero *ad Fam.* 5.2.8; Cassius Dio 37.42–43; Plutarch *Cicero* 23.4–6.

108. Wiseman (1994: 358–59); Habicht (1990: 38).

109. Plutarch *Cicero* 23.6.

110. Plutarch *Cicero* 23.4; cf. Cicero *Pro Sulla* 21–22.

111. Sumner (1963: 216).

112. Cassius Dio 37.40.1; Stockton (1971: 141).

113. Sallust *BC* 59.4; Cassius Dio 37.39.3.

114. Cicero *Pro Sulla* 6, 7, 18, and 71; cf. Lintott (1968: 217–18).

115. Habicht (1990: 33–34).

116. May (1988: 57–58).

117. See Scullard (1965: 13).

118. Cassius Dio 37.45; cf. Wiseman (1994: 361); Stockton (1971: 159); Tatum (1999: 64–86).

119. The widespread view that Crassus was involved in both financing and facilitating Clodius' payments to the jury has been disputed by Tatum (1999: 82–85).

120. According to Plutarch (*Cicero* 29.1), Clodius had actually been a member of Cicero's personal bodyguard during the Catilinarian conspiracy. Although some scholars dispute this, it is at least clear that there had been no hostility between them; Tatum (1999: 65).

121. Tatum (1999: 76–80).

122. There is, in fact, some evidence that Cicero had already begun to do this; see Cicero *De domo* 41; Suetonius *Divus Julius* 20; and Stockton (1971: 168–69).

123. See Lintott (1968: 74–83) on the composition of these *collegia* and Clodius' use of them for organized political violence.

124. Velleius Paterculus 2.45.1: *qui civem Romanum indemnatum interemisset, ei aqua et igni interdiceretur.*

125. Habicht (1990: 47).

126. Wiseman (1994: 367); cf. Cicero *ad Att.* 2.1.3.

Appendix A

1. In preparing this schema, I have relied chiefly on Taylor (1949 and 1966), Lintott (1999), and Cloud (1994), as well as the appropriate articles in *OCD3*. The quotation is from Lintott (1999) 2.

2. Cloud (1994: 491).

3. Millar (1998: 2).

4. See, for example, the discussion in Millar (1998: 197–209).

5. For a discussion of the term *novus homo*, see Historical Essay I.5.

6. *Intercessio* was the right of any Roman magistrate to block the actions of another magistrate of equal or lesser power. This is different from the veto power held by the tribunes, in that a tribune could block the actions of all magistrates, even senior ones, as well as the decisions of legislative bodies. See the section on tribunes below.

7. *RE* 2.A2, col. 1695.

8. Literally this means "the court for diminishing the majesty of the Roman people." This court is usually referred to simply as the *quaestio de maiestate*.

Select Bibliography

Primary Sources

Appian. *Bella Civilia*
Asconius. *Commentaries on Five Speeches of Cicero*
Caesar. *Bellum Civile*
Cassius Dio. *The Roman History*
M. Cicero
   Orations (in chronological order): *Pro Roscio Amerino* (80 B.C.); *In Verrem I–II* (70 B.C.);
   Pro lege Manilia (66 B.C.); *In toga candida* (64 B.C.); *De lege agraria contra Rullum
   I–III* (63 B.C.); *Pro Rabirio perduellionis* (63 B.C.); *In Catilinam I–IV* (63 B.C.); *Pro
   Murena* (63 B.C.); *Pro Sulla* (62 B.C.); *De domo sua* (57 B.C.); *Pro Caelio* (56 B.C.); *De
   provinciis consularibus* (56 B.C.); *In Pisonem* (55 B.C.).
   Works on Oratory: *De Oratore* (55 B.C.); *Brutus* (46 B.C.); *Orator* (46 B.C.).
   Philosophical Works: *De Republica* (54–51 B.C.); *De finibus* (45 B.C.); *De natura deorum*
   (45 B.C.).
   Letters: *Epistulae ad Atticum, Epistulae ad Quintum Fratrem, Epistulae ad Familiares*
[Q. Cicero] *Commentariolum Petitionis*
Plutarch. *Tiberius Gracchus; Gaius Gracchus; Marius; Sulla; Sertorius; Cicero; Crassus.*
Sallust. *Bellum Jugurthinum; Bellum Catilinae; Histories.*
Suetonius. *Divus Julius.*
Valerius Maximus. *Facta et Dicta Memorabilia*
Velleius Paterculus. *Historiae Romanae*

Secondary Sources

Africa, T. 1982. "Worms and the Death of Kings: A Cautionary Note on Disease and
   History." *Classical Antiquity* 1: 1–17.
Albertoni, M. et al. 2000. *The Capitoline Museums.* Trans. D. Arya and S. Mari. Milan:
   Electa.
Albrecht, M. von. 2003. *Cicero's Style: A Synopsis.* Leiden: Brill.
Astin, A. E. 1958. *The Lex Annalis before Sulla.* Collection Latomus, vol. 32. Brussels:
   Latomus. Also published as *Latomus* 16 (1957): 588–613.
———. 1967. *Scipio Aemilianus.* Oxford: Oxford University Press.
Barnes, E. J., and John T. Ramsey. 1988. *Cicero and Sallust: On the Conspiracy of Catiline.*
   New York: Longman.
Beard, M., J. North, and S. Price. 1998. *Religions of Rome. Volume 1: A History.* Cambridge:
   Cambridge University Press.

Bennett, C. E. 1908. *New Latin Grammar*. Boston: Allyn and Bacon. Rpt. Wauconda, Ill: Bolchazy-Carducci, 1994.

———. 1922. *Selections from Cicero: Orations, Letters, and de Senectute*. Boston: Allyn and Bacon. Rpt. 1964.

Benson, J. M. 1986. "Catiline and the Date of the Consular Elections of 63 B.C." In C. Deroux, ed., *Studies in Latin Literature and Roman History IV*, 234–46. Collection Latomus, vol. 196. Brussels: Latomus.

Berger, A. 1953. *Encyclopedic Dictionary of Roman Law*. Philadelphia: American Philosophical Society.

Bober, P. P., and R. Rubinstein. 1986. *Renaissance Artists and Antique Sculpture*. London: Harvey Miller Publishers; and Oxford: Oxford University Press.

Brunt, P. A. 1957. "Three Passages from Asconius." *Classical Review* 71 (n.s. 7): 193–95.

———. 1971a. *Italian Manpower 225 BC–AD 14*. Oxford: Oxford University Press.

———. 1971b. *Social Conflicts in the Roman Republic*. Oxford: Oxford University Press.

———. 1982. "Nobilitas and Novitas." *Journal of Roman Studies* 72: 1–17.

Cancik, H., and H. Schneider. 1997. *Der Neue Pauly: Enzyklopädie der Antike*. Stuttgart and Vienna: J. B. Metzler.

Cape, R. W., Jr. 1985. "The Rhetoric of Politics in Cicero's *Fourth Catilinarian*." *American Journal of Philology* 116: 225–77.

Cary, M. 1932. "Rome in the Absence of Pompey." Chapter 11 in *CAH* 9[1]: 475–505.

Cary, M., and H. H. Scullard. 1975. *A History of Rome*. New York: St. Martin's Press.

Clark, A. C. 1905. *M. Tulli Ciceronis Orationes*. Vol. 1. Oxford Classical Texts. Oxford: Oxford University Press.

———. 1907. *Q. Asconii Pediani Orationum Ciceronis quinque enarratio*. Oxford: Oxford University Press.

Cloud, D. 1994. "The Constitution and Public Criminal Law." Chapter 13 in *CAH* 9[2]: 491–530.

Connolly, P., and H. Dodge. 1998. *The Ancient City: Life in Classical Athens and Ancient Rome*. Oxford: Oxford University Press.

Crawford, J. W. 1994. *M. Tullius Cicero: The Fragmentary Speeches. An Edition with Commentary*. Atlanta, Ga.: Scholars Press.

Dorey, T. A., ed. 1965. *Cicero*. Studies in Latin Literature and Its Influence. New York: Basic Books, Inc.

Duncan, D. E. 1998. *Calendar: Humanity's Epic Struggle to Determine a True and Accurate Year*. New York: Avon Books.

Eagle, E. D. 1949. "Catiline and the Concordia Ordinum." *Phoenix* 3: 15–30.

Evans, J. K. 1981. "Wheat Production and Its Social Consequences in the Roman World." *Classical Quarterly* 75 (n.s. 31): 428–42.

Everitt, A. 2001. *Cicero: The Life and Times of Rome's Greatest Politician*. New York: Random House. Orig. published in England in 2001 by John Murray Publishers.

Frayn, J. M. 1979. *Subsistence Farming in Roman Italy*. London: Centaur Press Ltd.

Frerichs, K. 1997. *Cicero's First Catilinarian Oration, with Introduction, Running Vocabulary and Notes*. Wauconda, Ill.: Bolchazy-Carducci.

Fuhrmann, M. 1992. *Cicero and the Roman Republic*. Trans. W. E. Yuill. London and Cambridge, Mass.: Blackwell Publishers Ltd. First published 1990 as *Cicero und die römische Republik*.

Gabba, E. 1976. *Republican Rome: The Army and the Allies*. Trans. P. J. Cuff. Oxford: Oxford University Press.

———. 1994. "Rome and Italy: The Social War." In *CAH* 9²: 104–28.

Gelzer, M. 1923. "Sergius Catilina, L." Columns 1693–1711 in *RE,* vol. 2, part A2. First published 1923.

———. 1969. *The Roman Nobility.* Trans. R. Seager. Oxford: Oxford University Press.

Gildersleeve, B. L., and G. Lodge. 1895. *Gildersleeve's Latin Grammar.* 3rd ed. London: Macmillan and Co., Ltd. Rpt. Wauconda, Ill: Bolchazy-Carducci Publishers, 2000.

Gruen, E. S. 1974. *The Last Generation of the Roman Republic.* Berkeley: University of California Press.

Habicht, C. 1990. *Cicero the Politician.* Baltimore and London: Johns Hopkins University Press.

Hall, U. 1977. "Notes on Fulvius Flaccus." *Athenaeum* 55: 280–88.

Hardy, E. G. 1924. *The Catilinarian Conspiracy in Its Context: A Re-Study of the Evidence.* Oxford: Basil Blackwell. Rpt. New York: AMS Press, 1976.

Haskell, F., and N. Penny. 1981. *Taste and The Antique: The Lure of Classical Sculpture 1500–1900.* New Haven and London: Yale University Press.

Hornblower, S., and A. Spawforth, eds. 1996. *OCD* ³. Oxford: Oxford University Press.

Jones, H. S., ed. 1912. *A Catalogue of the Ancient Sculptures Preserved in the Municipal Collections of Rome: The Sculptures of the Museo Capitolino.* Oxford: Clarendon Press.

———. 1926. *A Catalogue of the Ancient Sculptures Preserved in the Municipal Collections of Rome: The Sculptures of the Palazzo dei Conservatori.* Oxford: Clarendon Press.

Lanham, Richard A. 1991. *A Handlist of Rhetorical Terms,* 2nd ed. Berkeley: University of California Press.

Last, H., and R. Gardner. 1932. Chapters 1–4 and 6–7 in *CAH* 9¹: 1–209; 261–349.

Linderski, J. 1963. "Cicero and Sallust on Vargunteius." *Historia* 12: 511–12.

Lintott, A. W. 1968. *Violence in Republican Rome.* Oxford: Oxford University Press. 2nd ed. published in 1999, with a new introduction.

———. 1970. "The Tradition of Violence in the Annals of the Early Republic." *Historia* 19: 12–29.

———. 1972. "*Provocatio* from the Struggle of the Orders to the Principate." In *Aufstieg und Niedergang der Römischen Welt,* ed. H. Temporini and W. Haase, part 1, vol. 2, 226–67. Berlin and New York: W. de Gruyter, 1972–.

———. 1994. Chapters 1–3 in *CAH* 9²: 1–103.

———. 1996. "*senatus consultum ultimum.*" *OCD* ³: 1388–89.

———. 1999. *The Constitution of the Roman Republic.* Oxford: Oxford University Press.

Macadam, A. 2000. *City Guide: Rome.* 7th ed. Blue Guide Series. London: A. and C. Black; and New York: W. W. Norton.

MacDonald, C. 1977. *Cicero: In Catilinam I–IV, Pro Murena, Pro Sulla, Pro Flacco.* Cambridge, Mass: Harvard University Press.

Marshall, B. A. 1985. *A Historical Commentary on Asconius.* Columbia: University of Missouri Press.

May, J. M. 1988. *Trials of Character: The Eloquence of Ciceronian Ethics.* Chapel Hill and London: University of North Carolina Press.

———. 2002a. "Cicero: His Life and Career." Pages 1–21 in May 2002b.

———, ed. 2002b. *Brill's Companion to Cicero: Oratory and Rhetoric.* Leiden: Brill.

Millar, F. 1998. *The Crowd in Rome in the Late Republic.* Ann Arbor: University of Michigan Press.

Mitchell, Th. N. 1971. "Cicero and the *Senatus Consultum Ultimum.*" *Historia* 20: 47–61.

———. 1979. *Cicero: The Ascending Years.* New Haven: Yale University Press.

———. 1991. *Cicero: The Senior Statesman*. New Haven: Yale University Press.

Murray, R. J. 1966. "Cicero and the Gracchi." *Transactions and Proceedings of the American Philological Society* 96: 291–98.

Nicolet, C. 1994. "Economy and Society, 133–43 B.C." Chapter 16 in *CAH* 9²: 599–643.

Pelling, C. B. R. 1985. "Plutarch and Catiline." *Hermes* 113: 311–29.

Platner, S. B., and T. Ashby. 1929. *A Topographical Dictionary of Ancient Rome*. Oxford: Oxford University Press.

Presicce, C. P. 2000. *La Lupa Capitolina*. Rome: Commune di Roma.

Rawson, E. 1983. *Cicero: A Portrait*. London: Bristol Classical Press. First published 1975.

Richardson, L., Jr. 1992. *A New Topographical Dictionary of Ancient Rome*. Baltimore and London: Johns Hopkins University Press.

Scullard, H. H. 1965. "The Political Career of a *Novus Homo*." Pages 1–25 in Dorey (1965).

———. 1981. *Festivals and Ceremonies of the Roman Republic*. Ithaca: Cornell University Press.

Seager, R. 1964. "The First Catilinarian Conspiracy." *Historia* 13: 338–47.

———. 1994. Chapters 6–7 in *CAH* 9²: 165–228.

Sherwin-White, A. N. 1973. *The Roman Citizenship*. 2nd ed. Oxford: Oxford University Press. First published 1939.

Squires, S., trans. *Asconius Pedianus, Quintus: Commentaries on Five Speeches of Cicero*. Bristol, UK, and Wauconda, Ill.: Bristol Classical Press and Bolchazy-Carducci Publishers.

Stockton, D. L. 1971. *Cicero: A Political Biography*. Oxford: Oxford University Press.

———. 1979. *The Gracchi*. Oxford: Oxford University Press.

Sumner, G. V. 1963. "The Last Journey of L. Sergius Catilina." *Classical Philology* 58: 215–19.

Syme, R. 1939. *The Roman Revolution*. Oxford: Oxford University Press. Rpt. 1982.

Tatum, W. J. 1999. *The Patrician Tribune: Publius Claudius Pulcher*. Chapel Hill and London: University of North Carolina Press.

Taylor, L. R. 1949. *Party Politics in the Age of Caesar*. Berkeley and Los Angeles: University of California Press. Rpt. 1961.

———. 1966. *Roman Voting Assemblies*. Ann Arbor: University of Michigan Press.

Ungern-Sternberg, J. von. 1997. "Catilina." Columns 1029–31 of vol. 2 in Cancik and Schneider (1997).

White, K. D. 1970. *Roman Farming*. London: Thames and Hudson.

Wiseman, T. P. 1971. *New Men in the Roman Senate, 139 B.C. to A.D. 14*. Oxford: Oxford University Press.

———. 1994. Chapters 9–10 in *CAH* 9²: 327–423.

Yavetz, Z. 1963. "The Failure of Catiline's Conspiracy." *Historia* 12: 485–99.

Vocabulary

A

ab, a (prep. + abl.): by (personal agent), from

abdico, abdicare (often used with reflexive pronoun): to resign from office before the legal term expires, abdicate

abeo, abire, abii, abitum: to go away, depart

abhorreo, abhorrere, abhorrui (+ ab + abl.): to be unconnected with; to differ from; to be inconsistent with, to disagree with

abicio, abicere, abieci, abiectum: to throw down, cast down

abiectus, -a, -um: low, common, mean, contemptible; dejected, downcast

abs: an archaic form of **ab,** generally used only before **te**

abscondo, abscondere, abscondi, absconditum: to hide, conceal

absolutio, -onis, f: an acquittal (at law)

absum, abesse, afui, afuturus: to be away; to be absent, not present

abundantia, -ae, f.: abundance, plenty; prosperity, time of wealth

abutor, abuti, abusus sum (+ abl.): to abuse, misuse

ac (conj.): and

accedo, accedere, accessi, acessurus: to go to, come to, approach, come near

accelero, accelare: to hasten, hurry

accido, accidere, accidi, —: to happen

accipio, accipere, accepi, acceptum: to receive, welcome, accept

accubo, accubare: to recline (at table)

accuso, accusare: to accuse, reproach

acer, acris, acre (adj.): sharp, fierce, keen, energetic; (+ gen.) eager for, passionate for

acerbe (adv.): harshly, severely, cruelly

acerbissimus, -a, -um: superlative adjective of **acerbus**

acerbitas, -atis, f.: bitterness, harshness, severity

acerbus, -a, -um: bitter, harsh, violent, severe

acerrimus, -a, -um: superlative adjective of **acer**

acervus, -i, m: mass, pile, heap, great number, quantity

acies, -ei, f.: 1. point, sharp edge, sharpness; 2. battle line, front line of troops prepared for battle

acrior, -ius (comp. adj. of **acer**): harsher, more severe

ad (prep. + acc.): to, toward, for; for the purpose of, with a view to

adduco, adducere, adduxi, adductum: to lead to, bring before; to prompt, induce

adeo (adv.): actually, in fact; even

adeps, -ipis, m./f.: fat; corpulence

adfero, adferre, attuli, adlatum: 1. to bring *accusative* to *dative*, carry to; 2. to cause, cause to, produce

adficio, adficere, adfeci, adfectum: 1. to treat, affect; 2. to afflict, punish; 3. to honor *accusative* with *ablative*

adfinis, -e (adj.): adjoining, connected with, implicated in, accessory to

adfligo, adfligere, adflixi, adflictum: damage, hurt, injure, afflict, distress

adgrego, adgregare: to collect, bring together

adhibeo, adhibere, adhibui, adhibitum: to apply, use

adhuc (adv.): until now

adimo, adimere, ademi, ademptum: to take away, remove

adipiscor, adipisci, adeptus sum: to gain, obtain

aditus, -us, m.: approach, entrance

adiungo, adiungere, adiunxi, adiunctum: to join, attach, add on, accompany, to add *accusative* to *dative*

adiuvo, adiuvare, adiuvi, adiutum: to help, assist

administer, -tri, m.: assistant, helper

administro, administrare: to manage, guide, direct, control, regulate

admiror, admirari, admiratus sum: to wonder at, admire

admonitu, m. (only in abl. sing.): suggestion, request

adnuo, adnuere, adnui, —: to nod in agreement

adquiro, adquirere, adquisivi, adquisitum: to add to, acquire, gain, get in addition; to understand, comprehend

adsequor, adsequi, adsecutus sum: to follow up, overtake; to accomplish, effect, attain

adservo, adservare: to watch over, keep under guard

adsideo, adsidere, adsedi, —: to sit down

adsidue (adv.): continually, constantly

adsuefacio, adsuefacere, adsuefeci, adsuefactum: to train, accustom

adsum, adesse, adfui, adfuturum: to be present; to assist, help, aid

adulescens, -entis, m.: a youth, young man

adulescentulus, -i, m.: a young man, youth (diminutive of **adulescens,** B148.1)

adulter, -i, m.: adulterer, seducer

adultus, -a, -um: mature, full grown

adventus, -us, m.: a coming, approach, arrival

advesperascit (impersonal verb): it approaches evening, it is twilight

aedes, -is, f.: building, temple; in plural: a home, a house, dwelling

aedificio, aedificiare: to erect a building

aedificium, -i, n.: building

aeger, -gra, -grum: ill, sick, unwell, diseased

aeque (adv.): equally, in like manner, in an equal decree

aequitas, -atis, f.: fairness, justice

aequus, -a, -um: 1. even, flat; 2. equal, reasonable, fair; 3. calm, composed
    aequo animo: calmly, patiently, with equanimity, with indifference

aerarium, -i, n.: the treasury

aerarius, -a, -um: pertaining to a treasury
    tribunus aerarius: tribune of the treasury, an official in charge of public disbursement

aes, aeris, n.: copper, bronze; money; bronze tablet, on which laws were inscribed
    aes alienum: another's money (i.e., debt)

aestus, -us, m.: heat, fever

aetas, -tatis, f.: age, time of life

aeternus, -a, -um: lasting, enduring, permanent, eternal

afuit: see **absum**

ager, agri, m.: land, field, country

agnosco, agnoscere, agnovi, agnitum: to recognize, assent to, acknowledge

ago, agere, egi, actum: 1. to do, drive, act, accomplish; 2. to speak (*Cat.* 1.8); 3. plead (*Cat.* 1.18)

quid agis?: what are you doing?

agrarii, -orum, m pl.: the agrarian party, those seeking agrarian reforms

agrarius, -a, -um: of or pertaining to the land

agrestis, e (adj.): of the fields or countryside; rustic, uncultivated, boorish, coarse

aio (defective verb): to say
    aiunt: they say
    ut aiunt: as they say

alea, -ae, f.: dice, a game with dice; gambling

aleator, -oris, m.: gambler

alienigena, -ae, m.: one born in a foreign land; (as adj.) foreign

alienus, -a, -um.: belonging to another; foreign, strange

alienus, -i, m.: a foreigner, outsider

aliquando (adv.): finally, at length, now at last; at some time, at any time

aliquanto (adv.): by a little, a little

aliqui, aliqua, aliquod: 1. (indefinite adjective some, any; 2. (indefinite pronoun) someone, anyone, something

aliquis, aliqua, aliquid: 1. (indefinite pronoun) anyone, someone, anything, something; 2. (adjective) some, any, a certain

aliquo (adv.): to someplace, to somewhere

aliquot (indeclinable indefinite number): some, several, a few

alius, -a, -ud: other, another

Allobroges, -um, m. pl.: the Allobroges, a warlike people of Gaul

alo, alere, alui, altum or alitum: to nourish, support, sustain, maintain

altaria, -ium, n. pl.: an altar, altar for sacrifice to the gods

alter, altera, alterum: one another, the other (of two)
    alter . . . alter: the one . . . the other; the former . . . the latter

altior, altius: comparative adjective of **altus**

altus, -a, -um: high, lofty, tall; great, elevated

amans, -antis (adj.): affectionate, loving

amentia, -ae, f.: madness, frenzy

amicio, amicire, amicui, amictum: to cover, clothe, wrap, surround

amicus, -i, m.: a friend

amitto, amittere, amisi, amissum: to send away; to lose, let go

amo, amare: to love

amor, -oris, m.: love, affection

amplector, amplecti, amplexus sum: to embrace

amplifico, amplificare: to extend, enlarge, increase, amplify

amplissimus, -a, -um: superlative adjective of
amplus: most distinguished, most noble

amplitudo, -inis, f.: 1. breadth, size, bulk; 2.
greatness, dignity, grandeur

amplius: comparative adverb of **amplus:** more, further

amplus, -a, -um: full, abundant, copious, ample

an (conj.): or; introducing a question: Or? Or is it
the case that?

angulus, -i, m.: angle, corner

anhelo, anhelare: to breathe hard, gasp, pant; to
desire eagerly (**scelus**, *Cat.* 2.1)

anima, -ae, f.: breath, spirit, life

animadversio, -onis, f.: attention; punishment

**animadverto, animadvertere, animadverti, ani-
madversum:** 1. to pay attention to, attend to,
regard, observe; 2. to punish, enact a punishment against
in hunc animadvertere: to punish this man

animus, -i, m.: 1. mind, spirit; 2. determination,
resolve; 3. in plural: courage; 4) feeling, mind,
disposition

annus, -i, m: year

ante (adv.): before, previous, earlier
ante quam: sooner than, before

ante (prep. + acc.): before

antea (adv.): before

antelucanus, -a, -um: before dawn (i.e., lasting
all night)

antepono, anteponere, anteposui, antepositum
(+ acc. + dat.): to put *accusative* before *dative*,
to prefer

antiquissimus, -a, -um: superlative adjective of
antiquus, most ancient

antiquus, -a, -um: ancient, former, of old

aperio, aperire, aperui, apertum: to open,
uncover, disclose, reveal

aperte (adv.): openly, clearly, without disguise

apertus, -a, -um: uncovered, exposed, open

apparatus, -a, -um: magnificent, splendid, sump-
tuous

appello, appellare: to call, name

Appenninus, -i, m: the Apennine mountains

appropinquo, appropinquare: to come near,
approach

aptus, -a, -um: fit, suitable; proper

apud (+ acc. of person): among, at the house of;
equivalent to the French *chez*

Apulia, -ae, f.: a province of south-east Italy

aqua, -ae, f.: water

aquila, -ae, f.: an eagle; in war, a silver eagle, the
standard of a legion (carried by the senior centurion of the first cohort)

ara, -ae, f.: an altar

arbitror, arbitrari, arbitratus sum: to think,
suppose, believe

arceo, arcere, arcui, — (+ acc. + **ab** + abl.): to
keep *accusative* away from ab + *ablative*.

arcesso, arcessere, arcessivi, arcessitum: to
summon, call, send for

ardeo, ardere, arsi, arsum: to burn, be on fire

ardor, -oris, m.: a burning, flame

argenteus, -a, -um: made of silver, silver

argentum, -i, n.: silver; money; silver-plated
serving dishes

argumentum, -i, n.: evidence, ground, support,
proof

arma, -orum, n. pl.: arms, weaponry, weapons
in arma: in arms, under arms

armatus, -a, -um: armed, equipped with arms,
carrying weapon, under arms

arx, arcis, f.: citadel, summit, stronghold; in Rome,
the northern summit of the Capitoline Hill

ascendo, ascendere, ascendi, ascensum: to
mount, climb, ascend, reach

ascisco, asciscere, ascivi, ascitum: to add, adopt,
enlist

aspectus, -us, m.: sight, view; appearance, picture; aspect, countenance

aspicio, aspicere, aspexi, aspectum: to look at,
view, behold, regard
aspicere inter sese: to cast glances at one another

at (conj.): but

atque (conj.): and, and also
atque si: but if

atrocitas, -atis, f.: cruelty, harshness, bitterness

atrox, atrocis (adj.): savage, cruel, violent, horrible

attendo, attendere, attendi, attentum: to notice,
attend to, give heed

attribuo, attribuere, attribui, attributum (+ acc.
+ dat.): to assign *accusative* to *dative*, give,
grant, entrust

attuli: see **adfero**

auctionarius, -a, -um: pertaining to an auction

auctor, -oris, m.: author, originator, promoter

auctoritas, -atis, f.: 1. power, authority, influence;
2. will, resolve; 3. judgment, decision

audacia, -ae, f.: insolence, boldness, recklessness,
audacity, presumption

audacior, -ius: comparative adjective of **audax**

audacissimus, -a, -um: superlative adjective of
audax

audax, -acis (adj.): bold, daring, foolhardy, rash

audeo, audere, ausus sum: to venture, dare, be
bold

audiens, -entis, m.: a hearer, a listener

audio, audire, audivi, auditum: to hear

augeo, augere, auxi, auctum: to increase, make greater, extend

Aurelia Via: the Aurelian Way, which ran northwest from Rome

auris, -is, f.: ear

auspicium, -i, n.: 1. omen, auspices, divination by the flight of birds; 2. command, guidance, authority

aut (conj.): or

    aut . . . aut: either . . . or; both . . . and (*Cat.* 1.15)

autem (conj.): 1. (adversative) but, on the contrary, however; 2. (resumptive) furthermore, in addition

auxilium, -i, n.: help, aid, assistance; plural: auxiliary forces, auxiliary troops

aversus, -a, -um (+abl.): hostile to, blind to, opposed to

avus, -i, m.: grandfather, ancestor

B

bacchor, bacchari, bacchatus sum: to revel, rave, exult, rave like a bacchant (worshipper of Bacchus)

barbaria, -ae, f.: strange land, foreign country (as opposed to Greece and Italy)

barbarus, -a, -um: foreign, strange, barbarous, uncivilized

barbatus, -a, -um: bearded

beatus, -a, -um: 1. happy, blessed, fortunate; 2. wealthy, rich, opulent

bellum, -i, n.: war

bene (adv.): well

beneficium, -i, n.: service, kindness

benevolentia, -ae, f.: goodwill, favor, gratitude

benignitas, -atis, f.: kindness, goodness, favor

bibo, bibere, bibi, —: to drink

bipertito (adv.): in two parts

bis (adv.): twice

bona, -orum, n. pl.: goods, property

bonus, -a, -um: good, sound

brevis, -e (adj.): brief, short

breviter (adv.): briefly, in a few words

C

caedes, -is, f.: slaughter, massacre, murder

caelum, -i, n.: sky, heaven; air

calamitas, -atis, f.: misfortune, calamity, disaster

calliditas, -atis, f.: shrewdness, skill, cunning

campus, -i, n.: 1. plain, field, level place, open field; 2. frequently used for the Campus Martius, a large, grassy plain north of the Capitoline Hill that was used for military exercises and meetings of the **comitia centuriata** (including consular elections); see Map 2

cano, canere, cecini, —: to sing; to foretell, predict, prophesy

canto, cantare: to sing

capillus, -i, m.: hair, head of hair

capio, capere, cepi, captum: 1. to take, receive; 2. to hold, contain; 3. to strike, capture

capitalis, -e (adj.): deadly, dangerous, pernicious

Capitolium, -i, n.: the Capitol, the temple of Jupiter on the Capitoline Hill

caput, -itis, n.: head; capital punishment

carcer, -eris, m.: prison

careo, carere, carui, cariturus (+ abl.): to be without, be deprived of

carior, -ius: comparative adjective of **carus**, more dear

carus, -a, -um: dear, esteemed, beloved, valued

castra, -orum, n. pl.: army camp, military camp

castrensis, -e (adj.): of the camp, in the camp

casus, -us, m.: a chance event, chance; accident, mishap

    casu: by chance

causa, -ae, f.: cause, reason; motive; case, trial

    causa: (in abl. + preceding gen.): because of, for the sake of

cedo, cedere, cessi, cessum (+ dat.): to yield to, submit to, retreat before

celebro, celebrare: to celebrate, solemnize, keep

celeriter (adv.): swiftly, quickly

cena, -ae, f.: banquet, dinner, dinner party

censeo, censere, censui, censum: (of senators) to propose, vote, state their opinion

centurio, -onis, m.: centurion

cerno, cernere, crevi, cretum: to see, perceive, behold

certamen, -inis, n.: contest, struggle

certe (adv.): certainly, assuredly, to be sure

certior, certius: comparative adjective of **certus**

    certiorem facere aliquem: to inform someone

certissimus, -a, -um: superlative adjective of **certus**: most trustworthy, most loyal

certo, certare: to fight, contend, compete with, strive to outdo

certus, -a, -um: fixed, settled, definite, certain; certain, specified, particular

cervix, cervicis, f.: neck

ceteri, -ae, -a: the others, the rest, everyone/everything else, the remainder

cibus, -i, n.: food

cinis, -eris, m.: ashes, embers

circum (prep. + acc.): around, about

circumcludo, circumcludere, circumclusi, circumclusum: to shut in, hem in, surround, enclose

circumdo, circumdare, circumdedi, circumdatum: (+ acc. + dat.): to put *accusative* around *dative,* to surround

circumscriptor, -oris, m.: cheat, swindler

circumsedeo, circumsedere, circumsedi, circumsessum: to sit around, surround

circumspicio, circumspicere, circumspexi, circumspectum: to look at, watch out for; consider

circumsto, circumstare, circumsteti, —: to stand around, surround, besiege

Cisalpinus, -a, -um: on this side of the Alps

civilis, -e (adj.): of citizens, civil

civis, -is, m./f.: citizen

civitas, -atis, f.: state, citizenship, citizen's rights

clam (adv.): secretly, privately, in secret

clamo, clamare: to shout aloud, cry out

clarior, clarius: comparative adjective of **clarus:** clearer

clarissimus, -a, -um: superlative adjective of **clarus:** most famous, most distinguished

clarus, -a, -um: brilliant, glorious; famous

clemens, -entis (adj.): mild, merciful, lenient, compassionate

clientela, -ae, f.: clientship, patronage; plural: body of clients

coepi, coepisse, coeptus sum (appears only in the perfect and pluperfect tenses): to begin, commence

coerceo, coercere, coercui, coercitum: to restrain, check, repress; to correct

coetus, -us, m.: meeting, assembly

cogitatio, -onis, f.: thought, design, plan

cogito, cogitare: to think, plan, consider

cognitor, -oris, m.: advocate, sponsor, defender

cognosco, cognoscere, cognovi, cognitum: to recognize, acknowledge, identify, investigate, examine

cogo, cogere, coegi, coactum: to summon, convene; to force, compel

colonia, -ae, f.: colony, settlement of Roman citizens, colonial town

colonus, -i, m.: farmer, settler, colonist

color, -oris, m.: color, hue, tint

comes, -itis, m./f.: companion, associate, partner

comissatio, -onis, f.: revel, carousal

comitatus, -us, m.: escort, retinue, company

comitia, -orum, n. pl.: election

comitium, -i, n.: place of assembly, especially the **comitium,** an area adjoining the Forum, between the Curia Hostilia (Senate House) and the **rostra** (speaker's platform); (see Map 1)

comito, comitare: to accompany, follow, attend

commemoro, commemorare: 1. to remember, recall, keep in mind; 2. to mention, recount, relate

commendatio, -onis, f.: recommendation; excellence, worth

commendo, commendare: (+ acc. + dat.): to entrust *accusative* to *dative,* commit for protection

committo, committere, commisi, commissum: 1. to begin (a fight); 2. to act, do; 3. to commit, perpetrate, be guilty of a crime; 4) (+ acc. + dat.): to deliver, entrust, commit, yield

commoveo, commovere, commovi, commotum: to stir up, alarm, agitate, disturb

se commovere: to begin to disturb; to rouse oneself, make a disturbance

communis, -e (adj.): common, general, universal, public

commuto, commutare: to alter wholly, change entirely, change

comparo, compare: 1. to prepare, make ready; 2. to constitute, comprise; 3. to furnish, provide

compello, compellere, compuli, compulsum: to drive, force

comperio, comperire, comperi, compertum: to find out about, learn about, discover, ascertain

competitor, -oris, m.: rival, opposing candidate, competitor

complector, complecti, complexus sum: to embrace

complexus, -us, m.: embrace

complures, -ium: (adj. pl.): many, several, more than one

comprehendo, comprehendere, comprehendi, comprehensum: to seize, arrest; to detect, discover

comprimo, comprimere, compressi, compressum: to restrain, hinder, check, repress

conatus, -us, m.: attempt, endeavor, undertaking

concedo, concedere, concessi, concessum (+ acc. + dat.): yield *accusative* to *dative,* to submit, withdraw; to grant, defer

concido, concidere, concidi, —: to fall down, collapse, decline, decay

concipio, concipere, concepi, conceptum: to conceive, imagine, devise

concito, concitare: to stir up, arouse, excite

concordia, -ae, f.: harmony, agreement, concord

concupisco, concupiscere, concupivi, concupitum: to desire eagerly concurso, concursare: to run about, run to and fro

concursus, -us, m.: a gathering, a coming together

condemno, condemnare: (+ acc. of person + gen. of charge): to sentence, condemn, convict, find guilty

condicio, -onis, f.: agreement, condition, circumstances, position, situation

condo, condere, condidi, conditum: to found (a city)

confectus, -a, -um: weakened, impaired, exhusted

confero, conferre, contuli, conlatum: 1. to bring together, collect; 2. to bring, direct; 3. to compare; 4. to contribute

se conferre: 1. to betake oneself, to go; 2. to devote oneself

conferre in (+ a date): to assign to (a particular date), determine for

confertus, -a, -um: stuffed, packed, full

confessio, -onis, f.: confession, acknowledgment

confestim (adv.): immediately

conficio, conficere, confeci, confectum: 1. to complete, accomplish, fulfill; 2. to weaken, wear out, consume; 3. to destroy, kill

confido, confidere, confisus sum: to trust firmly, be confident that

confirmo, confirmare: 1. to affirm, confirm, give assurance; 2. to strengthen, make strong; 3. to declare, promise

confiteor, confiteri, confessus sum: to confess

conflagro, conflagrare: to burn, consume with fire; to be on fire, be consumed

confligo, confligere, conflixi, conflictum: to struggle, fight, contend

conflo, conflare: 1. to bring about, effect, produce, cause; 2. to bring together, make up, compose

confringo, confringere, confregi, confractum: to break into pieces, destroy

congrego, congregare: to assemble

conicio, conicere, conieci, coniectum: to throw, hurl; to drive, force

coniectura, -ae, f.: a conjecture, guess, inference, induction

coniunctio, -onis, f.: union, bond

coniungo, coniungere, coniunxi, coniunctum: to join, connect, unite

coniunx, -ugis, f./m.: husband, wife, spouse

coniuratio, -onis, f.: a conspiracy, plot

coniveo, conivere, conivi, —: to overlook, leave unnoticed, look the other way

conlega or collega, -ae, m.: partner in office, colleague, associate

conligo or colligo, conlegere, conlegi, conlectum: collect, gather, assemble; muster (of troops)

conloco, conlocare: to place, station, set up

conor, conari, conatus sum: to try, attempt

conroboro, conroborare: to strengthen, invigorate, make strong

conruo, conruere, conrui, —: to perish, fall in ruin

consceleratus, -a, -um: criminal, defiled with crime

conscientia, -ae, f.: 1. knowledge, consciousness, feeling, sense; 2. a sense of right, conscience; 3. a sense of guilt, remorse; guilty conscience

conscriptus, -i, m.: one enrolled

conscripti patres (originally patres et conscripti): i.e., senators, the regular way of addressing the members of the Senate

consecro, consecrare: (+ abl. of means): to make sacred

consensio, -onis, f.: agreement, unanimity, concord

consentio, consentire, consensi, consensum: to agree, unite, combine

consequor, consequi, consecutus sum: to pursue, overtake; to follow; to understand; to acquire, get, obtain

conservo, conservare: to preserve, save, keep intact, preserve

consilium, -i, n.: 1. plan, design; 2. advice, deliberation, counsel; 3. purpose, judgment; 4) determination, resolution; 5) council, body of counselors, deliberative assembly

consilium inire: to form a plan, conspire

consolor, consolari, consolatus sum: to console, comfort, cheer, encourage

conspectus, -us, m.: sight, view, range of sight

conspicio, conspicere, conspexi, conspectum: to look at, see, gaze upon

conspiratio, -onis, f.: harmony, unanimity, concord, union

constanter (adv.): firmly, steadily, constantly, resolutely

constantia, -ae, f.: firmness, steadfastness

constituo, constituere, constitui, constitutum: 1. to establish, decide, agree upon; 2. to designate, select, assign, appoint, decree; 3. to set up, establish, found (a colony), constitute, set in order

constringo, constringere, constrinxi, constrictum: to bind, shackle, restrain

consuetudo, -inis, f.: custom, habit, usage

consul, -ulis, m.: a consul, the highest magistrate on the Roman Republic; see Appendix A

consularis, -e: 1. (as adj.) of or pertaining to a consul, consular; 2. (as substantive) an ex-consul, one of consular rank

consulatus, -us, m.: the office of consul, consulship

consulo, consulere, consului, consultum (+ dat.): 1. to consult, deliberate; 2. to take thought for, consider the interests of; 3. to ask for advice, ask one's opinion

consultum, -i, n.: decree, decision
consultum senatus: a decree of the Senate

consumo, consumere, consumpsi, consumptum: to waste, use up, consume

contamino, contaminare: to corrupt, contaminate, defile

contego, contegere, contexi, contectum: to cover, protect, conceal, bury

contemno, contemnere, contempsi, contemptum: despise

contendo, contendere, contendi, contentum: to compare, contrast

contentio, -onis, f.: strife, struggle, rivalry, tension

contentus, -a, -um: content, satisfied

conticesco, conticescere, conticui, —: to become still, fall silent, cease speaking

continentia, -ae, f.: self-restraint

contineo, continere, continui, contentum: 1. to hold together, contain; 2. to hold back, limit, restrain; 3. to comprise, enclose

contingo, contingere, contigi, contactum: to touch; often used impersonally (+ inf. + dat. of person): to happen to

contio, -onis, f.: meeting, assembly; public oration, speech before the people

contionator, -oris, m.: one who addresses the people at a public meeting (**contio**); demagogue

contra (prep. + acc.): against
contra atque (conj.): other than, contrary to, different from, opposite to

contraho, contrahere, contraxi, contractum: to draw together, contract (debt); to bring about, accomplish, produce

controversia, -ae, f.: quarrel, question, dispute, controversy

contulisse: see **confero**

contumelia, -ae, f.: reprimand, reproach, insult, disgrace

convenio, convenire, conveni, conventum: 1. to come together, meet, assemble, gather; 2. impersonal (+ acc. + inf.): it is fitting

conventus, -us, m.: meeting, conference

converto, convertere, converti, conversum: to turn around, turn back, reverse, to face (in a direction), to fix, center, direct

se convertere: to turn oneself around, turn against

convinco, convincere, convici, convictum: to overcome, convict, refute, expose

convivium, -i, n.: banquet, feast

convoco, convocare: to summon, call together

copia, -ae, f.: supply, abundance; troops, forces

copiosus, -a, -um: wealthy, richly provided

corpus, -oris, n.: body

corrigo, corrigere, correxi, correctum: to correct, make straight, set right

corruptela, -ae, f.: a corruption, seduction, temptation

corruptor, -oris, m.: corruptor, seducer

corruptus, -a, -um: depraved, corrupted

cotidianus, -a, -um: daily, everyday

cotidie (adv.): every day, daily

credo, credere, credidi, creditum: 1. (+ dat. of person) to believe; 2. (+ acc. + dat.): to give *accusative thing* to *dative person*, entrust to

cresco, crescere, crevi, cretum: to grow, increase, be strengthened

cruciatus, -us, m.: torture, torment, pain

crudelis, -e (adj.): cruel, pitiless

crudelissimus, -a, -um: superlative adjective of **crudelis**

crudelitas, -atis, f.: harshness, cruelty

crudeliter (adv.): harshly, cruelly

crudelius: comparative adverb of **crudelis**: too cruelly

cruentus, -a, -um: bloody, covered with blood

cubile, -is, n.: bed, couch; bed-chamber, resting place

cuipiam: see **quispiam**

culpa, -ae, f.: fault, blame, guilt

cum (prep. + abl.): with

cum (conj.): when, at the time when
cum . . . tum: (correlatives) when . . . then; both . . . and; not only . . . but also

cumulo, cumulare: to heap up, pile up

cunctus, -a, -um: all whole, entire

cupiditas, -atis, f.: a longing, desire, passion

cupio, cupere, cupivi, cupitum: to long for, desire

cur (interrog. adv.): why?

cura, -ae, f.: care, concern

curia, -ae, f.: senate house, place of meeting of the Senate

curo, curare: to care for, take pains, attend to, take care that

currus, -us, m.: chariot

cursus, -us, m.: course, passage, direction, way

custodia, -ae, f.: watching, guard, protection, custody, confinement, surveillance

custodio, custodire, custodivi, custoditum: to watch, guard, protect

custos, -odis, m./f.: watchman, guard

D

damno, damnare: to condemn

de (prep. + abl.): 1. about, concerning, of, from among; 2. from, down from, out of (describing part of a whole)

debeo, debere, debui, debitum: 1. to owe; 2. (in passive) to be owed, be due; 3. (+ inf.) to be bound, be under obligation, should, ought; 4. to deserve to

debilis, -e (adj.): lame, disabled, crippled, infirm, debilitated

debilitatus, -a, -um: past participle of **debilito:** crushed, crippled, disabled

debilito, debilitare: to weaken, disable, to lame, debilitate

debitus, -a, -um: due, owing, appropriate

decedo, decedere, decessi, decessum: to go away, withdraw

decerno, decernere, decrevi, decretum: to decree, decide, determine

decimus, -a, -um: tenth

declinatio, -onis, f.: a bending aside, a turning away, a sideways movement

decoctor, -oris, m.: a spendthrift, ruined man, bankrupt

decretum, -i, n.: decree, formal, resolution

dedecus, -oris, n.: a shame, disgrace

deduco, deducere, deduxi, deductum: to lead away, draw out, turn aside; (of colonists) to conduct to, settle

defatigo, defatigare: to wear out, tire out, exhaust

defendo, defendere, defendi, defensum: to defend, justify, protect

defero, deferre, detuli, delatum: 1. to carry away, remove; 2. to bring, transfer, deliver; 3. to indict, charge; 4) to report

defetigo: see **defatigo**

deficio, deficere, defeci, defectum: 1. to fail, be wanting, be overwhelmed; 2. to desert, abandon, forsake

defigo, defigere, defixi, defixum: to plunge in, drive, fix plant

deflagro, deflagrare: to burn up, consume with fire

deicio, deicere, deieci, deiectum: to throw down, avert, turn away, repel

deinde (adv.): then, next (in a series)

delatus: see **defero**

delecto, delectare: to charm, please, delight

delectus, -us, m.: a chosen force, picked men; a recruited force

deleo, delere, delevi, deletum: to abolish, destoy, annihilate

deligo, deligere, delegi, delectum: to choose

delubrum, -i, n.: temple, shrine, sanctuary

demens, -entis (adj.): mad, out of one's senses, insane

dementer (adv.): foolishly, madly

dementia, -ae, f.: folly, madness

demigro, demigrare: to go away, migrate, move, depart

deminutio, -onis, f.: decrease, lessening, diminution

demonstro, demonstrare: to show, point out

demum (adv.): at last, finally, not until then

denique (adv.): finally, at last; in short, in a word

denuntio, denuntiare: to announce, declare, proclaim; to order, command

depello, depellere, depuli, depulsum: to drive away, expel, remove, strike down

dependo, dependere, dependi, depensum: to pay

deploro, deplorare: to weep bitterly for, lament, deplore

depono, deponere, deposui, depositum: to put down, set aside

deposco, deposcere, depoposci, —: to demand, claim

depravo, depravare: to corrupt, pervert, spoil; lead astray

deprecor, deprecari, deprecatus sum: to avert, plead against, seek to avoid

deprehendo (or **deprendo**), **deprehendere, deprehendi, deprehensum:** 1. to detect, find out, discover; 2. to take, catch, seize

derelinquo, derelinquere, dereliqui, derelictum: to forsake, abandon, desert

describo, describere, descripsi, descriptum: to define, assign, prescribe, fix

desero, deserere, deserui, desertum: to desert, abandon

desiderium, -i, n.: a longing, ardent desire, wish

desidero, desiderare: to long for, wish for, desire, lack

designo, designare: to point out; to appoint, choose, elect

consul designatus: consul designate, consul elect

desino, desinere, destiti, desitum (+ inf.): to leave off, cease, desist, stop

desisto, desistere, destiti, destitum (+ inf.): to leave off, cease, desist from

desperatio, -onis, f.: hoplessness, despair

desperatus, -a, -um: without hope, desperate, abandoned

despero, desperare: to despair of, give up hoping for

destringo, destringere, destrinxi, destrictum: to strip off; to unsheathe, draw

desum, deesse, defui, —: to be lacking, missing, absent; (with dat.) to be lacking to someone or something, to fail

detestor, detestari, detestatus sum: to denounce, avert, ward off

detraho, detrahere, detraxi, detractum: to draw off, take away

detrimentum, -i, n.: harm, loss

detuli: see **defero**

deus, -i, m.: (dat. pl. **dis, diis**; gen. pl. **deorum, deum**): a god, deity

devoveo, devovere, devovi, devotum: to devote, dedicate, consecrate

dextera, -ae, f.: right hand (originally **dextera manus**)

dico, dicere, dixi, dictum: to say, speak

dictator, -oris, m.: dictator

dictatura, -ae, f.: dictatorship

dictito, dictitare: to keep saying (frequentive of **dicere**)

didici: see **disco**

dies, -ei, m. (sometimes **f.** in sing.): 1. day; 2. a period of time, interval

difficilimus, -a, -um: superlative adjective of **difficilis**

difficilis, -e (adj.): difficult

difficultas, -atis, f.: difficulty, trouble

dignitas, -atis, f.: greatness, dignity, authority, self-respect, honor, reputation

dignus, -a, -um (+ abl.): worthy, deserving; proper, suitable

diiudico, diiudicare: to judge, decide; to resolve

dilectus, -us, m.: choice, selection

diligens, -entis (adj.): careful, diligent; hard-working, industrious

diligenter (adv.): attentively, diligently

diligentia, -ae, f.: diligence, hard work, industry

diligentissimus, -a, -um: superlative adjective of **diligens**

dilucesco, dilucescere, diluxi, —: to become light, approach dawn

dimicatio, -onis, f.: fight, combat, struggle, encounter

dimitto, dimittere, dimisi, dimissum: to break up, dissolve, dismiss

direptio, -onis, f.: a plundering, pillaging, sack

direptor, -oris, m.: pillager

diripio, diripere, diripui, direptum: to tear to pieces, plunder

discedo, discedere, discessi, discessum: to go apart, separate, scatter

discessus, -us, m.: departure, withdrawal

disciplina, -ae, f.: teaching, instruction

disco, discere, didici, —: to learn

discribo, discribere, discripsi, discriptum: distribute, divide, assign; arrange

discrimen, -inis, n.: critical moment, decision, determination

dispertio, dispertire, dispertivi, dispertitum: to distribute, divide, apportion

dissemino, disseminare: to sow, scatter, spread, extend

dissensio, -onis, f.: disagreement, dissention, discord, strife

dissentio, dissentire, dissensi, dissensum: to disagree, be at odds, differ

dissimilis, -e (adj.): unlike, different

dissimulo, dissimulare: to hide, conceal, disguise, pretend that something is not so, dissimulate

dissolutus, -a, -um: lax, remiss; negligent, careless, irresponsible

dissolvo, dissolvere, dissolvi, dissolutum: 1. to unloose, separate; 2. to pay, discharge; 3. to be released from debt

distribuo, distribuere, distribui, distributum: to divide, distribute, apportion

diu (adv.): a long time, a long while, for a long time

diutius: comparative adverb of **diu**, too long, rather long; longer, for a longer time, any longer

divello, divellere, divelli, divulsum: to tear away

diversus, -a, -um: different, various, diverse

divinitus (adv.): from heaven, by divine influence

do, dare, dedi, datum: to give

dolor, -oris, m.: pain, grief, resentment, distress, anguish, sorrow

domesticus, -a, -um: 1. of the family, domestic, household, private; 2. domestic, native

domesticum bellum: civil war

domicilium, -i, n.: home

dominatio, -onis, f.: rule, dominion, power; tyranny

domus, -us, f.: (abl. **domo**): home

domi (loc.): at home

dormio, dormire, dormivi, dormitum: to be asleep

dubitatio, -onis, f.: doubt, hesitation

dubito, dubitare: to doubt; (+ inf.) hesitate

dubius, -a, -um: doubtful, uncertain;
   sine dubio: without doubt, certainly
duco, ducere, duxi, ductum: to lead, guide, conduct; to draw (a sword)
dudum (adv.): for a long time
   iam dudum: now for a long time
duint: archaic present subjunctive of **do, dare**
dulcis, -e (adj.): sweet
dum (adv.): while, yet, still; as long as, provided that
   dum modo: if only, as long as, provided that
duo, duae, duo: two
dux, ducis, m.: leader, commander, general

E

ebriosus, -a, -um: drunk, drunken
ecquis, ecquid (interrog. pron. & adj.): 1. anyone? anything? any at all?; 2. in indirect questions: whether any
edictum, -i, n.: edict, proclamation
edo, edere, edidi, editum: to set forth, publish, write down
edoceo, edocere, edocui, edoctum: to explain, show exactly
educo, educere, eduxi, eductum: to lead out, bring forth
effero, efferre, extuli, elatum: 1. to carry away; 2. to raise up, elevate, exalt
effrenatus, -a, -um: unrestrained, unbridled
effugio, effugere, effugi, —: to flee from, escape from
egens, -entis (adj.): poor, needy
egeo, egere, egui, — (+ abl.): to need, lack, to want, to be without
egestas, -atis, f.: want, lack, destitution, poverty
egredior, egredi, egressus sum: to go out, come forth, depart
egregius, -a, -um: distinguished, extraordinary, superior
eicio, eicere, eieci, eiectum: throw out, hurl forth, cast out, drive away
   se eicere: to cast oneself out, go out, go away
eiectus, -a, -um (past participle of **eicio**): condemned, rejected, wrecked
elabor, elabi, elapsus sum: to slip away, escape
eludo, eludere, elusi, elusum: to elude, avoid; to escape; to mock, insult
emergo, emergere, emersi, emersum: to come forth, arise, extricate oneself, get free from
emitto, emittere, emisi, emissum: to send out, send away
emorior, emori: to die, decease
enim (explanatory conj., usually after the first word in its clause): for, because

eodem (adv.): to the same place
eques, -itis, m.: equestrian, horseman, member of the equestrian order
equitatus, -us, m.: cavalry
erga (prep. + acc.): toward
ergo (adv.): then, therefore
   quid ergo? what then?
eripio, eripere, eripui, ereptum: to snatch away, tear out, take away; to rescue, deliver
erro, errare: 1. to wander, to go astray; 2. to be mistaken, to err
eructo, eructare: to belch, belch forth; to make drunken threats about
erumpo, erumpere, erupi, eruptum: to burst forth, break out; be disclosed
et (adv. and conj.): (adverb) also; (conj.) and
etenim: (adv.) for, indeed, really; (conj.) for, truly, indeed, since, because
etiam (adv.): now too, yet, as yet, still, even, even though
Etruria, -ae, f.: a region of Italy northwest of Rome
evado, evadere, evasi, evasum: to go forth, escape
everto, evertere, everti, eversum: to overturn, overthrow, destroy
evocator, -oris, m.: a summoner, a recruiter
evomo, evomere, evomui, evomitum: to vomit forth, eject
ex (prep. + abl.): from, out of (before consonants, sometimes **ex** = **e**)
exaggero, exaggerare: to heap up, accumulate; to heighten, magnify, exalt
exanimatus, -a, -um: weakened, tired, exhausted; frightened, terrified
exaudio, exaudire, exaudivi, exauditum: to hear clearly, listen to, heed, regard
excedo, excedere, excessi, excessum: to go forth, depart, leave, withdraw
excelsus, -a, -um: high, lofty, elevated
excido, excidere, excidi, —: to fall from, fall away, slip away
excipio, excipere, excepi, exceptum: to take up, capture, receive; to take out, single out; to exclude, omit
excito, excitare: to stir up, rouse up, raise up
excludo, excludere, exclusi, exclusum: to shut out, exclude
excursio, -onis, f.: a running out, running away; attack, excursion
exeo, exire, exii, exitum: to go forth, set out; to go away, depart

exerceo, -ere, exercui, exercitum: to exercise, train, discipline

exercitatio, -onis, f.: training, exercise, practice, experience

exercitus, -us, m.: army

exhaurio, exhaurire, exhausi, exhaustum: to drain off, remove, exhaust

exigo, exigere, exegi, exactum: to complete, end, finish

exilium, -i, n.: exile

eximius, -a, -um: exceptional, outstanding, distinguished, extraordinary

existimo, existimare: to think, believe, consider, estimate, judge

exitiosus, -a, -um: deadly, dangerous, destructive

exitium, -i, n.: destruction, ruin

exitus, -us, m.: an outcome, result, conclusion, end

expectatio, -onis, f.: expectation; eagerness, concern, anticipation

expello, expellere, expuli, expulsum: to drive out, drive away, eject, expel

expono, exponere, exposui, expositum: to set forth, explain

expromo, expromere, exprompsi, expromptum: to practice, exert; exhibit, display

exsilium, -i, n.: exile

exsisto, exsistere, exstiti, —: to emerge, appear; to exist, be

exspecto, exspectare: to expect, wait for

exstinguo, extinguere, extinxi, extinctum: to kill, put out, quench, destroy, blot out, extinguish

exsto, exstare, exstiti, —: to appear, arise, exist, be found

exsul, -is, m.: exile

exsulto, exsultare: to rejoice, exult

extermino, exterminare: to drive out, drive away, expel

externus, -a, -um: external, foreign

extorqueo, extorquere, extorsi, extortum: to twist out, wrench away

extremum, -i, n.: end

extulit: see effero

F

facile (adv.): easily

facilius: comparative adverb of facile: more easily

facinorosus, -i, m.: criminal, vicious man

facinus, -oris, n.: crime, villainy

facio, facere, feci, factum: to make, do

factum, -i, n.: deed, act

facultas, -atis, f.: power, means, opportunity, resource

falcarius, -i, m.: scythe-maker

inter falcarios: at the scythe-makers' quarter, a district in Rome

fallo, fallere, fefelli, falsum: to deceive, mislead, trick; to disappoint

falsus, -a, -um: false, not true

fama, -ae, f.: 1. reputation; 2. rumor, report; 3. good reputation, fame

fames, -is, f.: hunger

familia, -ae, f.: household, family; group of slaves

mater familias: the lady of the house; familias is an archaic genitive

familiariter (adv.): very closely, familiarly, on intimate terms

fanum, -i, n.: shrine, sanctuary

fascis, is, m.: bundle; plural fasces: a bundle of rods with an ax, carried before the highest magistrates as a symbol of authority

fatalis, -e (adj.): ordained by fate, destined, decreed

fateor, fateri, fassus sum: to admit, confess, grant, acknowledge

fatum, -i, n.: fate, destiny; ill-fate, calamity, death; prediction about the future, that which is ordained

fauces, -ium, f. pl.: 1. jaws; 2. mountain passes

faveo, favere, favi, fauturus: to be favorable, well disposed; to favor

fax, facis, f.: 1. torch, firebrand; 2. meteor, comet, shooting star; 3. incitement, stimulus

febris, -is, f.: fever

fefellit: see fallo

fere (adv.): almost, practically, nearly

fero, ferre, tuli, latum: 1. to bear, endure, tolerate; 2. to cast a vote, give an opinion; 3. (of speech) to report, say, tell

ferramenta, -orum, n. pl.: arms, weapons, iron implements

ferreus, -a, -um: made of iron; hard-hearted, unfeeling

ferrum, -i, n.: iron; sword

fidelis, -e (adj.): trustworthy, faithful

fides, -ei, f.: faith, trust; loyalty, credit, confidence, reliance

fides publica: a promise of protection, pledge of safety, immunity from prosecution

filia, -ae, f.: daughter

filius, -i, m.: son

fingo, fingere, finxi, finctum: to fashion, invent, imagine

finis, -is, m.: limit, boundary, termination; plural: territory

quem ad finem: to what end? how long?

fio, fieri, factus sum: to be made, become; to happen, occur, be done

firmo, firmare: to make firm, strengthen, fortify

firmus, -a, -um: secure, reliable, strong

fixus, -a, -um: fixed, firm, rooted

flagitiose (adv.): disgracefully

flagitiosissime: superlative adverb of **flagitiose**, most disgracefully

flagitiosus, -a, -um: shameful, disgraceful

flagitium, -i, n.: shameful act, disgraceful deed

flagito, flagitare: to demand

flamma, -ae, f.: flame, blaze, fire

flecto, flectere, flexi, flexum: to turn aside, turn away

florens, -entis (adj.): flowering, blooming; prosperous

floreo, florere, florui, —: to bloom, blossom; to flourish, be prosperous, be distinguished

flos, floris, m.: flower

focus, -i, m.: fireplace, hearth

foedissimus: superlative adjective of **foedus**

foedus, -a, -um: foul, defiled, impious

foedus, -eris, n.: treaty, league, compact, alliance

foras (adv.): out of doors

fore: shortened (syncopated) form of the future active infinitive **futurus, -a, -um esse**

foris (adv.): out of doors, outside; outside the city (*Cat.* 2.4)

formido, -inis, f.: fear, dread

fors, fortis -adj: strong

fortasse (adv.): perhaps

forte (adv.): by chance

fortis, -e (adj.): strong, firm, steadfast; brave, courageous, spirited, bold

fortissimus, -a, -um: superlative adjective of **fortis**: most honorable (*Cat.* 1.21)

fortiter (adv.): bravely, strongly, courageously

fortitudo, -inis, f.: strength, firmness, courage, fortitude

fortuna, -ae, f.: 1. fortune, luck, circumstances, fate; 2. good fortune; 3. state, condition; 4. plural: possessions, property, goods

fortunatissimus, -a, -um: superative adjective of **fortunatus**

fortunatus, -a, -um: fortunate, lucky, blessed

forum, i, n.: an open space, public place, market place; at Rome, the Forum Romanum, between the Capitoline and Palatine Hills

frango, frangere, fregi, fractum: to break, break down, soften, weaken

fraudatio, -onis, f.: deception, fraud, cheating

frequens, -entis (adj.): in great number, crowded, in a crowd

frequentia, -ae, f.: crowd, multitude, throng

frequento, frequentare: to fill with a multitude, bring together in a crowd, fill, crowd

fretus, -a, -um (+ abl.): relying on, trusting in

frigus, -oris, n.: cold, coldness, chill

frons, frontis, f.: forehead

fructus, -us, m.: fruit, profit, enjoyment; gratification; achievements, benefits, rewards

fruor, frui, fructus sum (+ abl.): to enjoy, have the benefit of

fuga, -ae, f.: flight, fleeing, running away, exile

fugio, fugere, fugi, fugitum: to flee, fly, run away

fugitivus, -i, m.: fugitive, runaway slave

fulgeo, fulgere, fulsi, —: to shine brightly, gleam

fulmen, -inis, n.: lightning flash, stroke of lightning, thunderbolt

functus: see **fungor**

fundamentum, -i, n.: foundation

fundo, fundare: to found, set up, establish

funestus, -a, -um: deadly, fatal, destructive

fungor, fungi, functus sum (+ abl.): to perform, fulfill

furiosus, -a, -um: mad, raging, wild

furo, furere, —, —: to rage, rave, be out of one's mind

furor, -oris, m.: rage, fury, madness, passion

furtim (adv.): furtively, secretly, like a thief

furtum, -i, n.: theft, robbery; deceit

G

ganeo, -onis, m.: glutton, profligate, debauchee

gaudium, -i, n.: gladness, enjoyment, joy

gelidus, -a, -um: cold, icy cold

gener, -eri, m.: son-in-law

gens, gentis, f.: race, clan, tribe, people

genus, -eris, n.: tribe, kind, class, type; family, birth, descent

gero, gerere, gessi, gestum: to carry; to accomplish, do, manage, perform
with **bellum:** to wage war; with **se:** to act, behave, comport oneself

gladiator, -oris, m.: gladiator; fighter, cutthroat

gladiatorius, -a, -um: gladiatorial

gladius, -i, m.: sword

gloria, -ae, f.: glory, honor, praise, renown

gradus, -us, m.: a step, stage, grade

gratia, -ae, f.: favor, gratitude; plural: thanks
gratias agere (+ dat. of person): to give thanks to a person
gratiam referre: to return thanks, show gratitude
gratiam habere (+ dat. of person): to give thanks to a person

gratulatio, -onis, f.: joy, congratulation, rejoicing, public thanksgiving

gratus, -a, -um: pleasing, welcome

gravis, -e (adj.): serious, heavy, weighty, burdensome

gravissimus, -a, -um: superlative of **gravis:** heaviest, most severe, most important, most influential

graviter (adv.): seriously, gravely

gravius: compartive adverb of **gravis,** more heavily

grex, gregis, m.: flock, herd

gubernatio, -onis, f.: direction, management, steering, government

H

habeo, habere, habui, habitum: 1. to have, hold; 2. to celebrate (a festival); 3. to hold, convene, cause to take place

   orationem habere: to deliver a speech

   gratiam habere (+ dat. of person): to give thanks to

haereo, haerere, haesi, haesum (+ **in** + abl.): to cling to, remain fixed in, abide, continue

haesito, haesitare: to hesitate, be at a loss, be irresolute

haruspex, haruspicis, m.: soothsayer, diviner, prophet

hebesco, hebescere: to grow dull

hesternus, -a, -um: of or concerning yesterday

hic (with a long i; adv.): in this place, here

hic, haec, hoc (demonst. pron. or adj.): this

hice, haece, hoce: older form of **hic, haec, hoc;** used for emphasis

hiems, hiemis, f.: winter

hinc (adv.): hence, from this place, from this (reason), from (on) this side

hodiernus, -a, -um: of today, today's

homo, hominis, m.: human being, man, person

honestas, -atis, f.: honor, good reputation, good chraracter, merit

honeste (adv.): honorably

honestissimus, -a, -um: superlative adjective of **honestus**

honesto, honestare: to honor, dignify, adorn, grace

honestus, -a, -um: honorable, distinguished, noble

honor, -oris, m.: 1. honor, repute, distinction; 2. high office, public honor

honos: see **honor**

horribilis, -e (adj.): horrible, dreadful, terrible

hortor, hortari, hortatus sum: to urge, encourage, exhort

hospitum, -i, n.: hospitality, ties of hospitality

hostis, -is, m./f.: enemy, especially a public enemy

huc (adv.): hither, to this point

humanitas, -atis, f.: kind consideration, kindness, humanity

humanus, -a, -um: human, cultured, refined

humus, -i, f.: earth, ground, soil

   humi: (loc.): on the ground

I

iaceo, iacere, iacui, —: to lie, lie down, be in an inferior position, be at a disadvantage

iacio, iacere, ieci, iactum: to throw, hurl; to send forth, utter, declare

iacto, iactare: to throw, toss, throw about, toss about, torment

   se iactare: 1. to brag, boast, show off; 2. to advance one's own cause

iactus, -us, m.: throwing, casting, hurling

iam (adv.): 1. (with present tense) now, right now; 2. (with past tense) already

   nulla iam, non iam: no longer

   iam pridem (adv.): now for a long time, long ago

Ianuarius, -a, -um: of January

   Kalendae Januariae: the Kalends of January, the first day of January, New Year's Day

ibi (adv.): there, in that place

idcirco (adv.): on that account, for this reason

idem, eadem, idem (pron.): the same

Idus, Iduum, f. pl.: Ides, middle of the month (the fifteenth or thirteenth day; see B371, Gp. 491); debts and interest on loans were often due on the Ides.

igitur (conj.): therefore, accordingly

ignavia, -ae, f.: laziness, cowardice

ignis, ignis, m.: fire

ignominia, -ae, f.: shame, dishonor

ignoro, ignorare: to not know, be unacquainted with

ignotus, -a, -um: unknown, not known

ille, illa, illud (demonstr. pron. and adj.): this, that (sometimes has a positive connotation)

illinc (adv.): on that side, from that side

imago, -inis, f.: likeness, picture, image

imberbis, -e (adj.): beardless

immanis, -e (adj.): enormous, immense; monstrous

immanitas, -atis, f.: enormity, excess; savageness, fierceness, barbarism

immaturus -a, -um: unripe, premature, too early, untimely

immineo, -ere (+ dat. of person): to threaten

immitto, immittere, immisi, immissum: to send in, send against

immo (adv.): nay, on the contrary

immo vero (adv.): nay, rather indeed

immortalis, -e (adj.): immortal, imperishable, eternal

impedio, impedire, impedivi, impeditum: hinder, prevent

impello, impellere, impuli, impulsum: to urge on, encourage, impel

impendeo, impendere (+ dat. of person): to hang over, be imminent, threaten, impend

imperator, -oris, m.: commander, general

imperitus, -a, um: unskilled, ignorant

imperium, -i, n.: chief command, power, authority; empire

impero, imperare: to order, command

impertio, impertire, impertivi, impertitum: to bestow, give a share, give, impart

impetro, impetrare: to gain one's end, succeed, prevail

impetus, -us, m.: an attack, assault

impius, -a, -um: impious, wicked, shameless

impius, -i, m.: an impious, wicked person

imploro, implorare: to entreat, beg, beseech, implore

importunissimus, -a, -um: superlative adjective of **importunus**

importunus, -a, -um: 1. troublesome, cruel, savage; 2. unsuitable, unnatural; 3. unmannered, rude

improbissimus, -a, -um: superlative adjective of **improbus**

improbitas, -atis, f.: wickedness, dishonesty

improbus, -a, -um: wicked, base, shameless

improbus, -i, m.: wicked person, rogue, criminal

impubes, -eris (adj.): youthful, young, not full-grown

impudens, -entis (adj.): shameless, without shame, extremely bold, impudent

impudenter (adv.): shamelessly, without shame, impudently

impudentia, -ae, f.: rashness, boldness; shamelessness, impudence, effrontery

impudicus, -a, -um: unchaste, shameless

impunitus, -a, -um: unpunished

impurus, -a, -um: unclean, impure

in (prep.): (+ abl.) in, on, in the case of; (+ acc.) into, against

inanis, -e (adj.): empty, vain

inauratus, -a, -um: gilded, overlaid with gold

incendium, -i, n.: burning, fire, conflagration

incendo, incendere, incendi, incensum: to set fire to, burn

incensio, -onis, f.: a burning

inceptum, -i, n.: beginning, undertaking

incertus, -a, -um: not fixed, unsettled, doubtful, uncertain

incido, incidere, incidi, —: (from **cado:** to fall) to fall into, incur (debt)

incido, incidere, incidi, incisum: (from **caedo:** to cut): to cut through

incipio, incipere, incepi, inceptum (+ inf.): to begin

inclino, inclinare: to learn, tend

includo, includere, inclusi, inclusum: to shut in, inclose, confine

incolumis, -e (adj.): safe, unharmed

incredibilis, -e (adj.): unbelievable, unparalleled

increpo, increpare, increpui, increpitum: to make a sound, rattle, rustle

incumbo, incumbere, incubui, incubitum: to bend to (the oars); apply oneself to, pay attention to

indemnatus, -a, -um: uncondemned, unsentenced

index, indicis, m./f.: informer, witness, spy

indicium, -i, n.: proof, evidence, sign, mark

indico, indicare: to disclose, inform, betray; to inform against, accuse

indico, indicere, indixi, indictum: to appoint, announce, declare publicly

bellum indicere: to declare war

induco, inducere, induxi, inductum: 1. to lead on, influence, induce; 2. to ensnare, delude

inducere animum: to persuade oneself

industria, -ae, f.: hard work, diligence, industry

ineo, inire, inii, initum: to begin, attempt, undertake

consilium inire: to form a plan, to plot, conspire

iners, -ertis (adj.): lazy, sluggish, cowardly

inertia, -ae, f.: inactivity, idleness, laziness; lack of skill

infamis, -e (adj.): of ill-repute, shameful, disreputable, infamous

inferi, -orum, m. pl.: the dead, shades, inhabitants of the lower world

apud inferos: among those below, (i.e., among the dead)

infero, inferre, intuli, inlatum (+ acc. + dat.): 1. to bring *accusative* to *dative*, to carry to, introduce; 2. to inflict on, bring against

inferus -a, -um: low, below

infestissimus, -a, -um: superlative adjective of infestus

infestus, -a, -um: hostile, dangerous, troublesome, threatening

infimus, -a, -um: the lowest, last, most humble; masculine plural: slaves

infinitus, -a, -um: not limited, infinite; countless, indefinite

infirmus, -a, -um: weak, feeble, infirm

infitiator, -oris, m.: a denier, defaulter, one who repudiates a debt

infitior, infitiari, infitiatus sum: to deny, contradict

inflammo, inflammare: to inflame, kindle; to arouse, excite

ingenium, -i, n.: natural talent

ingens, -entis (adj.): huge, enormous

ingenuus, -i, m.: freeborn man, free man who has free parents

ingravesco, ingravescere: to increase, grow worse

ingredior, ingredi, ingressus sum: to advance, go forward, march, proceed

inhio, inhiare (+ dat.): to open the mouth to

inhumanissimus, -a, -um: superlative adjective of inhumanus

inhumanus, -a, -um: brutal, cruel, inhuman

inicio, inicere, inieci, iniectum: to throw onto; to thrust upon, cause, bring about

inimicitiae, -arum, f. pl.: enmity, hostility

inimicus, -i, m.: enemy, especially a personal enemy (opposed to hostis: public enemy)

iniquitas, -atis, f.: inequality, unfairness, injustice

iniquus, -a, -um: unfair, unjust

iniri: see ineo

initio, initiare: to initiate, consecrate

initum: see ineo

iniuria, -ae, f.: (abl. sing. as adv.): wrongly, unjustly

inlecebra, -ae, f.: charm, enticement, allurement

inlustris, -e (adj.): bright, brilliant; famous, honorable, renowned

inlustro, inlustrare: to bring to light, reveal, disclose; to illuminate, make clear

inopia, -ae, f.: want, lack of resources, scarcity, poverty, indigence

inquam: I say (only has present forms, so present is used for past)

inquis: you say

inretio, inretire, inretivi, inretium: to catch in a net, ensnare, entangle

inscribo, inscribere, inscripsi, inscriptum: to write upon, inscribe

insepultus, -a, -um: unburied

insidiae, -arum, f. pl.: plot, snare, trap; ambush

insidiator, -oris, m.: spy, assassin, one who lies in wait

insidior, insidiari, insidiatus sum (+ dat. of person): lie in wait for, plot against

insidiosus, -a, -um: deceitful, treacherous, dangerous

insigne, -is, n.: mark, indication, proof, sign, token

insimulo, insimulare: to charge, accuse

insolenter (adv.): immoderately, haughtily, insolently

insolentius (adv.): comparative of insolenter

insperatus, -a, -um: unhoped for, unexpected

instituo, instituere, institui, institutum: to intend, decide; to begin

insto, instare, institi, instaturus: to draw near, approach, be at hand

instrumentum, -i, n.: (in plural): implements, tools, instruments

instruo, instruere, instruxi, instructum: to arrange, set in order, marshal

integer, integra, integrum: intact, untouched, whole; open, undecided

intellego, intellegere, intellexi, intellectum: to understand, perceive, think

intendo, intendere, intendi, intentum: to plan, intend; to aim

inter (prep. + acc.): between, among

intercedo, intercedere, intercessi, intercessum: to intervene, come between

interea (adv.): meanwhile, in the meantime

intereo, interire, interii, intertium: to die, perish

interest: see intersum

interficio, interficere, interfeci, interfectum: to kill, slay

interim (adv.): meanwhile

interimo, interimere, interemi, interemptum: to destroy, kill, slay

interitus, -us, m.: destruction, overthrow, ruin, annihilation

internicio, -onis, f.: massacre, slaughter, carnage, destruction

interrogo, interrogare: to ask, enquire

intersum, interesse, interfui, interfuturum: 1. to be between, lie between; 2. to differ, be different; 3. interest (impersonal): it is of interest, it concerns

interventus, -us, m.: coming in, intervention

intestinus, -a, -um: internal; civil

intimus, -a, -um: intimate, close to

intra (prep. + acc.): within, inside

introduco, introducere, introduxi, introductum: to lead in, being in

intueor, intueri, intuitus sum: to look upon, gaze at

intulisset: see **infero**

intus (adv.): on the inside, within

inuro, inurere, inussi, inustum (+ dat.): to burn into, brand into

inusta: see **inuro**

invenio, invenire, inveni, inventum: to find, discover, devise, invent

investigo, investigare: to find out, discover, investigate

inveterasco, inveterascere, inveteravi, —: to grow old, become established, be rooted

invictus, -a, -um: unconquered, invincible

invidia, -ae, f.: 1. envy, jealousy; 2. ill-will, prejudice, hatred, unpopularity

invidiosus, -a, -um: arousing hatred, causing hatred

invidus, -i, m.: envious person, hater

invito, invitare: 1. to invite, treat, feast, entertain; 2. to ask, request

invitus, -a, -um: unwilling

ipse, ipsa, ipsum (intensive pron. and adj.): self

is, ea, id (demonstr. pron. and adj.): this, that; such, of such a kind

iste, ista, istud: 1. (demonstr. adj.) this, that, such, of such a kind (frequently with a pejorative or negative implication); 2. (demonstr. pron.) he, she, it (frequently pejorative)

ita (adv.): thus, so, in this way, in such a way

Italia, -ae, f.: Italy

itaque (conj.): and so, and thus

item (adv.): likewise, also, in the same way

iter, itineris, n.: path, route

iterum (adv.): again, a second time

iubeo, iubere, iussi, iussum: to order, command; desire, entreat, propose, wish

iucundus, -a, -um: pleasant, agreeable, delightful, pleasing

iudicium, -i, n.: judgment, decision, lawsuit, trial, court, tribunal

iudico, iudicare: to judge, form an opinion

iugulum, -i, n.: throat

iungo, iungere, iunxi, iunctum: to join together

iure (adv.): by right, with justice, justly, deservedly

ius, iuris, n.: right, justice; law

iura, n. pl.: rights

ius iurandum, iuris iurandi, n.: an oath

iussero: see **iubeo**

iussu, m. (only in abl. sing.): order, command, decree

iustior, -ius: comparative adjective of **iustus**

iustus, -a, -um (adj.): just, right, fair, righteous, honorable

iuventus, -utis, f.: 1. period of youth, youth; 2. a young man

K

Kalendae, -arum, f. pl.: Kalends, first day of the month

Kalendae Novembres: first day of November

L

labefacio, labefacere, labefeci, labefactum: to weaken, cause to shake

labefacto, labefactare: to cause to totter, undermine, weaken

labor, -oris, m.: 1. labor, work, effort, exertion; 2. hardship, trouble, pain

lacesso, lacessere, lacessivi, lacessitum: to challenge, provoke

lacrima, -ae, f.: tear

lacto, lactare: to take milk, suck milk

laedo, laedere, laesi, laesum: to hurt, wound, injure, damage

laetitia, -ae, f.: joy, exultation, gladness, happiness, pleasure

laetor, laetari, laetatus sum: to rejoice, be glad

lamentatio, -onis, f.: wailing, grief, lamentation

lamentor, lamentari, lamentatus sum: to lament, bewail

languidus, -a, -um: weak, sluggish, dull, languid

largitio, -onis, f.: giving freely, generosity, granting

largitor, -oris, m.: lavish giver, spendthrift

late (adv.): widely

lateo, latere, latui, —: to lie hidden

latius: comparative adverb of **late:** more widely

lator, -oris, m.: one who proposes a law, proposer

latro, -onis, m.: robber, thief

latrocinium, -i, n.: 1. robbery, piracy, brigandage; 2. band of robbers

latrocinor, latrocinari, latrocinatus sum: to be a robber, practice robbery

latus, -eris, n.: side, flank; body

laudo, laudare: to praise, give praise to

laus, laudis, f.: praise

lectissimus, -a, -um: superlative adjective of **lectus**

lectulus, -i, m.: couch, bed

lectus, -a, -um: distinguished

lectus, -i, m.: couch, bed, sofa

legatus, -i, m.: ambassador, legate

legio, -onis, f.: legion

lego, legere, legi, lectum: to read

lenio, lenire, lenivi, lenitum: to soften, to soothe, relieve

lenior, -ius: comparative adjective of lenis: milder, more gentle

lenis, -e (adj.): mild, gentle, lenient, mercful

lenissimus, -a, -um: superlative adjective of lenis

lenitas, -atis, f.: 1. softness, gentleness, mildness; 2. clemency, mercy, leniency

leno, -onis, m.: agent; pimp, procurer

lentus, -a, -um: slow, sluggish

lepidus, -a, -um: delicate, effeminate

levior, -ius: comparative adjective of levis

levis, e (adj.): 1. light, not heavy; 2. of character, light-minded, capricious, fickle, untrustworthy

levitas, -atis, f.: lightness, fickleness; shallowness, superficiality

levo, levare: to lift, lighten, relieve, mitigate, ease, lessen

lex, legis, f.: law

libenter (adv.): gladly, willingly, cheerfully, with pleasure

liberi, -orum, m. pl.: children

libero, liberare: (+ abl.): to free from, liberate, free

libertas, -atis, f.: freedom, liberty

libertinus, -a, -um: pertaining to a freedman or ex-slave

libertinus, -i, m.: a freedman or ex-slave

liberus, -a, -um: free

libet (impers. verb + dat. of person + inf.): it is pleasing to *dative person* to do *infinitive*, it is agreeable to, it is desirable to

libido, -inis, f.: passion, lust, license; desire, longing

licet, licere, licuit (impers. verb + dat. of person + inf.): it is permitted, it is possible

licet ut (+ subj.): it is permitted that

linum, i, n.: linen, linen thread

liquefacio, liquefacere, liquefeci, liquefactum: to melt

litterae, -arum, f. pl.: letter, epistle, written works, literature, history

loco, locare: 1. to determine, fix, establish; 2. assign a contract

locuples, -etis (adj.): rich, wealthy, opulent; responsible, trustworthy

locupletior, -ius: comparative adjective of locuples

locus, -i, m.: 1. place, spot; 2. occasion, fitting time

longe (adv.): a long way off, far

quam longe: how far?

longinquus, -a, -um: distant, remote

loquor, loqui, locutus sum: speak, say, mention

luctus, -us, m.: sorrow, grief, affliction

ludus, -i, m.: game, spectacle, show; school

lugeo, lugere, luxi, luctum: to grieve, mourn

lupinus, -a, -um: of a wolf

lux, lucis, f.: light, brightness; day

luxuria, -ae, f.: rankness, luxuriance, extravagance

M

machinator, -oris, m.: contriver, designer, engineer, architect

machinor, machinari, machinatus sum: to devise, plan

macto, mactare: to punish, afflict

maeror, -oris, m.: grief, sadness, sorrow

magis (adv.): more

magistratus, -us, m.: magistrate, public official

magnifice (adv.): nobly, generously, richly

magnitudo, -tudinis, f.: size, large size, great extent, magnitude, greatness, importance, gravity

magno opere (adv.): greatly, utterly

magnus, -a, -um: large, great

maior, maius: comparative adjective of magnus: greater

maiores, maiorum, m pl.: ancestors

mos maiorum: custom of the ancestors

disciplinae maiorum: teachings of the ancestors

male (adv.): badly, scarcely, not at all

maleficium, -i, n.: an evil deed, wickedness, offense, crime

malleolus, -i, m.: a fire-dart, incendiary missile

malo, malle, malui, —: (+ inf.): to choose rather, prefer

malum, -i, n.: evil, misfortune, calamity, mischief

mandatum, -i, n.: command, order, instruction

mando, mandare: (+ acc. + dat.): to hand *accusative* over to *dative*, sentence, entrust, commit

mane (adv.): early in the morning

maneo, manere, mansi, mansum: to remain

manicatus, -a, -um: having long sleeves

manifesto (adv.): openly, clearly, evidently, manifestly

manifestus, -a, -um: clear, plain, obvious, evident, manifest

mano, manare: to drip, trickle, flow, spread, extend

manus, -us, f.: 1. hand; 2. handwriting; 3. band of men

mare, -is, n.: sea

maritus, -i, m.: husband

mater, -tris, f.: mother

mater familias: lady of the house

matuor, matuari, matuatus sum: to hasten

mature (adv.): 1. early, soon; 2. at the proper time

maturitas, -atis, f.: ripeness, maturity

maturius: comparative adverb of **mature**

mavis: second person singular, present indicative active of **malo**

maxime (adv.): in the highest decree, most, exceedingly

maximus, -a, -um: superlative adjective of **magnus**, greatest, largest

mecum = cum me

medicina, -ae, f.: medicine, remedy, relief

mediocris, -e (adj.): moderate; limited, existing within bounds or limits

mediocriter (adv.): moderately, slightly

meditor, meditari, meditatus sum: to consider, give attention to; to practice

medius, -a, -um: middle

ex media morte: from the threshold of death

me hercule! (interjection): by Hercules!

melior, -ius: comparative adjective of **bonus**, better

memini, -isse: to remember (this verb has only perfect forms, but translate as present)

memor, -oris (adj. + gen.): mindful, aware, remembering, heedful

memoria, -ae, f.: memory, remembrance

mendicitas, -atis, f.: beggary, poverty, destitution

mens, mentis, f.: 1. mind, thought, plan, purpose, opinion; 2. mind, feeling, heart, soul

aliqua mens: a change of mind, change of plan

mereor, mereri, meritus sum: to deserve, merit, be entitled to

merito (adv.): deservedly, justly

meritum, -i, n.: merit, service, kindess, benefit, favor

-met (enclitic pronoun added to personal pronouns): self

metuo, metuere, metui: to fear

metus, -us, m.: fear, anxiety, dread

meus, -a, -um: my

mihi (personal pronoun + dat.): to me

miles, -itis, m.: soldier

militaris, -e (adj.): pertaining to a soldier, military

minae, -arum, f. pl.: threats

minime: superlative adverb, least of all

minimus, -a, -um: superlative adjective of **parvus**, smallest, least

minitor, minitari, minitatus sum (+ dat. of person): threaten

minor, minus: comparative adjective of **parvus**, less

minuo, minere, minui, minutum: to make small, lessen, diminish

minus (comp. adv.): less

misceo, miscere, miscui, mixtum: to mix, circulate; concoct, prepare

miser, -a, -um: miserable, wretched, pitiable

miseras: see **mitto**

miseria, -ae, f.: misery, distress, misfortune

misericordia, -ae, f.: pity, compassion, sympathy, mercy

misericors, -cordis (adj.): merciful, compassionate; sympathetic

miseror, miserari, miseratus sum: to pity, feel compassion

miserrimus: superlative adjective of **miser**

mitior, -ius: comparative adjective of **mitis**

mitis, -e (adj.): mild, gentle, considerate

mitissimus, -a, -um: superlative adjective of **mitis**

mitto, mittere, misi, missum: to send

mixtus, -a, -um: mixed, varied, motley

modo (adv.): only; merely

modo (conj.): if only, provided that, on condition that

non modo . . . sed etiam: not only . . . but also

non modo . . . sed ne quidem: not only . . . but not even

non modo . . . verum etiam: not only . . . but even

modus, -i, n.: way, manner, mode, measure; type, sort, kind

nullo modo: in no way

quodam modo: in a certain way

moenia, -ium, n. pl.: city walls, defensive walls

moles, -is, f.: 1. a massive structure, weight, burden; 2. difficulty, labor, toil

molior, moliri, molitus sum: 1. to undertake, to build; 2. to plot, contrive; 3. to set in motion, try, attempt

mollis, -e (adj.): soft, gentle, mild

moneo, monere, monui, monitum: to advise, warn

monstrum, -i, n.: repulsive character, monster, abomination

monumentum, -i, n.: memorial, monument, statue, memorial statue

mora, -ae, f.: delay

morbus, -i, m.: sickness, disease, illness

morior, mori, mortuus sum: to die

mors, mortis, f.: death

mortuus, -a, -um: dead

mos, moris, m.: custom, usage, practice, habit
  mores, morum, m. pl.: conduct, behavior, morals, character
  mos maiorum: the custom of the ancestors, customary practice, hallowed tradition
motus, -us, m.: 1. movement, motion; 2. disturbance, political uprising
moveo, movere, movi, motum: to move, stir; to concern, trouble, disturb, influence
mucro, mucronis, m.: sword, the point of a sword
mulier, -eris, f.: woman
muliercula, -ae, f.: little woman, mistress
multitudo, -inis, f.: great number; multitude, crowd, throng; the common people
multo, multare: to punish
multus, -a, -um: much, many
municeps, -cipis, m.: citizen of a **municipium** (free town), townsman, fellow-citizen
municipium, -i, n.: town; **municipia** were original Italian communities that held Roman citizenship as well as a local self-government
munio, munire, munivi, munitum: to fortify, defend
munitus, -a, -um: defended, fortified
murus, -i, m.: wall, city wall
muto, mutare: to change
mutus, -a, -um: mute, unspeaking, unable to speak, still, silent

N

nam (conj.): for (explanatory, introduces a reason)
nanciscor, nancisci, nactus sum: to find, get, obtain
nascor, nati, natus sum: to be born, to grow
natio, -onis, f.: race, tribe, people, nation
natura, -ae, f.: nature
naufragus, -i, m.: shipwrecked person, bankrupt, ruined person
-ne (adv.): added to the end of the first word of a sentence to form a question
nec or **neque** (adv. and conj.): and not, also not; nor
  nec ... nec: neither ... nor
necessario (adv.): unavoidably, by necessity
necessarius, -i, m.: relative, kinsman; friend, client, patron
necesse (indeclinable adj.): necessary
  necesse est: it is necessary
necessitas, -atis, f.: need, necessity
neco, necare: to kill, to put to death
nefandus, -a, -um: impious, heinous, abominable
nefarie (adv.): unlawfully, impiously, wickedly
nefarius, -a, -um: wicked, unlawful, impious, criminal

neglego, neglegere, neglexi, neglectum: to be indifferent to, disregard, not care about, neglect
nego, negare: to say no, deny, refuse
negotium, -i, n.: business, business affair; difficulty, pains, trouble
nemo, m./f. (dat. **nemini,** acc. **neminem,** plural gen. and abl. sing. from **nullus**): no one
nepos, -otis, m.: grandson; spendthrift, prodigal
nequam (indeclinable adj.): worthless, good-for-nothing
nequior, -ius: comparative adjective of **nequam**
nequitia, -ae, f.: worthlessness, vileness, wickedness
nescio, nescire, nescivi, —: to not know, be ignorant
  nescio an: I do not know whether (i.e., I am inclined to think)
nex, necis, f.: murder, slaughter, violent death
nihil: 1. (indeclinable noun) nothing; 2. (as adv.) in no way
nimis (adv.): too much, excessively
nimium (adv.): too much, exceedingly
nimius, -a, -um: too much, excessive
nisi (conj.): if not, unless
niteo, nitere, nitui, —: to shine, glisten
nitidus, -a, -um: shining, bright
nix, nivis, f.: snow
nobilis, -e (adj.): distinguished, noble
nobiscum = cum nobis
nocens, -entis (adj.): guilty; (as noun) guilty one, culprit
noceo, nocere, nocui, nociturus (+ dat.): to hurt, harm
nocturnus, -a, -um: occurring at night, nocturnal
nolo, nolle, nolui, —: to be unwilling, not wish
nomen, nominis, n.: a name, appellation
nominatim (adv.): by name
nomino, nominare: to name, call
non (conj.): no, not
  non solum ... sed etiam: not only, but also
  non iam (adv.): no longer
nondum (adv.): not yet
nonne (interrog. adv.; expects affirm. answer): would not? surely not? did not?
nonnullus, -a, -um: some
nos, nostrum (1st pers. pl. pron.): we, us
noster, -tra, -trum (possess. adj.): our
nota, -ae, f.: mark, stamp, brand
noto, notare: to mark, designate
notus, -a, -um: well-known, famous
November, -bris, -bre (adj.): of November
  Kalendae Novembres: Kalends or first day of November

novus, -a, -um: recent, new
  novae res: new things, revolution
nox, noctis, f.: night
nudius (adv. of time, used only in phrases of time with an ordinal number): it is now . . . (from **nunc dies est**)
  nudius tertius: it is now the third day (i.e., the day before yesterday)
nudus, -a, -um: naked, bare
nullus, -a, -um: not any, none, no
num: 1. (interrog. particle expecting a neg. answer) surely not?; 2. in indirect questions) whether
numen, -inis, n.: divine power
numerus, -i, m.: number
numquam (adv.): never
  non numquam (adv.): not never, sometimes, frequently, from time to time
nunc (adv.): now, at this time
nuper (adv.): recently, lately
nuptiae, -arum, f. pl.: a wedding marriage
nutus, m.: (no gen.; abl. sing. **nutu**): nod; command, will

O

ob (prep. + acc.): on account of
obeo, obire, obivi, obitum: 1. to travel over; 2. to surround; 3. to attend to; 4. to go to meet, engage in
oblatum: see **offero**
obligo, obligare: to bind; pledge mortgage
oblino, oblinere, oblevi, oblitum: to daub, smear
oblitus, -a, -um (+ gen.): forgetful, unmindful, not remembering
obliviscor, oblivisci, oblitus sum (+ gen.): to forget
obscure (adv.): secretly, stealthily, in the dark; darkly, obscurely, in a way that is difficult to understand
obscuro, obscurare: to cover up, hide, obscure
obscurus, -a, -um: hidden, secret, obscure
obses, -idis, m./f.: hostage; surety, pledge, assurance, guarantee
obsideo, obsidere, obsedi, obsessum: 1. to besiege, surround; 2. to watch for, wait for
obsides, -idis, m.: hostage, pledge
obsidio, -onis, f.: siege, blockade, besieging
obsto, obstare, obstiti, obstitum (+ dat.): to thwart, hinder, prevent
obstupefacio, obstupefacere, obstupefeci, obstupefactum: to stupefy, amaze
obstupesco, obstupescere, obstupui, —: to be astonished, dumbstruck, amazed, thunderstruck

obsum, obesse, obfui, —: (+ dat.): to be harmful to, hurt, injure
obtempero, obtemperare: to comply, obey
obtineo, obtinere, obtinui, obtentum: to assert, maintain, prove, demonstrate
obtingo, obtingere, obtigi, —: to befall, happen, occur
obtuli: see **offero**
occasus, -us, m.: ruin, destruction, downfall
occido¹, occidere, occidi, occisum: to strike down; to kill, slay, murder
occido², occidere, occidi, occasum: to fall, to go down, to set
occludo, occludere, occlusi, occlusum: to shut up, close
occulte (adv.): in secret, in concealment, secretly
occultus, -a, -um: adj-concealed, secret
occupo, occupare: to take possession of
occurro, occurrere, occurri, occursum (+ dat.): to run to meet; to oppose, resist
oculus, -i, m.: eye
odi, odisse (defective verb): to hate
odium, -i, n.: hatred, ill-will, enmity
offendo, offendere, offendi, offensum: to offend, displease, repel, vex
offero, offerre, obtuli, oblatum (+acc + dat.): to offer, give; to expose *accusative* to *dative*
officium, -i, n.: service, duty, function
omen, -inis, n.: omen, sign of the future
omitto, omittere, omisi, omissum: to omit, disregard; to pass over, say nothing of
omnis, -e (adj.): all, every
opera, -ae, f.: effort, work, labor, service, pains, exertion, assistance
  operae pretium est: it is worthwhile
opinio, -onis, f.: opinion, expectation, common belief, general impression
opinor, opinari, opinatus sum: to think, believe, be of the opinion
  ut opinor: as I think
oportet (impers. verb): it is right, it is proper, it is fitting
  oportebat (imperf. tense + acc. person + infinitive): it was fitting for *accusative person* to have done *infinitive*
oppeto, oppetere, oppetivi, oppetitum: to meet, encounter
oppono, opponere, opposui, oppositum (+ acc. + dat.): to put *accusative* against *dative*
opprimo, opprimere, opressi, opressum: 1. to crush, to overwhelm, put down; 2. to suppress, subdue, check, restrain, overpower; 3. to press upon, burden, oppress

ops, opis, f.: help, aid, support; plural: resources

optimates, optimatium, m. pl.: the optimates, the aristocratic party

optimus, -a, -um: superlative adjective of **bonus:** the best, best

opto, optare: desire, wish for; pray for

opus, operis, n.: work, labor, toil; occupation, trade

opus est (+ inf.): there is need of

oratio, -onis, f.: speech, oration

orbis, -is, m.: round surface, circle

orbis terrae or **orbis terrarum:** earth, world, universe

ordo, ordinis, m.: 1. row, line, series, order, rank; 2. class, rank, degree, body (there were three main orders of citizens of Rome: senatorial, equestrian, and plebian)

orior, oriri, ortus sum: to rise

ornamentum, -i, n.: equipment, decoration, mark of honor, ornament, adornment; in plural: resources

orno, ornare: to equip, furnish, supply, adorn; to honor, dignify

ortus, -us, m.: rising, rise

os, oris, n.: mouth; face, countenance

ora, n. pl.: faces

ostendo, ostendere, ostendi, ostentum: to show

ostento, ostentare: to show, display

otiosus, -a, -um: 1. leisurely, quiet, peaceful; 2. carefree, unconcerned

otium, -i, n.: leisure, quiet, peace

P

paco, pacare: to subdue, pacify

pactam: see **pango**

pactum, -i, n.: an agreement, stipulation, contract

pacto (abl. in adv. phrases): manner, way, means

isto pacto: in that way

nullo pacto: in no way

paene (adv.): almost

paenitet (impers. verb + acc. of person + gen. obj.): it causes regret to *accusative person* for *genitive object* (B 209)

palam (adv.): openly

pango, pangere, pepigi, pactum: to fix, settle, determine, agree upon

par, paris (adj.): equal

paratus, -a, -um: prepared, ready

paratus, -us, m.: preparation, provision

parco, parcere, peperci, parsum (+ dat.): to spare, preserve by sparing

parens, -entis, m./f.: parent, father, mother

pareo, parere, parui, — (+ dat. of person): to obey

paries, -etis, m.: wall of a house, house wall

pario, parere, peperi, partum: 1. to bear, bring forth, give birth; 2. to produce, create; 3. to acquire, obtain; 4. passive: to accrue, result

paro, parare: to prepare, make ready, provide; acquire, obtain

parricida, -ae, m.: parricide, murderer of his father, desperate criminal

parricidium, -i, n.: parricide, murder of a father; murder, destruction

pars, partis, f.: 1. part, portion, share; 2. party, faction, side

particeps, -cipis, m. (+ gen.): partner, participant in

partim (adv.): partly

parum (adv.): too little, not enough; insufficiently

parvolus, -a, -um (or **parvulus, -a, -um):** very little, very small

parvus, -a, -um: small

pastor, -oris, m.: herdsman, shepherd

patefacio, patefacere, patefeci, patefactum: to throw open, disclose, bring to light

pateo, patere, patui, —: to lie open, be clear, be plain

pater, -tris, m.: father

pater familias: father of the family, head of the household

patres conscripti: see **conscripti patres**

patientia, -ae, f.: patience, endurance

patior, pati, passus sum: suffer, allow, endure, permit

patria, -ae, f.: fatherland

patricius, -i, m.: patrician, nobleman, man from the upper class

patricii, -orum, m. pl.: patricians, upper class, nobility

patrimonium, -i, n.: inheritance from a father, paternal estate

paucus, -a, -um: few; **pauci, m. pl.:** a few men

paulisper (adv.): for a little while, for a short time

paulo (adv.): a little, by a little

paulo ante: a little earlier, a little while ago

paulum, -i, n.: a little, trifle, small amount

paulus, -a, -um: a little

pecto, pectere, pexi, pexum: to comb

pecunia, -ae, f.: money; plural, riches

pecus, pecudis, f.: sheep, cattle

pedester, pedestris, pedestre (adj.): on foot, pedestrian

pedestres copiae, f. pl.: infantry soldiers

pello, pellere, pepuli, pulsum: to beat, strike, hurl, impel; to drive away

Penates, -ium, n.: household gods; guardian gods of the family

penitus (adv.): deeply. deep within

peperit: see **pario**

per (prep. + acc.) 1. (describes personal agency) through, by, through the efforts of, by the agency of; 2. (in oaths and adjurations) by

percello, percellere, perculi, perculsum: to strike down, overthrow, destroy

percipio, percipere, percepi, perceptum: to learn, understand, know

percutio, percutere, percussi, percussum: to strike

perditus, -a, -um: ruined, profligate, lost, corrupt

perdo, perdere, perdidi, perditum: to ruin, destroy

perduco, perducere, perduxi, perductum: to lead through, bring, conduct

pereo, perire, perii, peritum: to perish, be destroyed

perfero, perferre, pertuli, perlatus: 1. to bring, convey, carry through; 2. to bear, put up with, endure, allow; 3. to report

perficio, perficere, perfeci, perfectum: to complete, bring about, accomplish, finish, bring to pass

perfringo, perfringere, perfregi, perfractum: to break thoroughly, violate, infringe

perfruor, perfrui, perfructus sum (+ abl.). to enjoy fully

perfugium, -i, n.: place of refuge, shelter

pergo, pergere, perrexi, perrectum: to go on, go forward, march, proceed

perhorresco, perhorrescere, perhorrui, —: to be terrified at, shudder at

periclitor, periclitari, periclitatus sum: to put in peril, endanger

periculum, -i, n.: danger, risk; **periculo** (+ gen.): at the risk of

perlatum: see **perfero**

permagnus, -a, -um: very large, very great

permaneo, permanere, permansi, permansurus: to remain, stay

permitto, -mittere, -misi, -missum (+ acc. + dat.): to entrust *accusative* to *dative of person*

permodestus, -a, -um: very modest, extremely shy

permoveo, permovere, permovui, permotum: to move deeply, arouse, excite, disturb

permultus, -a, -um: very much; plural: very many

pernicies, -ei, f.: danger, destruction, calamity, ruin; (+ dat.) destruction for

perniciosus, -a, -um: dangerous, destructive, ruinous, harmful, pernicious

perpetuus, -a, -um: perpetual, continuous, lasting, permanent

in perpetuum (tempus): for all time, forever

persaepe (adv.): very often

perscribo, perscribere, perscripsi, perscriptum: to write out; to record, register

persequor, persequi, persecutus sum: to pursue, hunt down, chase, overtake

perspicio, perspicere, perspexi, perspectum: to see clearly, perceive, understand, observe, mark, note

perterreo, perterrere, perterrui, perterritum: to frighten thoroughly, terrify

pertimesco, pertimescere, pertimui, —: to become thoroughly frightened, to fear terribly, tremble, dread

pertineo, pertinere, pertinui, —: to pertain to, have reference to, concern, tend to, apply to, relate to

perturbo, perturbare: to disturb, throw into confusion, discompose, embarrass

pervenio, pervenire, perveni, perventum: to reach, come to, arrive at

pestis, -is, f.: disease, plague, pest; destruction, ruin

petitio, -onis, f.: blow, thrust, attack

peto, petere, petivi, petitum: 1. to seek for, aim at; 2. to attack, assault

petulantia, -ae, f.: impudence, wantonness, petulance

pietas, -atis, f.: loyalty, sense of duty

placeo, placere, placui, placitum (+ dat. of person): to please, suit, satisfy; often used impersonally

placo, placare: (+ acc. + dat.): to reconcile *accusative* to *dative*, to calm, placate, pacify, appease

plane (adv.): plainly, clearly

plebs, plebis, f.: the common people

plenus, -a, -um: full, crowded, thronged

plurimus, -a, -um: superlative adjective of **plus:** most, very many

quam plurimos: as many as possible

plus, pluris (adj.): more

plus quam: more than

poena, -ae, f.: punishment, penalty

polliceor, polleri, pollicitus sum: to promise

pono, ponere, posui, positum: to put, place

pons, pontis, m.: bridge

pontifex, pontificis, m.: priest
   pontifex maximus: the chief priest
popina, -ae, f.: tavern
popularis, -e (adj.): pertaining to the people, democratic, popular, devoted to the people, populist
populus, -i, m.: people, nation
porta, -ae, f.: city-gate, gate
possessio, -onis, f.: property, possession, holding, having
possum, posse, potui, —: to be able
post (prep. + acc.): after
postea (adv.): afterward, after this, later, after that, often
posteri, -orum, m. pl.: coming generations, descendants, posterity
posteritas, -atis, f.: the future, future time, after ages
posterus, -a, -um: future, subsequent, ensuing
   in posterum: for the future
posthac (adv.): after this, hereafter, henceforth, in the future, afterward
postremo (adv.): finally
postremus, -a, -um: last, final
postulo, postulare: to ask, demand, request, desire
potens, -entis (adj.): powerful
potentissimus, -a, -um: superlative adjective of **potens**
potestas, -tatis, f.: power; ability, opportunity
potior, potiri, potitus sum (+ gen.): to take possession of, gain, acquire
potius (comp. adv.): rather
   potius quam (conj.): rather than
prae (prep. + abl.): in front of; in comparison with
praebeo, praebere, praebui, praebitum: to give, grant, offer
praeceps, -cipitis (adj.): headlong, rash, inconsiderate, hasty
praecipio, praecipere, praecepi, praeceptum: to consider beforehand; to advise, warn; to order, command
praecipue (adv.): especially, chiefly, principally
praeclarus, -a, -um: very famous, distinguished, outstanding, extraordinary; splendid, admirable, excellent
praecurro, praecurrere, praecucurri, praecursus (+ dat.): to run before; to surpass, outstrip
praedator, -oris, m: plunderer, robber
praedico, praedicare: 1. to proclaim, boast, claim, declare; 2. to praise, laud; 3. to say first, begin by saying
praedico, praedicere, praedixi, praedictum: to say beforehand, predict, foretell

praedium, -i, n.: farm, estate
praefectura, -ae, f.: prefecture, city governed by a prefect
praefero, praeferre, praetuli, praelatum: to place before, offer, present
praemitto, praemittere, praemisi, praemissum: to send ahead
praemium, -i, n.: a reward, recompense
Praeneste, -is, f.: Praeneste (modern Palestrina), a town about twenty miles southeast of Rome
praescribo, praescribere, praescripsi, praescriptum: to instruct, give instructions, direct
praesens, -entis (adj.): 1. present, at hand, in person; 2. powerful, influential; helpful; *Cat.* 3.21: providential; 3. (of time) present, contemporary, existing
praesentia, -ae, f.: presence
praesertim (adv.): especially, particularly
praesideo, praesidere, praesedi, —: (+ dat.): to guard, watch, protect, defend
praesidium, -i, n. (often plu.): garrison, guard; defense, protection; armed escort, troops
praesto (adv.): at hand, ready, present
praesto, praestare, praestiti, praestitum: to stand in front, be responsible
praestolor, praestolari, praestolatus sum (+ acc. or dat.): to wait for, expect
praeter (prep. + acc.): except for, besides, apart from; against, contrary to
praeterea (adv.): besides, furthermore
praetereo, praeterire, praeterii, praeteritum: to pass over, pass by
praetermitto, praetermittere, praetermisi, praetermissum: to let pass by, let slip, neglect, omit
praeterquam (adv.): beyond, besides, except, other than
praetor, -oris, m.: praetor; Roman magistrate who acted as a judge; the **praetor urbanus** judged cases concerning Roman citizens (see Appendix A)
praetoria cohors: praetorian guard, the bodyguard of the praetor or general
praetorius, -a, -um: pertaining to a praetor or general; praetorian
praetuli: see **praefero**
praetura, -ae, f.: praetorship, office of the praetor
precor, precari, precatus sum: to pray to, invoke, entreat, beg
premo, premere, pressi, pressum: to press, overwhelm
pretium, -i, n.: price; bribe
   operae pretium est: it is worthwhile

pridem (adv.): long ago, for a long time
   iam pridem: now for a long time
pridie (adv.): on the day before
primo (adv.): at first
primum (adv.): first
primus, -a, -um: first, foremost
   quam primum: as soon as possible
princeps, -cipis, m.: chief, leader, foremost man
principium, -i, n.: beginning, commencement, origin
pristinus, -a, -um: former, ancient
priusquam (comp. adv.): before, earlier than
privatus, -a, -um: private, not public; out of office
privatus, -i, m: private citizen (as opposed to a public official, such as a consul or a praetor)
privo, privare: (+ acc. + abl.): to deprive *accusative* of *ablative*
pro (prep. + abl.): on behalf of, in return for, in place of
probo, probare: 1. to approve, recommend; 2. to prove, to make clear
procella, -ae, f.: storm, squall
procul (adv.): formerly, once
procuratio, -onis, f.: superintendency, charge, management
prodigium, -i, n.: 1. omen, portent, prodigy; 2. a monster, unnatural being, unnatural crime
prodigus, -a, -um: wasteful, lavish, prodigal, spendthrift
proelium, -i, n: battle, fight
profectio, -onis, f.: setting out, departure, going away
profecto (adv.): certainly, assuredly
profero, proferre, protuli, prolatum: to bring forward
proficio, proficere, profeci, profectum: to accomplish
proficiscor, proficisci, profectus sum: to set out, depart
profiteor, profiteri, professus sum (+ two acc.): to declare publicly that one is, to avow oneself to be, claim to be
profligo, profligare: to overthrow, overcome
profugio, profugere, profugi, profugitum: to flee, run away, escape
profundo, profundere, profudi, profusum: to pour forth; squander
progredior, progredi, progressus sum: to go forward, proceed, advance, go
prohibeo, prohibere, prohibui, prohibitum: to hold back, prevent, obstruct

proicio, proicere, proieci, proiectum: to hurl forth, throw out
proinde (adv.): therefore, accordingly
prolato, prolatare: to postpone, put off
propago, propagare: (+ acc. or dat.): to increase, prolong, preserve; establish, ordain
prope (adv.): nearly, almost, about
propono, proponere, proposui, propositum: to put forward, present, propose; to consider
proprius, -a, -um (+ gen.): one's own, peculiar to, proper to, appropriate for
propter (prep. + acc.): on account of
propulso, propulsare: to drive back, drive off, ward off, avert, repel
proscriptio, -onis, f.: proscription, confiscation
prosequor, prosequi, prosecutus sum: to follow, pursue, accompany, escort
prospicio, prospicere, prospexi, prospectum (+ acc. or dat.): to foresee, see beforehand, provide for, take precautions for
prostratus, -a, -um: on the ground, prostrate; powerless
prosum, prodesse, profui, — (+ dat.): to be useful to, benefit, profit, serve
providentia, -ae, f.: wisdom, foresight
provideo, providere, providi, provisum (+dat.): to foresee; to care for, provide for, to take precautions, prepare
provincia, -ae, f.: province, territory governed by a magistrate from Rome
provincialis, -e (adj.): of or pertaining to a province, in a province
proximus, -a, -um: 1. nearest, next; 2. most recent, last; 3. following, ensuing, upcoming
prudens, -entis (adj.): prudent, discreet, wise
prudentia, -ae, f.: foresight, wisdom, prudence
pruina, -ae - f.: frost, cold
publicatio, -onis, f.: confiscation
publice (adv.): publicly, in public
publico, publicare: to confiscate, take away; to make public
publicus, -a, -um: of the people, public, for the common good, common
pudor, -oris, m.: modesty, sense of shame, decency
puer, -eri, m.: boy, young man
pugna, -ae, f.: fight, battle, combat
pugno, pugnare: to fight
pulcher, -era, -erum: beautiful
pulcherrimus, -a, -um: superlative adjective of **pulcher**
pulvinar, -aris, n.: couch of the gods, cushioned seat on which images of the gods were placed during a **lectisternium** (feast of the gods)

punctum, -i, n.: point, moment
punio, punire, punivi, punitum: to punish
purgo, purgare: to clean out, cleanse, purify, purge
purpura, -ae, f.: purple
purpuratus, -a, -um: wearing purple (i.e., a king, a member of the royal court)
puto, putare: to think, believe, consider

Q

quaero, quaere, quaesivi, quaesitum: to seek, to look for, to strive to attain
quaesitio, -onis, f.: 1. a question, inquiry; 2. judicial investigation, trial, court of law
quaesitor, -oris, m.: investigator, examining magistrate, prosecuting officer
quaeso (only in first person pres.) I beg, I pray, I beseech
quaestus, -us, m.: business, employment, occupation, trade
qualis, -e (adj.): such as, of such a kind
quam (adv., with comparatives): than
quam (adv.): in what manner, how
  quam diu: how long?
  quam primum: as soon as possible
  quam ob rem: and for this reason, and therefore
quamquam (conj.): although; and yet (at the beginning of a sentence)
quantus, -a, -um: how much, how great
quapropter (adv.): for this reason, wherefore, on this account
quartus, -a, -um: fourth
-que (enclitic conj.): and (attached to the second of two words to be joined)
querimonia, -ae, f.: complaint
queror, queri, questus sum: to complain about
qui, quae, quod (relative pron.): who, which, what
quia (conj.): because
quicquid: see **quisquis**
quicumque, quaecumque, quodcumque: whoever, whatever, all, every
quid (interrog. adv.): why? how? what? in what respect?
quidam, quaedam, quoddam (indef. pron. + adj.): some, certain, a certain one, certain ones
quidem: (adv.): indeed
quies, -etis, f.: rest, repose, peace, quiet, inaction, freedom from exertion
quiesco, quiescere, quievi, quietum: to keep quiet, be inactive, be at peace

quietus, -a, -um: peaceful, at rest
quintus, -a, -um: fifth
Quirites, m. plu.: citizens
quis, quid (interrog. pron. and adj.): who? what? what kind of?
quispiam, quaepiam, quodpiam (indef. pron.): anyone, anything
quisquam, quidquam (quicquam): 1. (adj.) some, any; 2. (indef. pron.) someone, anyone; something, anything
quisque, quaeque, quidque: each, each person, each one
  unus quisque: each and every one
quisquis, quicquid (quidquid) (indef. pron.) whoever, whatever
quo: 1. (adv.) to this place; 2. (conj.) to what place, to where, whither; 3. (conj.) to what point? how long?
quoad (adv.): as long as, until
quocumque (adv.): to wherever, in whatever direction, whithersoever
quondam (adv.): formerly, once, at one time
quoniam (adv.): since, seeing that, because
quoque (conj.): also, too
quot (indeclinable adj.): how many
quotiens (adv.): how many times; as often as, as many times as
quotienscumque (adv.): as many times as, af often as

R

rapina, -ae, f.: plundering, robbery, pillage, rapine
rapio, rapere, rapui, raptum: 1. to seize and carry off; 2. to drive, impel, push
ratio, -onis, f.: 1. method, reason, rational thinking; 2. mode, manner, way; 3. pursuit, business matter; 4. plan (*Cat.* 2.13)
recens, recentis (adj.): recent, fresh
recipio, recipere, recepi, receptum: 1. to promise, pledge oneself, take responsibility, undertake, agree; 2. to take back, receive, accept; 3. to receive, welcome
recito, recitare: to read out, read aloud
recognosco, recognoscere, recognovi, recognitum: to recall to mind, recollect, review
reconciliatio, -onis, f.: reestablishment, restoration, reinstatement
recondo, recondere, recondidi, reconditum: to put away, hide, conceal
recordor, recordari, recordatus sum: to think over, remember, recollect, call to mind
recreo, recreare: to restore, refresh; with reflexive pronoun, translate as middle or passive

recta (adv.): straightway, directly (originally **recta via**)

recte (adv.): rightly, properly, suitably, appropriately, correctly

recusatio, -onis, f.: a declining, a refusal

recuso, recusare: to refuse

redeo, redire, redii, reditum: to go back, return

redimio, redimire, redimii, redimitum: to bind around, crown

redundo, redundare: 1. to run over, overflow, be in excess, be abundant; 2. to wash back over, overwhelm, redound

refero, referre, rettuli, relatus: 1. to carry back; 2. to report; 3. to refer, show, submit for consideration

    gratiam referre: to return thanks, show gratitude

regie (adv.): regally, tyrannically

regio, -onis, f.: a territory, province, district, area, region; boundary-line, limit

regno, regnare: to reign, rule as king

regnum, -i, m.: rule, authority, sovereignty, supreme power

relatus: see **refero**

relevo, relevare: to relieve, free, lighten; to free from a burden

relinquo, relinquere, reliqui, relictum: to leave behind

reliquus, -a, -um: remaining, the rest, left over, left

remaneo, remanere, remansi, remansum: to remain, remain behind, be left

remissio, -onis, f.: relaxation, diminishing, easing, lessening, lowering

remissior, -ius: comparative adjective of **remissus**

remissus, -a, -um.: relaxed, slack, loose; negligent, remiss

remoror, remorari, remoratus sum: to hold back; to be delayed, deferred

removeo, removere, removi, remotum: to exclude *accusative* from *ablative*, to take away, set aside, withdraw, remove

repello, repellere, reppuli, repulsum: to drive back, drive away, repulse; to drive away from, keep away from

repente (adv.): suddenly

repentinus, -a, -um: sudden

reperio, reperire, repperi, repertum: to find out, discover

reprimo, reprimere, repressi, repressum: to check, restrain, curb

repudio, repudiare: to spurn, refuse, put aside, reject

res, rei, f.: thing, affair, fact, circumstance, reason, matter, business

    res publica: the Roman Republic (literally, the public thing)

reseco, resecare, resecui, resectum: to cut away

reservo, reservare: to preserve, save, keep

resideo, residere, resedi, —: to be left, stay behind, remain

resisto, resistere, restiti, —: 1. to stand still, remain behind; 2. to withstand, oppose, resist

respondeo, respondere, respondi, responsum (+ acc + dat.): to reply to, respond to, answer *accusative thing* to *dative person*

responsum, -i, n.: an answer, reply, response; opinion, advice

restinguo, restinguere, restinxi, restinctum: to extinguish, put out

restituo, restituere, restitui, restitutum: to restore

resto, restare, restiti, —: to be left, remain; (+ dat.): to oppose, resist, withstand

reticeo, reticere, reticui, —: to be silent

retineo, retinere, retinui, retentum: to hold back, maintain, preserve

retorqueo, retorquere, retorsi, retortum: to twist back, turn back

rettundo, rettundere, rettudi, retusum: to beat back, weaken, blunt, dull

reus, -i, m.: person accused, defendant

revertor, reverti, reversus sum: to return, come back

revoco, revocare: to call back, recall, divert

rex, regis, m.: king

robur, -oris, n.: oak tree; strength

robustus, -a, -um: strong, hardy

rogo, rogare: to ask, request

    sententiam rogare: to ask someone's opinion

    legem rogare: to pass or enact a law

Romanus, -a, -um: Roman, of or belonging to Rome

ruina, -ae, f.: a downfall, ruin, catastrophe

rumpo, rumpere, rupi, ruptum: to burst, break

rusticus, -a, -um: pertaining to the country, rustic, rural

S

sacra, sacrorum, n. pl.: sacred rites, religious rituals

sacrarium, -i, n.: shrine, sanctuary

sacrosanctus, -a, -um: sacred, inviolate; untouched, safe

saeculum, -i, n.: age, century

saepe (adv.): often

saepio, saepire, saepsi, saeptum: to hedge in, fence around; protect

saepius: comparative adverb of saepe: very often

sagacissimus, -a, -um: superlative adjective of sagax

sagax, sagacis (adj.): intellectually quick, keen, acute, sagacious

salto, saltare: to dance

salus, -utis, f.: health, safety

saluto, salutare: to greet, welcome, hail, pay respects to
    ad me salutatum: to greet me (accusative supine showing purpose)

salvus, -a, -um: safe, unharmed; solvent, free from debt

sancio, sancire, sanxi, sanctum: 1. to make sacred; 2. to decree, ordain

sanctissimus, -a, -um: superlative adjective of sanctus: most sacred; very upright, conscientious

sane: truly, indeed, by all means

sanguis, -inis, m.: blood

sano, sanare: to heal, cure, make healthy

sanus, -a, -um: sound, sane, healthy

sapiens, -entis, m.: wise man, philosopher

satelles, satellitis, m./f.: 1. attendant, follower; 2. accomplice, partner

satis (indeclinable noun + gen.): enough, sufficient
    satis facere: to do enough

saucius, -a, -um: wounded

scaena, -ae, f.: stage, scene; theatre

scelerate (adv.): wickedly, criminally

sceleratus, -a, -um: wicked, criminal, impious

sceleratus, -i, m.: scoundrel, criminal

scelus, -eris, n.: a wicked deed, crime, sin

scientia, -ae, f.: knowledge

scilicet (adv.): you may know, you may be certain; clearly, surely, certainly

scio, scire, scivi, scitum: to know, be aware of

scortum, -i, n.: harlot, prostitute

scriba, -ae, m.: clerk, secretary, accountant, career, civil servant

se or sese (third person reflexive pron., acc. /abl., sing. /pl.): him/herself, themselves

secedo, secedere, secessi, secessum: to withdraw, go away

secerno, secernere, secrevi, secretum: to separate, segregate, seclude

securis, -is, f.: ax

sed (conj.): but

sedes, -is, f.: a seat, chair; dwelling-place, residence

seditio, -onis, f.: a rebellion, insurrection; sedition, treason

sedo, sedare: to settle, stop, bring to an end

seiungo, seiungere, seiunxi, seiunctum: to disunite, disjoin, separate, part

sella, -ae, f.: chair, bench, work-stool

semel (adv.): once

semen, seminis, n.: seed

seminarium, -i, n.: breeding ground, hot-bed

semper (adv.): always, ever

sempiternus, -a, -um: everlasting, perpetual, eternal

senatus, -us, m.: the senate, the Roman Senate

senex, senis, m.: old man

sensus, -us, m.: sense of perception, feelings, sense, consciousness, emotion

sententia, -ae, f.: 1. opinion, judgement; 2. plan, purpose, resolve; 3. intention, will, desire

sentina, -ae, f.: bilge water (the filthy water that collects in the bottom of a ship), refuse, sewage; the lowest of the people, dregs, rabble

sentio, sentire, sensi, sensus: perceive, feel, sense; think, realize, know

sepelio, sepelire, sepelivi, sepultum: to bury; to destroy, ruin

sequor, sequi, secutus sum: to follow, pursue; to adopt, act on, put into effect

serius: comparative adverb of serus: too late

sermo, -onis, m.: 1. talk, conversation, discourse, speech; 2. rumor, report

serpo, serpere, serpsi, serptum: to creep along, crawl, glide

serta, -orum, n. pl.: wreaths of flowers, garlands

serus, -a, -um: late

servio, servire, servii, servitum (+ dat.): 1. to serve, be a slave; 2. to labor for, gratify; 3. to aim at, have regard to

servitium, -i, n.: slavery; plural: a body of slaves, class of slaves, slaves

servo, servare: to save, make safe, deliver, rescue, preserve

servus, -i, m.: a slave, servant

severior, -ius: comparative adjective of severus

severitas, -atis, f.: seriousness, gravity, strictness, severity

severus, -a, -um: serious, strict, stern, severe

si (conj.): if

sic (adv.): so, thus, in such a way

sica, -ae, f.: dagger

sicarius, -i, m.: assassin, murderer

sicut (adv.): as, just as

significatio, -onis, f.: sign, indication; omen, portent

signum, -i, n.: 1. sign, mark; 2. a seal, the impression of a seal-ring (or signet ring); 3. image, picture, statue; 4. plural: military standards

silentium, -i, n.: silence

sileo, silere, silui: to be silent; to not speak of, suppress

silvestris, -e (adj.): wooded, of the woods

similis, -e (adj.): like, resembling, similar

simul (adv.): at the same time

simul atque: adv.): as soon as

simulacrum, -i, n.: image, statue

sin (conj.): but if, if not, if however, if on the contrary

sine (prep. + abl.): without

singularis, -e (adj.): single, extraordinary, unprecedented

singuli, -ae, -a (pl. adj.): one by one, individual; one to each, separate

in dies singuli: day by day, each successive day

sino, sinere, sivi, situm: to permit, allow

sinus, -us, m.: curve, fold; bosom

sitis, -is, f.: thirst

sive . . . sive: if . . . or if

sobrius, -a, -um: sober

societas, -atis, f.: fellowship, alliance, association

socius, -i, m.: companion, ally, partner; accomplice

sodalis, -is, m./f.: close friend, intimate, boon companion

sol, solis, m.: the sun

soleo, solere, solitus sum (+ inf.): to be accustomed

solitudo, solitudinis, f.: isolation, solitude

sollicitatio, -onis, f.: inciting, instigation

sollicito, sollicitare: to stir, rouse up, excite, incite, provoke

sollicitus, -a, -um: excited, alarmed, anxious, worried

solum (adv.): only

non solum . . . sed etiam: not only . . . but also

non solum . . . verum etiam: not only . . . but even, not only . . but also

solum, -i, n.: soil, ground

solus, -a, -um (gen. **solius**): alone, only

solutior, solutius: comparative adjective of **solutus**

solutus, -a, -um: careless, lax, remiss

somnus, -i, m.: sleep; inactivity, laziness

sors, sortis, f.: 1. fate, lot; 2. wages, pay

spargo, spargere, sparsi, sparsum: to scatter, to sprinkle

species, -ei, f.: appearance, look; outward appearance

speculor, speculari, speculatus sum: watch

spero, sperare: to hope, expect, believe

spes, -ei, f.: hope

spiritus, -us, m.: breath, air

spiritus caeli: the breath of air (i.e., life)

spolio, spoliare: to rob someone (acc.) of something (abl.); strip, deprive, plunder

sponte (f. abl. sing. only): free will, accord

sponte sua: of his/her own accord

sponte tua: of your own accord

stabilio, stabilire, stabilivi, stabilitum: to make firm, establish, assure

statim (adv.): at once, immediately, right away

statua, -ae, f.: image, statue, monumental figure

statuo, statuere, statui, statutum: 1. to set up, erect, place, stand; 2. to decide, choose, resolve, decree

status, -us, m.: condition, situation, status

stirps, stirpis, f.: stem, stalk, root; source, origin

sto, stare, steti, statum: to stand, remain firm

studeo, studere, studui, —: 1. (+ inf.) to be eager to do; 2. (+ dat.) to be eager for, desire

studiosus, -a, -um (+ gen.): interested in, devoted to, fond of

studium, -i, n.: eagerness, zeal, inclination, desire; plural: pursuits, interests

stultissimus, -a, -um: superlative adjective of **stultus**

stultitia, -ae, f.: foolishness, simplicity

stultus, -a, -um: foolish, stupid

stuprum, -i, n.: lewdness, outrage; incest, lust; shame, adultery

suadeo, suadere, suasi, suasum: to advise, urge, recommend

subeo, subire, subivi, subitum: to undergo, endure

subicio, subicere, subieci, subiectum (+ acc. + dat.): to bring *accusative* to *dative*

subiector, -oris, m.: forger

subigo, subigere, subegi, subactum: to crush, suppress, overpower, subdue

subito (adv.): suddenly

subsellium, -i, n.: low bench, seat; a senator's seat

subsidium, -i, n.: assistance, support, help, aid, reinforcement

succedo, succedere, successi, successum (+ dat.): to approach, march to, draw near

suffero, sufferre, sustuli, sublatum: suffer, undergo, endure

sui (gen.), **sibi** (dat.), **se** or **sese** (acc. + abl.) (third person reflexive pron.): himself, herself, themselves

sum, esse, fui, futurus: to be

summa, -ae, f.: precedence, chief rank, leadership, supreme power; the highest welfare, the greatest good

summus, -a, -um: highest, extreme; most important, most eminent

sumo, sumere, sumpsi, sumptum: to take in hand, claim; to exact or inflict punishment

sumptuose (adv.): expensively, sumptuously

sumptuosius: comparative adverb of **sumptuose**; comparatives often have the meaning of too much, excessively (i.e., at *Cat.* 2.20, line232).

sumptus, -us, m.: expense

superfuturus: see **supersum**

superior, -ius: comparative adjective of **superus:** 1. higher; 2. former, previous, earlier; 3. most recent

noctem illam superiorem: that night before last (*Cat.* 1.8)

supero, superare: to surpass, conquer

supersum, superesse, superfui, superfuturus: to be left, remain, remain alive

superus, -a, -um: higher, above

suppedito, suppeditare: to supply, provide abundantly

supplex, -icis, m.: suppliant, supplicant, humble petitioner

supplicatio, -onis, f.: public thanksgiving, thanksgiving day, festival

supplicium, -i, n.: 1. humble entreaty, petition, supplication; 2. punishment, penalty

surgo, surgere, surrexi, surrectum: to stand up

suscipio, suscipere, suscepi, susceptum: to undertake, take upon oneself; incur, bear

suspicio, suspicere, suspexi, suspectum: to mistrust, suspect

suspicio, suspicionis, f.: suspicion

suspicor, suspicari, suspicatus sum: to mistrust, suspect

sustento, sustentare: to procrastinate, put off, defer, delay; to support, depend upon

sustineo, sustinere, sustinui, sustentum: to endure, tolerate, sustain

suus, -a, -um: (reflex. possess. adj.): his/her own, its own, their own (see B86.1)

T

tabella, -ae, f.: writing tablet, waxed tablet for writing; sometimes used metaphorically for the letters that were written on such tablets

taberna, -ae, f.: shop, inn, tavern

tabesco, tabescere, tabui, —: to waste away, pine away

tabula, -ae, f.: 1. board; 2. writing tablet, letter; 3. plu.): public records; 4. an auction placard, auction sale

tabulae novae: new account books (i.e., the cancellation of debt)

taceo, tacere, tacui, tacitum: to be silent, say nothing

taciturnitas, -atis, f.: a keeping silent, silence, taciturnity

tacitus, -a, -um: silent, secret, hidden, concealed

taeter, -tra, -trum: foul, loathsome

talaris, -e (adj.): reaching to the ankles

talis, -e (adj.): such, of such a kind, of such a sort

tam (adv.): so, such, so much

tam diu (adv.): so long

tamen (adv.): nevertheless

tametsi (conj.): nevertheless

tamquam (adv.): as much as; as if, as though

tandem (adv.):finally, at last; in questions: I ask you, pray tell

tango, tangere, tetigi, tactum: to strike at, smite, hit

tantum (adv.): so much, only so much

tantus, -a, -um: so much, so great; of so great a size, such great

tarde (adv.): late, last, slowly

tardissime: superlative adverb of **tarde:** last of all, finally

tarditas, -atis, f.: slowness, tardiness

tardus, -a, -um: slow, late, tardy

tectum, -i, n.: roof; house, dwelling, abode

tecta, -orum, n.: houses

tecum = cum te

telum, -i, n.: a missile weapon, spear, javelin

temere (adv.): rashly, heedlessly, too boldly, imprudently, unwisely

temeritas, -atis, f.: rashness, boldness, heedlessness, thoughtlessness, foolhardiness, recklessness, indiscretion

temperantia, -ae, f.: moderation, temperance, self-control

tempestas, -atis, f.: a storm, tempest

templum, -i, n.: a place dedicated to a deity, temple, shrine

tempto, temptare: 1. to try, test, attempt; 2. to attack, assail

tempus, -oris, n.: 1. time, occasion, time of need, emergency, crisis; 2. plural: the times, conditions, circumstances

O tempora!: Oh, the times!

tendo, tendere, tetendi, tentum: to hold out, stretch out

tenebrae, -arum, f. pl.: darkness

teneo, tenere, tenui, tentum: to hold, catch; to maintain, preserve

tenuis, -e (adj.): thin, slender humble, poor

tenuissimus, -a, -um: superlative adjective of **tenuis**

termino, terminare: to set bounds, bound, limit, set limits, define, determine

terminus, -i, n.: limit, border, boundary

terra, -ae, f.: land

tertius, -a, -um: third

testamentum, -i, m.: will, testament

Tiberis, -is, m.: the River Tiber; **Tiberis** at *Cat.* 3.5 is nominative

timeo, timere, timui, —m: to fear, to be afraid of, dread

timidus, -a, -um: fearful, afraid, faint-hearted

timor, -oris, m.: fear, dread

toga, -ae, f.: toga (outer garment worn only by male Roman citizens that was a mark of citizen status)

togatus, -a, -um: wearing the toga (i.e., wearing a civil, nonmilitary dress)

togatus, -i, m.: citizen, civilian

tolerabilis, -e: bearable, endurable, tolerable, not extremely harsh

tolero, tolerare: to tolerate, endure, allow

tollo, tollere, sustuli, sublatum: 1. to lift up, raise up, elevate, exalt; 2. to remove, destroy, take away, abolish

tot (indeclinable adj.): so many

totiens (adv.): so often, so many times

totus, -a, -um (gen. **totius**): all, the whole, total, entire

tracto, tractare: to handle, manage, conduct

se tractare: to conduct oneself

trado, tradere, tradidi, traditum: to hand over, deliver

Transalpinus, -a, -um: on the other side of the Alps

transcendo, transcendere, transcendi, transcensum: to climb over, make one's way across, cross over

transfero, transferre, transtuli, translatum: to convey, direct, transfer

transigo, transigere, transegi, transactum: to accomplish, carry out, put into effect

transtuli: see **transfero**

tribunal, tribunalis, n.: platform, raised platform for the seats of magistrates

tribunus, -i, m.: commander, chief representative

tribunus aerarius: paymaster, official in charge of making payments from the public treasury, tribune of the treasury

tribunus plebis: tribune of the people; see Appendix A

triduum, -i, n.: a three-day period

triumpho, triumphare: to celebrate a triumph; rejoice, be glad

triumphus, -i, m.: triumphal procession; triumph, victory

trucido, trucidare: to slaughter, slay, kill, murder

tu (pers. pron.): you

tuba, -ae, f.: trumpet

tueor, tueri, tutus sum: to guard, maintain, protect; to look at

tulisses: see **fero**

tum (adv.): at that time; thereupon, next, afterwards

tum . . . cum (correl. adv.): 1. at that time . . . when; 2. both . . . and; 3. not only . . . but also

tumultus, -us, m.: disturbance, disorder, rebellion, insurrection

tumulus, -i, m.: heap of earth, mound, hill

tunica, -ae, f.: tunic (undergarment worn by both men and women and could be sleeved or sleeveless)

turbulentus, -a, -um: restless, stormy, troublesome

turpis, -e (adj.): shameful, disgraceful

turpissime: superlative adverb of **turpiter,** most shamefully

turpiter (adv.): shamefully, disgracefully, dishonorably

turpitudo, -inis, f.: baseness, shamefulness, dishonor, disgrace

tuto (adv.): safely, safe

tuus, -a, -um: your

tyrranus, -i, m.: tyrant, absolute ruler, despot

U

uber, -eris, n.: a teat, udder, breast

ubinam (interrog. adv.): where? where in the world?

ulciscor, ulcisci, ultus sum: to take vengeance on, take revenge against, to avenge; to punish

ullus, -a, -um: any, any one, any at all

ultro (adv.): voluntarily, of one's own accord, unasked, spontaneously

umquam (adv.): at any time, ever

una (adv.): along with, together with

undique (adv.): from all sides, from everywhere

unguentum, -i, n.: ointment, unguent, perfume

unice (adv.): uniquely, singularly, especially

universus, -a, -um: all together, entire, whole

unus, -a, -um (gen. **unius**): one, alone, a single

unus quisque: each and every one, each individual

urbanus, -a, -um: urban, pertaining to the city

urbs, urbis, f.: city

usque (adv.): all the way

usura, -ae, f.: use, enjoyment; in business, interest

usurpo, usurpare: to use, employ

ut (adv.): 1. (+ indic.) when, as; 2. (+ subj.) that, namely, that; in order that, with the result that, etc.

uterque, utraque, utrumque: each of two, both

uti = ut

utilior, utilius: comparative adjective of **utilis:** more useful

utilis, utile (adj.): useful, profitable

utilitas, -atis, f.: usefulness; benefit, profit, advantage, welfare

utinam (adv.): (introduces a wish) would that, if only

utor, uti, usus sum (+ abl.): 1. use, enjoy; 2. to treat, to deal with; 3. find (*Cat.* 2.18, line 207)

utrum . . . an (conj.): whether . . . or

uxor, -oris, f.: a wife

V

vacillo, vacillare: to sway to and fro, stagger, reel; to vacillate

vacuefacio, vacuefacere, vacuefeci, vacuefac-tum: to make empty, make clear, make vacant

vacuus, -a, -um: empty, free

vadimonium, -i, n.: bail, security, bail-bond; promise of appearance secured by bail

vagina, -ae, f.: scabbard, sheath for a sword

valde (adv.): very much, exceedingly

valeo, valere, valui, valitum: be strong, powerful

varietas, -atis, f.: difference, diversity; change

varius, -a, -um: different, various, varied

vastatio, -onis, f.: devastation

vastitas, -atis, f.: devastation, destruction, ruin

vasto, vastare: to lay waste, devastate, destroy

vates, -is, m.: poet, prophet, soothsayer

vectigal, -alis, n.: tribute, tax, revenue

vehemens, -entis (adj.): 1. vigorous, strong, forceful, powerful; 2. eager, active; 3. violent, impestuous

vehementer (adv.): strongly, vehemently, violently

vehementior, -ius: comparative adjective of **vehemens**

vehementissime: (superl. adv.): most eagerly, most earnestly; strongly, most forcefully

vehementius: comparative adverb of **vehemens:** more strongly, more ardently, more violently

vel . . . vel: either . . . or

velum, -i, n.: cloth, covering, awning, curtain, veil

vena, ae, f.: vein, blood vessel

veneficus, -i, m.: poisoner

venenum, -i, n.: poison

veneror, venerari, veneratus sum: to venerate, worship, pray to, reverence, adore, honor

venio, venire, veni, ventum: to come

verbum, -i, n.: word; plural - language

vere (adv.): 1. truly, really; 2. properly, rightly

vereor, vereri, veritus sum: 1. to fear, be afraid; 2. to revere, respect, reverence

vero (adv.): in truth, certainly, to be sure, truly, in fact, but, although, however, on the other hand

verso, versare: 1. to turn often, to keep turning, to twist; 2. (in passive) to live in, dwell, remain, stay

versor, versari, versatus sum (passive of **verso**): 1. to be, be situated in, exist; 2. to be busied, be employed, be engaged in; 3. to move about, keep turning; 4. to be around, be among, belong; 5. to live in, dwell

verum (adv.): truly, indeed; but yet, still, however

verum, -i, n.: the truth, reality, fact

verus, -a, -um: true, real, genuine

vesperia, -ae, f.: evening

Vesta, -ae, f.: the goddess Vesta, daughter of Saturn and Ops

vester, vestra, vestrum: your, yours

vestigium, -i, n.: footprint, trace; plural: ruins

vetus, -eris (adj.): old, ancient, of old, of a former time, of long standing

vexatio, -onis, f.: annoyance, outrage, insult, harassment

vexo, vexare: to harass, vex, trouble

via, -ae, f.: way, course, policy

vibro, vibrare: to move to and fro, to brandish

vicesimus, -a, -um: the twentieth

vicinus, -i, m.: neighbor

victor, -oris, m.: a conqueror, victor

victoria, -ae, f.: victory

videlicet (adv.): one may see, it is evident, clearly, plainly

video, videre, vidi, visum: 1. to see; 2. (in passive) to seem; to be seen

vigilans, -antis (adj.): watchful, vigilant, careful

vigilia, -ae, f.: 1. a watching, wakefulness, lying awake; 2. watch, guard, night watch; 3. lack of sleep

vigilo, vigilare: to watch, keep awake, be wakeful; stay up late for, do at night

villa, -ae, f.: a country-house, farm, villa

vinclum: see vinculum

vinco, vincere, vici, victum: conquer, defeat, vanquish

vinculum, -i, n.: bond, fetter; imprisonment

vindex, -icis, m.: an avenger, punisher

vindico, vindicare: to punish

vinum, -i, n.: wine

violo, violare: to threat with violence, injure, dishonor, outrage, violate

vir, -i, m.: man, husband

virgo, -inis, f.: maiden; Vestal Virgin

virtus, -utis, f.: 1. courage, bravery, valor; 2. strength, vigor; 3. virtue, moral goodness

vis, vis, f.: force, strength, power, violence

viscus, visceris, n.: internal organs, viscera, guts, entrails

vita, -ae, f.: life, way of life

vitium, -i, n.: fault, crime, vice

vito, vitare: to avoid

vituperatio, -onis, f.: blame, reproach, accusation, censure

vivo, vivere, vixi, victum: to live, have life, be alive

vivus, -a, -um: alive, living, having life

vix (adv.): with difficulty, barely, hardly, scarcely

vixdum (adv.): barely, scarcely

voco, vocare: to call, summon; to convoke, convene

volito, volitare: to fly about, go to and fro **volnero:** see **vulnero**

volnus, -eris, n.: wound

volo, velle, volui: to wish, want, will, desire

voltus, -us, m.: face, look; appearance, expression

voluntas, -atis, f.: 1. wish, will, desire, choice, inclination; 2. disposition, consideration; 3. goodwill, favor

voluptas, -atis, f.: pleasure, satisfaction, enjoyment

vos: accusative plural of **tu:** you

votum, -i, n.: vow, prayer; wish, promise

vox, vocis, f.: voice, sound; word, saying, speech

vulnero, vulnerare: to wound, hurt, injure, maim

CPSIA information can be obtained
at www.ICGtesting.com
Printed in the USA
LVHW040442190822
726304LV00002B/220